UFC

A VISUAL HISTORY

Written by
THOMAS GERBASI

TABLE OF CONTENTS

UFC
A VISUAL HISTORY

Foreword

In 2011, we released the *UFC Encyclopedia*. Going through that book brought back a lot of memories about the story of UFC and mixed martial arts.

What stuck with me the most was how so much had changed in such a short time. From 1993 to 2011, UFC went from spectacle to sport, from an outlaw event to one that packed more than 55,000 people into a baseball stadium in Toronto.

Yet as you look through the book you have in your hands now, it's almost mind-blowing to see how much more has changed since 2011. Since the last book was released, we secured deals with FOX and Reebok that have altered the landscape of the sport forever, we've introduced women's divisions into UFC, we've gone to even more countries around the world and we're on the right track to my ultimate goal of MMA being the biggest sport on the planet.

What is it about UFC that has captivated fans, cutting across demographics and cultures? What I've always believed is that fighting is in our DNA. No matter who you are, if there's a fight going on, you're going to watch it over anything else. Of course that's easy to say, but how do you capture that in 400 pages? This is not just the history of the sport, the fights and the athletes. It's the feeling you get when you see two highly skilled fighters putting it all on the line in the Octagon.

You don't just tell someone about it; you show them. In *UFC: A Visual History*, you won't just read the stories of your favorite fighters and classic fights; you will see what it looked like on those memorable nights in the Octagon.

From that first night in Denver in 1993 to UFC 129 in Toronto in 2011 and to all the great fight nights in Las Vegas, Brazil, Canada, Dublin and beyond, this book will make you feel like you're there, watching history being made.

This is still just the beginning. We've got a lot of history left to make.

Enjoy the book,

Dana White
UFC President

1993

It started off simple enough: businessman Art Davie had an idea for a martial arts tournament that was inspired by a video series entitled *Gracies in Action*. In this series, members of Brazil's Gracie family, creators of their own form of jiu-jitsu, showed the history of their art and how effective it was, both in sanctioned and unsanctioned combat situations. An intrigued Davie contacted Rorion Gracie, the oldest son of family patriarch Helio, as well as Gracie student John Milius, a respected director and screenwriter. Davie pitched his idea of an eight-man, single elimination tournament to determine which martial arts style was most effective in a real fight.

That's all it took. Gracie and Milius were in, and when they learned that Semaphore Entertainment Group (SEG), home to Campbell McLaren and Bob Meyrowitz, was willing to air the event, the Ultimate Fighting Championship was born.

Gracie's family had already traveled from Brazil to California to help build awareness of Gracie jiu-jitsu, and Rorion obviously had his own motives for wanting to see UFC succeed. While many assumed that he would select his imposing brother Rickson to represent the family, he instead chose younger brother Royce, a 26-year-old who would never be described as imposing.

"It was pretty much Rorion and my father's decision," Royce said. "I was at the right weight at the right time, and I wasn't too big or too small. I'm glad they gave me a chance. I was dying for the opportunity."

It was an opportunity attached to plenty of pressure, though. A loss by Gracie would effectively kill off the benefits of having an entire Pay-Per-View broadcast to spread the word about Gracie jiu-jitsu. But Royce had ice water in his veins.

"At the same time that I knew there was pressure, they were also taking away the pressure by giving me enough confidence," he said. "That's what Gracie jiu-jitsu gives to you; it gives you confidence. It's like you've seen that movie before; it's just about getting in there and doing it. They were telling me, 'When you get in there, it's just one man against another. It's just you and him.' And there was no mystery in that. You're not fighting five people; you're fighting one guy only, so don't worry about it."

GERARD GORDEAU
THE HAGUE, NETHERLANDS

DEBUT: UFC 1, NOVEMBER 12, 1993

Gerard Gordeau made his name in Europe as a premier savate and Kyokushin karate practitioner, but stateside, he will always be remembered as the man who introduced mixed martial arts to the world in the opening bout on the UFC 1 broadcast. Future UFC lightweight Dale Hartt said, "I watched the first UFC, and I thought it was gonna be like pro wrestling and be fake. Then Gerard Gordeau kicks Teila Tuli in the face. All of a sudden, I see that tooth flying out. I was sold."

Gordeau won two bouts that night in 1993 before being submitted by Royce Gracie in the tournament final. He only fought once more, in 1995 in Japan, before retiring.

While commentator and kickboxing legend Bill "Superfoot" Wallace may have gotten it wrong in the televised intro by calling it the "Ultimate Fighting Challenge," the fighters thankfully got it right in the Octagon during the first Ultimate Fighting Championship event at McNichols Sports Arena in Denver on November 12, 1993. Each competitor played a key role in giving the world its first dose of the sport of mixed martial arts.

But the undisputed star of UFC 1 was Royce Gracie. His introduction of "the gentle art" to the world stunned three bigger, stronger and faster opponents who had no defense for his submission wizardry.

In the final of the first eight-man, one-night tournament, Gracie forced savate specialist Gerard Gordeau to submit to a rear-naked choke in one minute and 44 seconds. The victory capped a night which began with Gordeau's soccer kick knockout of 400-pound Teila Tuli, who lost a tooth in the 26-second bout thanks to the Dutchman.

The next quarterfinal bout was a back-and-forth affair. Kevin Rosier shook off some rough moments in the early going against Zane Frazier to roar back and halt his opponent at the 4:20 mark, causing Frazier's corner to throw in the towel.

Following this bout, the world got its first glimpse of the gi-wearing Gracie, a member of what eventually became known as fighting's First Family. Standing across the cage from him was pro boxer Art Jimmerson, who bizarrely prepared for battle with one boxing glove. Shortly after the opening bell, Gracie closed the distance with a kick and then took Jimmerson to the canvas. Jimmerson, who was baffled and unable to escape, tapped out 2:18 into the match.

Joining the final four in the semifinals was Ken Shamrock, who was already a veteran of Japan's Pancrase organization. He needed just 1:49 to submit Patrick Smith with a heel hook. If anyone had a chance at figuring out Gracie's mysterious style, it was Shamrock, who was both physically imposing and had submission experience.

Gracie was not about to be figured out, though. In his semifinal bout with his fellow future UFC Hall of Famer, he took Shamrock down and slipped in a choke. Shamrock tapped out at the 57-second mark.

The two would meet again, but there was other business to be taken care of first. After Gordeau won his semifinal bout with a 59-second TKO of Rosier, Gracie squared off against the lanky European in the final bout of the tournament.

Fans again wondered what Gracie would do with the devastating striker, but the Brazilian had the answer, and it was the one he had all night: takedown, choke, game over. This time, he used a rear-naked choke to end his opponent's evening. At 1:44 of the bout, Royce Gracie was 3-0, was holding a check for $50,000 and had just started a revolution—one that may not have gone anywhere if he had not won that night in Colorado.

"I can't say for sure that it wouldn't continue, but I don't think it would have grabbed people the way it did if Royce wasn't the guy," said John McCarthy, who became one of the premier referees in mixed martial arts in the ensuing years. "Royce is not a small guy, but he was perfect in that he didn't even look like an athlete. He's strong, but he's super thin, and it's because he won that I think people said, 'Whoa, you've got to see this.' If Ken Shamrock had won, a lot of people would have looked at it and said, 'Well, look at him.' So I think it had a lot to do with it taking off."

"I think the sport would have continued," Gracie added. "Gracie jiu-jitsu would have been a little harder. But the sport would have gone on, no matter who won. It would have just given more credibility to the other arts. But by winning, Gracie jiu-jitsu got all the credibility."

PATRICK SMITH
DENVER, CO

DEBUT: UFC 1, NOVEMBER 12, 1993

In six early UFC fights, Patrick Smith only lost twice—to future UFC Hall of Famers Ken Shamrock and Royce Gracie. A feat that is impressive in and of itself. But what may have gotten lost in the shuffle was that Smith, a black belt in several martial arts, including taekwondo and Kenpo karate, made a concerted effort to learn the ground game after his UFC 1 loss to Shamrock. By the time he returned to the Octagon, he was able to submit two of three foes in the UFC 2 tournament before losing in his fourth bout of the night to Gracie. Following a submission of Rudyard Moncayo at UFC 6, Smith continued to fight until 2009.

ROYCE GRACIE

DEBUT: UFC 1, NOVEMBER 12, 1993
UFC 1, 2 AND 4 TOURNAMENT WINNER

RIO DE JANEIRO, BRAZIL

"This is my house," said Royce Gracie in 2006. "I built it."

A bold statement, indeed, but as boxing great Muhammad Ali once said, "It ain't bragging if you're telling the truth." And Gracie was unquestionably telling the truth.

The standard bearer for Gracie jiu-jitsu since his UFC debut in 1993, the Rio de Janeiro native always had the confidence to step into competition and the skills to succeed. Perhaps more importantly, he had broad enough shoulders to carry the Gracie name into each fight, knowing that a loss could cripple the mystique of fighting's First Family. However, he never saw it as an issue.

Royce was the son of the legendary Helio Gracie, who founded the art that eventually became known internationally as Brazilian jiu-jitsu with his brother Carlos. Royce and his own brothers Rickson, Royler, Relson and Rorion, practically grew up on the canvases of their father's academy in Brazil.

On the night of November 12, 1993, few people in the United States knew who the Gracies were, and even fewer knew what to expect from an event called the Ultimate Fighting Championship. Ironically, Royce's older brother Rorion created the event partly to show the world which style of martial arts was most effective in a real fight. Rorion Gracie obviously believed that his family's art form, jiu-jitsu, was the most effective. It had been proven over the years in countless challenge matches in Brazil, but now it was time to take Gracie jiu-jitsu worldwide. The McNichols Sports Arena in Denver, Colorado, was the first stop.

The question was who would represent the family in this first competition? The Gracies chose Royce, a skinny and unassuming 26-year-old. Many shielded their eyes, fearing for his safety against his more visually imposing opposition.

Once the tournament began, Art Jimmerson, future UFC Hall of Famer Ken Shamrock and Gerard Gordeau all went down in defeat on that single night. Gracie's style amazed viewers, and his ease in defeating three opponents in one evening shocked them. But it was no fluke. Four months after his first tournament victory, he did it again at UFC 2, submitting four opponents (Minoki Ichihara, Jason DeLucia, Remco Pardoel and Patrick Smith) to take home a second tournament title.

On September 9, 1994, at UFC 3, Gracie finally ran into a challenge from imposing Kimo Leopoldo. However, despite being pushed to his limits, Gracie submitted his foe with an armlock 4:40 into the fight. Forced to withdraw from his next UFC 3 tournament fight against Harold Howard due to exhaustion, Gracie rebounded in the UFC 4 tournament, recording three more submission wins over Ron Van Clief, Keith Hackney and Dan Severn to take his third title.

Following a 36-minute draw in his April 1995 rematch with Ken Shamrock at UFC 5, Gracie disappeared from the fight game for nearly five years. He returned to the ring in Japan for three PRIDE fights in 2000, which included his first loss after a 90-minute epic battle with Kazushi Sakuraba. Two more bouts in Japan followed before he made the stunning 2006 announcement that he was returning to UFC to face longtime welterweight champion Matt Hughes in a non-title bout.

This was an uphill climb: the athletes had improved in mixed martial arts and the rules were different from when Gracie had last competed in UFC 10 years prior. At 39 years old, he was giving up seven years to his opponent.

At UFC 60 in May 2006, Gracie made the walk to the Octagon once again. He fell short of victory, getting stopped via strikes, at 4:39 of the first round. But during the bout, he displayed what was perhaps his greatest attribute—heart—in refusing to tap out to a tight submission, locked in by the longtime welterweight champion. When it was all over, the appreciative crowd gave him a rousing ovation, a fitting tribute for a man who meant so much to so many.

Gracie, along with old rival Ken Shamrock, was inducted into the UFC Hall of Fame on November 21, 2003.

KEN SHAMROCK

DEBUT: UFC 1, NOVEMBER 12, 1993
UFC SUPERFIGHT CHAMPION

MACON, GA

In the early days of UFC, if you were going to build a prototype of a fighter, you probably would have come up with someone who looked like "The World's Most Dangerous Man" Ken Shamrock. Skilled in all aspects of MMA, Shamrock made a hybrid style of fighting essential to success in the sport. But his impact went far beyond a win-loss record. While fighters like Royce Gracie and Randy Couture conducted their business in a low-key fashion, Shamrock built a base of fans that either loved him or hated him, as he was the master of promoting a fight and inciting fans to have a reaction toward him.

"Honestly, I believe it's the way I carry myself, the way I respect the fans, the way I respect the sport and the way I respect myself and my family," Shamrock said. "I've been brought up on respect, and respect is a very big part of my training, of my fighters' training, in my family and also with the fans. So I think that over the years I've been fighting, that has touched a lot of fans out there, and therefore, they stay pretty loyal to me. There are some out there that want the bad boy image, and I just don't fit into that. So I have my good fans, and then I have the ones that don't like me, but everybody does know me."

From his first UFC bout in 1993, when he submitted Patrick Smith with a heel hook in just a minute and 49 seconds, Shamrock was not only a world-class fighter, but he looked and acted the part. Scowl on his face, shoulders barely able to fit through doors, Shamrock's swagger was one of the earliest memories for UFC fans, and it rubbed plenty of his peers the wrong way. Then again, that was the idea. Shamrock's bad blood matchups both here and abroad elevated his profile to a level of stardom few fighters enjoyed.

"You have to have rivalries," he said. "People enjoy rivalries, whether it's in football, baseball or boxing. There are so many ways to have a rivalry. It doesn't even have to be an anger rivalry; it could be someone who is undefeated against another person who is undefeated. That's something you can build on."

The biggest feud of them all was between Shamrock and Tito Ortiz. Though they buried the hatchet after Ortiz' second consecutive first-round win (his third stoppage victory in as many fights against his rival), when the gloves were on, the animosity was real.

But beyond the bluster, Shamrock was a fighter, one who scored wins over Bas Rutten, Matt Hume, Dan Severn, Kimo Leopoldo (twice) and Maurice Smith. He also fought Royce Gracie to a draw after losing to him in their first bout. Shamrock also had an influential role as the leader of the Lion's Den fight team that launched the careers of his adopted brother Frank, Guy Mezger, Vernon White, Jerry Bohlander and Tra Telligman, among others.

While age and injuries eventually caught up to Shamrock, there's no questioning his influence on the sport. It was no surprise when he joined Gracie as the first two fighters inducted into the UFC Hall of Fame in 2003.

"One thing I learned along the way was that you have one thing, and one thing that nobody can ever take away from you—and you never let anybody try to take it away from you—and that's your honor," he said. "It's the thing inside that makes you who you are. Honor is not about winning; honor is about you stepping up and standing for what you believe in, and that's it. That's what I do: if somebody says something to me or does something to me, I will stand up."

FIGHTS OF THE YEAR

UFC 1

| GRACIE | WSUB1 | SHAMROCK |

KNOCKOUTS OF THE YEAR

UFC 1

| GORDEAU | TKO1 | TULI |

SUBMISSIONS OF THE YEAR

UFC 1

| GRACIE | WSUB1 | GORDEAU |

DEBUTS

UFC 1

ROYCE GRACIE	ART JIMMERSON
GERARD GORDEAU	ZANE FRAZIER
KEN SHAMROCK	TEILA TULI
KEVIN ROSIER	JASON DELUCIA
PATRICK SMITH	TRENT JENKINS

THE OWNERS

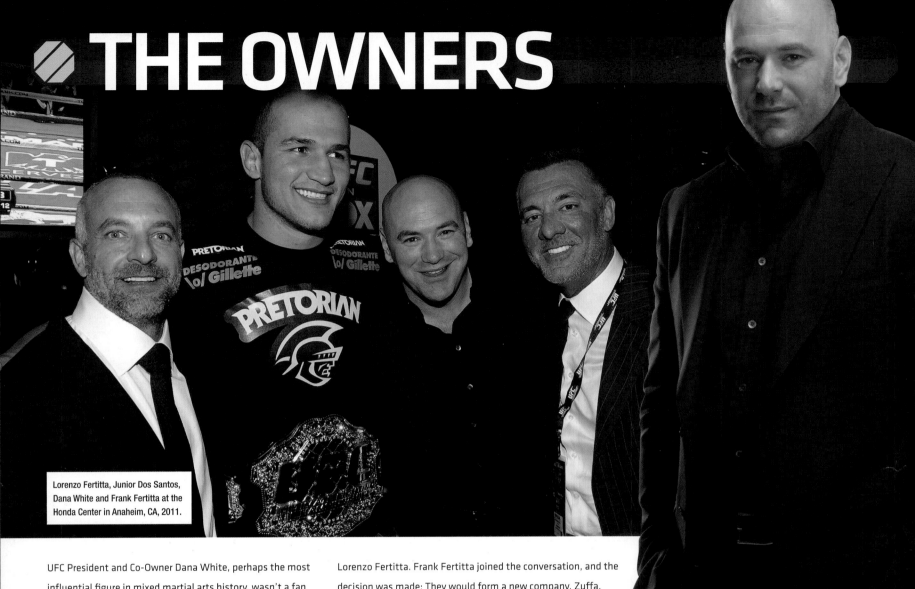

Lorenzo Fertitta, Junior Dos Santos, Dana White and Frank Fertitta at the Honda Center in Anaheim, CA, 2011.

UFC President and Co-Owner Dana White, perhaps the most influential figure in mixed martial arts history, wasn't a fan the first time he saw the sport back in 1993.

"I had seen the first two, and then I stopped watching," said White. "I was a boxing guy. A bunch of us from the gym got together and rented it on Pay-Per-View and watched it. The stuff that [Royce] Gracie was doing you didn't understand, and then I watched the second one and there wasn't really ground fighting, but laying and stalling on the ground."

Fast forward a few years.

Dana White had moved from Boston back to Las Vegas, where he had attended high school. White was managing fighters and gyms in the area, when he soon reconnected with an old classmate, Lorenzo Fertitta, who ran the Station Casinos along with his brother, Frank Fertitta III. One night, the three were at the Hard Rock Casino when they ran into John Lewis, a mixed martial artist and jiu-jitsu black belt. One thing led to another, and Lewis began instructing the trio in Brazilian jiu-jitsu. They were immediately hooked and enthralled with MMA, and quickly became interested in the UFC.

But UFC was in trouble, on the verge of bankruptcy and extinction. White discovered that it was for sale and told

Lorenzo Fertitta. Frank Fertitta joined the conversation, and the decision was made: They would form a new company, Zuffa, and buy the promotion—which they did in January of 2001.

That was the easy part.

The hard part was taking a damaged brand and not only reviving it, but bringing it to another level as a sport, rather than as a spectacle. With unified rules already in place, Zuffa began the task of running toward regulation instead of running away from it. The goal was to get the sport back on cable and get it sanctioned by athletic commissions from around the world so that fights in England and Australia would be fought under the same rules as bouts in New Jersey and Las Vegas.

It was a difficult task, but one the Zuffa trio was prepared to undertake. Slowly, the walls began coming down. The sport was sanctioned in the fight capital of the world, Nevada, and state after state followed. The media, once content to write MMA off as "human cockfighting," began to write about it as a true sport, focusing on the lives and journeys of the fighters. With matchmaker Joe Silva consistently putting on compelling fights, the events got bigger and bigger.

But eventually, the resurrection of UFC hit a snag when Lorenzo Fertitta decided that the company was simply losing too much money to remain viable.

> **"I HAD SEEN THE FIRST TWO, AND THEN I STOPPED WATCHING. I WAS A BOXING GUY."**
> —DANA WHITE

One night, he told White to look for a buyer. The next morning, however, he changed his mind and told his partner that he was willing to give it one more shot.

That shot had to hit its mark. In 2005, Zuffa's last-ditch effort was a reality show titled *The Ultimate Fighter*. Remarkably, it worked, as the show was a ratings hit. However, it wasn't until the live finale and the unforgettable war between Forrest Griffin and Stephan Bonnar that White believed his company had reached its tipping point. Even today, he doesn't hesitate to say that, "The biggest thing to ever happen to us was Forrest Griffin and Stephan Bonnar."

The UFC was alive and on its way to being successful, which would have been the signal for most businessmen to take their foot off the gas. Instead, White and the Fertittas pushed the pedal to the metal, building a brand that is a juggernaut of the sports world.

White is the front man, a tireless worker and a media favorite for his no-nonsense approach and uncanny ability to tell it like it is. Lorenzo Fertitta and Frank Fertitta are content letting White take the lead while they work their magic behind the scenes. It is a synergistic relationship where one part can't function without the other two.

"If you look throughout history, anything that's started to fail, people start pointing fingers real quick," said White. "They [the Fertittas] never did that. And when it flipped and everything started to get successful, and you look at how much my life changed and how well known I became, there was never any ego, never anything about money or who's getting press or who's doing this. We never fight about anything, and never did they say, 'What are you doing?' 'What are you saying?' 'Why did you do this?' 'Why did you do that?' They let me be me and run this thing."

Now sanctioned in all but one of the states with athletic commissions in the U.S., UFC airs in over 800 million homes on television in 129 countries, and is home to shows in Brazil, England, Australia, Canada, Germany, Ireland, Japan, Sweden, China, Singapore, New Zealand, Mexico and Abu Dhabi. UFC has become not just an American phenomenon, but an international one.

"It's about building a sport, and our goal is to make this thing a sport everywhere," said White.

In 2008, to aid in the UFC's global expansion, Lorenzo Fertitta stepped down as the chairman of Station Casinos to work full time with Zuffa. White calls it one of his personal highlights.

UFC President Dana White presents the TapouT awards at UFC 45.

"The thing was getting so big and we had these goals, but I was one guy," he said. "I was stretched as thin as you could possibly stretch a human being. There was no way we were going to do what we needed to do with just me over here. So when the day came that Lorenzo actually left Station Casinos to come work for the UFC, it was a proud moment for me."

There would be more—a lot more.

In April 2011, the organization presented a show at Toronto's Rogers Centre that sold more than 55,000 tickets, a North American record. UFC shows no signs of slowing down, as historic deals with FOX and Reebok, more international events and the creation of the streaming service UFC FIGHT PASS take the brand to a new level. But when it comes down to it, what matters to White and the Fertittas is bringing the best fights and fighters to fans around the world while wrapping it in the best live sports experience around. That's something you can never put a price tag on.

"This company's so big and it's so different than it used to be when it started, and there are a lot of things that I've given up control on," White said. "But I will never give up control or the product itself and what happens that night in the arena and on TV. It's that experience that I really watch over."

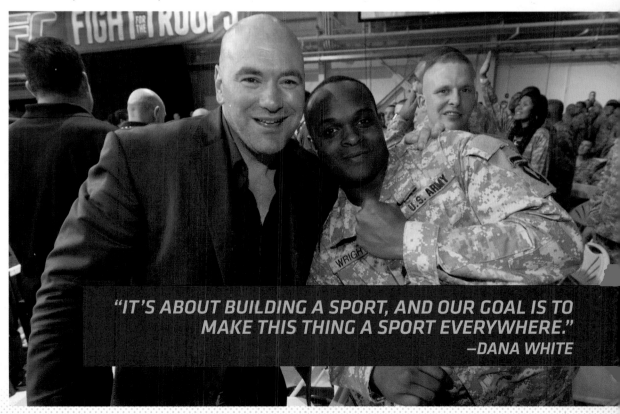

"IT'S ABOUT BUILDING A SPORT, AND OUR GOAL IS TO MAKE THIS THING A SPORT EVERYWHERE."
—DANA WHITE

◈1994

The first UFC event in November 1993 was a rousing success, so it was no surprise that four months later, it was back. The event remained in Colorado, this time held at Mammoth Gardens in Denver. Although the venue had changed, the result was the same: Brazil's Royce Gracie tore through the field at UFC 2 to win his second consecutive tournament.

This time around, Gracie submitted Minoki Ichihara, Jason DeLucia, Remco Pardoel and Patrick Smith in perhaps his most impressive one-night run. There was a lack of star power around the jiu-jitsu wizard, but UFC 2 did introduce one of the Octagon's most notable figures: referee John McCarthy. Oddly enough, "Big" John was almost one and done that March night.

"The first fight was Sean Daughtery vs Scott Morris," McCarthy remembered. "Scott Morris submits him in 20 seconds, neck cranks him, and he taps. The next one is a guillotine choke, and I'm thinking, 'This is easy.' But from that point on, my life was a living hell. I was scared because I wasn't supposed to stop this thing."

> ## "I WAS SCARED TO DEATH BECAUSE I WASN'T SUPPOSED TO STOP THIS THING."
> — "BIG" JOHN McCARTHY

At that point in UFC's history, the only way a fight could end was a knockout, a submission, or a towel being thrown in. The referee was unable to stop a fight. When the event was over, a frazzled McCarthy told Rorion Gracie—one of UFC's co-founders—that he was done.

"I can't stand there and let someone get beat to death while I stand there looking stupid," he said. "If someone cannot defend themselves, I have to be able to stop the fight. He [Gracie] finally agreed to it, and I did number three, but I was mortified in the beginning."

At UFC 3 on September 9, 1994, the Octagon traveled to Charlotte, North Carolina, with an eight-man tournament highlighted by the return of Royce Gracie and his rival from UFC 1, Ken Shamrock. The hope was that the two would meet in the tournament finals, and Shamrock did his part by defeating Christophe Leininger. Gracie's foe in the quarterfinals was mysterious newcomer Kimo Leopoldo, who entered the Octagon with a full-sized wooden cross draped across his back.

Kimo was no eccentric novelty act. He could fight and, for the first time, Gracie was pushed to his limit, taking plenty of punishment before he submitted his foe at the 4:40 mark. The bout drained Gracie so much that he withdrew from the tournament before his semifinal matchup with Canada's Harold Howard. Shamrock went on to earn a spot in the finals with a submission of Felix Lee Mitchell, but Shamrock was sidelined by injury.

GUY MEZGER
HOUSTON, TX

DEBUT: UFC 4, DECEMBER 16, 1994, UFC 13 LIGHTWEIGHT TOURNAMENT WINNER

During the late '90s and beginning of the new millennium, Guy Mezger was perhaps the most visible mixed martial arts fighter in the United States, appearing on VH1 and FOX television, as well as writing a book on kickboxing.

"To be honest, I've had such an incredibly lucky life, and there's probably a real good reason why this happened this way, and that's the way I look at it."

He could also fight, as evidenced by his four UFC wins, including one over Tito Ortiz at UFC 13 in 1997. But after losing to Ortiz in their 1999 rematch, the former Pancrase star returned to Japan, where he fought much of his early career. Mezger starred in PRIDE from 1999 to 2002, fighting the likes of Wanderlei Silva, Chuck Liddell, Ricardo Arona and Rogerio Nogueira.

In 2004, Mezger was scheduled to face Ortiz a third time at UFC 50, but he withdrew from the bout due to stroke-like symptoms. He retired shortly after, but remains involved in the martial arts world.

Enter police officer Steve Jennum, an alternate who was given a finals berth against Howard despite not fighting earlier in the night. Jennum made the most of his shot, stopping Howard in 87 seconds to win the UFC 3 tournament.

After that bizarre and anticlimactic ending, UFC brass was hoping for a better outcome for the next event at the Expo Square Pavilion in Tulsa, Oklahoma, on December 16th. Gracie was again presented as the main attraction, but also entering the UFC 4 tournament was a 35-year-old former All-American wrestler named Dan Severn.

"When I walked out there in 1994, I was looking at this and going, 'Just one event,'" Severn said with a laugh.

But Severn's performance that night was no laughing matter, at least not for his opponents. In the quarterfinals, he suplexed Anthony Macias over and over, before finishing him with a rear-naked choke in under two minutes. Marcus Bossett lasted less than a minute in the semis, sending Dan "The Beast" Severn to the finals.

Waiting for him was Gracie, who showed off his usual submission magic in dispatching Ron Van Clief and Keith Hackney. However, as soon as the final match began, Severn took Gracie down and kept him there, stunning both the fans in attendance and those watching on Pay-Per-View. For nearly 15 minutes, it was all Severn who was dominant, but he was ultimately unable to finish the resilient Brazilian.

"If you watch the match from my perspective, it was just going fine my way," Severn said. "I took the man down, and I would rather rain down any day than rain up. It wasn't until several minutes into the match before I realized, you know, I may have to hit this guy. But I had to think about it because it was not in my repertoire; I had never practiced it before, and I was going against 26 years of rules, regulations and sportsmanlike conduct. So that was difficult for me. I struggled more with my conscience than I ever did with an opponent. I'm out there as a sportsman; I don't have to create any anger issues or things of that nature. I'll shake his hand before, I'll shake it after; there's no hard feelings."

It appeared that Severn was going to end the Gracie's unbeaten streak, though. As Severn closed in on victory, he noticed Royce staring at the patriarch of the family, his father Helio Gracie, at Octagonside.

"They say the eyes are a window to a man's soul, and I'm staring through this man's soul," Severn said. "And he's looking at his dad [Helio Gracie] outside the cage, and I could read exactly what was going through his mind. It's kinda like, 'Dad, I'm hangin' in there, but if you would throw that towel in, I wouldn't hold it against you.' So my eyes go from Royce's to the old man, and he's got the towel in his hand, and he raises the towel and crosses his arms and shakes his head no."

Severn chuckles at the memory, because after 15 minutes of Severn controlling the fight, Gracie found his opening and submitted "The Beast" at 15:49 of the bout. The Gracie streak continued, but Dan Severn would be heard from again very soon.

KEITH HACKNEY
ROSELLE, IL

DEBUT: UFC 3, SEPTEMBER 9, 1994

Poor Keith Hackney. At just 200 pounds, the black belt in taekwondo and Kenpo karate was about to get wiped out by 600-pound Emmanuel Yarborough at UFC 3 in 1994. But then the horn sounded, and Hackney exploded with a right hand that sent Yarborough to the canvas. The sumo wrestler would shake off the shot, but he couldn't weather the next attack of flying fists, as Hackney stunned onlookers with a TKO win.

Unable to continue in that night's tournament due to a broken hand, Hackney defeated Joe Son three months later at UFC 4 before losing to Royce Gracie the same night. In his final bout, the cult hero was submitted by Marco Ruas at the Ultimate Ultimate '95 event.

HAROLD HOWARD
ONTARIO, CANADA

DEBUT: UFC 3, SEPTEMBER 9, 1994

Whether it was his ever-present mullet, missing teeth, or the immortal line, "We have a saying back home that if you're coming on, COME ON," odds are that you didn't forget Canada's Harold Howard once you saw him in the Octagon.

That's impressive considering that he only had four MMA fights in a career that lasted from 1994 to 1996. Two of those fights came at UFC 3, where he knocked out Roland Payne in 46 seconds and was submitted due to strikes by Steve Jennum. In between, he gained most of his notoriety for a bout he didn't fight: the UFC 3 tournament semifinal against Royce Gracie, from which the UFC legend withdrew due to exhaustion before a single blow was thrown.

STEVE JENNUM
OMAHA, NE

DEBUT: UFC 3, SEPTEMBER 9, 1994
UFC 3 TOURNAMENT CHAMPION

Ninjitsu fighter Steve Jennum sat back and watched the UFC 3 tournament in 1994 unfold as an alternate, not expecting to get called into action. However, when Ken Shamrock couldn't continue in his final match, the Nebraska police officer got the opportunity of a lifetime. Jennum made the most of it, defeating Harold Howard in 87 seconds to win the tournament with just one fight.

UFC tournament rules were changed after the bout, and while Jennum submitted Melton Bowen in his first bout at UFC 4, an injury kept him from advancing. He would go on to lose the three remaining fights in his MMA career before retiring in 1997.

KIMO LEOPOLDO
MUNICH, WEST GERMANY

DEBUT: UFC 3, SEPTEMBER 9, 1994

Kimo Leopoldo was one of the most recognizable fighters from the early days of UFC. That's not much of a surprise, considering he entered the Octagon for the first time at UFC carrying a full-sized wooden cross. In the Octagon, Kimo's battering of the formerly untouchable Royce Gracie earned him instant acclaim. That first bout turned into six more fights in the organization, including two bouts with Ken Shamrock, both of which he lost. At UFC 43 in 2003, Kimo earned his biggest victory when he submitted Tank Abbott in less than two minutes. Despite rumors in 2009 to the contrary, he is still alive and well.

ANTHONY MACIAS
OKLAHOMA CITY, OK

DEBUT: UFC 4, DECEMBER 16, 1994

The unfortunate recipient of repeated suplexes from Dan "The Beast" Severn in both fighters' 1994 UFC debuts, Anthony "Mad Dog" Macias was more than just a foil for the future UFC Hall of Famer, even if his record didn't reflect it.

A hard-nosed Oklahoma native who fought like he was double-parked, it was feast or famine for the "Mad Dog," who only saw three of his 41 pro fights go the distance. In the Octagon, Macias dusted himself off from the UFC 4 loss to Severn to defeat He-Man Gipson by submission due to strikes at UFC 6. However, he lost his next tournament match that night to Oleg Taktarov in just nine seconds.

REMCO PARDOEL
OSS, NETHERLANDS

DEBUT: UFC 2, MARCH 11, 1994

Despite hailing from the kickboxing capital of the world, Holland's Remco "Grizzly" Pardoel instead focused on Brazilian jiu-jitsu, which he parlayed into a visit to UFC in 1994.

On that first night, Pardoel submitted Alberto Cerra Leon. He then delivered one of the most frightening knockouts in UFC history as he elbowed Orlando Wiet into defeat in just 89 seconds. Next was his first true test: a UFC 2 tournament final bout against Royce Gracie. However, Pardoel wasn't ready, and was submitted in 91 seconds. Pardoel would return for UFC 7 a year later, losing a semifinal bout to Marco Ruas. While this was his last Octagon bout, he continued to compete until 2003.

DAN SEVERN

DEBUT: UFC 4, DECEMBER 16, 1994
UFC 5 TOURNAMENT WINNER
ULTIMATE ULTIMATE '95 TOURNAMENT WINNER
UFC SUPERFIGHT CHAMPION
UFC HALL OF FAME (2005)

COLDWATER, MI

If you ask Dan "The Beast" Severn his first impression of UFC, he doesn't hesitate in his response.

"'Awe' might be one of the best words to sum it up," he said. "To do this type of competition in the United States, I was almost flabbergasted. I knew if it survived, it would gather a great deal of attention." And while Coldwater, Michigan, didn't have Pay-Per-View back in 1993, a buddy of Severn's in Detroit did. When he brought the VHS tape over, the die was cast.

"He showed it to me and said, 'You ever think about doing this stuff?' The rest is history."

At the time, Severn, a two-time All-American wrestler at Arizona State University and a competitor in the 1984 and 1988 Olympic trials, was 35 years old. As far as he was concerned, his best days had passed him by.

"If anybody wants to call me 'The Beast' now, then their sights were not all that high in the first place," he said. "If they wanted to see a real animal, they should have seen me from 1984 to 1986 because I ruled the world, hands down."

Still, he wanted to give mixed martial arts a try. His debut was set for UFC 4 on December 16, 1994, in Tulsa, Oklahoma. There was just one catch: due to previous commitments, he only had five days to train.

In his first match against Anthony Macias, Severn suplexed his opponent before submitting Macias with a rear-naked choke in 1:45. His next opponent, Marcus Bossett didn't get that far, lasting just 52 seconds. Then, Severn would face UFC's undisputed superstar, Royce Gracie, in the night's tournament final. Early in the match, things went according to plan as he took the jiu-jitsu expert to the canvas and kept him there.

WORLD CHAMPIONSHIP

Eventually, Severn started firing off some strikes, and as the bout went from five minutes to 10, to nearly 15, it looked like just a matter of time until Gracie would be forced to give in. But at the 15:49 mark, Gracie found his opening and forced Severn to tap out to a triangle choke.

After his loss to Gracie, Severn's inner competitor wouldn't let him stop. He signed on for UFC 5, but this time, he wouldn't train for only five days. When he returned in April 1995, there was no stopping him as he tore through Joe Charles, Oleg Taktarov and Dave Beneteau to win the UFC 5 tournament. After a submission loss to Ken Shamrock at UFC 6, three more victories against Paul Varelans, Tank Abbott and Taktarov earned him the Ultimate Ultimate '95 tournament crown. Five months later, Severn avenged the loss to Shamrock with a 30-minute split decision that was dreadful to watch, but added a superfight championship belt to his trophy case.

Following the Shamrock fight, Severn would only fight twice more in the Octagon, losing a heavyweight title fight to Mark Coleman in 1997, and then getting stopped on leg kicks by Pedro Rizzo at UFC 27 in 2000.

Before and after the Rizzo bout, Severn stayed active, fighting anyone and everyone, whenever asked. In 2013, at 54, "The Beast" retired with a remarkable 101-19-7 record. His final tally included the names Cal Worsham, Victor Valimaki, James Thompson, Seth Petruzelli, Forrest Griffin, Marcus Silveira, Josh Barnett, Kimo Leopoldo, Paul Buentello, Jeremy Horn and Pat Miletich.

While Severn doesn't strap on the gloves in competition anymore, he continues running his training facility in Michigan and working with local schools as a strong advocate for education. As for the sport of MMA, he doesn't think about his influence too much, but he does appreciate when it's brought to his attention that he was the one who made it safe for wrestlers to make their move into the sport. Severn was inducted into the UFC Hall of Fame on April 16, 2005.

FIGHTS OF THE YEAR

UFC 4
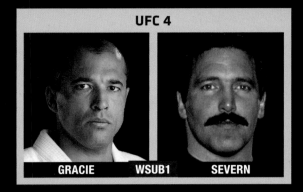

| GRACIE | WSUB1 | SEVERN |

UFC 3

| GRACIE | WSUB1 | KIMO |

UFC 3
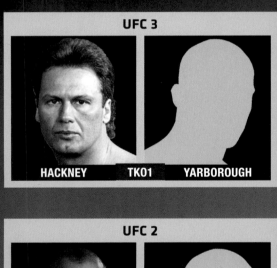

| HACKNEY | TKO1 | YARBOROUGH |

UFC 2

| GRACIE | WSUB1 | ICHIHARA |

UFC 3

| JENNUM | WSUB1 | HOWARD |

KNOCKOUTS OF THE YEAR

UFC 3

| HACKNEY | TKO1 | YARBOROUGH |

UFC 1
| SMITH | TKO1 | MORRIS |

UFC 2
| PARDOEL | KO1 | WIET |

UFC 4
| BOSSETT | KO1 | XAVIER |

UFC 3
| HOWARD | KO1 | PAYNE |

SUBMISSIONS OF THE YEAR

UFC 4

| GRACIE | WSUB1 | SEVERN |

UFC 3
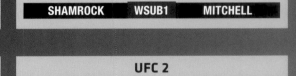

| GRACIE | WSUB1 | KIMO |

UFC 2

| GRACIE | WSUB1 | PARDOEL |

UFC 3
| SHAMROCK | WSUB1 | MITCHELL |

UFC 2
| GRACIE | WSUB1 | DELUCIA |

DEBUTS

UFC 2	UFC 3	UFC 4
REMCO PARDOEL	STEVE JENNUM	DAN SEVERN
JOHNNY RHODES	FELIX LEE MITCHELL	MARCUS BOSSETT
JASON DELUCIA	KIMO LEOPOLDO	ANTHONY MACIAS
ORLANDO WIET	ROLAND PAYNE	MELTON BOWEN
FRED ETTISH	CHRISTOPHE LEININGER	JOE SON
SCOTT MORRIS	KEITH HACKNEY	RON VAN CLIEF
MINOKI ICHIHARA	HAROLD HOWARD	JASON FAIRN
SCOTT BAKER	EMMANUEL YARBOROUGH	GUY MEZGER
ALBERTO CERRA LEON		ELDO DIAS XAVIER
ROBERT LUCARELLI		JOE CHARLES
THADDEUS LUSTER		
FRANK HAMAKER		
DAVID LEVICKI		
RAY WIZARD		
SEAN DAUGHTERY		

THE HISTORY OF THE
UFC CHAMPIONSHIP BELT

Some athletes fight for glory; some do it for the paycheck. Others do it just to quench their thirst for competition. But for whichever reason they choose to fight, when an athlete reaches the pinnacle of his or her profession and earns the right to be called champion of the world, it's nice to get a memento. Nothing signifies being at the top of the game better than a world championship belt.

In UFC, the precious and coveted gold belt measures 48 inches in length by 12 inches tall and weighs in at 12 pounds. While the belt is currently the one accessory every fighter wants to own, in the early days of the organization, tournament winners like Royce Gracie were awarded medals for their efforts.

It wasn't until UFC 5 that the winner of the superfight championship bout between Gracie and Ken Shamrock expected to receive a championship belt. But when the bout was ruled a draw, the belt stayed in its case. After that point, tournament champions continued receiving belts until UFC 12, when medals were brought back for most tourney winners.

At UFC 12 in 1997, Mark Coleman became the first UFC heavyweight champion. From that event until UFC 48, champions received a new title belt for each successful defense.

By the time Zuffa took over, the belts were slowly redesigned until they became the championship belts worn today by UFC's best of the best. Although it has been a long journey to get to this point, whether a fighter received a belt in 1997 or 2015, each champion can rest assured that he or she earned it. That is something no one can ever take away.

1995

After the fiasco of UFC 3 in which alternate Steve Jennum walked into the tournament final and won while Royce Gracie and Ken Shamrock dealt with exhaustion and injury respectively, UFC officials ensured that the first event of 1995 would have Gracie and Shamrock on the card. This would be the first time the two were going to meet since UFC 1 in 1993.

To accomplish this, UFC set up a superfight—the first in the promotion's history. There would still be a tournament at Independence Arena in Charlotte, North Carolina, on April 7, 1995, but the main attraction would be the clash between the two longtime rivals, who were UFC's biggest stars at the moment. UFC 5 was also notable for being the first event with time limits. The superfight and the tournament final were both set for 30 minutes or less; the quarterfinal and semifinal matches in the tournament received a 20-minute limit.

As the superfight proved, the new time limit procedure was a work in progress. Despite the anticipation for Gracie vs Shamrock II, the match didn't live up to expectations, instead turning into a war of attrition that ended in a draw.

Gracie attacked with leg kicks early, with Shamrock shooting for and getting a takedown. Gracie waited for an opening for submissions from the bottom, but Shamrock stayed close, even as the Brazilian chopped away with kicks to the back. This went on for quite some time, with periodic bursts of action as Shamrock and Gracie traded shots on the canvas.

As the bout approached the 16-minute mark, Gracie began making his move, but Shamrock kept him pinned to the canvas. The pattern continued as neither was willing to take the risks necessary to break the fight open. Surprisingly, at the 30-minute mark, the bout kept going, and at the 31:06 mark, referee John McCarthy restarted the bout in the standing position and implemented a five-minute overtime period. However, after a hard right from Shamrock, the two hit the canvas again and remained there until the five minutes were over; drawing boos from a crowd that had just witnessed—at 36:06—the longest fight in UFC history.

There was compelling action in North Carolina that night, mainly thanks to Dan "The Beast" Severn. He followed up an impressive UFC 4 performance—capped off by his near-win over Gracie—with three dominant wins over Joe Charles, Oleg Taktarov and Dave Beneteau that earned him his first tournament title.

After the dust settled at UFC 5, the big news out of the UFC camp was that Rorion Gracie was cutting ties with the promotion and bringing his brother Royce with him. Feeling that the introduction of rules and time limits were diluting his original vision, the co-founder's decision left UFC without its biggest star.

The solution? Crown a champion, which is what UFC attempted to do for a second time at the Casper Events Center in Wyoming on July 14, 1995. After the draw between Gracie and Shamrock in the first UFC superfight, Shamrock would get another crack at the vacant crown against the promotion's other most marketable athlete: Dan Severn.

This time, Shamrock, "The World's Most Dangerous Man," made the most of his opportunity, submitting Severn in a little over two minutes. Using crisp striking and—most importantly—stellar takedown defense to keep Severn guessing, Shamrock was able to catch his opponent's neck in a guillotine choke, culminating in a tapout 2:14 into the bout.

UFC now had someone to push to mainstream audiences. The charismatic and imposing Shamrock was the perfect fit, even though his greatest rival, Gracie, had left the building.

In the UFC 6 tournament, Russia's Oleg Taktarov ran the field, defeating Dave Beneteau, Anthony Macias and Tank Abbott to pick up the crown and earn a future shot at Shamrock.

Oddly enough, with Shamrock taking over the mantle as UFC's top name, Severn following right behind him and Taktarov showing potential, Huntington Beach newcomer David "Tank" Abbott may have captivated fans the most.

MARCO RUAS

DEBUT: UFC 7, SEPTEMBER 8, 1995
UFC 7 TOURNAMENT WINNER

RIO DE JANEIRO, BRAZIL

Rio de Janeiro's Marco Ruas could have lost every one of his 15 professional mixed martial arts fights, and would still be remembered, if only for what was one of the best nicknames in the history of the game: "The King of the Streets."

With a moniker like that, you better know how to fight. Ruas' ease in competition came from years of training and the development of a style he called "Ruas Vale Tudo." *Vale tudo* means "anything goes," and that's what the Brazilian delivered.

Debuting in UFC at the age of 34 in 1995, he submitted Larry Cureton and Remco Pardoel in his first two bouts before finishing his night by chopping down "The Polar Bear," Paul Varelans, in 13:17 to win the UFC 7 tournament.

Three months later, he was back for the Ultimate Ultimate event, but after submitting Keith Hackney, he lost the first bout of his career to Oleg Taktarov via decision. After the Taktarov bout, Ruas fought three times in the World Vale Tudo Championship event, defeating UFC veterans Steve Jennum and Pat Smith and engaging in another scrap with Taktarov. The bout with Taktarov was declared a draw after 31 minutes and 12 seconds. Still a big name in the sport despite age and injuries creeping up on him, Ruas returned to UFC to face Maurice Smith in 1999 following two PRIDE fights. However, he was forced to retire in his corner due to a knee injury.

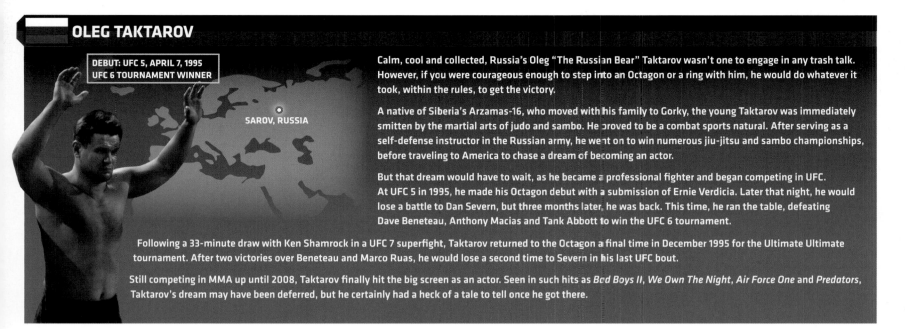

OLEG TAKTAROV

DEBUT: UFC 5, APRIL 7, 1995
UFC 6 TOURNAMENT WINNER

SAROV, RUSSIA

Calm, cool and collected, Russia's Oleg "The Russian Bear" Taktarov wasn't one to engage in any trash talk. However, if you were courageous enough to step into an Octagon or a ring with him, he would do whatever it took, within the rules, to get the victory.

A native of Siberia's Arzamas-16, who moved with his family to Gorky, the young Taktarov was immediately smitten by the martial arts of judo and sambo. He proved to be a combat sports natural. After serving as a self-defense instructor in the Russian army, he went on to win numerous jiu-jitsu and sambo championships, before traveling to America to chase a dream of becoming an actor.

But that dream would have to wait, as he became a professional fighter and began competing in UFC. At UFC 5 in 1995, he made his Octagon debut with a submission of Ernie Verdicia. Later that night, he would lose a battle to Dan Severn, but three months later, he was back. This time, he ran the table, defeating Dave Beneteau, Anthony Macias and Tank Abbott to win the UFC 6 tournament.

Following a 33-minute draw with Ken Shamrock in a UFC 7 superfight, Taktarov returned to the Octagon a final time in December 1995 for the Ultimate Ultimate tournament. After two victories over Beneteau and Marco Ruas, he would lose a second time to Severn in his last UFC bout.

Still competing in MMA up until 2008, Taktarov finally hit the big screen as an actor. Seen in such hits as *Bad Boys II*, *We Own The Night*, *Air Force One* and *Predators*, Taktarov's dream may have been deferred, but he certainly had a heck of a tale to tell once he got there.

Claiming before his first bout that he was "going to be the most athletic person that's ever stepped into the Octagon," the 6'0," 280-pound Abbott certainly didn't fit that description. Nevertheless, the self-described "pit fighter" was an unrepentant brawler who had the power and wrestling skills to give anyone fits. But mainly, it was his power, and when Abbott caught his opponents clean, it was lights out. The fans loved it, as well as Tank's anti-hero demeanor. He wasn't a squeaky clean all-American boy; he was the stereotype of the guy coming off the bar stool and into the Octagon. Such an image would hurt the sport down the line, but for now, everyone ate it up.

Fans also quickly embraced Brazil's Marco Ruas, who won the UFC 7 tournament in Buffalo, New York, on September 8, 1995, with a well-rounded and unique style, aptly titled "Ruas Vale Tudo." The Rio de Janeiro native, who finished Larry Cureton, Remco Pardoel and Paul Varelans on his way to the tourney crown, also introduced fight fans to the best nickname in the sport: "The King of the Streets."

In UFC 7's main event, Ken Shamrock successfully defended his superfight title by engaging in a 33-minute draw with Oleg Taktarov. It was far from an aesthetic success, though, as the bout lacked any sustained or compelling action. Shamrock seemed content to do just enough while standing and on the canvas to keep Taktarov at bay. Taktarov's offense was virtually non-existent, as he was unable to find an opening from his back for a submission against the defensively sound Shamrock. Although he was able to land some shots while standing, that was not enough to hinder Shamrock. UFC was going to be in trouble if it didn't start imposing rules to avoid stalemates like this, and the promotion knew it.

Now two years into its run, UFC again tried to shake things up for its two-year anniversary, putting together an event called The Ultimate Ultimate on December 16. The eight-man tournament featured the most notable stars from past events. Though fighters like Gracie and Shamrock weren't involved, it was still an interesting evening, one made better by the introduction of judges who would select a winner if the bouts went the distance.

In terms of timing for the event, quarterfinal bouts were scheduled for 15 minutes, semis for 18 minutes, and the final for 27 minutes with a three-minute overtime. The quarterfinals did not need the judges, with Taktarov, Ruas, Severn and Abbott all finishing their foes. From there on, it was decision time, with Taktarov getting the nod over Ruas and Severn defeating Abbott. In the final, Severn picked up another tournament title by winning the decision over Taktarov, clearly establishing himself as the most dominant fighter in UFC.

PAUL VARELANS
SUNNYVALE, CA

DEBUT: UFC 6, JULY 14, 1995

Few nicknames are as apt as the one given to Mr. Paul "The Polar Bear" Varelans. One look at the 6'8," 300-pounder, and you would instantly agree that "The Polar Bear" fits the bill. However, beyond his moniker, Varelans was a staple of the early UFC broadcasts. This powerful and effective fighter was resilient in the face of danger and was able to consistently beat fighters like Cal Worsham, Mark Hall and Joe Moreira.

But when Varelans stepped up against the next level of competition, UFC standouts like Tank Abbott, Marco Ruas, Dan Severn and Kimo Leopoldo always prevailed.

CAL WORSHAM
FOLSOM, CA

DEBUT: UFC 6, JULY 14, 1995

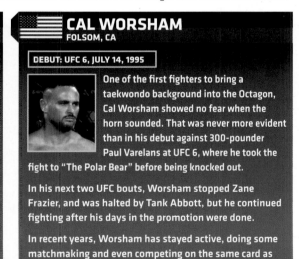

One of the first fighters to bring a taekwondo background into the Octagon, Cal Worsham showed no fear when the horn sounded. That was never more evident than in his debut against 300-pounder Paul Varelans at UFC 6, where he took the fight to "The Polar Bear" before being knocked out.

In his next two UFC bouts, Worsham stopped Zane Frazier, and was halted by Tank Abbott, but he continued fighting after his days in the promotion were done.

In recent years, Worsham has stayed active, doing some matchmaking and even competing on the same card as his son, Hunter. In his last bout, he lost a decision to UFC Hall of Famer Dan Severn in 2011.

DAVE BENETEAU
WINDSOR, CANADA

DEBUT: UFC 5, APRIL 7, 1995

He eventually became a criminal lawyer in his native Canada, but back in the early days of UFC, "Dangerous" Dave Beneteau laid down the law of a different sort. Scoring two quick wins in his UFC 5 debut over Asbel Cancio and Todd Medina which lasted a combined 2:33, Beneteau was considered to be a serious threat to future UFC Hall of Famer Dan "The Beast" Severn. However, "The Beast" emerged victorious in that night's tournament, submitting Beneteau in 3:01. Back-to-back losses to Oleg Taktarov and a nearly two-year break followed, but Beneteau finished his UFC career on a high note with a UFC 15 win over Carlos Baretto in 1997.

FIGHTS OF THE YEAR

KNOCKOUTS OF THE YEAR

SUBMISSIONS OF THE YEAR

UFC 5

TAKTAROV   WSUB1   VERDICIA

UFC 6

VARELANS   KO1   WORSHAM

UFC 7

RUAS   TKO1   VARELANS

ULTIMATE ULTIMATE 95

SEVERN   WSUB1   VARELANS

UFC 6
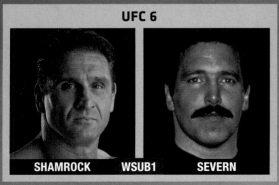
SHAMROCK   WSUB1   SEVERN

UFC 5
HESS   TKO1   ANDERSON

UFC 6
ABBOTT   KO1   MATUA

UFC 7
RUAS   TKO1   VARELANS

UFC 6
ABBOTT   TKO1   VARELANS

UFC 6
VARELANS   KO1   WORSHAM

UFC 6
SHAMROCK   WSUB1   SEVERN

UFC 5
TAKTAROV   WSUB1   VERDICIA

UFC 7
RUAS   WSUB1   CURETON

ULTIMATE ULTIMATE 95
SEVERN   WSUB1   VARELANS

UFC 6
TAKTAROV   WSUB1   MACIAS

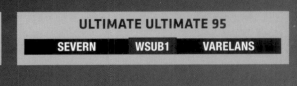

DEBUTS

UFC 5	UFC 6	UFC 7
DAVE BENETEAU	JOEL SUTTON	MARK HALL
ASBEL CANCIO	JACK MCGLAUGHLIN	RYAN PARKER
OLEG TAKTAROV	HE-MAN GIPSON	GERRY HARRIS
TODD MEDINA	TANK ABBOTT	DAVID HOOD
ERNIE VERDICIA	JOHN MATUA	SCOTT BESSAC
LARRY CURETON	PAUL VARELANS	ONASSIS PARUNGAO
JON HESS	CAL WORSHAM	FRANCESCO MATURI
ANDY ANDERSON	RUDYARD MONCAYO	GEZA KAHLMAN JR.
JOHN DOWDY		MARCO RUAS

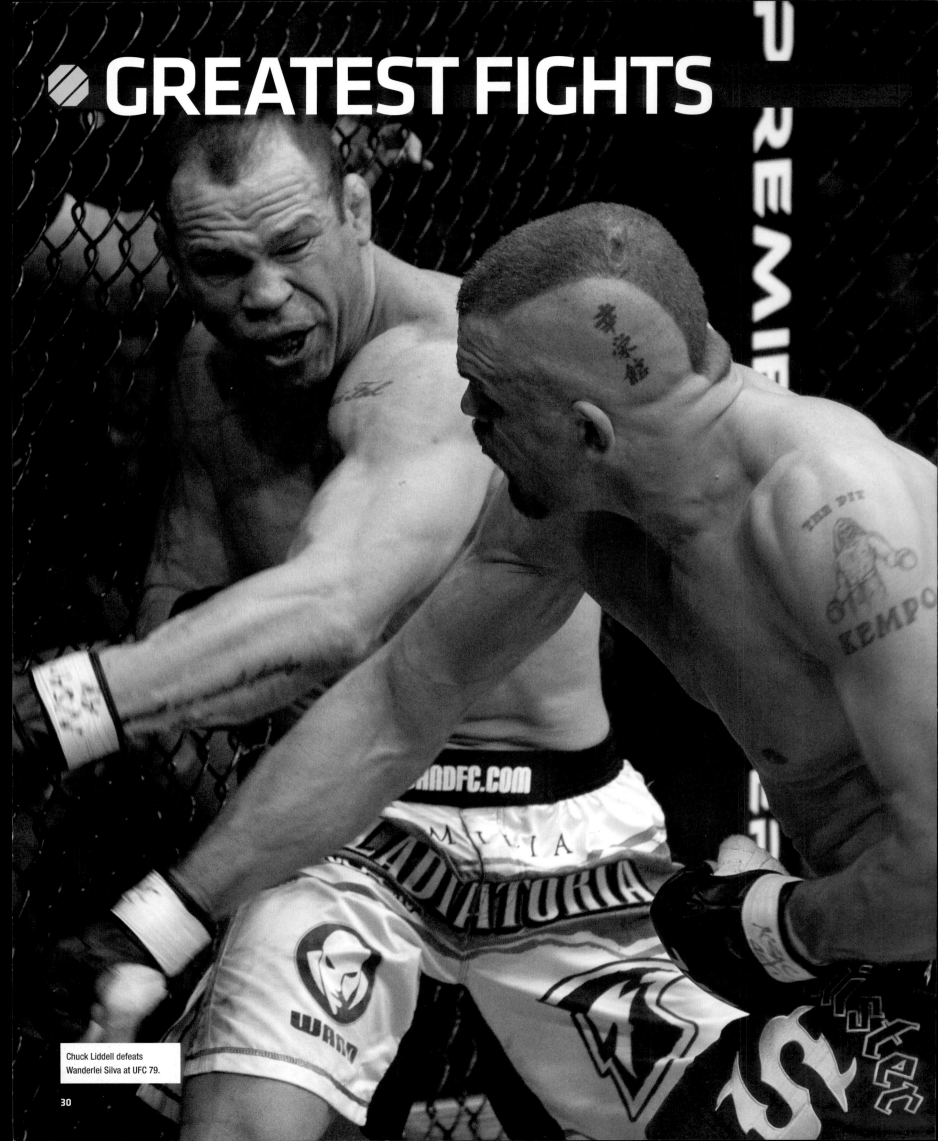

Chuck Liddell defeats
Wanderlei Silva at UFC 79.

UFC 4
ROYCE GRACIE vs DAN SEVERN

With dominant finishes of Anthony Macias and Marcus Bossett, world-class wrestler Dan "The Beast" Severn emerged at December 16, 1994's UFC 4: Revenge Of The Warriors event as perhaps the only person capable of giving superstar Royce Gracie a fight. And what a fight he gave, battling hard for more than 15 minutes until Gracie finally locked in the finishing triangle choke to win his third UFC tournament title.

UFC 22
FRANK SHAMROCK vs TITO ORTIZ

This was one of the most memorable fights from the early UFC shows and—in the eyes of many—the best of the pre-Zuffa era. Tito Ortiz and Frank Shamrock went to war for three rounds, where it was safe to say that either man had a good chance of eventually winning the fight. By the fourth round, though, Ortiz was losing steam, and his conditioning betrayed him. Shamrock pounced and stopped him, defending his title for the fourth time in his final UFC bout. However, Ortiz learned a valuable lesson that day. Never again would conditioning be an issue for "The Huntington Beach Bad Boy," who instead adopted a Spartan philosophy for his future fight preparations.

UFC 31
RANDY COUTURE vs PEDRO RIZZO I

Heavy-handed Brazilian Pedro Rizzo was regarded as the heir apparent to the heavyweight crown held by Randy "The Natural" Couture, and once again, many considered "The Natural" the underdog. When the horn sounded, though, it was Couture's will and heart that ruled the day as he pounded out a close but well-earned unanimous decision over "The Rock." Want to know how much heart he showed that night? Ask anyone who was at the post-fight conference. Couture was barely able to walk to his seat on the podium after enduring Rizzo's hellacious leg kicks for five rounds.

UFC 35
JENS PULVER vs BJ PENN I

To most observers, this fight should have been over before it started. No one gave reigning lightweight champ, "Lil' Evil," Jens Pulver, a chance of beating "The Prodigy," BJ Penn, in this matchup. Yet in one of the grittiest performances in UFC history, "Lil' Evil" successfully defended his crown by beating Penn via a five-round decision. The loss crushed Penn, the heavily favored Hawaiian. "I didn't know what I was going to do with my life or my career," Penn remembered. "Everything was in shambles. I didn't know what to think, I didn't know where to go. The only thing I was sure about was that it was a great learning experience."

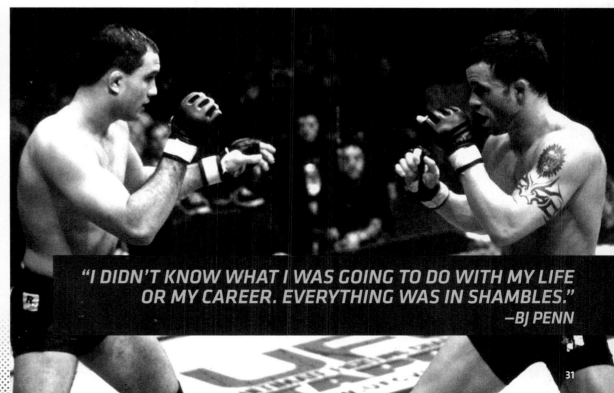

"I DIDN'T KNOW WHAT I WAS GOING TO DO WITH MY LIFE OR MY CAREER. EVERYTHING WAS IN SHAMBLES."
—BJ PENN

THE ULTIMATE FIGHTER 1 FINALE
FORREST GRIFFIN vs STEPHAN BONNAR I

In a pitched battle between two scrappers who fought as if a six-figure UFC contract was on the line—and it was—Forrest Griffin and Stephan Bonnar gave fight fans a brawl they will always remember. Add in the fact that this standup war was being televised live to millions on TV, and the impact of the bout was even more profound. It was bombs away from the opening horn, with both fighters growing progressively more tired as the rounds passed, but refusing to give ground. In the end, the decision went to Griffin, but there were no losers in the Octagon. After the decision was announced, contracts were awarded to both fighters.

UFC 52
MATT HUGHES vs FRANK TRIGG II

Just one week after Forrest Griffin and Stephan Bonnar waged war and put UFC on the mainstream map, veterans Matt Hughes and Frank Trigg showed mixed martial arts fans a war of their own. This time, the battle was at the highest levels of the sport, with the UFC welterweight crown on the line. As soon as the pre-fight staredown ended, these two 170-pound standouts got down to business. Trigg stunned Hughes with strikes (and an inadvertent low blow) early and locked in a rear-naked choke seconds later, but the champion escaped. After slamming Trigg to the mat, he locked in a choke of his own, ending the frenetic instant-classic at the 4:09 mark.

UFC 58
GEORGES ST-PIERRE VS BJ PENN I

The big question about Georges St-Pierre entering into a fight against prodigal son BJ Penn was how he would react in the face of adversity. The first time he faced it against Matt Hughes, St-Pierre folded. Against Penn in a first round that saw him bloodied and battered, the Canadian bit down on his mouthpiece and went to war, winning the next two rounds to eke out a close decision and earn a rematch with Hughes. It was stirring stuff from GSP in a bout that was tense from start to finish as two of the best 170-pounders in the world matched wits and fists for 15 minutes.

THE ULTIMATE FIGHTER 3 FINALE
KENDALL GROVE vs ED HERMAN

The fact that UFC awarded contracts to both Kendall Grove and Ed Herman—the first time that happened since Forrest Griffin and Stephan Bonnar waged war at The Ultimate Fighter 1 Finale—should immediately tell you how good this bout was. Herman controlled the first round, while Grove came back in the second. Both fighters fought like they had everything to lose in a third round that had more twists and turns than a rollercoaster. Each combatant was seemingly seconds away from victory or defeat, depending on the moment, and it was a memorable fight, to say the very least.

UFC 63
MATT HUGHES vs BJ PENN II

BJ Penn was at the top of his game for 10 minutes against Matt Hughes in their September 2006 rematch. Hughes, who had lost his title the first time to "The Prodigy," appeared to be on his way to another defeat. He even turned to prayer to help him out of a tight submission lock by Penn in the second round. But you can never underestimate the heart of a champion, and Hughes roared back to stop Penn in the third round and avenge his loss to the Hawaii native. Hughes later said, "I knew I had lost the first two rounds; that just meant I had three left."

"I KNEW I HAD LOST THE FIRST TWO ROUNDS; THAT JUST MEANT I HAD THREE LEFT."
—MATT HUGHES

UFC FIGHT NIGHT 6
DIEGO SANCHEZ vs KARO PARISYAN

Elite 170-pounders Diego Sanchez and Karo "The Heat" Parisyan locked horns in a bout that shows skeptics proof of what mixed martial arts is all about. Although the then-unbeaten Sanchez' true arrival as one of the best welterweights in the world came at Parisyan's expense via decision, "The Heat" should never hang his head for this performance. He landed his judo throws on Sanchez and continued to battle, even as the seemingly indefatigable Albuquerque native kept attacking for 15 torrid minutes. If you can't appreciate this fight for its technical and visceral brilliance, you're watching the wrong sport.

UFC FIGHT NIGHT 10
SAM STOUT vs SPENCER FISHER II

The rematch between lightweight standouts Spencer Fisher and Sam Stout made their exciting first fight look like a boring three-round waltz. Think of Forrest Griffin vs Stephan Bonnar, sped up and with even more flush shots landed. Fisher and Stout left it all in the Octagon that June night in Florida. While they only had the bruises and cuts to show for it, they also had the type of battle that will be remembered long after Fisher's three-round decision win is forgotten.

THE ULTIMATE FIGHTER: TEAM HUGHES VS TEAM SERRA FINALE
ROGER HUERTA vs CLAY GUIDA

To be considered "great," a fight must have more than frantic action and back-and-forth momentum swings—though those attributes don't hurt. What a fight truly needs to enter the realm of the classics, is drama. The bout between Roger Huerta and Clay Guida lived up to that standard spectacularly. Down two rounds to none on all three judges' scorecards, Huerta needed to stop or submit Guida in the final round to win. He did exactly that, stunning Guida with a knee before getting his foe's back and sinking in a fight-ending rear-naked choke. It was a fight in which everybody in attendance rose in unison to salute the most memorable battle of 2007.

UFC 79
CHUCK LIDDELL vs WANDERLEI SILVA

Six years in the making, the showdown between Chuck Liddell and Wanderlei Silva—the most dominant light heavyweights of this era—was worth the wait. Punctuated by brutal close-range exchanges, this was a fight that had patrons at the Mandalay Bay Events Center on their feet and people at home jumping off their couches. In the end, Liddell revived his career with a three-round win. In defeat, Silva remained one of the sport's true action heroes.

RAMPAGE JACKSON vs FORREST GRIFFIN

This UFC light heavyweight battle was everything you hoped for in a championship fight. For five rounds, Forrest Griffin and Rampage Jackson fought as if nothing else mattered. Filled with knockdowns, tactical stalemates, bone-rattling power shots, submission attempts and drama, this fight had it all. Even though there were rumblings in certain sectors about the decision, this was a close fight that could have gone either way. Griffin didn't have to explain himself for winning, and Jackson should not have felt ashamed in his defeat; both men did the sport proud on this night.

THE ULTIMATE FIGHTER: UNITED STATES VS UNITED KINGDOM FINALE
DIEGO SANCHEZ VS CLAY GUIDA

If Diego Sanchez and Clay Guida stood in opposite corners and didn't engage for 14 minutes and 30 seconds, the first 30 seconds of their bout still would have earned them a spot here; that's how exciting the frenetic toe-to-toe opening was. Luckily for us, they kept the pace high throughout the three-round battle, and this fight had something for everyone. If someone ever wonders why the lightweights are considered the most exciting division in the sport, show them this fight.

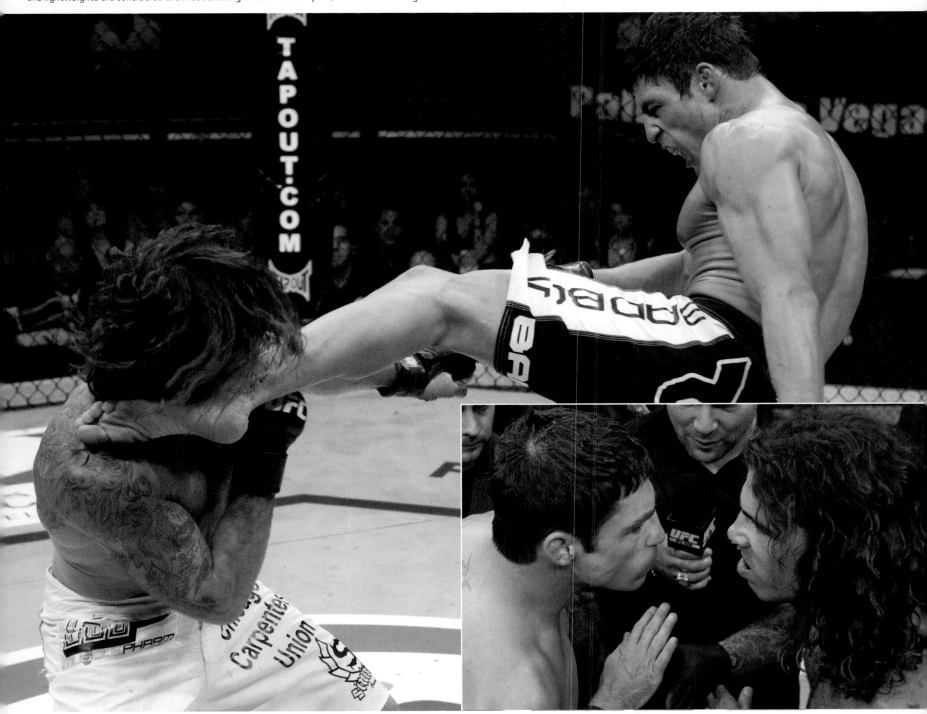

UFC 102
RANDY COUTURE VS MINOTAURO NOGUEIRA

At Octagon-side that August night in Portland, some likened this fight to the 1975 "Thrilla in Manila" between Muhammad Ali and Joe Frazier, and that opinion still stands today. Minotauro Nogueira and Randy Couture may have been in the final third of their storied careers. When you put two great fighters together, there's just something that turns the clock back and lets you see what made them so special. This was 15 minutes of fighting that anyone who saw it wouldn't soon forget, and it was also a primer for the rest of those young bucks out there on how to represent the sport and themselves when the horn sounds.

UFC 116
CHRIS LEBEN VS YOSHIHIRO AKIYAMA

On a stellar card that featured several Fight of the Night-worthy bouts, Chris Leben and Yoshihiro Akiyama took that competition as a challenge. They went on to perform not only the UFC 116 Fight of the Night, but one of the best to date. Featuring fierce toe-to-toe action, changes in momentum, and a shocking and exciting finish, this bout didn't disappoint. In the process, Leben, fighting (and winning) for the second time in two weeks, completed his transformation from MMA's problem child to a legit middleweight contender.

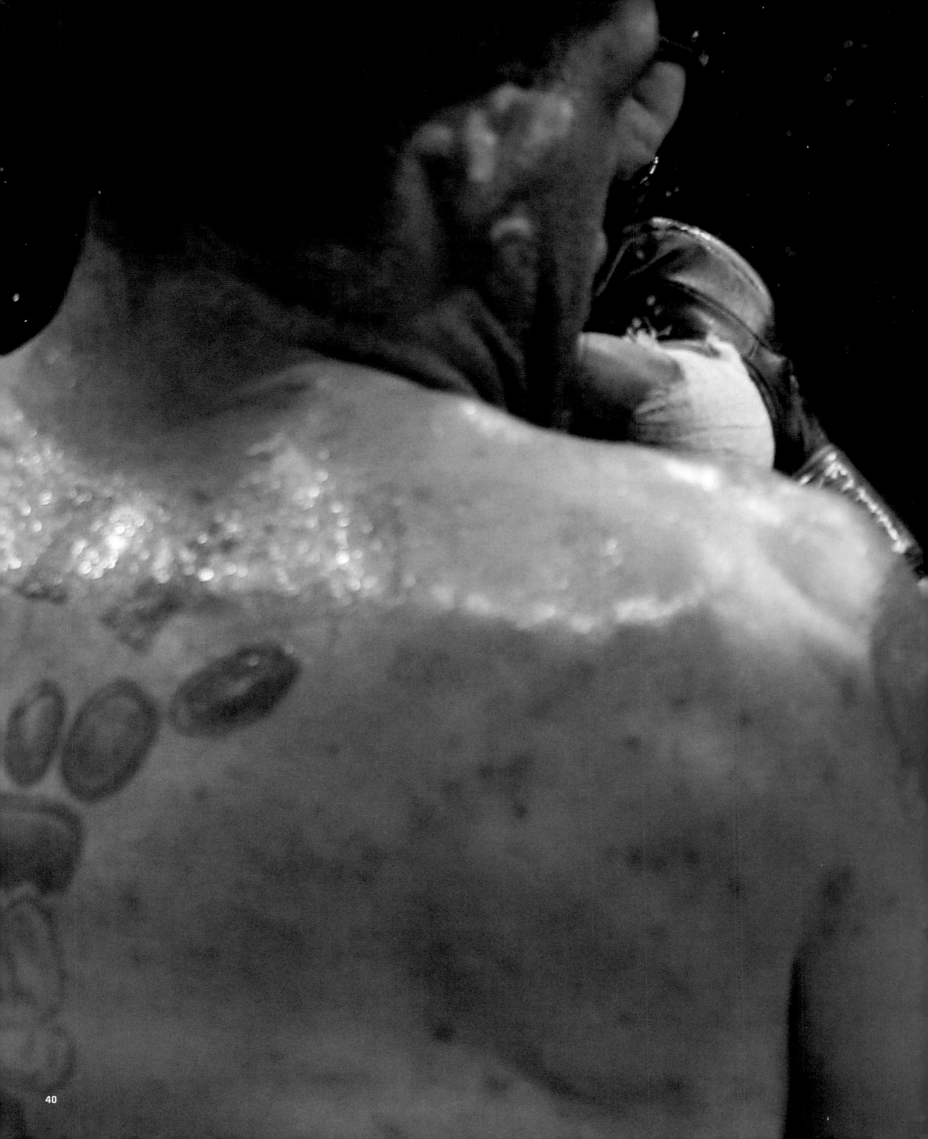

UFC FIGHT NIGHT: HUNT VS BIGFOOT
MARK HUNT vs BIGFOOT SILVA

No one expected the December 2013 heavyweight clash between Mark Hunt and Antonio "Bigfoot" Silva to last five rounds; most thought getting into the second round would be a stretch. But not only did these former training partners go the 25-minute distance, they also delivered an epic back-and-forth battle where the only fair decision—a draw—should have been rendered. And it was, leaving no losers in Brisbane, Australia. Of course, Silva's test after the bout for elevated testosterone levels put a damper on the post-fight euphoria, but the memories of the bout itself remain intact.

UFC 117
ANDERSON SILVA vs CHAEL SONNEN I

The drama before this UFC 117 bout took place couldn't hold a candle to what happened on fight night, as Anderson Silva and Chael Sonnen engaged in a championship fight for the ages. Sonnen dominated the majority of the bout with his ground-and-pound attack. However, each moment before he would take the previously untouchable title holder to the mat was filled with tension as Silva unleashed the strikes many believed would end the fight. Even though he got rocked on a few occasions, Sonnen was resolute in his attack. As the seconds ticked by, he got closer and closer to one of the sport's great upsets and the realization of a dream. Then, like the truest of true champions, Silva pulled off a fifth-round submission. Calling it a spectacular comeback simply doesn't do it justice.

UFC 125
FRANKIE EDGAR vs GRAY MAYNARD II

Perennial underdog Frankie Edgar, filled that role once again when he defended his lightweight crown for the second time against Gray Maynard, the only man to beat him. In the first round, it looked like the end of Edgar's reign, as "The Bully" knocked him down multiple times. Yet amazingly, Edgar roared back, and the two lightweights traded shifts of momentum until a fair draw verdict was rendered at the end of five fast-paced rounds.

UFC 139
SHOGUN RUA vs DAN HENDERSON I

If you watch a fight with top-level technique, an action-packed brawl or an amazing display of heart, you'll undoubtedly be happy to see at least one of the three. Two? That's a Fight of the Year candidate. All three, like we saw in the UFC 139 bout between Dan Henderson and Shogun Rua, in November 2011? That's all-time great territory, and that's what this fight was. From start to finish, everything that makes mixed martial arts great was on display, with two of the sport's superstars fighting in San Jose as if there were more than a win on the line. For nearly half an hour, Henderson and Shogun traded blows that would have knocked out lesser men, pulled off amazing escapes and comebacks, and truly left everything they had in the Octagon. Even before Henderson left the Octagon with the decision victory, it was clear that this match was something special.

UFC: SILVA VS STANN
WANDERLEI SILVA vs BRIAN STANN

Most expected the bout between Wanderlei Silva and Brian Stann to be a standup battle. No one could have forecasted the intense slugfest that the two light heavyweights delivered for nine minutes and eight seconds until Silva, the legendary "Axe Murderer," emerged with a stirring knockout victory. Calling it epic would be an understatement.

JON JONES VS ALEXANDER GUSTAFSSON

Jon Jones was on the verge of setting a new light heavyweight record for successful title defenses. Jones' performances in the Octagon made him appear unbeatable, but he found a worthy rival in Sweden's Alexander Gustafsson. For five rounds at UFC 165 on September 21, 2013, the two battled it out on nearly even terms. With Jones in danger of losing his crown, a late surge allowed him to escape with a decision and his title.

UFC 171

JOHNY HENDRICKS VS ROBBIE LAWLER I

The disappointment of Johny Hendricks' November 2013 loss to Georges St-Pierre vanished in the space of two words at the American Airlines Center on March 15, 2014. When Bruce Buffer said, "AND NEW...", declaring Hendricks the new UFC welterweight champion after a five-round classic with Robbie Lawler, the 170-pound division had its new king. Many believed Hendricks should have held that crown a few months earlier after his controversial split decision defeat to GSP, who later vacated the belt. But if you ask Hendricks, he will undoubtedly say that finally getting the belt was worth the wait, even if he had to walk through fire to get it.

JOSE ALDO vs CHAD MENDES II

After getting knocked out in a single round during his first championship match against Jose Aldo in 2012, Chad Mendes had a huge mountain to climb to get back to a featherweight title fight. He did just that, winning five straight fights to earn a rematch against Aldo in Brazil on October 25, 2014. This wasn't the same fighter, though, and this most certainly wasn't the same fight. This time around, it was 25 minutes' worth of war, and although Aldo retained his belt again, the Brazilian knew he was had passed one of the toughest tests of his career.

1996

Don Frye wins the 8-man tournament at UFC 8.

Entering UFC's first event in Puerto Rico on February 16, 1996, 410-pound Thomas Ramirez, the only local Puerto Rican fighter on the card, was advertised as being 200-0. In eight seconds, debuting Don Frye made that 200-1 with a knockout that stood for years as the fastest in UFC history. From that moment on, UFC had the new star it needed. The fledgling promotion had been trying to replace its first star, Royce Gracie, who had left the company after UFC 5, just 10 months earlier.

The 30-year-old Frye, a former college wrestling standout, had the look of a Hollywood action hero and the real-life swagger to match. By the end of his first night in the Octagon at UFC 8, Frye introduced himself to the world by defeating Ramirez, Sam Adkins and Gary Goodridge—all by knockout—winning the event's tournament.

Ken Shamrock was still splitting his schedule between fights in the United States and battles in Japan's Pancrase promotion. Regardless, he found time to return to the Octagon to defeat Kimo Leopoldo via submission in their UFC 8 superfight.

Giving up 65 pounds to Leopoldo, Shamrock used his superior MMA experience to level the playing field by taking his foe down to the mat. Shamrock kept himself in the dominant top position for much of the bout, eventually finding an opening to nab an ankle lock and force a tapout at the 4:24 mark.

The event marked certain changes to the rules, with time limits changed to 10 minutes per fight in the first two rounds of tournament bouts, and 15 minutes in superfight and tournament final bouts. Judges' decisions were also implemented for fights that reached the entire time limit. Unlike the future 10-point must system, three judges simply held up the name of the competitor they believed had won the fight.

Despite these nuances, debutants like Gary "Big Daddy" Goodridge and 21-year-old Jerry Bohlander didn't need judges. Goodridge knocked out Paul Herrera in one of the most dominant finishes in UFC history, and Bohlander submitted 330-pound Scott Ferrozzo a little over nine minutes into their bout.

The next event was scheduled for three months later, on May 17, 1996, at Cobo Arena in Detroit, Michigan. The UFC 9 main event was expected to be a good one, with local hero Dan "The Beast" Severn taking on Shamrock in a rematch that would be the evening's superfight.

As the bout drew closer, the promotion came under fire from Arizona senator John McCain, who famously referred to mixed martial arts as "human cockfighting" before starting a letter writing campaign designed to ban the sport.

This campaign hit Michigan, which put the upcoming UFC 9 event in danger of being cancelled. Ultimately, UFC 9 was allowed to proceed at 4:30 p.m. on the day of the show.

The catch? No closed-fist strikes to the head and no headbutts were allowed. Fighters attempting to use those maneuvers did so under the threat of arrest.

The show went on—fists included—but the event would later be remembered for how its main event resulted in what was perhaps the worst bout in organization (and maybe even MMA) history. Severn and Shamrock rarely engaged in their highly anticipated rematch, opting instead to circle each other for 30 minutes before the judges awarded "The Beast" the bout via split decision. This allowed him to even the score with Shamrock, who had submitted him at UFC 6.

The crowd was restless almost from the start, and rightfully so, with the lack of action. At the bout's halfway point, Severn scored a takedown, but he was unable to keep Shamrock on the ground. A second attempt was more successful, at least until Shamrock and Severn changed controlling positions on the mat. Eventually, Severn landed some shots that cut his opponent, but that was the extent of the action. The rest of regulation time and two overtime periods were unable to decisively settle anything.

"THE FIRST TIME I SAW IT, I THOUGHT IT WAS THE GREATEST THING I HAD EVER SEEN IN MY LIFE. AND I DIDN'T THINK I WAS THE ONLY ONE THINKING THAT WAY."
—MARK COLEMAN

DAVID ABBOTT

DEBUT: UFC 6, JULY 14, 1995

HUNTINGTON BEACH, CA

"I'm going to be the most athletic person that's ever stepped into the Octagon." With those words, the UFC career of David "Tank" Abbott began. And while he wasn't going to live up to that statement, he established himself not only as one of the most popular figures in UFC, but also as a legitimate knockout artist.

Entering the Octagon at UFC 6 in 1995 with a style described as "pit fighting," Abbott kept it quiet that he was an accomplished high school and junior college wrestler. Despite graduating from Long Beach State University with a degree in history, he was content to play the role of barroom brawler.

His discretion paid off, as his chilling 18-second knockout of John Matua set the stage for a career that—win or lose—saw him captivate fans for years.

On that first July night in UFC, Abbott stopped Matua and Paul Varelans before being submitted by Oleg Taktarov. The pattern of Tank's career was set: If you let him be the bully, he would beat you; if you bullied him or got him to the canvas, the fight was over.

That didn't stop fans from tuning in whenever Abbott fought. Through 1995 and 1996, he was one of the organization's most reliable attractions, able to beat most foes, but unable to deal with world-class competitors like Dan Severn, Don Frye and Vitor Belfort.

Even with back-to-back losses against Frye and Belfort, Abbott was awarded a heavyweight title shot against Maurice Smith at UFC 15 in October 1997. Not surprisingly, Smith finished Abbott in 8:08.

After a knockout loss to Pedro Rizzo at UFC Brazil in 1998, Abbott took a break from the sport for nearly five years. He returned at UFC 41, where he was submitted by Frank Mir in 46 seconds. After two more Octagon defeats, Abbott left UFC but remained a high-profile name for the résumés of up-and-coming fighters.

MARK COLEMAN

DEBUT: UFC 10, JULY 12, 1996
UFC 10 TOURNAMENT WINNER
UFC 11 TOURNAMENT WINNER
UFC HEAVYWEIGHT CHAMPION (1997)
UFC HALL OF FAME (2008)

FREMONT, OH

Mark "The Hammer" Coleman was 31 years old. He had a stellar amateur wrestling career that saw him win an NCAA championship in 1988 for Ohio State University, earn All-American status twice and compete for the United States in the 1992 Olympics. But the competitive fires still burned, and he had no idea where his athletic career would lead him.

Then he turned on the television, saw UFC and knew immediately that was what he was going to do. While adding striking to his wrestling wasn't going to be the easiest thing to do (at least on paper), Coleman and his fellow wrestlers saw that as a mere formality-a minor detail on their way to greatness in the Octagon.

Talent, athleticism and unbelievable strength and technique didn't hurt, either. In Coleman's UFC debut on July 12, 1996, in Birmingham, Alabama, he displayed all these traits in romping over Moti Horenstein, Gary Goodridge and Don Frye in one night. He won the UFC 10 tournament and become an instant star in mixed martial arts. The Frye victory in particular was special to Coleman, who notes it as the highlight of his UFC career.

Just two months later, Coleman was back in the Octagon and, even more impressive, beating Julian Sanchez and Brian Johnston in a combined 3:05 to win the UFC 11 tournament in Augusta, Georgia. In February 1997, he capped off his amazing run with a 2:57 win over UFC standout (and fellow Hall of Famer) Dan Severn to become the first UFC heavyweight champion.

While the wins were impressive, Coleman was so dominant that many thought he would never be beaten.

However, the streak did come to an end at UFC 14, when Coleman lost by unanimous decision against Maurice Smith. Although he left the organization following subsequent setbacks at the hands of Pete Williams and Pedro Rizzo, you couldn't keep "The Hammer" down. After a brief break, he traveled to Japan to compete in the PRIDE organization, where he resurrected his career.

In 2000, he defeated Masaaki Satake, Akira Shoji, Kazuyuki Fujita and Igor Vovchanchyn in succession to win the PRIDE Grand Prix finals, re-establishing himself as one of the best heavyweights in the world. Bouts against the likes of Minotauro Nogueira, Fedor Emelianenko, Mirko Cro Cop and Shogun Rua followed, captivating the MMA world.

But his heart always stayed with UFC, and in March 2008, Coleman was inducted into the UFC Hall of Fame. The ceremony took place in his beloved hometown of Columbus. Later on the night of his induction, he announced that he was returning to active duty in the Octagon. In his first bout back, at UFC 93 in January 2009, he lost a Fight of the Night battle via third-round TKO to Shogun in a rematch of their 2006 PRIDE fight that Coleman had won. But less than six months later, Coleman returned and showed off the moves that earned him the title of "Godfather of Ground-and-Pound," as he won a three-round unanimous decision over Stephan Bonnar at UFC 100.

Coleman would lose his last UFC bout via submission to Randy Couture in February 2010, but he will forever remain "The Hammer" in the eyes of his legion of fans. As for the warriors of the Octagon, they all owe a debt to Coleman—one of the sport's true innovators for his ability to translate wrestling into mixed martial arts success.

JERRY BOHLANDER
NAPA, CA

DEBUT: UFC 8, FEBRUARY 16, 1996
UFC 12 LIGHTWEIGHT TOURNAMENT WINNER

A member of Ken Shamrock's Lion's Den team, Jerry Bohlander was one of the organization's first "golden boys." A tenacious battler who specialized in submissions, Bohlander debuted in the UFC in 1996. Though his two opponents on the "David vs Goliath" card outsized him, he still submitted Scott Ferrozzo before getting stopped by Gary Goodridge. When he returned later that year, he would go 3-0 and win the UFC 12 lightweight tournament title. Bohlander's last UFC win would come over Kevin Jackson at UFC 16, with his 1999 cut-induced loss to Tito Ortiz being his last appearance in the Octagon.

SCOTT FERROZZO
SHAKOPEE, MN

DEBUT: UFC 8, FEBRUARY 16, 1996

One of the appeals of the early UFC events was that there were just as many characters as there were fighters. Scott Ferrozzo had a little bit of both in him. Managed by the future "Voice of The Octagon," Bruce Buffer, Ferrozzo was submitted in his first Octagon bout by Jerry Bohlander at UFC 8. Seven months later, he earned an alternate spot in the UFC 11 tournament with a win against Sam Fulton. When Bohlander fell out due to injury, the 300-pounder made the most of it, edging Tank Abbott in a bout still debated to this day. Ferrozzo retired after a 43-second loss to Vitor Belfort at UFC 12.

BRIAN JOHNSTON
SAN JOSE, CA

DEBUT: UFC 10, JULY 12, 1996

One of the first hybrid fighters to enter the Octagon in the early days of UFC, Brian Johnston could handle himself standing or on the mat. In 1996, he shined in victories over Scott Fiedler and Reza Nasri. Unfortunately, most of the Californian's bouts came against the elite of UFC, leading him to losses against Don Frye, Mark Coleman and Ken Shamrock. After leaving UFC and competing everywhere from Brazil to Hawaii, he returned for UFC 14 in 1997, where he faced Dan Bobish. A stroke cut his career short, but he has thankfully recovered.

ROBERTO TRAVEN
RIO DE JANEIRO, BRAZIL

DEBUT: UFC 11, SEPTEMBER 20, 1996

Roberto Traven was a gifted jiu-jitsu prodigy who earned his black belt in just four years. As one of the top grapplers in the world, he won numerous titles. Likewise, he tore out of the gate in MMA, winning his first five fights—including an 83-second finish of Dave Berry in his pro debut at UFC 11 in 1996. An injury kept Traven from continuing on in that night's tournament, and it would prove to be his final moment of glory in the Octagon. He wouldn't be back until 2001, when he was submitted by rookie (and future world champion) Frank Mir at UFC 34.

After UFC 9, there would be no more superfights in the Octagon, at least not ones dubbed as such, and some wondered if the embattled promotion would continue at all. However, Semaphore Entertainment Group (SEG) was nothing if not resilient and stubborn, and on July 12, 1996, UFC 10 found a home at the Fairgrounds Arena in Birmingham, Alabama.

Earlier that year, a fan in Ohio named Mark Coleman watched UFC. While he enjoyed the action, he wanted to take things to a new level by participating in the sport. But Coleman was no ordinary fan.

"I was immediately attracted to it, and I knew immediately that it was what I was gonna do," said Coleman, a 1988 NCAA wrestling champion for Ohio State University and a member of the 1992 United States Olympic team. "The first time I saw it, I thought it was the greatest thing I had ever seen in my life. And I didn't think I was the only one thinking that way."

A few months later he was in the Octagon, blasting out Moti Horenstein in 2:43 while introducing the world to a style of fighting known as ground-and-pound. Coleman defeated Gary Goodridge later that night before finishing up with a shocking TKO of Don Frye that earned the man dubbed "The Hammer" the UFC 10 tournament title.

Coleman said of the win over Frye, "My goal growing up as a little kid was always to be a professional athlete, and at that moment, I really felt like I was a professional athlete. It was so overwhelming when I finally did beat him; it was surreal."

Mark Coleman defeats Stephan Bonnar at UFC 100.

This victory was confirmation that although Royce Gracie's jiu-jitsu dominated the early days of UFC, Coleman, Severn and Frye had ushered in the era of the wrestler.

"Back in 1996, me and a bunch of wrestlers may have been naive, but we just really believed that we were gonna get in there and win these things," Coleman laughed. "I guess that was a good thing because confidence will take you a long way in this sport."

Two months after his stirring debut, Coleman was back for UFC 11 at the Augusta Civic Center in Augusta, Georgia. With fan favorite David "Tank" Abbott back in action for the first time since December 1995. The hope was that "The Hammer" would meet "Tank" in the finals of that night's tournament.

GARY GOODRIDGE
SAINT JAMES, TRINIDAD AND TOBAGO

DEBUT: UFC 8, FEBRUARY 16, 1996

Gary "Big Daddy" Goodridge has always been a fighter's fighter. He doesn't ask who, he doesn't ask how much. He just asks where. A mixed martial artist since UFC 8 in 1996, the Trinidad and Tobago native's record reads like a Who's Who of the sport. Mark Coleman, Marco Ruas, Don Frye, Alistair Overeem, Igor Vovchanchyn, Oleg Taktarov, and Fedor Emelianenko were all in with Goodridge, and one of his strengths was his willingness to fight anyone.

"It's just a warrior attitude," Goodridge said in 2001. "If you're going to war, you've got to be able to go to war with anybody. The sport is not big enough for people to start pointing and choosing whom they will and will not fight. Every fight I turn down, I will not get that fight back."

His debut match with Paul Herrera was quick. And as a barrage of elbows rendered Herrera unconscious, a star—and a career—was born. 4-4 in the Octagon, with wins over Herrera, Jerry Bohlander, John Campatella and Andre Roberts, "Big Daddy" went on to become an even bigger attraction in Japan, where he fought in PRIDE rings from 1997 to 2003.

Coleman did his part, submitting Julian Sanchez and Brian Johnston in a little over three minutes combined. However, after Abbott finished Sam Adkins, he ran into an alternate named Scott Ferrozzo, who upset the fan favorite via decision after 18 minutes.

The brawlers engaged immediately, with Abbott landing some good shots, but Ferrozzo answered right back as the fans roared. A little over a minute in, Ferrozzo was cut over the right eye as Abbott pinned him to the fence. The two exchanged in some trash talk between punches, and knees by Ferrozzo drew even more of a reaction before the two proceeded to throw more wild shots.

Following a quick break for the Octagon-side physician to check Ferrozzo's cut, the match offered more of the same, with each fighter having his moments. Despite being held against the fence, Ferrozzo's knees were scoring and taking their toll. "The Pit Bull" kept imploring Abbott to let him loose, but to no avail.

After the 15-minute time limit expired, the overtime period started with some fury as Abbott tried to turn things around. However, he soon resorted to pushing the fight back to the fence, where Ferrozzo continued to pound away and secure the decision win.

But the grueling win came with a price, as Ferrozzo was unable to continue in the tournament due to exhaustion and the cut over his eye. With no one left to fight, Coleman won the tournament by default—an anti-climactic ending that seemed to epitomize the promotion's struggles at the time.

Tank Abbott punches Pedro Rizzo at UFC Ultimate Brazil.

Heading to Fair Park Arena in Birmingham, Alabama, on December 7, 1996, UFC presented its second Ultimate Ultimate event. Although storm clouds were all around, for one night at least all was well in the world of mixed martial arts. The leading competitors came out in force, including Shamrock, Abbott and Leopoldo. But in the end, the star of the night was Don Frye, returning to form after the Coleman loss by earning his second tournament title with three consecutive wins. In the final, Frye survived an early knockdown from Abbott to roar back and submit the popular brawler in a war that packed plenty of action into just 83 seconds.

Seconds after the opening horn, a left jab by Abbott sent Frye sprawling to the mat. Frye immediately got to his feet but was swarmed by Abbott, who continued to rock him with the left hand. Frye instinctively fired back, but after a quick clinch, Abbott looked to be on the verge of finishing his foe. Moments later, Abbott lost his footing and was pushed to the mat. Frye, seeing his opening, took Abbott's back and eventually sunk in a rear-naked choke that forced Abbott to tap out at the 1:23 mark.

This event was a glowing reminder of why people loved this growing sport. But before the rest of the world got on board there would be dark days ahead for UFC.

 DON FRYE

DEBUT: UFC 8, FEBRUARY 16, 1996
UFC 8 TOURNAMENT WINNER
ULTIMATE ULTIMATE '96 TOURNAMENT WINNER

SIERRA VISTA, AZ

When he first set foot in the Octagon at UFC 8 in 1996, Don "The Predator" Frye looked like he came directly from central casting. Built like a truck, with a Tom Selleck-esque mustache and a swagger that immediately resonated among fans of the relatively new sport of mixed martial arts, Frye was an instant star. He was a fighter with no quit in him, and he had the power to back up any boasts.

The confidence came from a stellar amateur wrestling career, where he worked with UFC legends Dan Severn and Randy Couture. He also held a black belt in judo, along with some pro boxing experience.

His UFC debut didn't last long, as he needed just eight seconds (a record at the time) to knock out Thomas Ramirez. Two more wins over Sam Adkins and Gary Goodridge followed on the same night in Puerto Rico. In a little over three combined minutes, Frye had won the UFC 8 tournament.

After a UFC 9 TKO of the highly touted Amaury Bitetti, Frye competed in the UFC 10 tournament in July 1996 in Alabama. He defeated Mark Hall and Brian Johnston before an upset loss in the night's final to newcomer Mark Coleman.

Frye's perfect record was gone, but it would be the last time he lost in the Octagon. To cap off a hectic year of action, Frye got back to business at December 1996's Ultimate Ultimate tournament, submitting Gary Goodridge, Mark Hall and Tank Abbott to earn his second UFC tournament title.

FIGHTS OF THE YEAR

ULTIMATE ULTIMATE '96

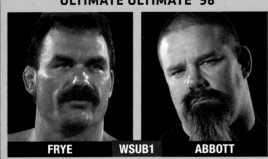

| FRYE | WSUB1 | ABBOTT |

UFC 10

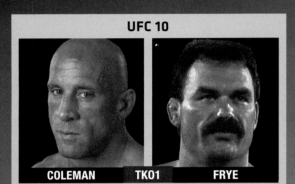

| COLEMAN | TKO1 | FRYE |

UFC 8

| GOODRIDGE | TKO1 | BOHLANDER |

UFC 9

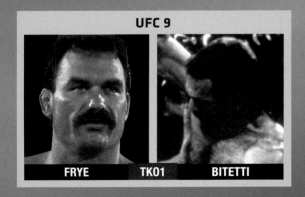

| FRYE | TKO1 | BITETTI |

UFC 11

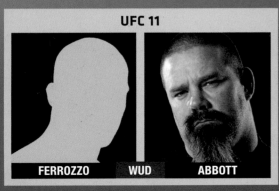

| FERROZZO | WUD | ABBOTT |

KNOCKOUTS OF THE YEAR

UFC 8
| GOODRIDGE | KO1 | HERRERA |

ULTIMATE ULTIMATE '96
| ABBOTT | KO1 | NELMARK |

UFC 10
| COLEMAN | TKO1 | HORENSTEIN |

UFC 9
| HALL | TKO1 | KITAO |

UFC 11
| JOHNSTON | TKO1 | NASRI |

SUBMISSIONS OF THE YEAR

UFC 8
| BOHLANDER | WSUB1 | FERROZZO |

ULTIMATE ULTIMATE '96
| FRYE | WSUB1 | HALL |

UFC 8
| SHAMROCK | WSUB1 | LEOPOLDO |

UFC 11
| COLEMAN | WSUB1 | SANCHEZ |

ULTIMATE ULTIMATE '96
| FRYE | WSUB1 | ABBOTT |

DEBUTS

UFC 8

SAM ADKINS

JERRY BOHLANDER

SCOTT FERROZZO

DON FRYE

GARY GOODRIDGE

PAUL HERRERA

KEITH MIELKE

JOE MOREIRA

THOMAS RAMIREZ

UFC 9

MATT ANDERSEN

AMAURY BITETTI

TAI BOWDEN

RAFAEL CARINO

KOJI KITAO

STEVE NELMARK

MARK SCHULTZ

UFC 10

JOHN CAMPETELLA

MARK COLEMAN

SCOTT FIEDLER

MOTI HORENSTEIN

BRIAN JOHNSTON

UFC 11

DAVE BERRY

SAM FULTON

FABIO GURGEL

REZA NASRI

JULIAN SANCHEZ

ROBERTO TRAVEN

ULTIMATE ULTIMATE '96

JACK NILSSON

BRUCE BUFFER

Bruce Buffer knew that he had found his calling in life. The only dilemma was finding a way to convince SEG, then-owners of Ultimate Fighting Championship, that he was the man to be "the Voice of the Octagon."

"I BLOCK OUT THE AUDIENCE TO A DEGREE. I FEED OFF THEIR ENERGY, BUT I'M NOT LOOKING AT THEM. TO ME, IT'S THE FIGHTERS AND ME, AND THAT'S IT."
—BRUCE BUFFER

The Oklahoma native had already established himself in the business world as the manager of renowned boxing ring announcer Michael Buffer, of "Let's get ready to rumble" fame. However, as a martial artist himself, Bruce felt an immediate affinity for MMA.

Bruce filled in on undercards and made one-off appearances, yet a full-time gig eluded him. Then, an appearance on the hit NBC sitcom *Friends* with UFC fighter Tank Abbott and referee John McCarthy gave him the leverage he needed. Buffer negotiated his way into a steady job beginning with UFC 13 in May 1997.

Since then, Buffer has become synonymous with UFC, with his "It's time" catchphrase and signature move of "The Buffer 180" distinguishing him from his peers in the announcing business. He also survived the "dark ages" of UFC, with the turning point coming when Forrest Griffin and Stephan Bonnar put on an epic battle in the finale of the first season of *The Ultimate Fighter* in 2005.

"The tide started to turn when I realized that when Dana [White] and the Fertitta brothers rolled the dice on *The Ultimate Fighter*, we started to really capture the hearts and minds of the 18- to 34-year-olds," Buffer said. "It started to bring in millions of new fans. But at the same time, the nucleus of fans that we had all along that had watched us since they were 12, they grew up. They come up to me now and say, 'I grew up watching you.' It's just a matter of timing."

Now there are video games, trading cards, a best-selling biography, more than 200,000 followers on Twitter and a weekly radio show. But if you ask Buffer about the best part of his success, he narrows it down to the time spent in the Octagon with two fighters waiting to do battle.

OTHER ANNOUNCERS

JOE MARTINEZ

This respected boxing and MMA announcer was the former voice of the WEC until December 2010. He has since made four appearances inside the UFC Octagon.

ANDY FRIEDLANDER

UFC announcer for international events.

MANNY GARCIA

Worked the Ult mate Ultimate 2 and UFC 12 in 1996-1997.

RICH GOINS

A cult favorite among fight fans to this day, the "G-Man" was the most recognizable person in the middle of the Octagon in the early days of the UFC.

RON JEREMY

Ron Jeremy worked the Octagon as the announcer for UFC 5.

MICHAEL BUFFER

The man known for the immortal phrase "Let's get ready to rumble," Michael Buffer took a break from his work in boxing for a couple of turns in UFC. Eventually, his brother Bruce Buffer took over as "the Voice of the Octagon."

SENSHIRO MATSUYAMA

Worked UFC 23 and UFC 29 in Japan.

JOE ROGAN

Joe Rogan has experienced plenty of success in the entertainment business: his popular stand-up act, the television series *Fear Factor* and as a cast member of *NewsRadio*. But it's the role as UFC's color commentator that may have garnered the taekwondo black belt and jiu-jitsu brown belt the most acclaim. It's not something he expected when he first began working as an interviewer for previous UFC owners SEG, beginning with UFC 12 in Dothan, Alabama.

"In the old SEG, we were in weird little [venues] in the middle of nowhere," he recalled. "You're in a 10,000-seat arena, and there are like 2,000 people in there, scattered. That was the real dark ages."

The gig didn't last long, but when Zuffa took over UFC in 2001, Rogan and some of his friends got tickets for an event.

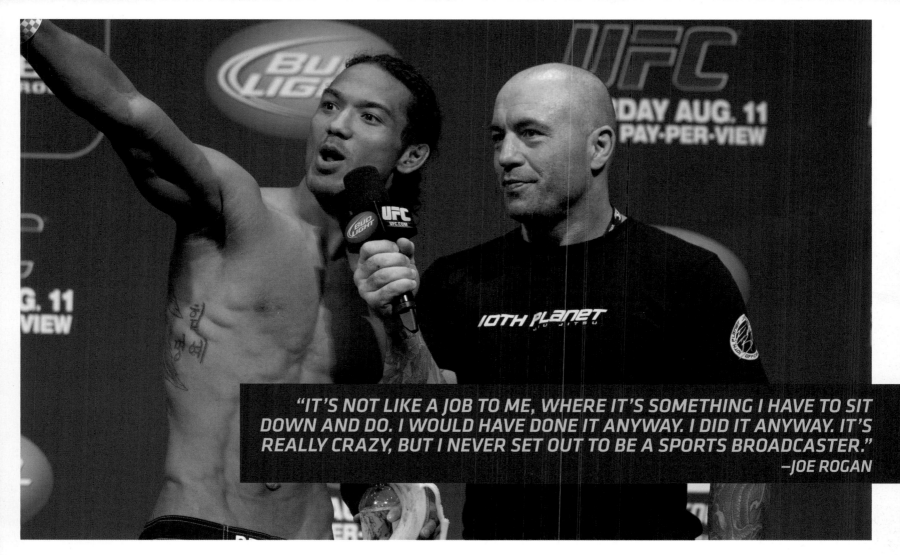

"IT'S NOT LIKE A JOB TO ME, WHERE IT'S SOMETHING I HAVE TO SIT DOWN AND DO. I WOULD HAVE DONE IT ANYWAY. I DID IT ANYWAY. IT'S REALLY CRAZY, BUT I NEVER SET OUT TO BE A SPORTS BROADCASTER."
—JOE ROGAN

One conversation with the diehard MMA fan convinced UFC president Dana White that Rogan was the man for the commentator's chair.

"He [White] was talking to me about fights, and I was just going off about this and that, and he asked me if I ever thought about doing commentary," Rogan said. "I told him that I just wanted to watch. He said, 'Just do it once for me, as a favor.' I said, 'Sure.' I did it once; I did it again and then I wound up doing all of them."

Rogan's commentary mixes the enthusiasm of a fan with the knowledge of someone well versed in combat sports. Many media members can say without a hint of shame that his knowledge of the ground game has saved them on more than one occasion when they looked at a submission and wondered, "What the heck is that?"

"When I do UFC," Rogan said, "my preparation is that I'm a huge MMA fan, and I watch all of them and pay attention to everything.

There are a lot of match-ups that really interest me 100 percent. That's my preparation—it's my life. It's not like a job to me, where it's something I have to sit down and do. I would have done it anyway. I did it anyway. It's really crazy, but I never set out to be a sports broadcaster. That was the criticism I got a lot in the beginning—'Well, he doesn't sound like a sports broadcaster.' Well, I'm not; I don't even know how I got the job."

This self-effacing honesty is a hallmark of Rogan's first love, comedy. To him, such honesty is a key to good comedy in general.

"Honesty and insight, two things that most people don't really have a whole lot of, make good comedy," he said. "What's really funny is stuff that you can relate to, the stuff someone points out that really makes sense to you. That's what's really funny. But in order to really do that correctly, you've got to be honest with yourself. And that's something that very few people really are, which is why there's so much bad comedy and why there are so many boring people.

"These people aren't really honest and they're not figuring life out; they're just pretending they figured life out. The best comedy is: Here's the world through my eyes, and I happen to have an unusual or unique point of view. There's other kinds of comedy, like Carrot Top stuff and other silly stuff—and I'm not knocking any of it, it's all fun and makes people feel better and enjoy the show—but there's a huge difference between a great stand-up comedian like Dave Chappelle and the boring kind of comedy. The boring kind of comedy is like point karate, and the kind of comedy I do is like MMA."

And it's as hard-hitting as the action he calls in the Octagon, making him the perfect man to command the UFC broadcast booth.

MIKE GOLDBERG

Fresh out of a job doing play-by-play for the Detroit Red Wings, Mike Goldberg needed some good news late in 1997. Little did he know that Bruce Connal, one of his producers at ESPN and with the Wings, would be playing Santa Claus that year.

"Goldie, you got a raw deal with the Wings, but I got a gig for you," Connal said. "You need to take a jiu-jitsu class; it's in Japan, but they'll pay you."

Goldberg, who was broadcasting anything and everything to get back on his feet, immediately accepted the job to do play-by-play for something called UFC.

"I had no idea what UFC was," he recalled. "But it was a gig, it was in Japan and it seemed pretty cool. I thought that maybe I'll get a second one out of the whole deal."

It has gone on a bit longer than that. Today, Mike Goldberg has become synonymous with mixed martial arts in general, and UFC in particular. Goldberg with UFC is like Vin Scully with MLB, Keith Jackson with college football or Marv Albert with NBA. You can't have one without the other.

Through his work in the gym, Goldberg has taken his immersion in MMA even further than just showing up on fight night.

Late in 2001, UFC president Dana White brought his play-by-play man down to the UFC Gym to get a taste of how fighters prepared for their fights. After four days of hitting the pads and working out with Bobby Stella, Goldberg was hooked. Since then, Muay Thai has been an integral part of his daily routine.

"It has helped me to see the sport the way I was able to see hockey when I was a hockey broadcaster because I had played hockey since I was seven-years-old," said Goldberg, who admits that he's still learning all the intricate details of the sport. It doesn't hurt having Joe Rogan by his side, either, considering the color commentator's history in jiu-jitsu and taekwondo.

"I look at it like I'm Al Michaels and Joe is John Madden," said Goldberg of his broadcast partner. "I didn't coach the game. I didn't play the game, so I still look at Joe as John Madden. But that being said, it's still important for me to bring more than a fork and a knife to the table. I've been able to achieve that because of my training and because of the time I've spent with the guys who have helped train me and helped me really understand the sport. But I still have a long way until I'm done because I'll always try to get better."

And whether it's show 1,150 or 1,000 for Mike Goldberg, the feeling is always the same when the arena lights go down.

"EVERY UFC EVENT IS THE SUPER BOWL, GAME SEVEN OF THE WORLD SERIES OR THE NCAA CHAMPIONSHIP. THAT TO ME, AS A BROADCASTER, IS WHAT EVERYBODY DREAMS OF."
—MIKE GOLDBERG

"That's when the work ends and the fun begins," he said. "At that point, I can't prep anymore, and the minute we call the first prelim, I get this sense of calm. Then we play that Who song, and I start jumping around like a little kid. That is truly when it's the highest of highs."

"The thing that makes UFC unique and, to me, the best gig in broadcasting today, is that every show is Game Seven," he continued. "I was the sideline guy with Michael Jordan and the Bulls during their first three titles. Every game watching Michael play was a privilege, but there were still Game 44 against a bad Charlotte team and Game 62 against a bad Sacramento team. We don't have those games. Every UFC event is the Super Bowl, Game Seven of the World Series or the NCAA Championship. That to me, as a broadcaster, is what everybody dreams of. You want to play in a Game Seven or broadcast a Game Seven, and I get to do several Game Sevens a year. That's why I've got the greatest job in the world."

JON ANIK

A New England native who joined the UFC broadcast team in 2011, Jon Anik is a respected broadcast journalist who first burst into the public's consciousness during his stint at ESPN. Once with UFC, Anik was put right to work, not just as a commentator, but as the host of the *Ultimate Insider* show and as a host of UFC pre- and post-fight and weigh-in shows. A true pro, Anik is a welcome addition to the UFC team.

KENNY FLORIAN

A former *The Ultimate Fighter* finalist who went on to become a top contender at 155 and 145 pounds in UFC, Kenny Florian may have been the best fighter to never win a UFC title. As astute an analyst of the fight game as he was a top-level fighter, "KenFlo" smoothly transitioned into the broadcast booth as a color commentator on fight nights as well as a host of the weekly *UFC Tonight* news show on FOX Sports 1.

BRIAN STANN

A decorated veteran of the United States Marine Corps, as well as a former WEC light heavyweight champion and UFC middleweight contender, Brian Stann is one of the busiest men in the fight game, even after his retirement as an active fighter. He has become a key member of the UFC broadcast team, with his insightful analysis and ease behind the microphone drawing the "All American" raves from fans and his fellow media members.

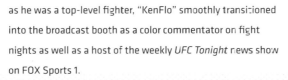

⬡ 1997

There was a young man who stuck around a little longer than Kerr, a 19-year-old Brazilian aptly nicknamed "The Phenom." At UFC 12 on February 7, 1997, the world got its first dose of Vitor Belfort.

Fighting on the undercard of a historic main event in which Mark "The Hammer" Coleman became UFC's first heavyweight champion by defeating Dan Severn, Belfort—a Carlson Gracie protégé—took a combined two minutes to defeat Tra Telligman and Scott Ferrozzo and win the UFC 12 heavyweight tournament. All blazing fists, Belfort's high-output and high-impact style were unlike anything seen in the Octagon previously. Although introducing UFC's first weight classes—heavyweight (200 pounds and over) and lightweight (199 pounds and under)—and crowning its first "real" champion were major milestones, it's likely that anyone who saw UFC 12 was talking about Belfort the next day.

"I knew what I was and always knew what my skills were and what I was capable of doing," Belfort said. "You have to know who you are and what you're capable of. It's very important."

"I WANTED TO REPRESENT MY SPORT OF WRESTLING REALLY WELL, AND I THINK MY YEARS OF WRESTLING EXPERIENCE PAID OFF."
—RANDY COUTURE

Not surprisingly, the buzz around Belfort only grew at UFC 13 in Augusta, Georgia, as he dispatched popular brawler Tank Abbott in less than a minute. It was the highlight of an event that launched the careers of two fighters who played a significant role in Belfort's career and in UFC history: Randy Couture and Tito Ortiz.

Ortiz, a brash young gun from Huntington Beach, California, debuted with a 31-second TKO of Wes Albritton before losing to Guy Mezger of the Lion's Den team in the lightweight tournament. The Mezger loss kicked off the first of several feuds that Ortiz became known for and that ultimately brought more attention to the sport.

Ortiz's star didn't truly begin to shine until later, when he became the face of UFC and the promotion's light heavyweight champion, but making an unlikely impact in Georgia that night was a debuting fighter only a month removed from his 34th birthday. Former wrestling standout Randy Couture won the UFC 13 heavyweight tournament with wins over Tony Halme and Steven Graham.

"I wanted to represent my sport of wrestling really well, and I think my years of wrestling experience paid off," Couture said after UFC 13. "I look forward to the next fight."

At the time, 1997 was just another year for UFC. The fledgling sport of mixed martial arts continued to battle against politicians looking to not just take it off television, but get rid of it entirely.

Yet in hindsight, the year was one of the most important of the pre-Zuffa era in terms of the establishment of weight classes and world championships. The talent entering the Octagon at this point in time was unparalleled; few years before or after could match it.

Of the 37 fighters who debuted in UFC in 1997, there were two future UFC Hall of Famers: Randy Couture and Tito Ortiz. There was also an Olympic gold medalist, Kevin Jackson; a soon-to-be Japanese legend, Kazushi Sakuraba; and four future UFC champions: Couture, Ortiz, Maurice Smith and Frank Shamrock.

Oddly enough, the man many believed would have similar accolades in UFC did not stick around long enough to find out. Mark Kerr displayed a fast start that had everyone wanting to see what he would do next.

A 1992 Division I national wrestling champion for Syracuse University, Kerr was an imposing physical force. Needless to say, mixed martial arts was a perfect fit. At UFC 14 in July 1997, he made his Octagon debut. Kerr tore through Moti Horenstein and Dan Bobish in a combined four minutes to win that night's heavyweight tournament.

Three months later, Greg Stott and Duane Cason fared even worse, lasting just a combined 70 seconds against Kerr, who picked up the UFC 15 heavyweight tournament crown. He should have been a natural to challenge for the promotion's world title. However, with Japan's PRIDE organization launching with hefty paychecks, and more security than what was available in UFC at the time, Kerr left. He fought 11 times for PRIDE over the next six years and never entered the Octagon again.

VITOR BELFORT

DEBUT: UFC 12, FEBRUARY 7, 1997
UFC 12 HEAVYWEIGHT TOURNAMENT WINNER
UFC LIGHT HEAVYWEIGHT CHAMPION (2004)

All it took was one look at 19-year-old Vitor "The Phenom" Belfort back at UFC 12 in February 1997, and fans were hooked. A black belt in jiu-jitsu under the legendary Carlson Gracie, Belfort instead used a blistering stand-up attack to stop Tra Telligman and Scott Ferrozzo in a combined two minutes. With that one-night tournament victory, a star was born.

Few challenged the aptly nicknamed "The Phenom" in those early UFC fights, and after his UFC 12 tournament win, Belfort crushed Tank Abbott in 52 seconds just three months later at UFC 13.

However, in this sport, all it takes is one bad night to overturn a perfect record. At UFC 15 in October 1997, Octagon newcomer Randy Couture taught Belfort a painful lesson. His ground-and-pound attack nullified the Brazilian's speed and power as Couture issued Belfort his first loss via TKO.

The reality check appeared to work, as Belfort bounced back with a submission of Joe Charles and a 44-second knockout of Wanderlei Silva. But as soon as he was back on track, Belfort left UFC to compete for Japan's PRIDE organization. In PRIDE, Belfort enjoyed great success from 1999 to 2001, defeating the likes of Heath Herring and Gilbert Yvel while only losing a decision to Kazushi Sakuraba.

RIO DE JANEIRO, BRAZIL

This hot streak prompted a return to UFC, and Belfort was immediately slotted for a light heavyweight championship fight against Tito Ortiz in the organization's debut in Las Vegas at UFC 33 in September 2001. Unfortunately, an injury forced Belfort out of the high-profile bout and delayed his comeback.

In June 2002, Belfort finally got back in the Octagon at UFC 37.5, losing a decision to the sport's newest star, Chuck Liddell. It was nearly a year before Belfort returned to action, but when he did, he showed true phenom form at UFC 43 as he knocked out Marvin Eastman in 67 seconds.

Back in the win column, Belfort was given a January 2004 title shot against old rival Couture. However, on January 9, just weeks before the bout, the joy of his December 2003 marriage to Joana Prado was shattered by the news that his sister, Priscila Vieira Belfort, had disappeared in Rio de Janeiro.

But at UFC 46, despite the emotional turmoil swirling around him, Belfort defeated Couture via first-round TKO due to a cut to win the UFC light heavyweight championship.

From 2004 to 2006, Belfort went into a tailspin in his professional life. He lost his championship to Couture via third-round TKO at UFC 49 in August 2004. He then went on to drop four of his next six bouts, including a decision to Ortiz at UFC 51, his last Octagon appearance for nearly five years.

Yet after his 2006 loss to Dan Henderson in PRIDE, Belfort began to show the focus he had lacked consistently over the previous years. When he stopped Rich Franklin in his victorious return to the Octagon at UFC 103 in 2009, the only thing remaining was for this more mature fighter to win another UFC title, a quest he is now in the midst of in the new middleweight division.

The rise of "The Natural" became even more prominent at UFC 15, but at UFC 14 in Birmingham, Alabama, on July 27, the heavyweight title changed hands five months after it was created. Former kickboxing star and Pancrase standout Maurice Smith entered the Octagon for the first time and stunned Coleman, winning a unanimous decision and the championship.

"Unfortunately, I started reading too many quotes, and I paid the price," Coleman said of his first pro loss. "The reason I did so well in [UFC] 10, 11 and 12 and in amateur wrestling was because I outworked my opponents. I wasn't used to the exposure and the fanfare, and I got caught up in it and started believing what I was reading too much, and it was a very humbling experience when I did finally lose."

Three months later, Smith successfully defended his crown for the first time with a win over Tank Abbott. The real story of the UFC 15 event

> "I WASN'T USED TO THE EXPOSURE AND THE FANFARE, AND I GOT CAUGHT UP IN IT AND STARTED BELIEVING WHAT I WAS READING TOO MUCH. IT WAS A VERY HUMBLING EXPERIENCE WHEN I DID FINALLY LOSE."
> —MARK COLEMAN

at Casino Magic in Bay St. Louis, Mississippi, wasn't the implementation of rules that forbade headbutts, groin strikes, strikes to the back of the neck and head, kicks to a downed opponent, small joint manipulation and hair pulling. Instead, it was the result of the heavyweight superfight between Couture and Belfort that saw Couture upset the seemingly unbeatable "The Phenom" via TKO in a little over eight minutes, shattering the Brazilian's aura of invincibility.

It was the key lesson of mixed martial arts: on any given night, any fighter can beat another. Couture epitomized that adage over the years, upsetting the odds more than once. After beating Belfort, his next challenge was Smith. During UFC's first visit to Japan for Ultimate Japan 1 on December 21, 1997, Couture brought home a world title for Christmas, as he defeated Smith for the heavyweight belt.

MARK KERR
TOLEDO, OH

DEBUT: UFC 14, JULY 27, 1997
UFC 14 HEAVYWEIGHT TOURNAMENT WINNER
UFC 15 HEAVYWEIGHT TOURNAMENT WINNER

Known at various times in his career as "The Specimen," "The Titan" and "The Smashing Machine," Mark Kerr was all of those things in the Octagon, where he dominated his opponents over a four-fight stint in 1997.

"I had no idea I had this in me: the capacity to get out there and fist fight with another man," Kerr said. "I always knew I was competitive, but I never knew that if you gave me a circumstance like this: you and me are going to get in the ring and you're either going to get beat up or beat somebody up; let's see what you're made of. And that's what it amounted to for me. I was able to tap into this really competitive nature in me where I can get real aggressive, real dominant, real physical, real primitive. It was just amazing."

Winning the UFC 14 and UFC 15 heavyweight tournaments in a little over five combined minutes, Kerr, a Division I national wrestling champion for Syracuse University, was seemingly destined for greatness. But it was not to be. Chasing glory in Japan's PRIDE organization, Kerr pounded his way to five wins and one no contest. However, after a loss to Kazuyuki Fujita, the wheels came off for Kerr, who only managed a 3-10 record over the next nine years.

TRA TELLIGMAN
FORT WORTH, TX

DEBUT: UFC 12, FEBRUARY 7, 1997

Tra Telligman was one of a long line of Lion's Den fighters to make their way through UFC, and with athleticism and stand-up power, it looked like he had the potential to go a long way. It didn't happen, though, as he only managed one win in the Octagon, a 1997 submission of Brad Kohler. Telligman experienced subsequent losses against Vitor Belfort, Tim Sylvia and Pedro Rizzo (twice). Telligman, who also dabbled in pro boxing, scored a huge win in the PRIDE organization in 2001, defeating top contender Igor Vovchanchyn in what was a personal milestone.

MAURICE SMITH

DEBUT: UFC 14, JULY 27, 1997
UFC HEAVYWEIGHT CHAMPION (1997)

SEATTLE, WA

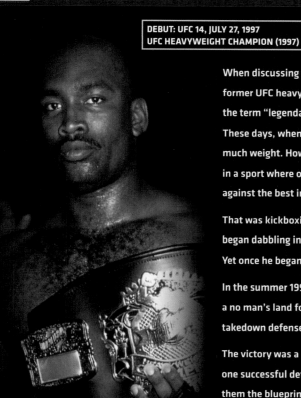

When discussing the kickboxing prowess of former UFC heavyweight champion Maurice Smith, the term "legendary" is usually attached at the front. These days, when the word is thrown out routinely, that doesn't hold much weight. However, in the case of the Seattle standout, consider that in a sport where one kick or punch can end your night, he went unbeaten against the best in the game for nearly 10 years.

That was kickboxing; mixed martial arts is a whole different animal. When Smith began dabbling in the sport as a competitor in Japan's Pancrase organization, he got bitten by that animal as he learned the ropes. Yet once he began to pick up takedown defense, it was a new day for Mr. Smith.

In the summer 1997, he was brought to UFC to face heavyweight champion Mark Coleman. Wrestlers like Coleman had made the Octagon a no man's land for strikers, just like Royce Gracie had done in early UFC matches. But Smith shocked the world at UFC 14, showing off his takedown defense, his solid ground game and, of course, his striking to win a unanimous decision and the title.

The victory was a high water mark for strikers in the Octagon, and though he would lose his title to Randy Couture at UFC Japan after just one successful defense (against Tank Abbott), the die had been cast. Strikers could survive in the Octagon, and Mo Smith had just given them the blueprint.

Smith never again rose to championship heights in UFC, going 2-2 in his final four bouts. He earned wins over Marco Ruas and Bobby Hoffman and had losses to Kevin Randleman and Renato "Babalu" Sobral. He remained active in MMA until 2008.

"I knew it was gonna be a very close fight," the new champion said. "A lot of guys come out and try to devastate Maurice right off, and he's too composed and too conditioned to do that. I knew it was gonna be a matter of being able to take him down and control him. I expected it to go long."

"All Randy did was hold me down really good," a disappointed Smith said. "That's all he did. He got a couple shots; I got a couple shots. A draw seemed about right."

UFC's first middleweight title—later to become light heavyweight—was also awarded that night in Yokohama. Longtime Japanese star Frank Shamrock, the brother of early UFC icon Ken Shamrock, made his debut with a title-winning effort over Olympic gold medal-winning wrestler Kevin Jackson that took just 16 seconds.

"I studied his fights. I studied his tape. He's an awesome wrestler and an elite athlete," Shamrock said. "I just saw a few holes in his wrestling ability and in his fighting style, and I capitalized on it. I think I got lucky, but I was prepared."

Also making his debut that night was Kazushi Sakuraba, a gentleman who fought only twice in UFC, both on December 21. Sakuraba fought Marcus "Conan" Silveira twice at Ultimate Japan, the first bout ending in a controversial no contest before Saku submitted Conan in their second meeting to win the card's heavyweight tournament. Sakuraba never fought in the Octagon again, instead becoming one of PRIDE's premier stars. The beloved fighter was later dubbed "The Gracie Hunter" for his defeats of Royce, Renzo, Royler and Ryan Gracie.

ANTHONY FRYKLUND
BOSTON, MA

DEBUT: UFC 14, JULY 27, 1997

One of the stalwarts of the Miletich Fighting Systems camp during its prime years, Anthony Fryklund made a career out of testing himself against big name opposition, competing in not only UFC, but in WEC and STRIKEFORCE, as well.

In July 1997, "The Freak" made his mixed martial arts debut with two fights in the UFC 14 tournament in Alabama. Both ended in under two minutes, with Fryklund submitting Donnie Chappell and then getting submitted by Kevin Jackson. He fought only twice more in the Octagon, going 1-1, but the rest of his fighting run included bouts with Matt Lindland, Anderson Silva and Cung Le.

KEVIN JACKSON
PHOENIX, AZ

DEBUT: UFC 14, JULY 27, 1997
UFC 14 MIDDLEWEIGHT TOURNAMENT WINNER

One of the United States' greatest wrestlers, Kevin Jackson was an Olympic gold medalist in 1992 and a world champion in 1991 and 1995. Jackson entered the world of MMA in 1997 and quickly ran off three wins, all in less than 1:30. His second and third victories came at UFC 14, earning him that event's middleweight tournament title.

In his next bout, in December 1997, he got a shot at Frank Shamrock's UFC title but was submitted in 16 seconds. Jackson finished his career with a win against Sam Adkins in an Extreme Challenge event in 1998. He currently serves as the head wrestling coach at Iowa State University.

RANDY COUTURE

DEBUT: UFC 13, MAY 30, 1997
UFC 13 HEAVYWEIGHT TOURNAMENT WINNER
THREE-TIME UFC HEAVYWEIGHT CHAMPION
TWO-TIME UFC LIGHT HEAVYWEIGHT CHAMPION
UFC HALL OF FAME (2006)

EVERETT, WA

"Not bad for an old man." The words from the mouth of 43-year-old Randy "The Natural" Couture came with a knowing smile just moments after he had shocked the world once again by soundly defeating 6'8" Tim Sylvia to win his unprecedented third UFC world heavyweight title in 2007. It was the kind of victory that you expected to be the last "time capsule" moment in the career of this ageless wonder, but in keeping to the form he had shown since his debut in 1997, he wasn't done thrilling fight fans.

A native of Everett, Washington, Randy Duane Couture served in the United States Army and then went on to become one of the nation's top wrestlers. But after seeing old college buddy Don Frye competing in a new venue called UFC, Couture was intrigued. Nine months later, he was stepping into the Octagon, and one of the sport's legendary careers was underway.

The UFC 13 tournament winner, Couture was just getting started, winning five UFC titles, three at heavyweight and two at 205 pounds. All the while, he defied the odds by defeating a who's who of mixed martial arts greats, including Chuck Liddell, Tito Ortiz, Kevin Randleman, Maurice Smith, Pedro Rizzo, Vitor Belfort and Mark Coleman.

In 2006, he retired, with his accomplishments earning "The Natural" a spot in the UFC Hall of Fame.

Not bad for an old man, indeed. But after returning to the sport in 2007 and winning his fifth UFC crown and five of his next seven bouts, a UFC 129 loss to Lyoto Machida in April 2011 prompted one of the greatest fighters of all time to retire from the sport for good, at 47, leaving a legacy that is hard to match.

TITO ORTIZ

DEBUT: UFC 13, MAY 30, 1997
UFC LIGHT HEAVYWEIGHT CHAMPION 2000-2003
UFC HALL OF FAME (2012)

HUNTINGTON BEACH, CA

Before Forrest Griffin and Stephan Bonnar kicked off the mixed martial arts explosion in 2005, there was Tito Ortiz, "The Huntington Beach Bad Boy," who was the face of UFC after Zuffa bought the company in 2001. He was brash, charismatic and he could fight, a triple threat that helped change the perception of the once outlawed sport.

Ortiz made his debut at UFC 13 as an alternate, defeating Wes Albritton in under a minute. An injury gave Ortiz a shot at Guy Mezger in the main draw that night, and although a controversial submission loss followed, the California native was hooked.

"I was a wrestler in high school, I wrestled in college and then I started training with Tank Abbott," Ortiz said. "When UFC first came out, it caught my eye right off the bat. There was always a dream in the back of my mind of being somebody, and being one of the best martial artists in the world really intrigued me into doing something about it."

He lost his first UFC title fight to Frank Shamrock in a 1999 classic, but seven months later, he defeated Wanderlei Silva to win the vacant championship. From 2000 to 2003, he ruled the 205-pound weight class with an iron fist, successfully defending his crown a record five times before losing it to Randy Couture at UFC 44.

Even through feuds with Chuck Liddell and Ken Shamrock, and frequently controversial stints as a coach on two seasons of *The Ultimate Fighter*, Ortiz' appeal never waned with the fans. While he never regained championship form, an inspiring victory over Ryan Bader in 2011 and an exciting trilogy with Forrest Griffin were apt closers to his UFC career. Before his final Octagon bout with Griffin in July 2012, Ortiz was inducted into UFC's Hall of Fame, cementing his legacy for all time.

FRANK SHAMROCK

DEBUT: ULTIMATE JAPAN 1, DECEMBER 21, 1997
UFC LIGHT HEAVYWEIGHT CHAMPION 1997-1999

SANTA MONICA, CA

Frank Juarez Shamrock began his fighting career in the shadow of his older adopted brother Ken, but that didn't last long. In fact, by the time he ended his five-fight string in UFC from 1997 to 1999, he was not only the king of the 205-pound weight class, but was considered by many to be the best pound-for-pound fighter in the sport.

Shamrock started his career in Japan's Pancrase organization in 1994, when, amazingly, he debuted against—and beat—future UFC heavyweight champion Bas Rutten. Over the next two years, he competed solely in Japan, winning most matches against the best fighters in the organization.

By 1997, he began to explore other options. After a memorable war with Enson Inoue in a Vale Tudo Japan bout that included a post-fight brawl with Inoue's brother Egan, Shamrock made his UFC debut on December 21, 1997. He needed just 16 seconds to submit world-class wrestler Kevin Jackson to win UFC's first middleweight title.

Sure, he was initially seen as Ken Shamrock's baby brother, but that didn't last long, and it ultimately didn't bother Frank.

"It's just the way it is," he said. "You're always going to have an older brother; you're always going to have the guy who made it first. You're always going to have that, and there's no way around it. And you become whoever you want to be. And if you live there, and you let that drag you down, that's your own business. I love my brother, and I'm very proud to be in the blood, and everything he's done and everything it's enabled me to do, that's a legacy."

As for Frank's own fighting legacy, it only grew during his time in UFC. For an encore after the Jackson bout, Shamrock slammed Igor Zinoviev into defeat in just 22 seconds at UFC 16 to move to 2-0 in the Octagon. Now, fans and pundits wondered not *when* someone would beat the champion, but *if*. Jeremy Horn and John Lober couldn't pull it off, but at UFC 22 in September 1999, rising star Tito Ortiz almost did, as he pushed Shamrock harder than he had ever been pushed in the Octagon over the first three rounds of their bout. But in round four, Shamrock turned the lights out, forcing the challenger to tap out due to strikes. It was Shamrock's finest hour, but also his last in UFC, as he retired immediately after the bout.

Like practically every fighter, though, retirements never last too long. While Shamrock didn't return to UFC, he did stay active in the STRIKEFORCE organization, falling short in two of his last three bouts against Cung Le and Nick Diaz. Age may have finally caught up to Frank Shamrock, but at his best, he was something to see.

1993   1994   1995   1996   1997   1998   1999   2000   2001   2002   2003   2004

FIGHTS OF THE YEAR

UFC 12
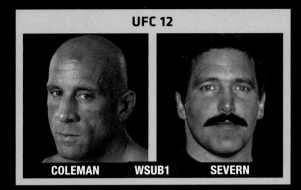
COLEMAN   WSUB1   SEVERN

UFC 13

MEZGER   WSUB1   ORTIZ

UFC 14
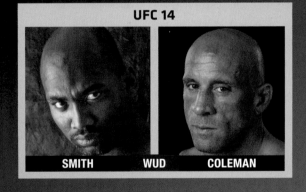
SMITH   WUD   COLEMAN

UFC 15
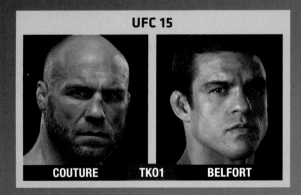
COUTURE   TKO1   BELFORT

UFC ULTIMATE JAPAN
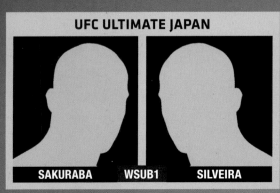
SAKURABA   WSUB1   SILVEIRA

KNOCKOUTS OF THE YEAR

UFC 12

BELFORT   TKO1   FERROZZO

UFC 13
BELFORT   TKO1   ABBOTT

UFC 12

BELFORT   TKO1   TELLIGMAN

UFC 14
KERR   TKO1   HORENSTEIN

UFC 15
KERR   KO1   STOTT

SUBMISSIONS OF THE YEAR

UFC 12

COLEMAN   WSUB1   SEVERN

UFC 13
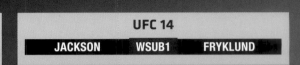
MEZGER   WSUB1   ORTIZ

UFC 14
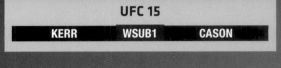
JACKSON   WSUB1   FRYKLUND

UFC 15
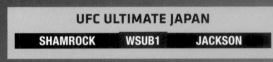
KERR   WSUB1   CASON

UFC ULTIMATE JAPAN
SHAMROCK   WSUB1   JACKSON

DEBUTS

UFC 12

- VITOR BELFORT
- NICK SANZO
- TRA TELLIGMAN
- JIM MULLEN
- WALLID ISMAIL
- YOSHIKI TAKAHASHI
- RAINY MARTINEZ
- ERIC MARTIN
- JUSTIN MARTIN
- JACKIE LEE

UFC 13

- TITO ORTIZ
- RANDY COUTURE
- WES ALBRITTON
- SAEED HOSSEINI
- ROYCE ALGER
- ENSON INOUE
- STEVEN GRAHAM
- DMITRI STEPANOV
- TONY HALME

UFC 14

- MARK KERR
- MAURICE SMITH
- ANTHONY FRYKLUND
- DONNIE CHAPPELL
- ALEX HUNTER
- YURI VAULIN
- KEVIN JACKSON
- TODD BUTLER
- DAN BOBISH

UFC 15

- HARRY MOSKOWITZ
- DUANE CASON
- HOUSTON DORR
- GREG STOTT
- CARLOS BARETTO
- KAZUSHI SAKURABA
- BRAD KOHLER
- YOJI ANJO
- MARCUS SILVEIRA
- FRANK SHAMROCK

ULTIMATE JAPAN 1

- KAZUSHI SAKURABA
- BRAD KOHLER
- YOJI ANJO
- MARCUS SILVEIRA
- FRANK SHAMROCK

UFC HALL OF FAME

JEFF BLATNICK

A 1984 Olympic Gold medal winner in Greco-Roman wrestling after battling cancer, Jeff Blatnick was a pioneering force in mixed martial arts who introduced countless people to the sport as a UFC commentator from UFC 4 through 32. Blatnick also worked closely with athletic commissions regarding the sport he loved, helping to create the rules that still govern MMA today. He also served as an MMA judge, even working several UFC events.

STEPHAN BONNAR

As one half of the most important match in UFC history, the fight against Forrest Griffin in 2005, Stephan Bonnar was no stranger to competing in big fights against the best of his era. The hard-nosed battler took on everyone from Hall of Famers Griffin and Mark Coleman to world champions Lyoto Machida, Rashad Evans, Jon Jones and Anderson Silva over the course of a career that endeared him to fight fans.

MARK COLEMAN

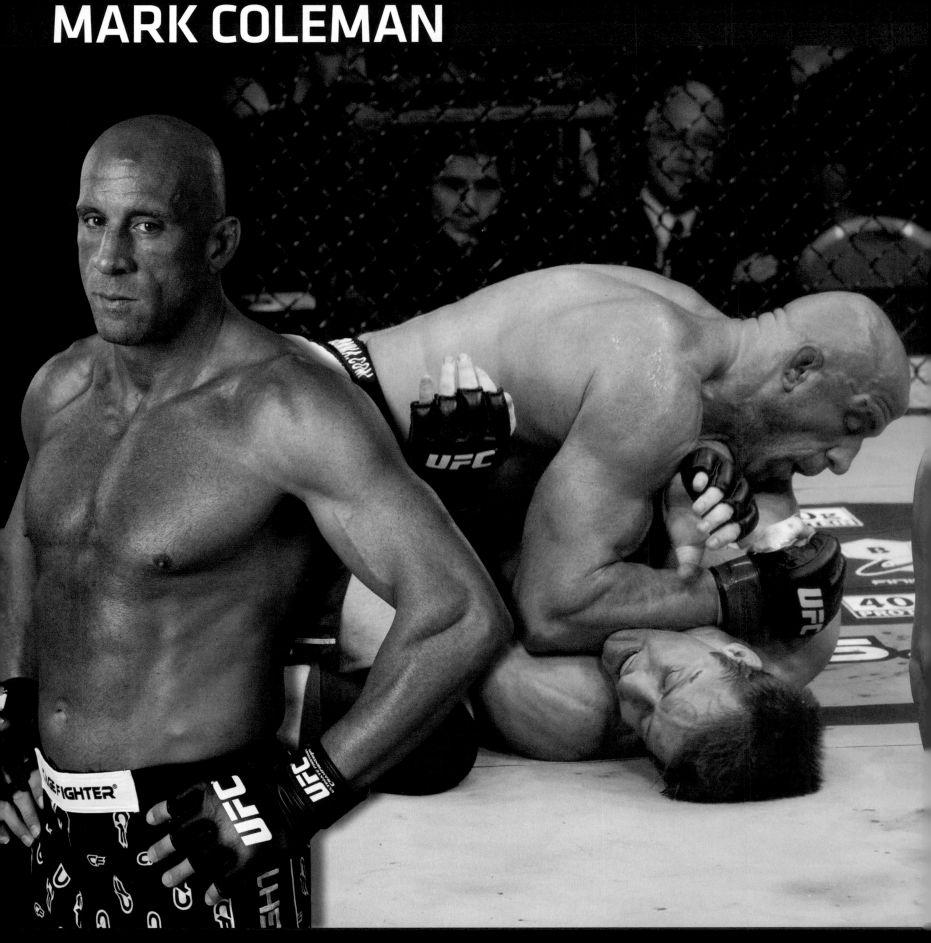

UFC's first heavyweight champion, Mark "The Hammer" Coleman virtually invented the ground-and-pound strategy that became his trademark. Fans will never forget his epic battles in the Octagon against legends including Stephan Bonnar, Shogun Rua, Dan Severn and Don Frye, as well as his classic bouts overseas in Japan's PRIDE organization. Coleman was a true original and one of MMA's pioneers.

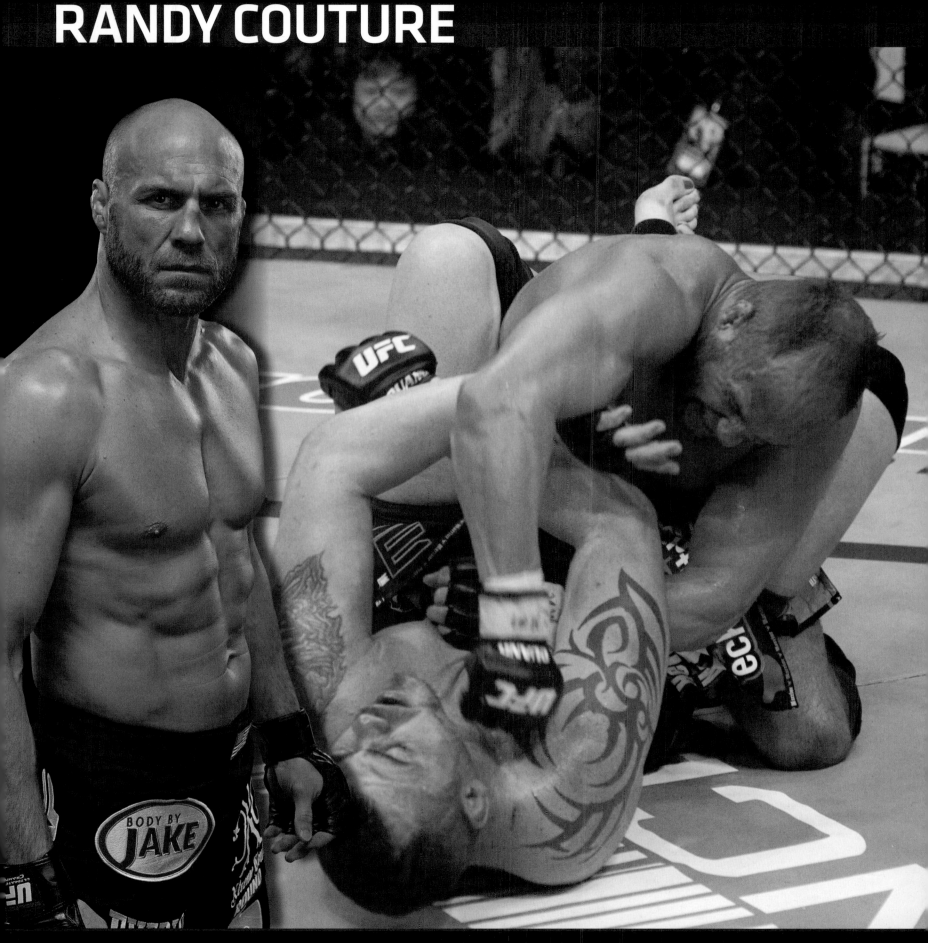

RANDY COUTURE

Mixed martial arts' ageless wonder Randy Couture did practically everything a fighter could do over the course of his Hall of Fame career. He won three heavyweight and two light heavyweight titles while facing a Who's Who of the sport that included Chuck Liddell, Vitor Belfort, Kevin Randleman, Josh Barnett, Tito Ortiz, Brock Lesnar, Minotauro Nogueira and Mark Coleman. In 2011, Couture retired from the sport at the remarkable age of 47.

ROYCE GRACIE

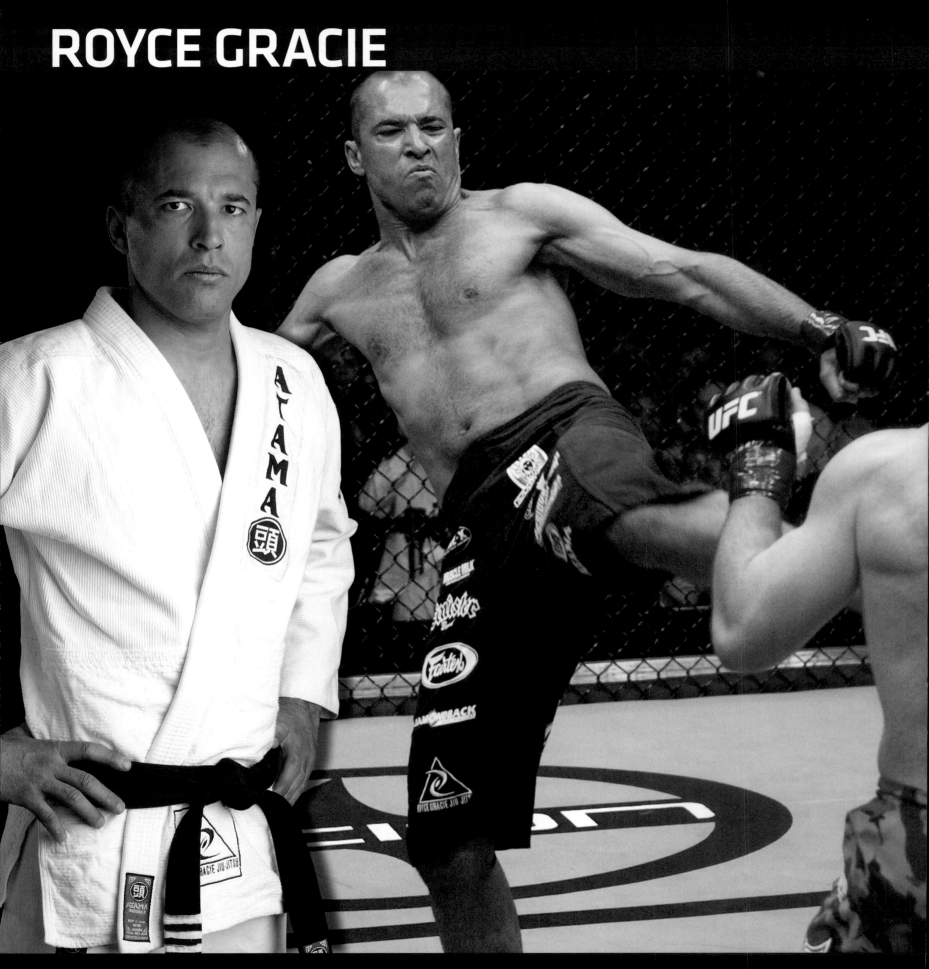

As the standard bearer for Gracie jiu-jitsu since his UFC debut in 1993, Royce Gracie always possessed both the confidence to step into competition and the skills to succeed. Maybe even more importantly, he had broad enough shoulders to carry the Gracie name into each fight, knowing that a loss could cripple the mystique of fighting's First Family. That liability was never an issue for him, as he won three UFC tournaments and practically built the sport of MMA.

FORREST GRIFFIN

With his humor and self-effacing attitude, Forrest Griffin seemed like the unlikeliest of mixed martial arts heroes. However, by the time his career ended in 2013, he had won the first season of the groundbreaking *The Ultimate Fighter* series, won a UFC light heavyweight championship and engaged in some of the best fights the sport had ever seen against Stephan Bonnar, Rampage Jackson and Shogun Rua. That's a legacy to be proud of.

MATT HUGHES

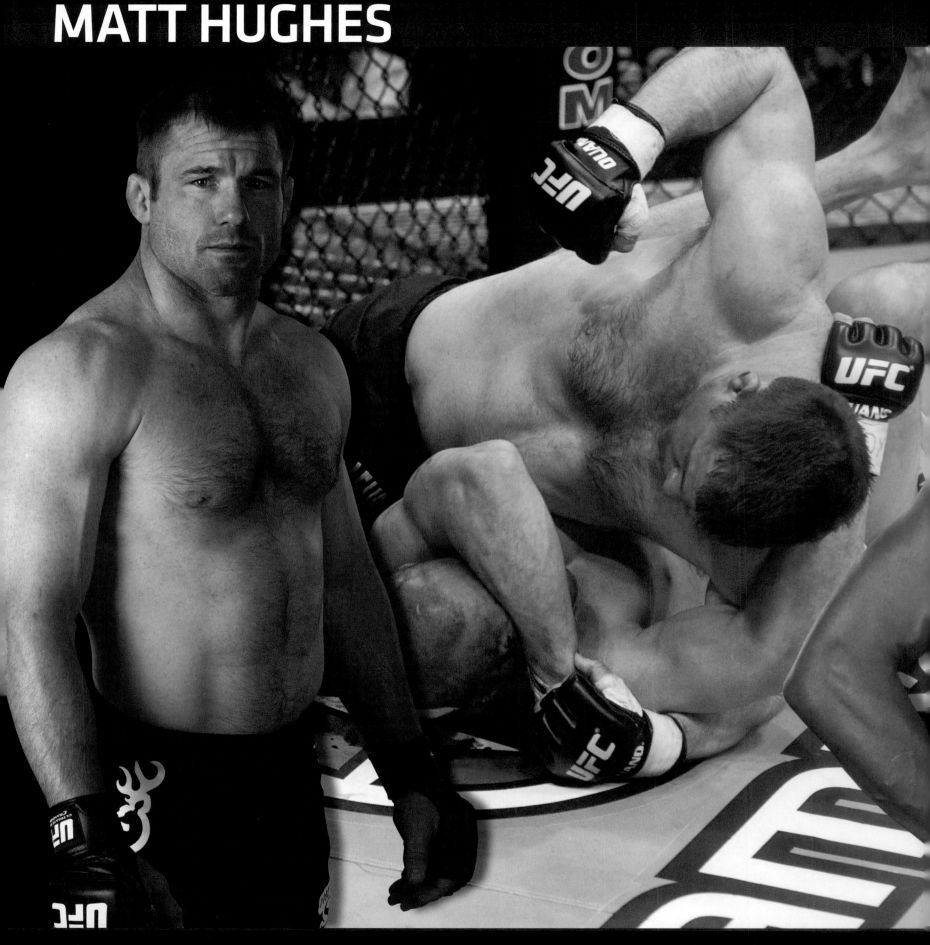

While he humbly downplays himself as just a country boy from Illinois, Matt Hughes' résumé says otherwise, as the former two-time welterweight champion was one of the most dominant 170-pound fighters of all-time. This powerhouse wrestler, with an underrated ground game, defeated the best, including BJ Penn, Georges St-Pierre, Royce Gracie, Carlos Newton, Frank Trigg, Sean Sherk, Renzo Gracie and Matt Serra.

CHARLES "MASK" LEWIS

He started out by selling t-shirts out of the trunk of his car, but Charles "Mask" Lewis took his vision and his love for mixed martial arts and turned TapouT into a premier clothing brand of the sport. Although his life was tragically cut short in an automobile accident in 2009, the legacy of this UFC Hall of Famer lives on through his brand and in the hearts of those who knew him.

CHUCK LIDDELL

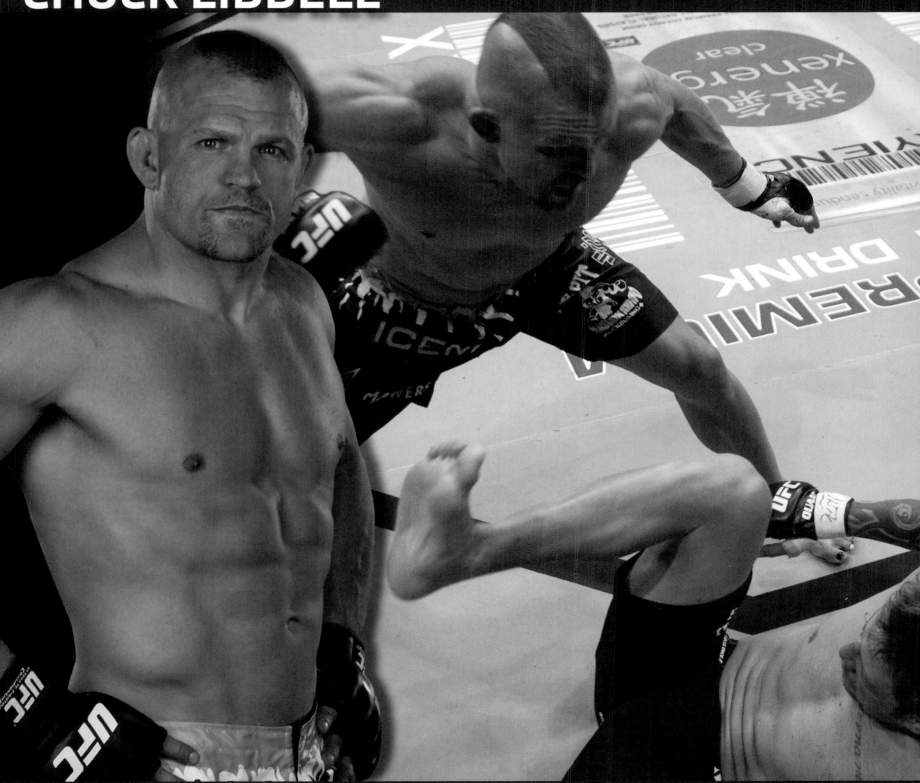

"The Iceman" held a nearly two-year reign atop the light heavyweight division that included knockout victories over Randy Couture, Tito Ortiz and Jeremy Horn. His résumé also includes victories over Wanderlei Silva, Vitor Belfort and Kevin Randleman. With the most knockouts in UFC history with 13, Chuck "The Iceman" Liddell was destined for the UFC Hall of Fame. In July 2009, this recognition was made official as he was inducted during the historic UFC 100 weekend.

PAT MILETICH

UFC's first welterweight champion, Pat Miletich, could do it all in the Octagon. His ability to strike or submit opponents made him a dominant titleholder. Besides his fighting prowess, "The Croatian Sensation" also changed the sport as the coach of the Miletich Fighting Systems team that included UFC champions Matt Hughes, Jens Pulver and Tim Sylvia, as well as Robbie Lawler, a future champion. Miletich received his Hall of Fame induction in 2014.

TITO ORTIZ

The second-longest reigning light heavyweight champion in UFC history, Tito Ortiz's slams, ground-and-pound and "bad boy" persona made him a crossover star in the early years of the UFC era. His memorable battles with Ken Shamrock, Chuck Liddell, Randy Couture and Forrest Griffin built a legacy that established him as one of the most popular fighters ever, earning him a spot in the UFC Hall of Fame in 2012.

One of only two men in UFC history to win world titles in separate weight divisions, BJ Penn's place in the record books is secure, but it's the Hawaiian's place in the heart of MMA fans around the world that may be even more notable. A fearless warrior whose talent earned him the nickname "The Prodigy," Penn won UFC titles at 155 and 170 pounds, facing the best the sport had to offer from his first bout to his last, including Matt Hughes, Georges St-Pierre, Nick Diaz, Frankie Edgar, Sean Sherk, Jens Pulver, Lyoto Machida and countless others.

BAS RUTTEN

A pioneering force who showed UFC fans what world-class striking and athleticism looked like, Bas Rutten may have only competed in the Octagon twice, but his impact was felt far beyond his wins over Tsuyoshi Kosaka and Kevin Randleman, as the former UFC heavyweight champion influenced countless fighters that came after him. Following his UFC career, the Netherlands native went on to be an ambassador for the sport through his commentary for several MMA organizations, including PRIDE.

DAN SEVERN

In the early days of UFC, former amateur wrestling star Dan Severn showed his grappling teammates that there was a place for world-class wrestlers in the Octagon. A two-time UFC tournament winner, "The Beast" earned wins over Tank Abbott, Ken Shamrock and Oleg Taktarov during the course of his Hall of Fame career in UFC. Amazingly, he kept competing on the local circuit until he retired in 2013 at age 54.

KEN SHAMROCK

If fans were going to build a prototype of a fighter when UFC launched in 1993, they probably would have come up with someone who looked like Ken Shamrock. Skilled in all aspects of MMA, Shamrock made a hybrid-style of fighting essential to success in the sport. His rivalries with Royce Gracie, Kimo Leopoldo and Tito Ortiz played a huge role in bringing MMA to the masses.

1998

After a year in which UFC introduced weight classes and world championships—and also welcomed a talented group of newcomers who would impact the sport for years to come—1998 should have been a bright one for the promotion. If you consider the action in the Octagon, and the talented individuals who entered the sport, it was.

But outside, looming storm clouds opened up. Cable television distributors refused to carry events, leaving fans only able to get their fix through satellite TV or in-person at the venue. Unfortunately, only two events were held stateside in 1998, with a third occurring in Brazil.

One of the most telling moments of the year came behind the scenes at UFC 17. The promotion's newly appointed commissioner, former Olympic gold medalist and current UFC color commentator Jeff Blatnick, referred to the beleaguered sport as "mixed martial arts" for the first time. Gone was the term "no holds barred," and the move from spectacle to sport continued.

Inside the Octagon, the year kicked off with the Battle in the Bayou event in New Orleans on March 13, 1998. In the featured bout of UFC 16, light heavyweight champion Frank Shamrock made it look like "The Big Easy" as he successfully defended his title for the first time with a 20-second finish of Igor Zinoviev courtesy of an Octagon-rattling slam.

"I train hard, I come prepared, and I've got luck and skill," 24-year-old Shamrock said at the time. "Igor is an awesome competitor; he's a friend of mine. The best man won tonight, but he'll be back, and I'm here to stay."

Also in action was popular early UFC heavyweight Kimo Leopoldo, who had his first bout in nearly two years spoiled by Japan's Tsuyoshi Kosaka in the night's heavyweight superfight. In the middleweight superfight, Jerry Bohlander submitted 1992 Olympic gold medalist Kevin Jackson.

UFC's first lightweight tournament took place at UFC 16, featuring fighters 170 pounds and under. In this event, future world champion and UFC Hall of Famer Pat Miletich defeated Chris Brennan, and Olympic silver medalist Townsend Saunders, to take the tourney victory in his Octagon debut.

"I TRAIN HARD, I COME PREPARED, AND I'VE GOT LUCK AND SKILL."
–FRANK SHAMROCK

Two months later, a star-studded array of future UFC standouts debuted at the Mobile Civic Center in Alabama, led by Chuck Liddell, Jeremy Horn, Carlos Newton and Dan Henderson. On that UFC 17 card, Liddell defeated Noe Hernandez via decision, while Horn lost his debut to Frank Shamrock via submission in a light heavyweight title bout. Newton and Henderson both won their debuts in that night's middleweight tournament semifinals before "Hendo" defeated "The Ronin" via split decision for the win.

 ## JEREMY HORN
OMAHA, NE

DEBUT: UFC 17, MAY 15, 1998

What more can you say about Jeremy Horn other than to give him his respect as one of the most experienced and talented fighters in the game? With more than 100 professional fights to his name, he earned his accolades the hard way: in competition.

"I was never really that gifted of an athlete or that physical, but I could look, see and think my way through a lot of things," said Horn. Horn's biggest UFC win was a finish of Chuck "The Iceman" Liddell at UFC 19, a result that "The Iceman" avenged in a title bout in 2005. "If I couldn't do it physically, I could find a way around it just by thinking. It got to be the way I fought, too."

A two-time world title challenger, Horn went 6-6 in his 12 Octagon bouts. Even after his last UFC match against Rousimar Palhares in 2009, the gifted strategist and student of the game continued impacting the sport as a coach to several UFC standouts like DaMarques Johnson and Sean O'Connell.

CHRIS BRENNAN
COMPTON, CA

DEBUT: UFC 16, MARCH 13, 1998

A respected Brazilian jiu-jitsu practitioner, Chris Brennan, earned many accolades for his mixed martial arts work in the early years of the sport. Brennan matched wits with some of the toughest fighters in the game, including Joe Stevenson, Antonio McKee, Joe Hurley, Steve Berger and Pat Miletich. In fact, it was Miletich (whom Brennan had already gone 0-1-1 against) who handed the Californian his first UFC loss at UFC 16 in 1998. Brennan had already beaten Courtney Turner earlier that night, but still went back to the local circuit. He returned only once more, at UFC 35 in 2002, where he lost a decision to fellow grappler Gil Castillo.

 ## MIKEY BURNETT
TULSA, OK

DEBUT: UFC 16, MARCH 13, 1998

Newer fans may remember Mikey "The Eastside Assassin" Burnett for running into the wall when he was a member of *The Ultimate Fighter* 4 cast, but the Oklahoman's legacy should really reflect his fight performances. He was one of the top welterweights of the late '90s, as well as a former Golden Gloves champion. Burnett was a tough out for anyone, a fact his opponents discovered the hard way. In March of 1998, he halted Eugenio Tadeu, earning a shot at Pat Miletich—and the first ever UFC 170-pound title. After 21 minutes, Miletich took a split decision win and the belt. While Burnett would defeat Townsend Saunders via decision three months later, he would never get another title shot.

 ## PEDRO RIZZO

DEBUT: ULTIMATE BRAZIL, OCTOBER 16, 1998

RIO DE JANEIRO, BRAZIL

Yet, despite all this action, the main attraction of UFC 17 was the comeback of former heavyweight champion Mark Coleman, making his first start since losing the belt to Maurice Smith nearly a year earlier. "The Hammer" was supposed to walk right back into a title shot against Randy Couture, the man who had beaten Smith.

"I was excited about the opportunity, and I saw it as a big challenge," Couture said of the meeting with Coleman. "In a lot of ways, that was really the peak of Mark's career."

Unfortunately, a rib injury took Couture out of the fight. Coleman was subsequently matched up with Lion's Den newcomer Pete Williams, who went on to score not just a huge upset, but also one of the greatest knockouts in UFC history. A head kick from Williams put the dream of a Couture-Coleman matchup on the back burner until the two met years later at UFC 109.

"I was looking forward to the fight and was disappointed that I didn't get a chance to compete because of the injury, and then seeing Mark turn around and get knocked out by Pete Williams, I was like, 'Damn. I probably could have won the fight,'" Couture said. "I've never been the knockout guy, so it wouldn't have been like Pete beat him, but I think I had a chance of beating him."

Coleman was similarly devastated. "I had been following Randy's career since he was wrestling," Coleman said. "I watched him wrestle many times, I did wrestle him in 1989 (winning the match), and I followed him throughout his career because I was coaching at Ohio State when he was wrestling at Oklahoma State. I almost had to coach against him in college, and I had been following him throughout his fight career, as well. So I was getting ready for him, and I was very confident that I was going to be able to beat him."

Pedro "The Rock" Rizzo should have been one of the greats. A skilled striker whose punishing leg kicks could make any fighter reconsider his vocation in life. The Rio de Janeiro native showed flashes of brilliance throughout his 14-fight UFC career. But in three shots at the heavyweight title, he came up empty. This wasn't because he wasn't good enough to win; it was because he just could not "pull the trigger" when the stakes were at their highest.

A protégé of "The King of the Streets" Marco Ruas, Rizzo made his way to UFC in 1998. In the organization's first Brazil event, he sent local fans home happy with a blistering knockout of Tank Abbott. Three wins later, all that was left was to win the title against Kevin Randleman. After an initial postponement of the bout, the two met up at UFC 26 in 2000. What followed was one of the worst fights in UFC history, a 25-minute study in tedium won by Randleman.

Vowing to show fans the "real" Pedro Rizzo, the Brazilian knocked out Dan Severn and Josh Barnett in successive bouts and was a heavy favorite when he took on Randy Couture in his second world title fight. Early on, he made the oddsmakers smile as he battered the champion, but Couture rebounded in the late rounds and retained the title. The loss seemed to take the life out of Rizzo's career, and he was blown out in three rounds by Couture in their rematch.

There would be no more title shots for Rizzo, only "what ifs."

CHUCK LIDDELL

DEBUT: UFC 17, MAY 15, 1998
UFC LIGHT HEAVYWEIGHT CHAMPION 2005-2007
UFC HALL OF FAME

SANTA BARBERA, CA

When you think of UFC, odds are that one of the first names to pop in your head is Chuck "The Iceman" Liddell. Whether it's his iconic Mohawk, knockout power, consistently exciting fights, or his post-fight scream, "The Iceman" is the one fighter who took mixed martial arts from a fringe sport to mainstream phenomenon.

A lifelong martial artist who also earned a degree in Business/Accounting at Cal Poly University, California's Liddell was hit with the inevitable decision of pursuing his fighting career (which he started in the form of kickboxing), or getting a "real job" by putting his degree to use after graduation. Liddell chose to put on the gloves. Training with John Hackleman, the only person to ever man his corner, Liddell compiled a 20-2 (16 KOs) record in kickboxing, grabbing two national titles as well as USMPA and WKA titles along the way.

Inspired by his kickboxing prowess and his budding jiu-jitsu training with John Lewis, Liddell threw his hat into the MMA ring. He made his UFC debut with a decision win over Noe Hernandez at UFC 17 in May of 1998.

Three months later, Liddell followed up with a victory over Jose Landi-Jons in the International Vale Tudo Championship. He was invited back to UFC to face Jeremy Horn, on March 5, 1999. Horn submitted the Californian, which was Liddell's first pro MMA defeat, but he wouldn't lose again for more than four years.

Undaunted by the loss, Liddell got back on track with three wins, but was still a huge underdog when he stepped into the cage with former UFC heavyweight champion Kevin Randleman at UFC 31.

78 seconds and a big right hand later, Randleman was stopped by Liddwell, and UFC had a new star. But the road to a championship still had some bumps to navigate along the way. Liddell had to combat the challenges of Murilo Bustamante, Amar Suloev, Vitor Belfort and Renato "Babalu" Sobral before putting himself firmly in line for a shot at the light heavyweight crown, held by Tito Ortiz.

The only problem was that Ortiz was having contract issues with the organization at the time, while also claiming that his friendship with Liddell made him unwilling to fight "The Iceman."

Unwilling to wait for Ortiz, Liddell was pitted against former heavyweight champion Randy Couture for the interim 205-pound crown at UFC 43 in June 2003. A heavy favorite, Liddell was upset by Couture and stopped in the third round.

Forced to regroup, Liddell was sent to Japan by UFC to represent the organization in the 2003 PRIDE Middleweight Grand Prix tournament. After a quarterfinal knockout of Alistair Overeem in August 2003, Liddell went back three months later hoping that he would win his semifinal match and meet PRIDE standout Wanderlei Silva in the finals. It was not to be, as Rampage Jackson stopped "The Iceman" in the second round.

Returning to the U.S. and UFC, Liddell got the one match he had been waiting for, when he headlined UFC 47 in April 2004, against Tito Ortiz. All the frustration of the previous years was released in five minutes and 38 seconds as Liddell stopped his rival and finished up with a post-fight scream that was in stark contrast to his usual soft-spoken demeanor.

The win over Ortiz kicked off a reign of terror in the light heavyweight division during the next three years that saw Liddell win seven fights in a row—all by knockout.

After defeating Vernon White at UFC 49 in August 2004, Liddell got a shot at redemption against Randy Couture. The bout followed Liddell's stint as a coach on *The Ultimate Fighter*, which put him in the nation's living rooms on a weekly basis.

In the UFC 52 rematch against "The Natural," Liddell not only became a champion for the first time, but his first-round knockout of Couture made him the face of mixed martial arts. Over the next few years, Liddell would become the first UFC fighter to appear on the cover of *ESPN The Magazine*, release a best-selling autobiography and make numerous movie and television cameos, including a memorable appearance on HBO's *Entourage*.

Despite his growing fame, his focus remained on his fighting. After defeating Couture, he defended his title with finishes of Jeremy Horn (the first man to beat him), Couture (in their 2006 rubber match), Sobral and Ortiz.

In May 2007, Liddell's reign ended at the hands of a familiar foe, Rampage Jackson, who knocked him out in the first round at UFC 71. This defeat kicked off a stint where Liddell—now in his late 30s—lost five of his last six bouts, albeit against top-notch competition like Jackson, Keith Jardine, Rashad Evans, Shogun Rua and Rich Franklin.

However, sandwiched between these losses was a stirring three-round victory over Wanderlei Silva at UFC 79 in December 2007.

In July 2009, Liddell was inducted into the UFC Hall of Fame. He fought once more, getting stopped in the first round by Rich Franklin at UFC 115 in June 2010 after a second stint as a coach on *The Ultimate Fighter*.

Liddell announced his retirement on December 29, 2010, and currently serves as UFC's Executive Vice President of Business Development.

LAVERNE CLARK
BETTENDORF, IA

DEBUT: UFC 16, MARCH 13, 1998

Plain and simple, Laverne Clark was a fighter. With more than 40 mixed martial arts bouts and 33 more in boxing's squared circle, Clark epitomized the "anywhere, anyone, anytime" mantra many fighters claim to have, but few actually adhere to. One of the Miletich Fighting Systems camp's early standouts, Clark fought a Who's Who on the Midwest circuit in the late 1990s and early 2000s, including Matt Hughes, Dave Menne and Shonie Carter. In between, he fought in several UFC bouts, defeating Josh Stuart, Frank Caracci, Fabiano Iha and Koji Oishi before losing his rematch with Iha at UFC 27 in 2000. It was Clark's last UFC bout, but he continued to compete in MMA until 2008.

TSUYOSHI KOSAKA
SHIGA, JAPAN

DEBUT: UFC 16, MARCH 13, 1998

A staple of UFC's heavyweight division in the late '90s, Tsuyoshi "TK" Kosaka—like his countryman Yuki Kondo—suffered from being in the Octagon during the organization's "Dark Ages." This almost guaranteed that he wouldn't get the respect he deserved from later generations of fight fans.

But for those who never saw him, rest assured that he was the real deal, a courageous fighter with legitimate skills, who never backed down. The first man to beat Fedor Emelianenko, Kosaka was a long-time training partner of Maurice Smith and Frank Shamrock. His UFC résumé included wins over Kimo Leopoldo, Pete Williams and Tim Lajcik.

MIKE VAN ARSDALE
WATERLOO, IA

DEBUT: UFC 17, MAY 15, 1998

A 1998 NCAA wrestling champion for Iowa State, as well as a U.S. Olympic alternate, Mike Van Arsdale has been a competitor his entire life—and a world-class one at that.

"Any athlete is going to compete to win," he said. "With proper training and with the right attitude, as long as everything comes together physically, and mentally you really want it when they put the heat on, of course I'm going to be thinking, 'I'm going to win this.'"

More often than not, he did, even in the world of mixed martial arts, where he traded blows with the likes of Randy Couture, Wanderlei Silva and Matt Lindland over the course of an eight-year career.

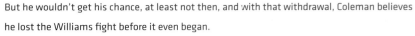

But he wouldn't get his chance, at least not then, and with that withdrawal, Coleman believes he lost the Williams fight before it even began.

"When he pulled out, it set off a chain," he recalled. "They changed opponents on me at least seven different times within the next two weeks. And I was just coming off my knee surgery, as well, so I was fairly messed up in the head, to say the least, back then."

UFC 17 would be the last live taste United States fans would have of UFC until January of 1999, as there would be no more stateside shows in 1998. Next was a trip to the Ginasio da Portuguesa in Sao Paulo for Ultimate Brazil on October 16, 1998.

By this time, Couture had declined a bout against the Netherlands' Bas Rutten, and instead signed with the Vale Tudo Japan promotion, forcing UFC to strip him of his heavyweight title. There was plenty of focus on the evening's championship bouts: Pat Miletich won the first UFC welterweight title—then called lightweight—against Mikey Burnett; and Frank Shamrock defended his crown successfully once more against John Lober. However, all eyes were on a young Brazilian named Pedro "The Rock" Rizzo.

Though Rizzo was forecast to be the next great Brazilian MMA fighter, many expected him to get tested immediately by veteran Tank Abbott. However, it didn't play out that way. "The Rock" used leg kicks to wear Abbott down.

PETE WILLIAMS
SAN LORENZO, CA

DEBUT: UFC 17, MAY 15, 1998

A high school wrestling teammate of UFC veteran Jerry Bohlander, Pete "El Duro" Williams followed his friend into mixed martial arts. As a member of Ken Shamrock's Lion's Den team, Williams won seven of his first eight bouts, competing both in the United States and in Japan's Pancrase and Rings organizations.

The success earned him a call from UFC. In his first Octagon bout, he delivered the defining moment of his career, as he knocked out Mark Coleman with a head kick at UFC 17 in 1998. However, a decision loss to Tsuyoshi Kosaka halted his momentum. Afterward, back-to-back wins against Jason Godsey and Travis Fulton earned him a UFC 23 title shot, which he lost via decision to Kevin Randleman. Williams retired after three UFC losses in 2001-2002.

ANDRE ROBERTS
TAMA, IA

DEBUT: UFC 17, MAY 15, 1998

With his ever-present Mohawk, Andre "The Chief" Roberts wasn't someone you would easily forget, and he certainly wasn't a fighter to be taken lightly. Clocking in at nearly 350 pounds, Roberts had a deceptive ground game, as evidenced by his nine wins via submission. However, it was his power that got him noticed, especially in his three-fight UFC stint. Roberts went 1-1 before engaging in a classic bout against Ron Waterman at UFC 21 in 1999. Battered for much of the early going, Roberts roared back, knocking out his opponent at 2:51 of the opening round. After that bout, "The Chief" went 4-1-1 before retiring in 2005.

The other match that Brazilians showed up for was the turf war between Rio de Janeiro's Vitor Belfort and debuting Curitiba native Wanderlei Silva. This one was no contest, as Belfort's blazing fists led him to victory in just 44 seconds.

The Octagon would not visit Brazil again until 2011. By then, UFC was in a much different place than it had been as it limped into 1999 after Ultimate Brazil: beat down, but not broken.

CARLOS NEWTON

DEBUT: UFC 17, MAY 15, 1998
UFC WELTERWEIGHT CHAMPION

NEWMARKET, ONTARIO, CANADA

When the sport of mixed martial arts was going through its years of growing pains, fighters were routinely stereotyped as barroom brawlers with little going on in their lives outside of punching their opponents in the face. But then came Carlos "The Ronin" Newton, and suddenly, the negative connotations that accompanied fighting went out the window.

A martial artist for much of his life, Newton was a quick study in the art of combat, eventually becoming a three-time Canadian jiu-jitsu champion and a two-time Canadian pankration titlist.

In UFC, Newton lost to Dan Henderson via a controversial decision at UFC 17. After a February 2001 loss to future middleweight champion Dave Menne in a local event, little chance was given to the Canadian when he took on longtime 170-pound champion Pat Miletich for the UFC title in May 2001.

A choke-out of Miletich changed everyone's opinion quickly, after which Newton rapidly shot to the top of the charts in the welterweight division. There would be little rest for the new champion. Six months after winning the belt, he was pitted against Miletich's teammate, powerhouse wrestler Matt Hughes.

On November 2, 2001, Newton caught the challenger, Hughes, in a triangle choke. Hughes proceeded to lift the champion over his head and prop him on the fence. After a few tense moments, Hughes slammed Newton to the canvas, knocking him out. There were some who believed Hughes was out first from the choke, but the result stood and the title changed hands.

Following a PRIDE win over Jose Landi-Jons three months later, Newton got a rematch with Hughes at UFC 38, but was defeated in four rounds.

The rematch with Hughes was the charismatic and dynamic Newton's final UFC title shot. Although he stayed busy against top-level competition around the world over the next eight years, "The Ronin" never again reached the heights he touched as a shooting star in 2001.

WANDERLEI SILVA

DEBUT: ULTIMATE BRAZIL, OCTOBER 16, 1998
PRIDE MIDDLEWEIGHT CHAMPION

From August 2000 to October 2004, Wanderlei "The Axe Murderer" Silva was the "baddest man on the planet." With a record of 15-0-1 with one no contest during that period, Silva was a tornado of terror in Japanese rings for the PRIDE organization, defeating the likes of Kazushi Sakuraba (three times), Rampage Jackson (twice), Dan Henderson, Ikuhisa Minowa and Guy Mezger.

Those four years cemented Silva in the history books as PRIDE's greatest 205-pounder ever. However, strangely enough, if you look back at his early career, Silva's eventual ascension was not necessarily a foregone conclusion, especially after getting stopped by Vitor Belfort in just 44 seconds in his UFC debut in 1998.

CURITIBA, PARANÁ, BRAZIL

Silva rebounded with a UFC win over Tony Petarra, and three wins in PRIDE. He then rolled the dice by going back to UFC, losing via decision in a title bout against Tito Ortiz, putting the 11-3 fighter's future in question.

After returning to PRIDE, he began an unstoppable reign that saw him go on a 17-fight unbeaten streak. Silva's confidence was at its peak when he battled Rampage Jackson in 2003 and 2004, walking away with two knockout victories.

Silva's second win over Jackson may have been his finest moment in PRIDE. Over the next two and a half years, the pace of fighting constantly against some of the best opponents in the world had seemingly caught up to him.

In 2007, Silva made the decision to move to the United States to live and train, and shortly thereafter, he re-signed with UFC. His first fight was one for the ages as he engaged in a classic hard-fought decision loss to Chuck Liddell at UFC 79. A 36-second knockout win over Keith Jardine at UFC 84 in 2008 followed. While he would go 3-4 in his next series of UFC bouts, win or lose, he always brought excitement to his loyal fan base.

DAN HENDERSON

DEBUT: UFC 17, MAY 15, 1998
UFC 17 MIDDLEWEIGHT TOURNAMENT WINNER
PRIDE WELTERWEIGHT CHAMPION
PRIDE MIDDLEWEIGHT CHAMPION
STRIKEFORCE LIGHT HEAVYWEIGHT CHAMPION

DOWNEY, CA

A native of Temecula, California, Dan "Hendo" Henderson turned to mixed martial arts in 1997 after a stellar Greco-Roman wrestling career that saw him represent the United States in the 1992 and 1996 Olympics. Henderson made his pro debut, with two fights in one night, on June 15, 1997. From there, the train just kept on rolling.

On May 15, 1998, he would make his Octagon debut, scoring consecutive victories over Carlos Newton and Allan Goes on the same night, at UFC 17. But for the next nine years, he would take his solid wrestling attack and devastating right hand overseas to compete. Henderson performed most notably in the PRIDE organization, where he defeated Renzo Gracie, Murilo "Ninja" Rua, Murilo Bustamante (twice), Yuki Kondo, Vitor Belfort and Kazuhiro Nakamura.

By early 2007, the Team Quest standout had established himself as one of the best pound-for-pound fighters in the world had taken home the PRIDE 183-pound championship for his efforts. He wasn't satisfied, though, and in February 2007, he moved up to the 205-pound class to face old rival Wanderlei Silva.

Henderson was on top of his game in that fight, knocking out Silva in the third round to add the PRIDE middleweight title to his welterweight crown—becoming the only fighter in history to own both titles simultaneously.

> "I WOULD NEVER TAKE A FIGHT WHERE I DIDN'T THINK I COULD BEAT THE GUY. AND HONESTLY, I THINK I CAN BEAT ANYBODY IN THE WORLD."
> —DAN HENDERSON

Following the bout, Henderson returned to UFC in search of another set of gold belts. He would fall short of that goal in back-to-back losses against Rampage Jackson and Anderson Silva. However, three consecutive wins over Rousimar Palhares, Rich Franklin and Michael Bisping showed that he had his mojo back.

"I've always been confident in myself and my abilities," Henderson said. "I would never take a fight where I didn't think I could beat the guy. And honestly, I think I can beat anybody in the world."

After his highlight-reel knockout of Bisping at UFC 100 in July 2011, Henderson took himself to the STRIKEFORCE organization. There, he shook off a decision loss to Jake Shields and won the promotion's light heavyweight title in 2011 with a TKO of Rafael Cavalcante.

For Henderson, home was always in the Octagon. After ending his STRIKEFORCE career with a thrilling first-round knockout of heavyweight superstar Fedor Emelianenko, Henderson graced the UFC roster once again. His first fight back, in November 2011, resulted in one of the greatest fights of all time, as he outlasted Shogun Rua over five rounds.

It was the crown jewel in a career that sees "Hendo" still battling it out with the best that UFC's light heavyweight and middleweight rosters have to offer. And he's hungrier than ever.

"I know I've accomplished quite a bit in the sport, but in my mind, I'm not gonna be satisfied with what I've done when I have bigger goals that I want to accomplish," he said. "Once I accomplish those goals, maybe I'll retire and be satisfied with that."

PAT MILETICH

DEBUT: UFC 16, MARCH 13, 1998
UFC 16 WELTERWEIGHT TOURNAMENT CHAMPION
UFC WELTERWEIGHT CHAMPION 1998-2001
UFC HALL OF FAME (2014)

DAVENPORT, IA

There's no denying the impact that Pat "The Croatian Sensation" Miletich had on the sport of mixed martial arts. A former UFC welterweight champion, who also led Matt Hughes, Jens Pulver and Tim Sylvia to world titles as a coach, he is one of the sport's pioneers, in and out of the Octagon. Miletich always believed that his success could be boiled down to one thing: hard work.

Involved in combat sports since he was a child, first in wrestling, then boxing and kickboxing, Miletich had the work ethic to outperform more naturally gifted competitors. He also had a keen eye for what was happening on the canvas or in the ring.

"I wrestled from the time I was in kindergarten through college, and I watched how different coaches had coached in all those different aspects of sports. I took the good aspects of coaching that I liked, because there were coaches that couldn't convey to me correctly the information that they were trying to get through my head, and there were other coaches that were really good at it. I just kind of modeled myself after them and tried to explain myself [to my own fighters] so that they could understand."

Eventually, Miletich sought an opportunity to put his wits and his fists to use in the budding sport of mixed martial arts and teamed up with Mark Hansen to get started in the gym.

"He was ranked among the top 10 heavyweights in the world and was a Davenport police officer," said Miletich of Hansen. "He and I were training partners for two, three years, at least, by ourselves before things got rolling. That was actually the first guy. He was a very dominant fighter and a really powerful guy, an All-American lineman at Northern Iowa."

On October 28, 1995, Miletich made his professional MMA debut with three wins in one night in a Chicago tournament. He continued to build his resume, and improve his fight game, on the Illinois/Iowa circuit, going 17-1-1 with the only loss coming against fellow MMA mastermind Matt Hume.

Then UFC called. On March 13, 1998, Miletich defeated Townsend Saunders and old rival Chris Brennan (they had fought twice previously) to win the UFC 16 tournament. Seven months later, Miletich was back, this time to fight for UFC's first lightweight—later converted to welterweight—title. In the opposite corner was scrappy Mikey Burnett, and though anticipation was high for the matchup, the match did not live up to the hype. Regardless of the lack of sustained action in the bout, Miletich eked out a 21-minute split decision to earn the championship belt.

Miletich successfully defended his belt four times over the next two years, defeating Jorge Patino, Andre Pederneiras, John Alessio and Kenichi Yamamoto, while battling an even tougher foe in the gym—a laundry list of mounting injuries.

Finally, in May 2001, the longtime champion surrendered his belt to Carlos "The Ronin" Newton via submission in what was a shocking upset at the time. However, less than two months later, Miletich was back, knocking out Shonie Carter with a head kick at UFC 32. But a rematch with Newton was not in the cards, as Matt Hughes seized the belt from "The Ronin" at UFC 34.

"The Croatian Sensation" moved up to middleweight for his next bout at UFC 36 in 2002, in which he was stopped by Matt Lindland. After the loss to Lindland, Miletich took a break from the sport to heal his injuries and focus on his gym.

At one time or another, standouts like Matt Hughes, Jens Pulver, Tim Sylvia, Jeremy Horn, Robbie Lawler, Drew McFedries, Rory Markham, Anthony Fryklund and Jason Black occupied Miletich's gym.

Miletich attempted comebacks in 2006 and 2008, losing to Renzo Gracie and then knocking out Thomas Denny. Currently, he provides expert commentary for various outlets, including Showtime and ESPN. He was inducted into the UFC Hall of Fame on July 6, 2014.

FIGHTS OF THE YEAR

UFC ULTIMATE BRAZIL

| SHAMROCK | WSUB1 | LOBER |

UFC 17

| HENDERSON | WSD | NEWTON |

UFC 16

| KOSAKA | WUD | KIMO |

UFC 17

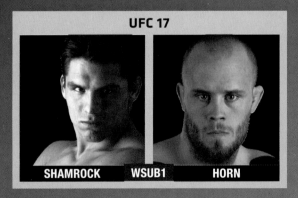

| SHAMROCK | WSUB1 | HORN |

UFC ULTIMATE BRAZIL

| RIZZO | KO1 | ABBOTT |

KNOCKOUTS OF THE YEAR

UFC 17

| WILLIAMS | KO1 | COLEMAN |

UFC ULTIMATE BRAZIL

| BELFORT | TKO1 | SILVA |

UFC 16

| SHAMROCK | KO1 | ZINOVIEV |

UFC 17

| ABBOTT | TKO1 | DUARTE |

UFC ULTIMATE BRAZIL

| RIZZO | KO1 | ABBOTT |

SUBMISSIONS OF THE YEAR

UFC 16

| BOHLANDER | WSUB1 | JACKSON |

UFC 16

| MILETICH | WSUB1 | BRENNAN |

UFC ULTIMATE BRAZIL

| BRAGA | WSUB1 | HORN |

UFC 17

| NEWTON | WSUB1 | GILSTRAP |

UFC 17

| SHAMROCK | WSUB1 | HORN |

Belfort defeats Silva at UFC Ultimate Brazil.

2005   2006   2007   2008   2009   2010   2011   2012   2013   2014   2015

DEBUTS

UFC 16
IGOR ZINOVIEV
TSUYOSHI KOSAKA
CHRIS BRENNAN
PAT MILETICH
TOWNSEND SAUNDERS
EUGENIO TADEU
MIKEY BURNETT
COURTNEY TURNER
LAVERNE CLARK
JOSH STUART

UFC 17
PETE WILLIAMS
JEREMY HORN
CARLOS NEWTON
DAN HENDERSON
HUGO DUARTE
JOE PARDO
MIKE VAN ARSDALE
BOB GILSTRAP
ALLAN GOES
ANDRE ROBERTS
CHUCK LIDDELL
NOE HERNANDEZ

ULTIMATE BRAZIL
CESAR MARCUSSI
PAULO SANTOS
TULIO PALHARES
ADRIANO SANTOS
EBENEZER FONTES BRAGA
PEDRO RIZZO
WANDERLEI SILVA
JOHN LOBER

GREATEST UPSETS

UFC 1
ROYCE GRACIE vs KEN SHAMROCK I

All fans needed to do was look at Royce Gracie and Ken Shamrock side-by-side to wonder how a skinny kid from Brazil could possibly beat a monster like Shamrock. Throw in the fact that Shamrock knew the "mysterious" submission game employed by Gracie, and the odds in his favor shot even higher. But on this night, Gracie was not to be denied. He put a new sport on the map with a brilliant three-fight/three-win performance, the highlight of which was his win in the middle over Shamrock.

UFC 3
KEITH HACKNEY vs EMMANUEL YARBOROUGH

In the early days of UFC, it was difficult to evaluate some of the competitors in this brand-new fighting venue; you usually judged fighters by their appearances. When 200-pound Keith Hackney faced off against 600-pound Emmanuel Yarborough, you feared for Hackney's safety. Well, at least you did until the fight started, and Hackney dropped his opponent with the first strike he landed. From there, it was all Hackney, who halted Yarborough in fewer than two minutes.

UFC 4
ROYCE GRACIE vs DAN SEVERN

With 10 wins and no losses in UFC, Royce Gracie was the undisputed king of the early Octagon. But the man many believed to have his number was Dan Severn, a former college wrestling star known as "The Beast." It was no surprise to anyone as Severn romped over his first two opponents in the 1994 tournament and then battered Gracie through the first 15 minutes of their final bout. But then Gracie pulled off a triangle choke at the 15:49 mark, the crowd roared and a legend's legacy was cemented.

UFC 14
MAURICE SMITH vs MARK COLEMAN

Just as jiu-jitsu ruled the early days of the Octagon, wrestling took over in 1996. As 1997 dawned, the man on the top of the heap was "The Godfather of Ground-and-Pound," Mark Coleman. But kickboxing star Maurice Smith was about to turn the MMA world on its ear at UFC 14, stunning observers with a style that was soon to be known as "sprawl and brawl." He tossed off Coleman's takedown attempts and pounded out a decision win that earned him the UFC heavyweight title and handed "The Hammer" his first loss.

UFC 15
RANDY COUTURE vs VITOR BELFORT I

Randy Couture made a career out of beating the oddsmakers, and it all began with his October 1997 thrashing of then-unbeaten Vitor Belfort. At the time, the question wasn't who would eventually beat "The Phenom," but if he would ever lose at all. Couture took all of eight minutes and 17 seconds to answer both questions as he notched up a TKO victory.

UFC 17
PETE WILLIAMS VS MARK COLEMAN

Despite his loss to Maurice Smith 10 months earlier, Mark Coleman was still "The Hammer" and remained a feared man in the Octagon. Originally scheduled to face fellow wrestler Randy Couture, Coleman was instead matched with young prospect Pete Williams. The Lion's Den product made an immediate name for himself with a highlight-reel head-kick knockout of an exhausted Coleman at the 12:38 mark of their 1998 bout.

UFC 35
JENS PULVER VS BJ PENN I

Despite his status as a UFC lightweight champion and a veteran competitor of the sport, Jens Pulver was a prohibitive underdog when he took on "The Prodigy," BJ Penn, at UFC 35 in 2002. For two rounds the oddsmakers were right, as Penn dominated and almost submitted the champion at the end of Round 2. But for the next three rounds "Lil' Evil" emerged, earning a five-round majority decision. That win stands as the defining moment in the career of the UFC's popular— and first—lightweight champion.

UFC 38
IAN FREEMAN VS FRANK MIR

In 2002, Frank Mir was UFC's golden boy, a charismatic young heavyweight with off-the-charts talent. Ian Freeman, competing in front of his countrymen in UFC's first visit to England, was a grizzled veteran fighting with a heavy heart due to his father's illness. Inspired, Freeman shocked Mir and the world with an emotional first-round TKO win. But the celebration was tempered by the news that Freeman's father had passed away shortly before the bout, with "The Machine" not being told until after the fight concluded.

UFC 43
RANDY COUTURE VS CHUCK LIDDELL I

After taking back-to-back losses at heavyweight to the much bigger Ricco Rodriguez and Josh Barnett, Randy Couture's drop to the 205-pound weight class was seen as a desperate move to save his career. Facing the feared Chuck Liddell in his first light heavyweight bout was just going to hasten Couture's demise. But the one person not counting Couture out was the man himself. Couture not only beat Liddell, he stopped him in the third round, beginning the second act of one of the fight game's most amazing careers.

UFC 46
BJ PENN VS MATT HUGHES I

BJ Penn came up short in his two previous shots at UFC gold, losing to Jens Pulver and drawing with Caol Uno. What made him think that he could beat Matt Hughes, and 15 pounds north at welterweight to boot? It's his confidence that made "The Prodigy" one of the greats, and he delivered a classic performance in submitting a stunned Hughes at 4:39 of the first round to win the UFC 170-pound title.

UFC 47
ROBBIE LAWLER VS NICK DIAZ

A no-nonsense knockout artist, "Ruthless" Robbie Lawler was turning into UFC's version of Mike Tyson, and the fans loved him for it. Even an injury-induced loss to Pete Spratt didn't quiet the buzz around Lawler. However, jiu-jitsu ace Nick Diaz certainly did the trick with his stunning one-punch finish of Lawler. But Diaz was no Buster Douglas, as he went on to a successful career of his own in the ensuing years.

UFC 57
MARCIO CRUZ VS FRANK MIR

Fewer than two years removed from a serious motorcycle accident that took his UFC heavyweight title and almost his life, Frank Mir returned to the Octagon in February 2006. There he met jiu-jitsu specialist Marcio Cruz at UFC 57. But this wasn't the same Mir who was on top of the world a couple of years earlier, and Cruz proved it by stopping the former champion in the first round. It wouldn't be until 2007 that the "real" Mir once again made his presence known.

UFC 63
JOE LAUZON VS JENS PULVER

After more than four years away, Jens Pulver's return to UFC in 2006 was supposed to be a celebration. And it was—for opponent Joe Lauzon. Lauzon knocked "Lil' Evil" out in less than a minute, momentarily derailing the former lightweight champion's comeback. As for Lauzon, he was back at work on Monday morning as an IT professional.

UFC 68
RANDY COUTURE VS TIM SYLVIA

After the former heavyweight and light heavyweight champion's year-long layoff—and knockout losses in two of his previous three fights—"The Natural" finally returned, but finding someone who was picking him to beat the 6'8" Tim Sylvia was nearly

impossible. However, Couture pulled off yet another miracle in winning a shutout five-round decision, delighting a packed house at the Nationwide Arena in Columbus, Ohio, in the process.

UFC 69
GEORGES ST-PIERRE vs MATT SERRA I

The year of the upset was definitely 2007. Matt Serra's stoppage of Georges St-Pierre was not only the biggest upset of that year, but of all-time. Matt Serra was given virtually no chance to take down a champion expected to reign atop his division for as long as he chose, but Serra succeeded this feat in astonishing fashion. The Renzo Gracie jiu-jitsu black belt did it with his fists, not his ground game, as he clipped GSP early and kept punching until referee John McCarthy halted the bout and raised the hand of the new welterweight champion.

UFC 70
MIRKO CRO COP vs GABRIEL GONZAGA I

Sure, Gabriel Gonzaga was an underdog against the feared Croatian striker, but there were more than a few people who figured the Brazilian jiu-jitsu black belt had the right stuff to beat Cro Cop—on the ground. But beating Cro Cop with a single kick to the head? Those are the kinds of odds that wouldn't even show up in Vegas. Still, Gonzaga pulled it off, winning with Cro Cop's signature move. He earned himself a shot at the heavyweight title and a permanent spot in UFC highlight reels.

UFC 76
SHOGUN RUA vs FORREST GRIFFIN I

No one thought that Forrest Griffin was going to win against high-profile PRIDE import Shogun Rua when they met in Anaheim in 2007. Griffin was going to show up, be competitive, swing for the fences, and eventually get put away by Shogun. At least that's what the Hollywood script called for, but Griffin didn't get the memo. He not only beat Shogun, he dominated him, putting the icing on the cake with a submission in the final minute to cap the upset victory.

UFC 76
CHUCK LIDDELL vs KEITH JARDINE

Before UFC 71, Chuck Liddell was the most dominant light heavyweight in the world. Keith Jardine was coming off a stoppage of Forrest Griffin and was apparently a couple of wins away from a title shot. What a difference one night makes. Even after Liddell lost to Rampage Jackson, he was still expected to make short work of Jardine, who had been defeated on that same night by Houston Alexander. However, with a disciplined game plan and some hellacious kicks, Jardine momentarily put Liddell's career on ice with a three-round split decision win.

UFC 90
JUNIOR DOS SANTOS vs FABRICIO WERDUM

If fans didn't know who Junior Dos Santos was before October 25, 2008, they were not alone. But if they still didn't know who this Brazilian bomber was after his 81-second demolition of Fabricio Werdum at UFC 90, where were they? In a little over a minute, Dos Santos smashed his way into the rankings with a ferocious knockout of the consensus Top 5 Werdum. Suddenly, this young man had plenty of fans around the MMA world waiting to see what he was going to do next.

MINOTAURO NOGUEIRA vs FRANK MIR I

Going into this 2008 battle of *The Ultimate Fighter* season eight, conventional wisdom said that Nogueira, one of the sport's all-time greatest heavyweights, was just too good for Mir. So when Mir started lighting up Nogueira on the feet almost as soon as the horn sounded, warning signs began flashing and the former UFC heavyweight champ grew more confident each time he knocked down the Brazilian. In the second round, he did what no fighter had ever done to the former PRIDE champ: he finished him to win the interim UFC heavyweight belt.

UFC 95

JOSH KOSCHECK vs PAULO THIAGO

At the time of this 2009 bout, it was assumed that the unbeaten but unknown Paulo Thiago would be dispatched fairly easily by highly regarded contender Josh Koscheck. The Brazilian had his supporters, but it would be safe to guess that not even Thiago's biggest fans would have expected their man to score with a right uppercut followed by a clean-up left hand to win by first-round knockout. This one stunned everyone, especially Koscheck.

UFC 112
FRANKIE EDGAR vs BJ PENN I

Few people outside of his native New Jersey gave Frankie Edgar a shot at defeating BJ Penn for the UFC lightweight title in their April 2010 bout. But with crisp striking and effective movement, as well as a couple of points-scoring takedowns, Edgar wowed fans in Abu Dhabi with a unanimous decision win. And if that wasn't enough, Edgar repeated the feat in a more dominant fashion four months later at UFC 118, proving that the first win was no fluke.

UFC 132
TITO ORTIZ vs RYAN BADER

If you picked 36-year-old Tito Ortiz to defeat Ryan Bader at UFC 132 in July of 2011, you probably did so just for sentimental reasons. The former light heavyweight champion had shown nothing in his previous five fights (a 0-4-1 stretch) that would make you think he could turn the tide against the young powerhouse. But he did, shocking Bader with a flush punch to the jaw and then finishing matters with a guillotine choke that ignited the MGM Grand Garden Arena crowd and resurrected Ortiz' career.

UFC 162
ANDERSON SILVA vs CHRIS WEIDMAN I

It's a daunting task to fight someone who hasn't lost in more than seven years in UFC, especially when that opponent has been deemed the greatest pound-for-pound fighter of all time. When undefeated Chris Weidman faced Anderson Silva for the 185-pound title in July 2013, the New Yorker was unmoved by the odds against him. He proved it on fight night, nearly submitting the Brazilian legend in the first round before scoring a stunning second-round knockout.

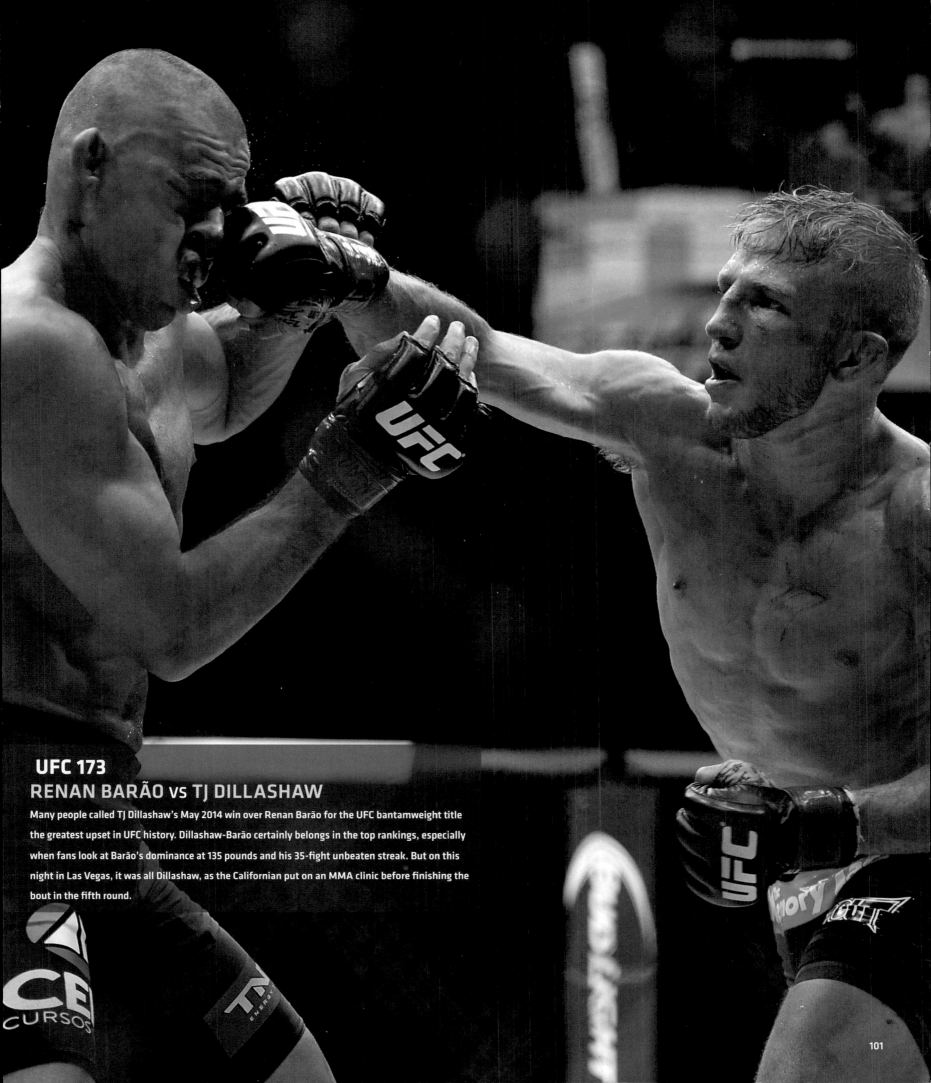

UFC 173
RENAN BARÃO vs TJ DILLASHAW

Many people called TJ Dillashaw's May 2014 win over Renan Barão for the UFC bantamweight title the greatest upset in UFC history. Dillashaw-Barão certainly belongs in the top rankings, especially when fans look at Barão's dominance at 135 pounds and his 35-fight unbeaten streak. But on this night in Las Vegas, it was all Dillashaw, as the Californian put on an MMA clinic before finishing the bout in the fifth round.

1999

Though UFC had plenty of talent and a growing fan-base, in 1999 the so-called "Dark Ages" were in full effect. UFC events were removed from cable television, politicians were still trying to ban UFC altogether, and the company was in trouble financially. However, owners SEG were nothing if not gutsy, and they continued to plug away, hoping for better days.

Of course, it didn't help that UFC's heavyweight division was thrown into disarray with the vacating of the title by champion Randy Couture. The hunt was on for a new star to rise to the top and claim the belt. A promising prospect would appear in the form of Holland's Bas Rutten, who made his Octagon debut after a long career in Japan's Pancrase organization. Rutten accomplished a hard-fought TKO win over Tsuyoshi Kosaka in the main event of UFC 18 on January 8 at the Pontchartrain Center in New Orleans.

Rutten had the personality and the talent to make some noise in UFC, and when you added rising Brazilian star Pedro Rizzo to the mix, the division was showing signs of life. At UFC 18, Rizzo scored the biggest win of his young career, taking a split decision over former champion Mark Coleman. While it wasn't a spectacular performance, it was enough to defeat the fading "Hammer," who would not grace the Octagon again for 10 years.

In the UFC 18 championship bout, UFC lightweight champion Pat Miletich continued to shut down all opposition, scoring a relatively uneventful unanimous decision over newcomer Jorge Patino in a 21-minute contest that didn't sit too well with fans in attendance that were craving action. It does take two to fight, though, and Patino didn't exactly conduct himself like a fighter trying to win a world championship. Outside of a tight guillotine choke in overtime, Miletich was in little trouble as he waltzed to another victory.

BAS RUTTEN

DEBUT: UFC 18, JANUARY 8, 1999
UFC HEAVYWEIGHT CHAMPION

TILBURG, NETHERLANDS

One of the most popular figures in MMA today, Bas "El Guapo" Rutten has garnered a huge fan base among a new generation of fans through his commentary work for the PRIDE organization and various other outlets. That in itself is fascinating, considering that these new fans may not know that the witty and gregarious Holland native was once one of the most feared fighters in the world.

Known for his devastating striking, Rutten wasn't a points fighter. Each shot he threw, whether with his fists or feet, was designed to knock an opponent out. During a 16-fight Muay Thai kickboxing career, all 14 of the taekwondo and Kyokushin karate black belt's wins ended via KO.

The next challenge for Rutten was mixed martial arts. He took to it like he had taken to kickboxing, adding ground fighting along the way to become a standout in Japan's Pancrase organization. Rutten would fight 30 times in Pancrase, going 25-4-1 with victories over the likes of Vernon White, Maurice Smith, Frank Shamrock, Guy Mezger and Masakatsu Funaki. The only person he couldn't seem to beat was Ken Shamrock, whom he lost to twice.

Firmly established in Japan, Rutten finally made the leap to America in 1999. Just a month shy of his 34th birthday, he battled Tsuyoshi Kosaka at UFC 18. Far behind on points, Rutten was looking at a decision loss as he began the overtime period, but he wasn't done yet.

At the 14:15 mark of the bout, Rutten finished Kosaka, earning a shot at the vacant heavyweight title against Kevin Randleman. This time, the bout went the full 21-minute distance, and despite a strong late surge from Rutten, it was assumed that Randleman would get the nod. He didn't, and with the split decision victory, Rutten was now the UFC heavyweight champion.

It was a short-lived reign, as Rutten vacated his title. Though he initially intended to chase Frank Shamrock in the middleweight division, he ultimately retired due to an accumulation of injuries.

Two months later, it was off to Casino Magic in Bay St. Louis, Mississippi, for UFC 19: Young Guns. Future UFC Hall of Famers Tito Ortiz and Chuck Liddell were in action, along with former Ohio State wrestling standout Kevin Randleman, who debuted with a decision win over former heavyweight champion Maurice Smith.

Making his second Octagon appearance, Liddell suffered his first pro loss as former middleweight title challenger Jeremy Horn secured his first UFC win in three tries. Horn sunk in an arm triangle choke in the closing seconds of regulation time that put Liddell to sleep as time ran out, ending the bout in his favor.

Still, the main event was certainly the biggest attraction that night, as rising star Ortiz evened the score with veteran Guy Mezger. Stepping in on late notice to replace the injured Vitor Belfort, Ortiz eagerly sought some payback against Mezger, and his smothering pace was unforgiving throughout. Eventually, Ortiz took the tired Mezger down to the canvas, and after a series of peppering ground strikes without a response from Mezger, referee John McCarthy stopped the fight at the 9:55 mark.

Kevin Randleman vs Maurice Smith at UFC 19.

The real fun took place after the bout, though, as Ortiz' post-fight gloating incensed Mezger's trainer, UFC pioneer Ken Shamrock. This set the stage for additional grudge matches in the coming years.

103

"You have to have rivalries," Shamrock said. "People enjoy rivalries, whether it's in football, baseball or boxing. There are so many ways to have a rivalry. It doesn't even have to be an anger rivalry; it could be someone who is undefeated against another person who is undefeated. That's something you can build on. Or even a rematch, you can build on that also. So it doesn't actually have to be anger or the way things are going between me and Tito [Ortiz]. You're not going to get those all the time. Most of the time, fighters are going to be respectful to each other. It's just the nature of our business. But at times, you have guys like Tito, who disrespects his opponents, especially after he beats them. He's got to dig the grave for them, and the fight's over. If you want to do stuff before the fight or during the fight, that's all good. But when you start doing things after the fight, I just think there's no place for that."

Kevin Randleman and Bas Rutten compete at UFC 20.

There was no bad blood between the headliners of UFC 20 at Boutwell Auditorium in Birmingham, Alabama, on May 7—at least not before their bout—but there was certainly plenty on the line when Rutten and Randleman were paired up to fight for Couture's vacated UFC heavyweight title.

Although Randleman apparently did everything necessary to fill the vacancy at the top of the heavyweight division, the judges didn't agree, awarding Rutten a split decision and the title.

"Randleman did real good in the first round, then he broke my nose and I was considering quitting, but I said, 'These last two rounds are gonna be my rounds,'" said Rutten. "'Even when he takes me down, I'm gonna fight him.' And I just unloaded."

"The Monster" had a different view of the 21-minute fight. "I beat Bas Rutten, and everyone knows it," said Randleman. "That's why they changed the rules. That's why they went to rounds. I made them go to rounds."

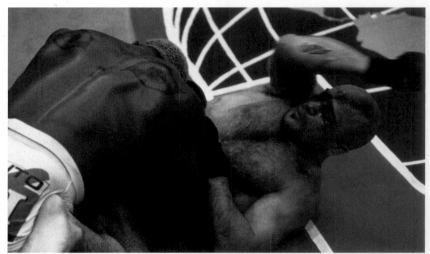

Bas Rutten wins the bout over Kevin Randleman via decision at UFC 20.

"I BEAT BAS RUTTEN, AND EVERYONE KNOWS IT. THAT'S WHY THEY CHANGED THE RULES. THAT'S WHY THEY WENT TO ROUNDS. I MADE THEM GO TO ROUNDS."
—KEVIN RANDLEMAN

Perhaps not solely because of Randleman vs. Rutten, but when UFC returned on July 16 in Cedar Rapids, Iowa, it did so with main card bouts consisting of three five-minute rounds and championship bouts scheduled for five five-minute rounds. The 10-point must system—first instituted in boxing—was also brought in, with points being awarded for Octagon control, effective striking, grappling and aggressiveness.

Those new rules brought mixed martial arts even closer to the realm of real sport, but oddly enough, none of the eight UFC 21 bouts needed judges. Main eventer Miletich defended his title yet again, stopping Andre Pederneiras in the second round.

UFC 22 took place at the Lake Charles Civic Center in Louisiana on September 24, 1999, and while the Octagon debut of future UFC Hall of Famer Matt Hughes was a landmark in MMA history, the main event more than held its own in terms of the record books. Frank Shamrock returned to defend his middleweight title (now known as light heavyweight) against young gun Tito Ortiz in what many consider to be the greatest fight of the pre-Zuffa era.

Battered from pillar to post by Ortiz, Shamrock was pushed to the limit by the challenger. However, when Ortiz' gas tank ran low, the champion roared back, submitting his opponent due to strikes in the fourth round. Ortiz was crushed by the defeat, but he knew as soon as the bout was over that he had been part of something special.

"I knew it right after the fight," Ortiz said. "Just competing against a five-time defending champion the way I did. I almost beat him, and I almost brought what it took to be the champion. I was completely hooked then. In my mind, losing to somebody was the worst thing that could ever happen. It was worse than the Guy Mezger loss; it was the worst loss I ever had. But I learned how to push myself to the limits, and I've got to thank Frank Shamrock. He helped me to become a champion because after losing to him, I never wanted to lose again."

As for Shamrock, he shocked UFC fans by retiring in the Octagon after the fight. "I came here to challenge myself, to fight all comers, and I feel like I've done that," said the long-reigning titleholder. "Who's left? I'm good right now just retiring my belt and concentrating on my marriage and doing a few other things. I think I'm gonna leave this belt in the ring here for the next crew to pick up, and retire my title tonight."

"I CAME HERE TO CHALLENGE MYSELF, TO FIGHT ALL COMERS, AND I FEEL LIKE I'VE DONE THAT."
—KEN SHAMROCK

When it rained, it poured on UFC. After Shamrock's retirement, Rutten vacated the heavyweight title and later left, as well. That left the door open for Randleman once more, and the Ohio native took advantage, defeating Pete Williams at UFC 23 in Tokyo on November 19, 1999, to finally get his hands on the championship belt.

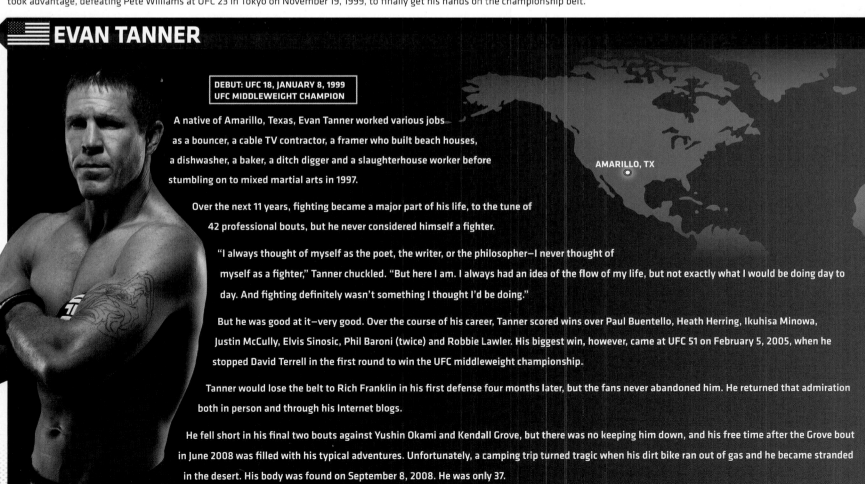

EVAN TANNER

DEBUT: UFC 18, JANUARY 8, 1999
UFC MIDDLEWEIGHT CHAMPION

A native of Amarillo, Texas, Evan Tanner worked various jobs as a bouncer, a cable TV contractor, a framer who built beach houses, a dishwasher, a baker, a ditch digger and a slaughterhouse worker before stumbling on to mixed martial arts in 1997.

AMARILLO, TX

Over the next 11 years, fighting became a major part of his life, to the tune of 42 professional bouts, but he never considered himself a fighter.

"I always thought of myself as the poet, the writer, or the philosopher—I never thought of myself as a fighter," Tanner chuckled. "But here I am. I always had an idea of the flow of my life, but not exactly what I would be doing day to day. And fighting definitely wasn't something I thought I'd be doing."

But he was good at it—very good. Over the course of his career, Tanner scored wins over Paul Buentello, Heath Herring, Ikuhisa Minowa, Justin McCully, Elvis Sinosic, Phil Baroni (twice) and Robbie Lawler. His biggest win, however, came at UFC 51 on February 5, 2005, when he stopped David Terrell in the first round to win the UFC middleweight championship.

Tanner would lose the belt to Rich Franklin in his first defense four months later, but the fans never abandoned him. He returned that admiration both in person and through his Internet blogs.

He fell short in his final two bouts against Yushin Okami and Kendall Grove, but there was no keeping him down, and his free time after the Grove bout in June 2008 was filled with his typical adventures. Unfortunately, a camping trip turned tragic when his dirt bike ran out of gas and he became stranded in the desert. His body was found on September 8, 2008. He was only 37.

MATT HUGHES

DEBUT: UFC 22, SEPTEMBER 24, 1999
TWO-TIME UFC WELTERWEIGHT CHAMPION
UFC HALL OF FAME (2010)

HILLSBORO, IL

Matt Hughes was probably tired of hearing about the topic, but as the two-time welterweight champion celebrated his induction into the UFC Hall of Fame on May 28, 2010, you couldn't help but remind him of his words before his Extreme Challenge bout against Chatt Lavender in 2001.

At that point, Hughes was 27 years old and already three years into his career. With a 2-1 record in UFC, prior to leaving, he seemed destined to return. However, the question for the former All-American wrestler from Eastern Illinois University was how long he saw himself competing in mixed martial arts.

"Two or three years maybe," said Hughes. "That's it. I was born and raised on a farm, and I want to go back there. I would like to win a UFC championship. If I've saved my money, and in two to three years, if it takes me that long to win that belt, it may very well be that I'll retire on the spot."

Well, things changed significantly. A decade after the Lavender fight, Hughes was still fighting. More importantly, with wins over Matt Serra, Renzo Gracie and Ricardo Almeida in 2009-2010, and just one loss to BJ Penn in November 2010, he was still relevant in the UFC welterweight division he had practically put on the map. His two title reigns saw him defend his title a combined seven times.

2005 2006 2007 2008 2009 2010 2011 2012 2013 2014 2015

But there are even more numbers that made Hughes' induction into the UFC Hall of Fame a no-brainer:

46 PRO WINS

18 UFC WINS

2 WELTERWEIGHT CHAMPIONSHIP REIGNS

7 SUCCESSFUL WELTERWEIGHT TITLE DEFENSES

9 CHAMPIONSHIP FIGHT WINS

5 KNOCKOUT WINS IN CHAMPIONSHIP FIGHTS

5 SUCCESSFUL CONSECUTIVE WELTERWEIGHT TITLE DEFENSES

12 WELTERWEIGHT CHAMPIONSHIP FIGHTS

3 SUBMISSION WINS IN WELTERWEIGHT CHAMPIONSHIP FIGHTS

6 WINS OVER FORMER OR CURRENT UFC CHAMPIONS (GEORGES ST-PIERRE, MATT SERRA, BJ PENN, DAVE MENNE, SEAN SHERK AND CARLOS NEWTON)

Even though this honor was no surprise, it did come as a shock to Hughes when he got the call from UFC President Dana White.

"I just never thought about it, to be honest, so yeah, it came out of the blue," said Hughes. "I've always been the type of guy who thought that somebody who gets inducted into the Hall of Fame needs to be a retired individual. That's just my train of thought. But I'm very privileged, and I thank UFC."

And if you know anything about him, you know that being a UFC Hall of Famer isn't going to prompt Hughes—who also coached two seasons of *The Ultimate Fighter*—to start sitting on the back porch and waxing poetic about his accomplishments.

It was a dream run for Hughes. After defeating Lavender via third-round submission, he put together two more wins and then was invited back to UFC to take on welterweight champion Carlos Newton at UFC 34 in November 2001. Hughes defeated Newton that night and began a title reign that saw him defeat Hayato Sakurai, Newton in a rematch, Gil Castillo, Sean Sherk and Frank Trigg.

Hughes would lose his crown to Penn at UFC 46 in 2004, but nine months later, he was back on top after beating soon-to-be welterweight great Georges St-Pierre. In Hughes' first defense of his second reign, he was pitted against Trigg again. What resulted was not only one of the greatest fights in UFC history, but the one fight that Hughes said he would pick if forced to choose a single fight that epitomized what he's all about.

That first-round submission win over Trigg could have been enough for Hughes to hang his hat on and walk into the sunset, but the pride of Hillsboro, Illinois, wasn't done yet. After that win, he defeated Joe Riggs, Royce Gracie, BJ Penn, Chris Lytle, Matt Serra, Ricardo Almeida and Renzo Gracie. His only losses came from St-Pierre (twice), Penn, Josh Koscheck and Thiago Alves.

In 2013, nearly three years after his UFC Hall of Fame induction, Hughes retired. He is currently UFC's Vice President of Athlete Development and Government Relations.

"I JUST NEVER THOUGHT ABOUT IT, TO BE HONEST, SO YEAH, IT CAME OUT OF THE BLUE."
—MATT HUGHES

JENS PULVER

DEBUT: UFC 22, SEPTEMBER 24, 1999
UFC LIGHTWEIGHT CHAMPION

SUNNYSIDE, WA

Jens "Lil' Evil" Pulver arrived in the fight game after battling through an abusive childhood and not only surviving, but thriving.

In 1999, he made his UFC debut, and by March 2000, he got his first Octagon victory over David Velasquez. Following subsequent wins over Joao Roque and John Lewis, he earned a shot to become the first ever UFC 155-pound champion when he took on Japanese star Caol Uno at UFC 30 on February 23, 2001. After five rounds, Pulver earned a unanimous decision over Uno. He was a world champion.

There was no downtime for the new champion. Just six months after winning the belt, he was back in the Octagon, defeating Dennis Hallman via five-round decision. Pulver was then matched up against the unbeaten BJ Penn, with most believing that the champion's Cinderella story was going to end in spectacular fashion on January 11, 2002.

Pulver wasn't among that crowd, though, and he took it as a personal insult that fans and the media wrote him off in the lead-up to the bout. What ensued over the next five rounds turned into one of the best fights of all time, as Pulver silenced the critics and took home a well-deserved majority decision.

Due to a contract dispute, this would be his last bout in UFC for more than four years. Over those four years, Pulver continued to fight, but there was always something missing for him. In 2006, he reached his apex when it was announced that he was returning to UFC.

Fights against Joe Lauzon and Penn followed, along with a stint as a coach on *The Ultimate Fighter* season five. Next up was a debut in the WEC's featherweight division, where he submitted Cub Swanson in 35 seconds in 2007.

A subsequent losing streak ended his WEC career, but no true fan cared. Pulver will always be a pioneer for the lighter weight classes in mixed martial arts.

KEVIN RANDLEMAN

DEBUT: UFC 19, MARCH 5, 1999
UFC HEAVYWEIGHT CHAMPION

SANDUSKY OH

Full of charisma, power and fury, Kevin "The Monster" Randleman was a shock to the system in UFC from 1999 to 2002. While his performances didn't always match his incendiary interviews, there was no denying his athleticism and wrestling ability in the Octagon.

A two-time Division I national wrestling champion for Ohio State University, Randleman followed his close friend and training partner Mark Coleman into mixed martial arts. He debuted in 1996 in Brazil, where he fought his first eight fights.

By March 1999, "The Monster" was in UFC, where he grounded-and-pounded his way to a decision victory over Maurice Smith. Just two months later at UFC 20, he was doing the same thing to Bas Rutten. But in one of the most controversial verdicts in UFC history, Rutten was awarded a split decision win and the vacant UFC heavyweight title.

When Rutten retired, Randleman was tagged to compete for the vacant crown against Pete Williams at UFC 23. This time, Randleman was awarded the decision and the UFC belt. In June 2000, he defended his title successfully against Pedro Rizzo in what was widely considered one of the most horrible fights in UFC.

Randleman lost his title to Randy Couture in his next fight at UFC 28. A drop to light heavyweight didn't help, as he was knocked out by Chuck Liddell at UFC 31. Randleman would only fight once more in UFC, but he left on a winning note, defeating Renato Sobral via decision at UFC 35.

In need of some new scenery, his next step would be Japan's PRIDE organization, where, like his friend Coleman, he resurrected his career in 12 fights over the next four years.

FABIANO IHA
FLORIANÓPOLIS, SANTA CATARINA, BRAZIL

DEBUT: UFC 20, MAY 7, 1999

When your nickname is "The King of The Armbar," you better be prepared to back up such a boast in the Octagon. Brazilian jiu-jitsu black belt Fabiano Iha certainly did—he finished six of his nine MMA wins by way of armbar.

"I know for sure that my armbar is better than anybody else's," said Iha in 2001. "It doesn't matter if he escapes from somebody else; I know I'll be able to get him anyway."

With a 3-4 UFC record from 1999 to 2001, Iha finished Laverne Clark (in a rematch), Daiju Takase and Phil Johns, but fell short against big names like Caol Uno and Dave Menne.

TIM LAJCIK
REDWOOD CITY, CA

DEBUT: UFC 21, JULY 16, 1999

A renaissance man who could legitimately list actor, stuntman, writer, wrestling coach and math teacher on his résumé—along with professional mixed martial artist—Tim "The Bohemian" Lajcik gave his all to his fighting career from 1998 to 2002. However, he wasn't able to elevate his game to where he could consistently put victories together.

Winless in UFC after kicking off his career with a 4-0 run that included a submission of Eugene Jackson, Lajcik lost Octagon matches to Tsuyoshi Kosaka and Jeff Monson, while drawing with Ron Waterman.

JOHN LEWIS
LAS VEGAS, NV

UFC 22, SEPTEMBER 24, 1999

A pioneering jiu-jitsu black belt whose impact stretched way beyond the Octagon or ring, John Lewis can be considered one of the most important figures in MMA history for introducing UFC owners Dana White, Lorenzo Fertitta and Frank Fertitta to the wonders of the ground game. In competition, Lewis was fearless, facing off with the likes of Jens Pulver, Laverne Clark, Rumina Sato (twice), Johil de Oliveira and Carlson Gracie Jr. But it was after his active career ended in 2000 that he began to really influence the fight scene. Lewis started coaching upcoming legends Chuck Liddell, Tito Ortiz, BJ Penn, Marc Laimon and the Inoue brothers.

DAIJU TAKASE
TOKYO, JAPAN

DEBUT: UFC 21, JULY 16, 1999

One of the hard luck stories in UFC history, Tokyo jiu-jitsu fighter Daiju Takase was a solid competitor who suffered from a case of poor career management, leading him into match after match against a killer series of opponents.

Winless in three UFC bouts against Jeremy Horn, Kenichi Yamamoto and Fabiano Iha, Takase was nonetheless able to make a decent living fighting at home for the PRIDE and Pancrase organizations. His 9-13-2 record was obviously nothing to brag about, but he will always have one great triumph. That moment was his 2003 triangle choke submission win over future UFC superstar Anderson Silva in PRIDE, a stunning upset that no one can ever take away.

RON WATERMAN
GREELEY, CO

DEBUT: UFC 20, MAY 7, 1999
WEC SUPER HEAVYWEIGHT CHAMPION

One of the more underrated heavyweights of the late 1990s was Ron Waterman. He was a hulking presence in the Octagon who parlayed his wrestling ability and strength into victories over Chris Condo and Satoshi Honma.

It wasn't until after he left the organization, following UFC 25 in 2000, that his career really took off, and he counted PRIDE wins over Valentijn Overeem and Kevin Randleman among his biggest. In 2003, he became the first and only WEC super heavyweight champion. In recent years, he has remained in the news for his work with former interim UFC heavyweight champion Shane Carwin, whom he also coached in high school.

FIGHTS OF THE YEAR

UFC 22

SHAMROCK   WSUB4   ORTIZ

UFC 18
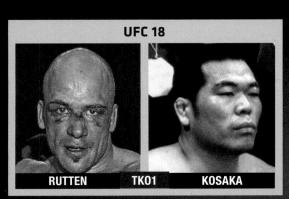
RUTTEN   TKO1   KOSAKA

UFC 21
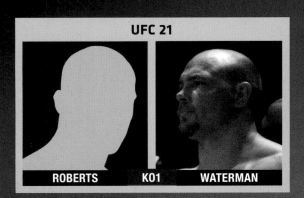
ROBERTS   KO1   WATERMAN

UFC 23

JACKSON   KO3   YAMAMIYA

UFC 19

HORN   TKO1   LIDDELL

KNOCKOUTS OF THE YEAR

UFC 16
RUTTEN   TKO1   KOSAKA

UFC 20
SILVA   KO1   PETARRA

UFC 21
JACKSON   KO2   ALGER

UFC 23
RIZZO   TKO3   KOSAKA

UFC 19
TANNER   TKO1   IGNATOV

SUBMISSIONS OF THE YEAR

UFC 19
HORN   WSUB1   LIDDELL

UFC 18
TANNER   WSUB1   GHOLAR

UFC 22
HORN   WSUB1   GODSEY

UFC 20
WILLIAMS   WSUB1   FULTON

UFC 21
JONES   WSUB1   MOURA

Rutten knocks out Kosaka at UFC 16

DEBUTS

UFC 18

- FRANK CARACCI
- DARREL GHOLAR
- EVAN TANNER
- JORGE PATINO
- BAS RUTTEN

UFC 19

- KEVIN RANDLEMAN
- SIONE LATU
- JOEY ROBERTS
- JASON GODSEY
- VALERI IGNATOV

UFC 20

- RON WATERMAN
- CHRIS CONDO
- FABIANO IHA
- MARCELLO MELLO
- DAVID ROBERTS
- TONY PETARRA
- TRAVIS FULTON

UFC 21

- DAVID DODD
- TIM LAJCIK
- FLAVIO MOURA
- PAUL JONES
- DAIJU TAKASE
- ANDRE PEDERNEIRAS

UFC 22

- JENS PULVER
- ALFONSO ALCAREZ
- JOHN LEWIS
- LOWELL ANDERSON
- MATT HUGHES
- STEVE JUDSON

UFC 23

- KATSUHISA FUJII
- MASUTATSU YANO
- KENICHI YAMAMOTO
- JOE SLICK

2000

If you want an idea of how day-to-day life was for UFC in 2000, look no further than the main event of its first show of the year at the Lake Charles Civic Center in Louisiana on March 10.

Originally scheduled to feature UFC heavyweight champion Kevin Randleman's highly anticipated first title defense against Pedro Rizzo, the show instead lost its main event due to an injury. This happened not a week or two before the bout, not even days before, but on fight night itself. Randleman slipped on several pipes while warming up backstage, fell to the concrete floor and hit his head, rendering him unconscious. He was rushed to a local hospital where he was diagnosed with a concussion, and UFC no longer had a main event. When you consider that 11 of the remaining 14 fighters on the card were making their Octagon debut, the fans weren't too happy.

A month later, UFC traveled to Tokyo for the Ultimate Japan 3 show on April 14. The goal at the Yoyogi National Gymnasium was to crown a new light heavyweight champion after Frank Shamrock's retirement in 1999. In one corner was an obvious choice, as Tito Ortiz had given

Shamrock one of the toughest fights of his career seven months earlier. Opposing "The Huntington Beach Bad Boy" was Brazil's "Axe Murderer" Wanderlei Silva. But when it was all over, Ortiz was crowned champion via a five-round unanimous decision. "I worked very hard for this, to make this belt happen," said the 25-year-old Ortiz, who would reign until 2003.

The crowning of a new champion was a high point for a promotion that needed any recognition it could get. Also, the addition of a new weight class for fighters under 155 pounds gave the new crop of talent a level playing field on which to compete in the Octagon.

"I WORKED VERY HARD FOR THIS, TO MAKE THIS BELT HAPPEN,"
–TITO ORTIZ

GAN McGEE
BISMARCK, ND

DEBUT: UFC 28, NOVEMBER 17, 2000

Trained by John Hackleman and a stablemate of Chuck Liddell, 6'10" Gan McGee seemingly had all the tools to win a heavyweight title. As a finisher, he had the fan support that could elevate a fighter to the next level. But things never clicked. After shaking off a UFC 28 loss to Josh Barnett with back-to-back stoppages of Pedro Rizzo and Alexandre Dantas, he lost his lone title shot to Tim Sylvia via knockout at UFC 44 in 2003.

MURILO BUSTAMANTE

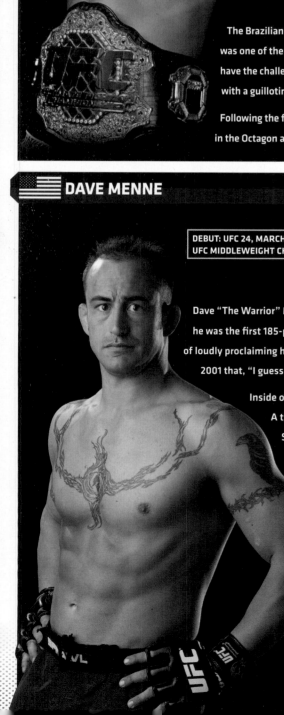

DEBUT: UFC 25, APRIL 14, 2000
UFC MIDDLEWEIGHT CHAMPION

ARPOADOR, RIO DE
JANEIRO, BRAZIL

You wouldn't know it by talking to the soft-spoken gentleman from Rio de Janeiro, but Murilo Bustamante was one of the MMA's most feared ground fighters during his heyday—a period in which he briefly reigned over the UFC middleweight division before leaving for Japan's PRIDE organization.

A fifth degree black belt in jiu-jitsu who earned his belt from Carlson Gracie, Bustamante used his ground skills in professional combat as early as 1991 in his native Brazil. But it was in 1996 that his mixed martial arts career truly kicked into gear. Unbeaten in his first six pro fights—including victories over Joe Charles, Chris Haseman and Jerry Bohlander—Bustamante made his UFC debut at UFC 25, submitting Yoji Anjo in the second round.

Two fights later, Bustamante was back, but he lost a close decision to Chuck Liddell at UFC 33. Bustamante didn't have to wait long to wear a championship belt, though. His next fight at UFC 35 on January 11, 2002, in which he won the UFC middleweight title with a second-round TKO of Dave Menne.

The Brazilian grappling king didn't wait long to defend his title. Four months later, he took on Matt Lindland at UFC 37 in May 2002. What resulted was one of the most bizarre fights in the organization's history. Bustamante appeared to submit Lindland with an armbar in the first round, only to have the challenger protest, leading referee John McCarthy to restart the fight. Bustamante did finish the fight for good in the third round, this time with a guillotine choke.

Following the fight, Bustamante and UFC were at an impasse when it came to contract negotiations. The Brazilian vacated the title and never fought in the Octagon again.

DAVE MENNE

DEBUT: UFC 24, MARCH 10, 2000
UFC MIDDLEWEIGHT CHAMPION

MINNEAPOLIS, MN

Dave "The Warrior" Menne once held the UFC middleweight title; in fact, he was the first 185-pound belt holder in the organization's history. But in terms of loudly proclaiming himself as the baddest man on the planet, he even admitted back in 2001 that, "I guess I'm an unlikely champion."

Inside of the Octagon, though, Menne was always one of MMA's fiercest competitors. A tireless worker, he came up the hard way, fighting close to 40 times en route to his title-winning effort over Gil Castillo at UFC 33 in September 2001.

On his way up the ranks, Menne was a regular in places like Indiana, Iowa, Wisconsin and his native Minnesota. He fought against the likes of Matt Hughes, Shonie Carter, Chris Lytle and Jose "Pele" Landi-Jons. What may have been even more impressive is that he did it all while training himself.

In March 2000, Menne got his first taste of UFC, defeating Fabiano Iha via decision at UFC 24. He wouldn't return for more than a year. When he did, he was competing for the UFC middleweight title against Castillo. Five rounds later, he was a world champion—vindication for years of hard work.

In his first defense at UFC 35, Menne lost his title via TKO to Murilo Bustamante. Then, just eight months later at UFC 39, Phil Baroni knocked out Menne in 18 seconds. Following a four-year break from the Octagon, he returned in 2006 but lost to Josh Koscheck and Luigi Fioravanti. Regardless, Menne holds a place in UFC lore as someone who may have been an unlikely champion but was still a top-level fighter.

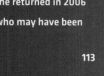

ANDREI ARLOVSKI

DEBUT: UFC 28, NOVEMBER 17, 2000
UFC HEAVYWEIGHT CHAMPION

MINSK, BELARUS

It was as far away from the top of the mixed martial arts world as you could get, and frankly, Andrei "The Pitbull" Arlovski had hit rock bottom in his professional fighting career. A native of Minsk, Belarus, Arlovski gave up a secure job as a police officer back home to roll the dice in a foreign country as a mixed martial artist. After starting his career at 3-1 (including a UFC win over Aaron Brink), he got stopped in back-to-back fights by Ricco Rodriguez and Pedro Rizzo.

The year was 2002, and everyone saw the potential of Arlovski. Standing 6'4" and weighing 240 pounds, Arlovski possessed the speed and athleticism of a middleweight with the power of a heavyweight. Add in a solid ground game that dwarfed most of his peers, and stardom should have been a given.

But something was lost in the translation between Arlovski's talent and what showed up in the Octagon on fight night. Still, beginning with a UFC 40 win over tough-as-nails Ian Freeman, Arlovski took over the heavyweight division, stopping Vladimir "The Janitor" Matyushenko and Wesley "Cabbage" Correira before he submitted Tim Sylvia with an Achilles lock in just 47 seconds at UFC 51 on February 5, 2005, to win the interim UFC heavyweight title.

Arlovski was later declared undisputed champion after his title defense against Justin Eilers (TKO1) at UFC 53. He then knocked out dangerous Paul Buentello in just 15 seconds.

His reign would end at UFC 59 on April 15, 2006; Sylvia stopped him in a single round in their rematch. A third bout fewer than three months later saw Sylvia emerge victorious again, this time by five-round decision.

Following the Sylvia rubber match, Arlovski finished off his UFC contract with three wins over Marcio Cruz, Fabricio Werdum and Jake O'Brien. He would not return until 2014.

JOSH BARNETT

DEBUT: UFC 28, NOVEMBER 17, 2000
UFC HEAVYWEIGHT CHAMPION

SEATTLE, WA

A talented athlete who could handle himself both on the ground and while standing, Seattle native Josh "The Warmaster" Barnett tore through his first six opponents, with a fourth-round submission win over Dan "The Beast" Severn in February 2000 earning him an invite to UFC.

While in the Octagon, Barnett didn't skip a beat, stopping Gan McGee at UFC 28 before suffering his first pro defeat three months later against Brazilian contender Pedro Rizzo. Yet, the bout was so well received that even after getting knocked out, Barnett's stock remained high. Following two comeback wins, Barnett was matched against Randy Couture at UFC 36 on March 22, 2002. After stopping Couture in the second round, Barnett became the youngest heavyweight champion in history at age 24— a record that still stands.

Four months later, Barnett was stripped of the title and suspended by the Nevada State Athletic Commission after testing positive for three anabolic agents. Barnett denied the charges, but for the time being, his time in UFC was over.

Eventually, Barnett resurfaced in Japan, where he had great success in the Pancrase and PRIDE organizations. However, when he returned to the United States for a 2009 Affliction bout against Fedor Emelianenko, he tested positive for anabolic steroids once again, canceling the match and the event.

Barnett soon found redemption in MMA, though, as a 2011 run in STRIKEFORCE brought him back to the U.S. for good. No longer "The Babyfaced Assassin," Barnett was now "The Warmaster." After going 3-1 in STRIKEFORCE, he returned to UFC in August 2013, defeating former two-time champion Frank Mir and proving that you can go home again.

But reality was never too far away, and while UFC had its share of anticipated main events that turned into duds, few hit rock bottom like the rescheduled UFC 26 headliner between Kevin Randleman and Pedro Rizzo in Cedar Rapids, Iowa, on June 9. It was a 25-minute war of nerves in which the winner via unanimous decision was the defending champion Randleman, but also in which the losers were the ones watching the dreadful five-rounder at the Five Seasons Events Center.

"I understand the boos, and I definitely deserve it," Randleman said after the bout. "But I can tell you this: I came in here to strike with a striker, not to come in here and wrestle him. I came in here with one plan: to stay on my feet, take him down when I could and box with him. I think Pedro and I just respected each other too much. I apologize."

> ## "I CAME IN HERE WITH ONE PLAN: TO STAY ON MY FEET, TAKE HIM DOWN WHEN I COULD AND BOX WITH HIM."
> ### —KEVIN RANDLEMAN

At least Pat Miletich kept his reign of excellence intact on the undercard, as he submitted John Alessio in the second round in front of his hometown fans. Other members of the Miletich Fighting Systems team who garnered wins were Matt Hughes and Jens Pulver, beginning to set the stage for an Iowa-based dynasty that would soon rule the MMA world.

Whether UFC would even be around in a few years was becoming a real question. A dud of a UFC 27 show on September 22 in New Orleans in which Pedro Rizzo stopped the returning Dan Severn in the first round didn't encourage too many people.

Yet, while SEG continued to hemorrhage money, a ray of light showed up in the form of UFC's first event in New Jersey on November 17, 2000. Held at the Trump Taj Mahal in Atlantic City, UFC 28 wasn't just a show being held in one of combat sports' most prestigious locations. It was the first one held under the newly created unified rules of mixed martial arts.

Accepted by the prestigious New Jersey State Athletic Control Board, the unified rules still govern the sport today. Containing several weight classes, judging criteria, ways to win, safety regulations and more than 30 fouls, these rules are the playbook by which MMA is run, focusing on fighter safety and fair play.

"Every show, something would happen, and we would make a rule about it. Or, I would learn something where I said, 'Don't ever do this, don't ever do that,'" said longtime referee John McCarthy, who, along with commentator Jeff Blatnick and matchmaker Joe Silva, helped develop the initial draft of the rules. "It was a progression, and luckily, over time, things evolved."

CHRIS LYTLE

DEBUT: UFC 28, NOVEMBER 17, 2000

INDIANAPOLIS, IN

For more than 12 years, if a young fighter had aspirations of getting to the next level in mixed martial arts, he had to get by seasoned veteran Chris "Lights Out" Lytle. More often than not, it was "lights out" for prospects like Kevin Burns, Paul Taylor, Kyle Bradley, Brian Foster and Matt Brown. But for Lytle, a former pro boxer who also fought the likes of Matt Hughes, Thiago Alves and Josh Koscheck, fighting was just a way of life.

A pro since 1999, the Indianapolis native saw the good, the bad and the ugly in the fight game. Lytle fought his way to UFC the hard way, as he competed consistently on the Midwest circuit before getting called to the Octagon in 2000. Lytle lost his debut to Ben Earwood, but he remained persistent, winning a callback three years later.

Again, Lytle fell short of victory against Robbie Lawler at UFC 45. After going 2-2 in the Octagon in his next four fights, he was able to use *The Ultimate Fighter* season four to catapult himself back into the sport's largest promotion.

Losing a controversial decision to Matt Serra in *The Ultimate Fighter* season 4 Finale, Lytle slowly worked his way back into the win column. As the fights wore on, it was evident Lytle wasn't just fighting to win; he was fighting to give the fans something to cheer about. As far as he was concerned, that was a great legacy.

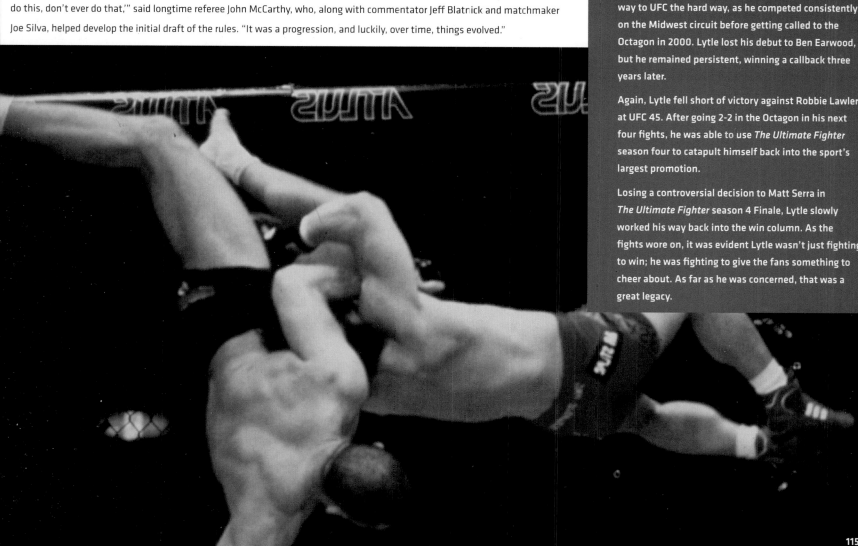

JOHN ALESSIO
VANCOUVER, CANADA

DEBUT: UFC 26, JUNE 9, 2000

With a 6-3 record and fewer than two years' experience, John "The Natural" Alessio admits that he was "a deer caught in headlights" in his UFC debut—a 2000 clash with Pat Miletich for the welterweight championship. Alessio was submitted at UFC 26, and he didn't return to the Octagon for six years, when he lost a close decision to Diego Sanchez at UFC 60. In between, the Canadian competed in PRIDE and other organizations. From 2006 to 2012, Alessio competed in UFC three more times, losing to Thiago Alves, Mark Bocek and Shane Roller.

SHONIE CARTER
CHICAGO, IL

DEBUT: UFC 24, MARCH 10, 2000

Shonie "Mr. International" Carter was ahead of his time. Charismatic, flamboyant and able to fight with the best, "Mr. International" was networking socially before there was such a thing. While he set the stage for the MMA explosion, he wasn't able to reap its benefits. "The new generation of fans don't know who I am," admitted Carter in 2005, when he returned to the Octagon after four years away to face Nate Quarry. He lost that fight, and he wasn't able to capitalize on a stint on *The Ultimate Fighter* season four, either. Still, diehard fans will always remember his spinning back-fist finish of Matt Serra in 2001 and his philosophy that fighting isn't just a sport; it's entertainment.

IAN FREEMAN
SUNDERLAND, UNITED KINGDOM

DEBUT: UFC 24, MARCH 10, 2000

The leading representative for British MMA long before the emergence of Michael Bisping, Ian "The Machine" Freeman was a tireless ambassador for the sport outside of competition and a fearless battler in it.

After a 2-1 start to his UFC career in 2000, a 2-6 run in his next eight bouts outside the Octagon had Freeman a heavy underdog when he took on undefeated rising star Frank Mir at UFC 38 in 2002.

But with his local fans cheering him on—and motivated by his seriously ill father—the 35-year-old delivered the performance of his career, stopping Mir at 4:35 of the first round. Tragically, it was later revealed that Freeman's father had passed away the day before from a battle with cancer, with the fighter not discovering this until after the bout.

DENNIS HALLMAN
OLYMPIA, WA

DEBUT: UFC 29, DECEMBER 16, 2000

It's a bold move to take the nickname "Superman." But considering that Dennis Hallman's career includes more than 60 wins, two submission victories over UFC Hall of Famer Matt Hughes and fights against Frank Trigg (twice), Denis Kang, Dave Menne and Caol Uno, it's clear that the ground-fighting wizard earned his moniker.

The only thing missing for the Washington native was a UFC championship belt, but fighting against the game's elite in the Octagon was never a bad substitute. "It [being in UFC] means that I get to fight the toughest guys at my weight and get proper recognition for doing so," Hallman said.

YUKI KONDO
NAGAOKA, NIIGATA PREFECTURE, JAPAN

DEBUT: UFC 27, SEPTEMBER 22, 2000

A 1-2 UFC record really doesn't tell the whole story when it comes to the 15-year career of Yuki Kondo. In fact, his UFC 27 win over Alexandre Dantas and Octagon losses to Tito Ortiz and Vladimir Matyushenko barely touch the surface when it comes to one of the most underrated fighters of his time. A Pancrase veteran who defeated Frank Shamrock, Semmy Schilt and Guy Mezger (among others), Kondo also starred in PRIDE, where his dance card included Wanderlei Silva, Dan Henderson and Igor Vovchanchyn. Even if he wasn't able to break out on the UFC scene, Kondo's impact will always be felt at home.

It was a monumental step forward for the sport. Now, SEG needed quality fights from quality fighters, and it also needed to cap it off with a main event worthy of a heavyweight championship if it wanted to attract Las Vegas for future shows. Well, the company and the crowd got what it needed, especially from heavyweight title combatants Randy Couture and Kevin Randleman.

For 14 minutes and 13 seconds, Couture and Randleman battled for Kevin's heavyweight title as if lives depended on the outcome. When it was all over, Couture walked away with the belt via third-round TKO, but both men left the arena with respect.

"This is not my time," Randleman said in a post-fight interview. "But I told you the only way I would be beaten is by a wrestler, and I got beat by one of the best wrestlers and best fighters in the world."

For Couture, it was a homecoming of sorts. He won the UFC heavyweight title, beating Maurice Smith at Ultimate Japan I in 1997. A contract dispute kept him out of the Octagon for almost three years, but what a way to return.

Also victorious in Atlantic City was "Lil' Evil" Pulver, who made a huge statement with a one-punch knockout of John Lewis. Heavyweights Josh Barnett and Andrei Arlovski also made impressive statements with finishes of Gan McGee and Aaron Brink, respectively.

It was a great night for UFC, but it was the final event SEG would put on in the United States. UFC 29 in Tokyo's Differ Ariake Arena would be the company's last, highlighted by successful title defenses by Tito Ortiz (over Yuki Kondo) and Pat Miletich (over Kenichi Yamamoto). A few weeks into the New Year, a new era would begin.

MATT LINDLAND
OREGON CITY, OR

DEBUT: UFC 29, DECEMBER 16, 2000

A U.S. Olympic gold medalist in 2000, Matt "The Law" Lindland was a top middleweight contender in the early days of the division in UFC. Lindland was a swarming wrestler who could nullify practically any opponent's game plan. An Oregon native who came up in the sport with Randy Couture and Dan Henderson, Lindland debuted in UFC in 2000. After winning four matches in a row, including bouts against Phil Baroni and Pat Miletich, he got a title shot against Murilo Bustamante at UFC 37. In this bout, he actually got submitted twice, with the second one sticking. He would go 5-2 over his next seven UFC bouts before being released in 2005.

JEFF MONSON
ST. PAUL, MN

DEBUT: UFC 27, SEPTEMBER 22, 2000

If you're good enough to win the Abu Dhabi submission wrestling world championship, you're a pretty special athlete. If you've done it twice, like Jeff "The Snowman" Monson did, you're on a whole other level. But instead of remaining content with his elite status in the grappling world, Monson chased after glory in the Octagon, as well. After some ups and downs while facing the likes of Chuck Liddell, Forrest Griffin and Ricco Rodriguez during his MMA career, "The Snowman" hit his stride in UFC in 2006, winning three straight bouts to earn a shot at the heavyweight title. Tim Sylvia ended Monson's year on a down note, though, defeating the challenger via decision over five rounds.

RENATO SOBRAL
RIO DE JANEIRO, BRAZIL

DEBUT: UFC 28, NOVEMBER 17, 2000

When you ask Renato "Babalu" Sobral what he learned from his 2002 loss to Chuck "The Iceman" Liddell, the answer comes as quickly as one of Babalu's triangle chokes.

"The most important thing I learned is that if you don't want to fight, stay home," Sobral said. He went on to reel off wins in 11 of 13 bouts after that defeat, losing only to Liddell in their 2006 rematch and to Jason Lambert. He was released from UFC after his win over David Heath at UFC 74, but Sobral's overall career was an impressive one, with wins against Jeremy Horn, Shogun Rua, Chael Sonnen and Trevor Prangley.

FIGHTS OF THE YEAR

UFC 28
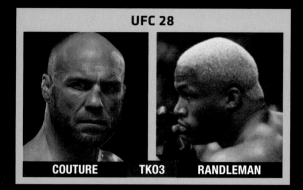
COUTURE   TKO3   RANDLEMAN

UFC 26
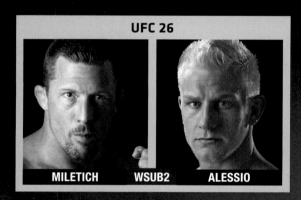
MILETICH   WSUB2   ALESSIO

UFC 25

ORTIZ   W5   SILVA

UFC 29
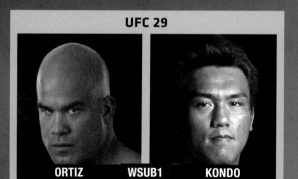
ORTIZ   WSUB1   KONDO

UFC 24
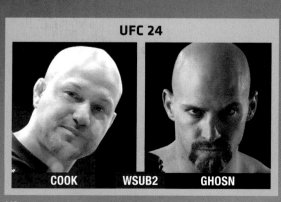
COOK   WSUB2   GHOSN

KNOCKOUTS OF THE YEAR

UFC 28

PULVER   KO1   LEWIS

UFC 25
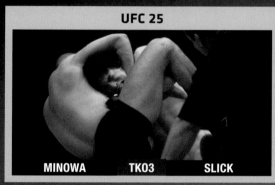
MINOWA   TKO3   SLICK

UFC 24
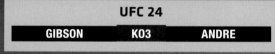
GIBSON   KO3   ANDRE

UFC 29
IHA   TKO1   TAKASE

UFC 27
KONDO   TKO3   DANTAS

SUBMISSIONS OF THE YEAR

UFC 25
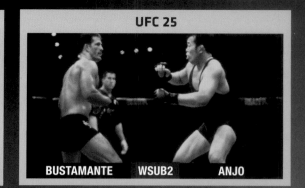
BUSTAMANTE   WSUB2   ANJO

UFC 24
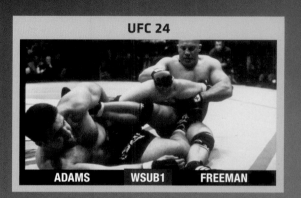
ADAMS   WSUB1   FREEMAN

UFC 29
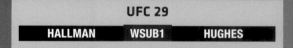
HALLMAN   WSUB1   HUGHES

UFC 27
IHA   WSUB1   CLARK

UFC 26
MILETICH   WSUB2   ALESSIO

DEBUTS

UFC 24

SHONIE CARTER	TIKI GHOSN
BRAD GUMM	DAVE MENNE
SCOTT ADAMS	LANCE GIBSON
IAN FREEMAN	JERMAINE ANDRE
DAVID VELASQUEZ	TEDD WILLIAMS
BOB COOK	

UFC 25

SATOSHI HONMA	SANAE KIKUTA
IKUHISA MINOWA	KOJI OISHI
MURILO BUSTAMANTE	

UFC 26

ADRIAN SERRANO
NATE SCHROEDER
JOAO ROQUE
MARCELO AGUIAR
ALEX ANDRADE
JOHN ALESSIO

UFC 27

CJ FERNANDES
JEFF MONSON
YUKI KONDO
ALEXANDRE DANTAS
BOBBY HOFFMAN

UFC 28

RENATO SOBRAL
GAN McGEE
JOSH BARNETT
ANDREI ARLOVSKI
CHRIS LYTLE
AARON BRINK
MARK HUGHES
ALEX STIEBLING
BEN EARWOOD

UFC 29

DENNIS HALLMAN
MATT LINDLAND

2001

Ortiz vs Tanner

Despite a strong end in 2000, UFC was dying. Owners SEG were losing more and more money, and the urge to continue fighting was diminishing. But on January 11, 2001, a company named Zuffa, manned by brothers Frank Fertitta III and Lorenzo Fertitta, along with their friend Dana White, purchased the struggling brand.

Zuffa means "fight" in Italian, and the new owners were ready to do precisely that. Aside from keeping mixed martial arts going in the United States, they wanted to regulate it both stateside and abroad, get it back on television and make it an international juggernaut. White was the front man, a tireless worker who told it like it was, whether anyone liked it or not. The Fertitta brothers, casino owners and gifted businessmen, worked outside of the media glare, encouraging White to run operations the way he saw fit. This brilliant strategy eventually made all of their goals come to fruition, but before Zuffa-owned UFC could take over the sporting world, it had to get through its first show on February 23, 2001.

 YVES EDWARDS
NASSAU, BAHAMAS

DEBUT: UFC 33, SEPTEMBER 28, 2001

A dynamic lightweight pioneer, Yves Edwards is someone who never shied away from fighting the best. He faced standouts like Aaron Riley, Pete Spratt, Nate Marquardt, Rumina Sato, Mike Brown and Duane Ludwig outside UFC.

In the Octagon, he compiled a 10-10, 1 NC record, with wins over John Gunderson, Cody McKenzie, Joao Marcos, Rich Clementi, Eddie Ruiz, Nick Agallar, Hermes Franca and Josh Thomson. And if you've been to a UFC event, you'll recognize the head kick that Edwards took Thomson out with; it's been immortalized in the organization's highlight-reel. Edwards retired in 2014.

"If anybody watches me fight, I want them to have enjoyed the experience," Edwards said. "I want people to ask Dana [White] or Joe [Silva], if they see them at restaurants or whatever, 'When's Yves Edwards gonna fight again?' To do that, you have to go out there and have exciting fights and once in a while get the flashy knockouts and the creative submissions. I want people to see the best of me and the best skills I have to offer."

The fighters on the UFC 30 card that winter night are household names to mixed martial arts fans today: Tito Ortiz, the late Evan Tanner, Jens Pulver, Caol (then known as Kaoru) Uno, Sean Sherk, Phil Baroni, Jeremy Horn, Josh Barnett and Pedro Rizzo. But back then they were fighters looking to find a place in a sport the mainstream didn't, and in many cases didn't want to, understand.

That perception was about to change. From the beginning, it was clear that for the new UFC to be successful, it needed a star. Huntington Beach, California's Tito Ortiz was that man. Like a main event fighter, the 205-pound champion knew how to close the show. In 30 seconds, Ortiz grabbed No. 1 contender Tanner in a bear hug, picked him up and slammed him to the canvas, knocking him unconscious in the process. Follow-up punches to the prone Tanner were just window dressing before referee John McCarthy was able to push Ortiz off his opponent and end the bout.

It was a stirring end to the first night of the Zuffa era, but there were other standouts that night: Pulver won the first UFC 155-pound title with a majority decision over Uno; Rizzo knocked out Barnett; and Australia's Elvis Sinosic upset Horn.

With the promotion staying in Atlantic City for UFC 31 on May 4, there were two more title bouts for fans hungry to see the best. In a memorable five-round war that headlined the event, Randy Couture and Pedro Rizzo waged a battle worthy of the heavyweight championship. In the end, Couture retained his title by a close but unanimous decision, but there were no losers in Zuffa's second UFC show at the Trump Taj Mahal.

Couture took home a victory the old-fashioned way: he earned it. The 37-year-old champ, who was never supposed to win—but just kept doing it—almost scored a spectacular first-round stoppage, executing his ground-and-pound strategy to perfection early on. Rizzo, caught under a barrage of punches, looked like he was done, and referee John McCarthy inspected the Brazilian very closely.

🇯🇵 CAOL UNO

DEBUT: UFC 30, FEBRUARY 23, 2001

YOKOSUKA, KANAGAWA PREFECTURE, JAPAN

One of the UFC lightweight division's first stars was Kanagawa, Japan's Caol Uno. He fought the elite during his first stint in UFC from 2001 to 2003, including BJ Penn (twice), Jens Pulver, Din Thomas, Yves Edwards and Hermes Franca. Uno came perilously close to winning the lightweight crown twice, losing a five-round decision to Pulver in 2001 and battling to a five-round draw with Penn in 2003.

Following his departure from UFC, he continued to face off against top-notch fighters like Joachim Hansen, Kid Yamamoto, JZ Cavalcante and Shinya Aoki in Japan, prompting a return to the organization after nearly six years away in 2009.

"I wanted to challenge in UFC again," said Uno. "This is the category where the best fighters meet, and I missed the unique atmosphere, which is very different from Japanese events."

This time around, Uno was unable to recapture the magic of his first go-round, as he could only manage an 0-2-1 record with losses against Spencer Fisher and Gleison Tibau.

The proud warrior wasn't through yet, though, as he continued to compete in high-profile shows in his native Japan following his 2010 release from UFC.

"I will keep winning one by one 'til I challenge the champion," said Uno. "The fans will always see my spirit in my fights."

🇺🇸 RICARDO ALMEIDA
NEW YORK CITY, NY

DEBUT: UFC 31, MAY 4, 2001

One of the most gifted grapplers in MMA, black belt Ricardo "Big Dog" Almeida used his skills on the canvas to befuddle some of the world's best fighters. His first time around in the Octagon wasn't a successful one, though, as he lost two of three bouts. Undeterred, he went to Japan and defeated Nate Marquardt for the Pancrase Middleweight Title—one of six consecutive wins that he compiled there. Following a nearly four-year break from the sport to focus on his family and his growing academy, Almeida returned to MMA and UFC in 2008. He went on to win five of eight bouts before announcing his retirement in 2011 after a loss to Mike Pyle.

FRANK MIR

DEBUT: UFC 34, NOVEMBER 2, 2001
TWO-TIME UFC HEAVYWEIGHT CHAMPION

LAS VEGAS, NV

The win was quick, decisive and career altering for Frank Mir, a talent-laden mixed martial artist who proved more than once that he needed a little adversity to truly show what he could do when the horn sounded in the Octagon.

On February 2, 2008, Mir was 2-2 in his previous four fights after a serious motorcycle accident broke his leg and stole almost two years from his career. He revived his MMA life with a 90-second submission of Brock Lesnar; a man who was crowned the UFC heavyweight champion just two fights later.

It was the latest chapter in the storied career of Las Vegas' Mir, who went from "Next Big Thing" to "damaged goods" to finally starting to realize the potential he had to become the best heavyweight on the planet.

That's the short version.

Seen as the future of the UFC division after two Octagon wins built his record to 4-0, Mir was upset in July 2002 by veteran Ian Freeman. His next bout was against the returning Tank Abbott, a one-dimensional but entertaining fighter who had been out of the Octagon for the previous five years.

His return met with snickers from the hardcore fans, but enough casual followers came on board to ensure that UFC 41 was going to be a big event. And Mir was the foil.

Forty-six seconds later, Mir wasn't just Abbott's foil; he was his conqueror, with a toehold ending the Californian's night in emphatic fashion. Mir went on to win his next three bouts, including a victory over Tim Sylvia in June 2004 that earned him the UFC heavyweight title.

But three months later, a motorcycle accident almost ended his career and his life. Luckily, Mir survived, but resurrecting his career took a little longer.

Mir finally returned to the Octagon almost two years later. He lost two bouts to Marcio Cruz and Brandon Vera, sandwiched around a lackluster decision win over Dan Christison. The losses were just the latest low points he had to fight through.

"I guess like anything else, there are highs and lows," said Mir. "But your family and friends get you through the low points, and you just ride it out. You keep pushing forward no matter how discouraging this all can be."

Just when it appeared that all Frank Mir's promise had truly ended on that Las Vegas road in September 2004 and that he was finished as a heavyweight contender, he rebounded, submitting Antoni Hardonk in 77 seconds in August 2007. This was his first submission win since beating Sylvia three years earlier. The win over the massive Lesnar was the true icing on the cake, though, and the victory that put him back in the title picture.

A stirring knockout of Minotauro Nogueira in December 2008 to win the interim UFC heavyweight championship was next. Although he lost his rematch with Lesnar at UFC 100 and an interim title bout against Shane Carwin in March 2010, Mir's resilience still sees him competing with the elite in the Octagon.

"I GUESS LIKE ANYTHING ELSE, THERE ARE HIGHS AND LOWS. BUT YOUR FAMILY AND FRIENDS GET YOU THROUGH THE LOW POINTS, AND YOU JUST RIDE IT OUT."

—FRANK MIR

The second round was a carbon copy of the first, but this time, it was Rizzo doing the damage, pounding a winded Couture with lefts, rights and stiff leg kicks. Couture staggered with practically every blow, but Rizzo's reluctance to pounce on the champ proved to be his downfall. Couture barely survived the second round, and at that moment, a distance fight seemed highly unlikely.

In the third and fourth rounds, Couture stood up with Rizzo, and the challenger refused to press his advantage. A stoppage by McCarthy to allow the doctor to check Couture's nose gave the champion the second wind he needed. As the pace slowed, he took the final two rounds and the fight.

In the co-main event, Carlos Newton and Pat Miletich waged the expected tactical battle. Newton won the war and the UFC welterweight title by choking out "The Croatian Sensation" at 2:50 of the third round to end one of the longest championship runs in the promotion's history.

But the memorable UFC 31 action didn't end there. Chuck Liddell gave a rude welcome to Kevin Randleman in the light heavyweight debut of "The Monster," stopping him with a left hook a mere 1:18 into the first round. Also in a night of great fights, Shonie Carter and Matt Serra produced one of the best, with Carter ending the bout suddenly with a spinning back-fist at the 4:51 mark of the third and final round.

Almost lost in all the high-impact action was the debut of a young Hawaiian prospect named BJ Penn, who stopped Joey Gilbert in a single round during a preliminary bout. Penn, nicknamed "The Prodigy," wouldn't be on the prelim card for long.

After the event, momentum was finally on UFC's side. With Zuffa putting on a full court press to the media in an effort to draw mainstream attention, UFC 32 at the Continental Airlines Arena in East Rutherford, New Jersey, on June 29, 2001, was a big deal.

Not surprisingly, the company's most notable star, Ortiz, delivered in the main event with a first-round TKO of Sinosic to retain his light heavyweight title. In the co-main event, Hawaiian wunderkind Penn drilled highly regarded Din Thomas with a right knee to the chin. He followed up with three hooks on his fallen opponent and scored a first-round TKO, his second in as many UFC appearances.

With so many good things happening for the new UFC regime, it was no surprise that after getting sanctioned in Nevada—the home of boxing's biggest events for decades—and also returning to television, Zuffa entitled the UFC 33 event "Victory in Vegas."

But soon, that old UFC bad luck began to resurface. First, headliner Vitor Belfort was injured and forced out of a light heavyweight title fight against Ortiz. Then, the terrorist attacks of September 11 put the September 28 event in jeopardy. But the biggest blow to the event's success came from the fights themselves. Featuring three title fights on the five-fight Pay-Per-View card, all five bouts went the distance: Dave Menne's middleweight title-winning effort against Gil Castillo; Pulver's first successful title defense against Dennis Hallman; and Ortiz' victory over late replacement Vladimir Matyushenko all lasted five rounds.

VLADIMIR MATYUSHENKO
REČYCA, BELARUS

DEBUT: UFC 32, JUNE 29, 2001

A native of Belarus, Vladimir "The Janitor" Matyushenko made his mark in the sports world in the United States, first as a two-time national junior college wrestling champion, and then as one of the premier mixed martial artists in the game.

A former world title challenger who scored wins over Yuki Kondo, Pedro Rizzo and Travis Wiuff, Matyushenko enjoyed great success in the six years between his UFC stints. He won nine of 10 bouts before returning to the Octagon in 2009 with victories against Igor Pokrajac and Eliot Marshall.

In 2010, Matyushenko saw his winning streak snapped at the hands of future light heavyweight champion Jon Jones. He scored knockouts of Alexandre Ferreira and Jason Brilz before a final UFC defeat to Alexander Gustafsson in 2011.

While this was bad enough aesthetically, the show ran long, with many viewers not even getting to see the conclusion of Ortiz-Matyushenko.

It wasn't the way Zuffa wanted its first Las Vegas show and its return to television to go, but any business inevitably has days like these. By November 2, the company was firing on all cylinders again with a UFC 34 event that featured two world title bouts and a blistering 11-second knockout of Caol Uno by BJ Penn.

The main event saw the continued reign of the grand old man of mixed martial arts, Randy Couture. Couture, 38, tightened his grip on his UFC heavyweight title with a dominant third-round TKO over a listless Pedro Rizzo in a main event that was hardly reminiscent of the five-round war the two had waged six months earlier.

But in the co-feature, there was plenty of drama. Iowa's Matt Hughes scored a stunning upset to win the welterweight title, knocking out Carlos Newton in two rounds. But the bout, dominated by Hughes, was not without a dose of controversy.

Hughes used his freakish strength to establish control from the outset. With slams, knees and strikes, Hughes easily won the first round and was dominating the second, when Newton was able to nab the Miletich team member in a triangle choke. The "oohs" and "aahs" could be heard throughout the MGM Grand Garden Arena when Hughes lifted Newton over his head and drove him into the fence.

The champion grabbed the top of the fence, but he soon let go after referee McCarthy admonished him. With Newton still over his head, and still sinking in the choke, Hughes took a step back and dropped his foe to the canvas. Slamming his head, Newton was out, and McCarthy stopped the bout. Simple enough, but Hughes was similarly dazed and needed to be told that he had won the fight and the title. So who was out first? In Newton's post-fight interview, he stated that he believed he had choked Hughes out. But upon viewing different replay angles of the final slam, Hughes obviously had the presence of mind to take a step back, thus removing Newton from the fence and allowing him to fall. Fans debate that call to this day, but it was one that stood, altering the course of welterweight history in the process.

More importantly, Zuffa's purchase of UFC gave a dying brand new life, with fans eager to see what was going to happen next.

BJ PENN

DEBUT: UFC 31, MAY 4, 2001
UFC WELTERWEIGHT CHAMPION
UFC LIGHTWEIGHT CHAMPION

KAILUA, HI

In 2006, BJ "The Prodigy" Penn was asked why, after all his ups and downs in the fight game, he still had the most diehard of fan followings. He paused, but only for a moment before responding:

"There's just something about BJ Penn that gets people amped up," he said. "You don't know what's gonna happen, but something's gonna happen. He might disappoint you, he might make you happy, he might make you cry, he might make you jump out of your chair, but he'll do something to you."

That, in a nutshell, describes the unforgettable odyssey of the fighter known to the world as "The Prodigy."

When Penn made his MMA debut in 2001—in UFC, no less—he was 22 years old, just a year removed from becoming the first non-Brazilian to win a gold medal in the Black Belt division of the Mundial World Jiu-Jitsu Championships. He was a prodigy in every way, shape and form.

He went on to walk through Joey Gilbert in his UFC debut, and he was even more impressive in stopping Din Thomas in the first round and knocking out Caol Uno in just 11 seconds. A lightweight title shot against then-champion Jens Pulver was a given, and Penn was expected to similarly blow through Pulver at UFC 35 in January 2002. However, Pulver proceeded to upset Penn and retain his title.

"Lil' Evil" left UFC over a contract dispute after the bout. But after Penn bounced back with wins over Paul Creighton and Matt Serra, he was again matched with Uno at UFC 41 in 2003, this time with the vacant belt on the line. Five rounds couldn't determine a winner that night, and a draw verdict was rendered.

In many ways, that draw sent Penn into a period of his career where his focus was scattered. Sure, he submitted Takanori Gomi in a non-UFC bout and then come back to the organization to win the welterweight title from Matt Hughes in 2004. But whether it was leaving UFC and his belt to fight elsewhere, or jumping to heavyweight to battle Lyoto Machida in 2005, Penn's career resembled that of a kid in a candy store who wanted to try everything but wound up with a toothache at the end of the day.

Eventually, Penn mended fences with UFC management and returned in 2006 with a split decision loss to Georges St-Pierre. A rematch with Hughes at UFC 63 served him with another defeat. But when he dropped back to 155 pounds to coach against Pulver on season five of *The Ultimate Fighter* and then fight him again (winning via second-round submission), Penn found his center again.

At UFC 80 on January 19, 2008, Penn finally won his lightweight title, submitting Joe Stevenson in the second round. A one-sided TKO of former champion Sean Sherk followed in Penn's first title defense, but then he got the itch to test the waters at 170 pounds again, and a January 2009 superfight was scheduled between him and old rival St-Pierre. However, a victory against GSP wasn't in the cards and Penn was defeated in four rounds.

Luckily for Penn, his faithful lightweight title belt was waiting at home for him, and there was no question that he was coming back to the Octagon to defend that belt. So when number-one contender Kenny Florian was brought to the table, Penn signed on the dotted line and silenced any doubts with a submission victory at UFC 101 in August 2009. Four months later, he shattered all lightweight title records with a TKO of Diego Sanchez. He was seemingly unstoppable again.

Enter unheralded Frankie Edgar, who beat Penn not once, but twice by decision in 2010, taking his lightweight crown in the process. Penn was crushed by the consecutive defeats, yet he opted to make one last stand at welterweight. In November 2010, he was pitted against Matt Hughes in a highly anticipated rubber match, and Penn ended the trilogy with a 21-second knockout win. It was the last victory for "The Prodigy," who retired after a 2014 loss to Edgar.

RICCO RODRIGUEZ

DEBUT: UFC 32, JUNE 29, 2001
UFC HEAVYWEIGHT CHAMPION

SAN JOSE, CA

Ricco "Suave" Rodriguez's career was on the line when he squared off against Andrei Arlovski at UFC 32 in 2001. But for him, it was no cliché; it was true. "If I would have lost that fight," he said at the time, "I pretty much would have been blackballed from the industry."

It had all happened so quickly for him. Blessed with good looks, charisma and a shockingly effective ground game, Rodriguez won the Abu Dhabi submission title at the ripe old age of 19. Soon, he duplicated his success in mixed martial arts, winning three straight PRIDE matches and the King of the Cage heavyweight title.

But with a daughter to feed, a girlfriend in the hospital recuperating from a serious accident, and bridges burned with the aforementioned organizations, Rodriguez had a one-fight UFC deal to face Arlovski. Win, and he could rebuild his life with the biggest MMA organization in the United States. Lose, and he would have to look for another line of work.

He won, stopping Arlovski in the third round. From there, it was your typical rags to riches tale. Rodriguez's next four fights all ended early, culminating with a gutsy fifth-round TKO win over Randy Couture at UFC 39 that made him a world heavyweight champion on September 27, 2002.

But the belt didn't prove to be the cure-all for Rodriguez's ills, as he let complacency and outside affairs enter through the cage door with him against Tim Sylvia. He lost the title in his first defense, getting stopped by "The Maine-iac" in the first round at UFC 41.

Two more consecutive losses followed: a controversial decision defeat to Minotauro Nogueira in a PRIDE bout and a listless three-round points loss to Pedro Rizzo in what proved to be his final UFC bout in November 2003.

MATT SERRA

DEBUT: UFC 31. MAY 4, 2001
UFC WELTERWEIGHT CHAMPION
THE ULTIMATE FIGHTER 4 WINNER

EAST MEADOW, NY

Following his decision loss to Karo Parisyan in June 2005, Matt "The Terror" Serra was at a crossroads in his career. As a veteran of the sport, he was coming off a defeat and starting to see a new generation of fighters make their way into UFC—courtesy of a new TV series called *The Ultimate Fighter*. He could stay home and run his two jiu-jitsu schools, but the fighter inside him couldn't bear to give up the competition.

Then he got a call about becoming a cast member for *The Ultimate Fighter*'s fourth season, entitled *The Comeback*. It was perfect. He could fight and, at the same time, he could get national television exposure for himself and his schools.

That wasn't the best part, though. The Renzo Gracie black belt not only won the show, but in his guaranteed welterweight title shot, he displayed his underrated power by stunning Georges St-Pierre via first-round TKO in April 2007. The popular New Yorker was a world champion.

Injuries kept him from a UFC 79 grudge match with Matt Hughes after their stint as coaches on season six of *The Ultimate Fighter*. After Serra lost his belt in the rematch to St-Pierre at UFC 83, he and Hughes met, with Hughes winning a close decision. Following the bout, Serra went 1-1, knocking out Frank Trigg and dropping a decision to the man he beat in The Ultimate Fighter 4 Finale, Chris Lytle. But whether he's winning or losing, you won't ever hear anyone complain about seeing "The Terror" in the Octagon.

"I decided to keep it simple," he said. "You like to fight, you're getting paid to fight, you made it to the big show, and God forbid you lose and you're out, at least you can say that you fought in UFC."

PHIL BARONI
LONG ISLAND, NY

DEBUT: UFC 30, FEBRUARY 23, 2001

Ask Phil "The New York Bad Ass" Baroni why he began fighting and he'll tell you it's because he "can't sing or dance." The popular fighter could scrap, though, and despite his losing UFC record, he always came to fight. Baroni began his UFC career quietly with a decision win over Curtis Stout at UFC 30 in 2001, but by the end of that year, he was making plenty of noise thanks to his memorable loss to Matt Lindland. Baroni bounced back with crushing knockouts of Dave Menne and Amar Suloev. Although the Menne win was his last victory in the Octagon, Baroni will always have a place in the hearts of UFC fans worldwide.

GIL CASTILLO
CONCORD, CA

DEBUT: UFC 33, SEPTEMBER 28, 2001

His UFC record is far from memorable, but when you consider that Gil Castillo's two Octagon losses came against Matt Hughes and Dave Menne it helps explain such a record. For a while, the Cesar Gracie jiu-jitsu brown belt was seen as one of the top fighters in the middleweight and welterweight divisions. After turning pro in 2000, Castillo ran off five wins without a loss, including back-to-back victories over Joe Hurley and Nate Marquardt. He had now earned himself a shot at UFC's newly created 185-pound title. Castillo dropped a five-round nod to Menne at UFC 33 in 2001, and a 2002 bout against Hughes finished via cuts, ending his championship dreams.

TONY DeSOUZA
LIMA, PERU

DEBUT: UFC 31, MAY 4, 2001

A native of Peru, Tony DeSouza grew up in Los Angeles, where he became a standout wrestler. He then discovered jiu-jitsu, learning under the wing of two of the game's best: Andre Pederneiras and John Lewis. In 2000, he moved to mixed martial arts. By his third fight, he was in UFC, defeating Steve Berger via decision at UFC 31 in 2001. Over the next six years, the stablemate of BJ Penn jumped around in his fighting career, finding the time to fit in some UFC bouts against the likes of Jutaro Nakao, Dustin Hazelett and Thiago Alves. DeSouza's last match was a TKO loss to Roan Carneiro in 2007.

SEMMY SCHILT
ROTTERDAM, NETHERLANDS

DEBUT: UFC 31, MAY 4, 2001

Semmy "Hightower" Schilt made his Pancrase debut in 1996 with a victory over Manabu Yamada, and over the next three years, he took on quality opponents like Masakatsu Funaki, Guy Mezger and Yuki Kondo. He won more than he lost, quickly gaining a following. In 2001, he had a brief stay in UFC, and the 6'11.5" giant quickly became a fan favorite. His devastating KO of Pete Williams at UFC 31 and his bloody loss to Josh Barnett at UFC 32 proved his worth as not only a tough competitor, but also an action fighter. A seven-fight stint in PRIDE and a record four K-1 World Grand Prix titles followed, cementing Schilt's place as one of the best fighters of his era.

ELVIS SINOSIC
CANBERRA, AUSTRALIA

DEBUT: UFC 30, FEBRUARY 23, 2001

If you ever get a chance to talk to Elvis "The King of Rock and Rumble" Sinosic, you will undoubtedly walk away knowing that he is one of the most accessible and classy athletes you could ever meet in professional sports. But when the horn sounds, the smile fades, and it's no more Mr. Nice Guy for Sinosic.

A black belt in Brazilian jiu-jitsu, shootfighting, taekwondo and Kai Shin, the Canberra native debuted in the Octagon with a stunning upset victory over Jeremy Horn at UFC 30. However, he remained winless over his next six bouts, despite delivering a supreme effort each time and a Fight of the Night battle with Michael Bisping in 2007.

DIN THOMAS
WILMINGTON, DE

DEBUT: UFC 32, JUNE 29, 2001

Din Thomas was one of a select group of fighters who helped put the lightweight division on the map in the United States in the late '90s and the early part of the new millennium. Along the way, he scored wins over Matt Serra, Jens Pulver and Fabiano Iha, losing only to elite fighters like Caol Uno and BJ Penn.

It's a track record few fighters can claim, and in contrast to most of those who were around as long as he was, the well-rounded Thomas remained relevant up until his retirement in 2014.

SEAN SHERK

DEBUT: UFC 30, FEBRUARY 23, 2001
UFC LIGHTWEIGHT CHAMPION

ST. FRANCIS, MN

With more than 40 fights and over a decade involved in the sport of mixed martial arts, there was little that Sean "The Muscle Shark" Sherk hadn't figured out when it came to professional fighting. He was a pro's pro; a stellar wrestler who—through fight experience and hard work—became a true mixed martial artist. But one thing had always eluded him: a world championship.

"The thought of winning that title belt and being the best in the world is what gets me up in the morning and makes me train three, four times a day," said Sherk, who lost a grueling five-rounder to Matt Hughes in a 2003 bout for the UFC welterweight title.

On October 14, 2006, Sherk's dream finally became a reality when he scored a unanimous five-round decision over Kenny Florian to win the UFC lightweight championship. But when he was stripped of the belt after failing a post-fight test for the banned substance Nandrolone following his first title defense against Hermes Franca, the dream became a nightmare. Sherk protested his innocence, and after returning in 2008, he was hungrier than ever to regain his belt, despite a UFC 84 loss to BJ Penn.

Injuries and a 2009 loss to Frankie Edgar slowed Sherk down, but a UFC 119 win over hot prospect Evan Dunham got "The Muscle Shark" back on track for what he hoped was the addition of some new hardware to his collection. Unfortunately, more injuries kept Sherk on the sidelines, forcing him to announce his retirement in 2013.

FIGHTS OF THE YEAR

UFC 34

| COUTURE | W5 | RIZZO |

UFC 30

| RIZZO | KO2 | BARNETT |

UFC 34

| LINDLAND | W3 | BARONI |

UFC 33

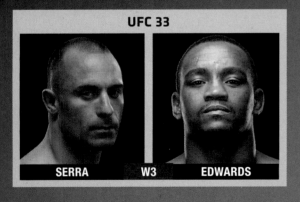

| SERRA | W3 | EDWARDS |

UFC 32

| RODRIGUEZ | TKO3 | ARLOVSKI |

KNOCKOUTS OF THE YEAR

UFC 31

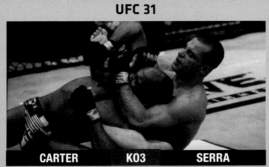

| CARTER | KO3 | SERRA |

UFC 34

| PENN | KO1 | UNO |

UFC 34

| HUGHES | KO2 | NEWTON |

UFC 30

| ORTIZ | KO1 | TANNER |

UFC 32

| MILETICH | KO2 | CARTER |

SUBMISSIONS OF THE YEAR

UFC 31

| NEWTON | WSUB3 | MILETICH |

UFC 34

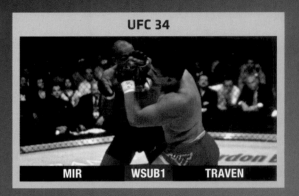

| MIR | WSUB1 | TRAVEN |

UFC 30

| SINOSIC | WSUB1 | HORN |

UFC 32

| BARNETT | WSUB1 | SCHILT |

UFC 33

| ALMEIDA | WSUB1 | JACKSON |

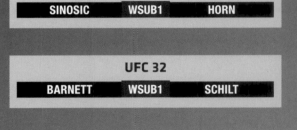

DEBUTS

UFC 30

| CAOL UNO |
| MARK ROBINSON |
| PHIL JOHNS |
| ELVIS SINOSIC |
| MARK ROBINSON |
| PHIL BARONI |
| CURTIS STOUT |
| SEAN SHERK |

UFC 31

| MATT SERRA |
| SEMMY SCHILT |
| RICARDO ALMEIDA |
| BJ PENN |
| TONY DESOUZA |
| STEVE BERGER |

UFC 32

| PAUL RODRIGUEZ |
| VLADIMIR MATYUSHENKO |
| RICCO RODRIGUEZ |
| DIN THOMAS |

UFC 33

| YVES EDWARDS |
| GIL CASTILLO |
| JUTARO NAKAO |

UFC 34

| FRANK MIR |
| HOMER MOORE |

Rashad Evans and Chuck Liddell face off at UFC 88.

UFC 6

TANK ABBOTT VS JOHN MATUA

In the early days of UFC, the knockouts came in a fast and furious fashion, and most were reminders that this was a contact sport. But few were as emphatic as Tank Abbott's introduction to the world—an 18-second display of fury and right hands that left John Matua down on the canvas, arms and legs outstretched.

UFC 8
GARY GOODRIDGE vs PAUL HERRERA

It was perhaps the most harrowing knockout in UFC history. After hearing that Paul Herrera had delivered some trash talk in his direction before their bout, Gary "Big Daddy" Goodridge responded by catching Herrera in a crucifix position moments into the fight. What followed was a crushing series of elbows that knocked Herrera out in just 13 seconds.

UFC 17
PETE WILLIAMS vs MARK COLEMAN

Exhausted after more than 12 minutes of fighting, former UFC heavyweight champion Mark Coleman was just trying to survive against young contender Pete Williams in their 1998 bout. Williams gave Coleman the rest he craved midway through that thirteenth minute with a flush kick to the head that became one of the most enduring images of early UFC action.

ULTIMATE BRAZIL
VITOR BELFORT vs WANDERLEI SILVA

One day they'd both be huge names in mixed martial arts, but at the time of their Ultimate Brazil bout in 1998, the undisputed star was Vitor Belfort, and Wanderlei Silva was just a raw newcomer. This prospect didn't get much time to settle in, though, as Belfort blitzed "The Axe Murderer" with a blinding series of rights and lefts en route to a 44-second TKO win.

UFC 40
CHUCK LIDDELL VS RENATO SOBRAL I

Everyone was rightfully scared of Chuck Liddell's right hand, and game plans centered on how to avoid getting posterized by the most dangerous weapon in UFC. Renato "Babalu" Sobral did an excellent job avoiding getting halted by Liddell's right. Instead, it was a left kick to the head that ended the Brazilian's night and put another notch in the belt of "The Iceman."

UFC 47
ROBBIE LAWLER VS NICK DIAZ

With only one injury-induced loss and concrete blocks for fists, Robbie Lawler wasn't only expected to be a future UFC champ, he was also the one guy no one wanted to stand with. Well, no one except brash groundfighter Nick Diaz. The Stockton, California native beat Lawler at his own game and stunned the MMA world by knocking him out with a single right hand that sent Lawler face first to the canvas.

UFC 49
YVES EDWARDS VS JOSH THOMSON

It was the last lightweight fight in UFC for nearly two years, but Yves Edwards ensured that fight fans would remember the 155-pounders. An attempted back fist by Josh Thomson was met by a flush right kick to the head by Edwards, and it was game over for "The Punk" and a spectacular knockout win for the master and creator of "thug-jitsu."

UFC 34
CARLOS NEWTON VS MATT HUGHES I

When UFC welterweight champion Carlos Newton sunk in a triangle choke on challenger Matt Hughes, it seemed only a matter of time until Newton retained his title. But Hughes took matters into his own hands, lifting Newton over his head. After some tense moments, he slammed his foe to the canvas, winning the fight and knocking out the 170-pound champion in the process.

RANDY COUTURE vs CHUCK LIDDELL II

For nearly two years, Chuck Liddell patiently waited for a shot at redemption following his 2003 upset loss to Randy Couture. In April 2005, he got it. With his trademark right hand, he exorcised his demons with a spectacular finish of "The Natural" to win the UFC light heavyweight championship.

THE ULTIMATE FIGHTER 4 FINALE
SCOTT SMITH vs PETE SELL

For pure aesthetic value, this unbelievable knockout wins every time. Smith and Sell became friends on the fourth season of *The Ultimate Fighter*, but they fought like enemies in their bout as they traded power shots. In the second round, Sell looked like he had pulled ahead when he nailed his opponent with a body shot that doubled Smith over in pain and sent him backpedaling to the fence. Sell ran in recklessly to land the finisher, but Smith caught him with a perfect right hand to the jaw. Seconds later, Smith had the TKO victory and one of those endings you truly have to see to believe.

UFC 69
GEORGES ST-PIERRE vs MATT SERRA I

As far as highlight-reel knockouts go, you can't help but give a nod to one that belongs on this list strictly for its historic and shock value. Matt Serra's upset of the seemingly unstoppable Georges St-Pierre definitely applies. A hard right hand that clipped a ducking St-Pierre took the champion's equilibrium. As St-Pierre tried to get his legs under him, Serra was calm, cool, collected and sending bombs down the pipe that kept the Canadian from getting back in the fight. Finally, a series of unanswered shots on the ground forced a halt to the bout, and the MMA world had a new champion in Matt "The Terror" Serra.

UFC 70
MIRKO CRO COP VS GABRIEL GONZAGA I

It's been said that if you live by the sword, you die by the sword. In a proverbial sense, feared Croatian striker Mirko Cro Cop certainly knew what that felt like after Brazilian jiu-jitsu black belt Gabriel Gonzaga turned the tables on him. Gonzaga knocked Cro Cop out in the first round with the weapon Cro Cop had made his name in the MMA world with—a kick to the head. When it landed, Cro Cop fell, twisting his knee and ankle in the process. Not only was it shocking, but it was spectacular.

UFC 77
ANDERSON SILVA VS RICH FRANKLIN II

It wasn't just one blow that ended Anderson Silva's rematch with Rich Franklin; the wide array of techniques displayed by the UFC middleweight champion were a thing of beauty. The stunning barrage left Franklin wondering what the best pound-for-pound fighter in the world was going to unleash on him next.

UFC 88
CHUCK LIDDELL VS RASHAD EVANS

In the first round, Rashad Evans fought the perfect fight against Chuck Liddell, using movement and quick flurries to frustrate "The Iceman." When Liddell came out recklessly and aggressively in the second stanza, Evans ended the perfect fight with the perfect punch, a right hand on the button that put the former light heavyweight king down and out.

UFC 92
RAMPAGE JACKSON VS WANDERLEI SILVA

With as cathartic a knockout as you'll find in this sport, Rampage Jackson finished off a rough 2008 campaign on a high note. Jackson scored not only a victory, but one over Wanderlei Silva—the man who had knocked him out twice in PRIDE. The fact that he dispatched his heated rival with a single left hook made the win even sweeter.

UFC 95

NATE MARQUARDT vs WILSON GOUVEIA

Nate Marquardt probably could have coasted in the third round of his bout against Wilson Gouveia at UFC 95 and just grabbed a decision win. But in that final stanza, it was as if something went off in his head that said "FINISH HIM." What followed was a dizzying array of fists, feet and knees that took Gouveia out at 3:10 of the round.

UFC 100

DAN HENDERSON vs MICHAEL BISPING

Yes, Michael Bisping talked a lot leading up to his UFC 100 showdown with Dan Henderson. But the Brit's mouth had nothing to do with his demise at the hands of Hendo. Instead, once the former two-division PRIDE champion realized that Bisping wasn't hurting him and that Bisping was pulling straight back *and* circling into his power hand, the end was inevitable. When Henderson's vaunted right hand crashed into Bisping's jaw in the second round, it was lights out for "The Count."

UFC 101

ANDERSON SILVA vs FORREST GRIFFIN

If at one point in your life you can say that you witnessed greatness in person, you're lucky. Those fans in attendance at the then-Wachovia Center in Philadelphia for UFC 101 had that opportunity. Middleweight champion Anderson Silva returned to the light heavyweight division and put on a clinic of precision striking in taking out former 205-pound titleholder Forrest Griffin at 3:23 of the first round. Call it over-the-top, but this performance was a potent mix of a Ted Williams swing, a John Coltrane solo and a Barry Sanders run out of the backfield.

UFC 114

TODD DUFFEE vs MIKE RUSSOW

Hot prospect Todd Duffee was on his way to another Octagon victory when he took on Mike Russow at UFC 114. But nothing's guaranteed until the fight is over, and Duffee learned that lesson the hard way. Russow pulled out a right hand from nowhere in the final round that starched Duffee at the 2:35 mark, stunning all in attendance at the MGM Grand Garden Arena.

138

UFC 126
ANDERSON SILVA vs VITOR BELFORT

Anderson Silva was more amped up than usual for his middleweight title defense against former training partner Vitor Belfort. He made sure that "The Phenom" was aware of his intentions as he knocked him out with a front kick to the face that Silva's friend—and action film star—Steven Seagal claimed to have taught him.

UFC 129
RANDY COUTURE vs LYOTO MACHIDA

In pre-fight interviews, UFC legend Randy Couture announced that he would be retiring after his UFC 129 bout against Lyoto Machida. Well, if Couture were having any second thoughts, Machida likely erased them with a flying front kick to the face in the second round that looked like it came directly from *The Karate Kid*.

UFC 129
JOHN MAKDESSI vs KYLE WATSON

One of the most creative standup fighters in UFC today, John "The Bull" Makdessi showed off a variety of techniques in his bout against Kyle Watson. Still, it was his picture-perfect spinning back-fist that will live on in highlight films forever. This move ended the bout in the third round, but Makdessi also craftily set it up with a fake that had Watson completely fooled before the final blow landed.

UFC LIVE: KONGO vs BARRY
CHEICK KONGO vs PAT BARRY

Many expected that Cheick Kongo would take Pat Barry down in their June 2011 bout, or that "HD" would even attempt to show off his own ground game against the Frenchman. Thankfully, the two decided to live up to their striking reputations. What followed was a tense trading of thudding leg kicks until all hell broke loose. Barry sent Kongo to the canvas twice, both times appearing to be seconds away from a stoppage victory. Just when all seemed lost for Kongo, he got to his feet, then threw two right hands. The first one stunned Barry, while the second put him on his back. When referee Dan Miragliotta halted the bout, Kongo had just delivered the most spectacular comeback win since Scott Smith finished Pete Sell in 2006.

UFC 142
EDSON BARBOZA vs TERRY ETIM

ESPN's *ESPYS* may have gotten it wrong in not awarding this knockout its 2012 Play of the Year award, but the finalist there was certainly a winner here. In a year with some spectacular knockouts, Edson Barboza's wheel-kick finish of Terry Etim at UFC 142 was far and away the best. It had it all: speed, power, technique, accuracy and pure "wow" effect. Etim was out the second he got caught by Barboza. But the scary part is that when asked about the finisher, the Brazilian Muay Thai expert said, "To be honest, no, I don't train that kick much. I like to train the basic things like body kicks or low kicks. But I've known how to do that kick since I was eight years old, when I started training Muay Thai. I think I have been keeping it inside of my mind, and when I need it, I throw it out."

> "TO BE HONEST, NO, I DON'T TRAIN THAT KICK MUCH...BUT I'VE KNOWN HOW TO DO THAT KICK SINCE I WAS EIGHT YEARS OLD, WHEN I STARTED TRAINING MUAY THAI. I THINK I HAVE BEEN KEEPING IT INSIDE OF MY MIND, AND WHEN I NEED IT, I THROW IT OUT."
> —EDSON BARBOZA

UFC 162
ANDERSON SILVA vs CHRIS WEIDMAN I

Seeing Anderson Silva lose for the first time in UFC was shocking enough. To see it happen by knockout doubled the trauma, but that's exactly what Chris Weidman did against the future Hall of Famer. Weidman stayed aggressive without getting reckless as Silva showboated. When the Brazilian icon dropped his hands one too many times, Weidman made him pay with a left hook that put Silva on the deck. He began the finishing sequence of strikes that kicked off a new era in the middleweight division.

2002

"THAT WAS THE THING THAT I NEEDED IN MY HEAD.
IF I GET BEAT, I GET BEAT, BUT I AIN'T GOING OUT LIKE THIS."
—JENS PULVER

The year that UFC was resurrected was 2001, thanks to the efforts of new owners, Zuffa, and a hungry roster of fighters eager to perform. But 2002 was going to prove whether the previous year's success was just a flash in the pan or if the company truly had staying power in a competitive market.

To do that, the promotion had to continue putting on events that felt like *events*, all the while introducing fans to a new breed of stars that didn't just perform on fight night, but also had compelling backstories.

One of those fighters was Hawaii's BJ Penn. Living up to his nickname, "The Prodigy," in every sense of the word; Penn ripped through his first three UFC opponents in under a round each. He was poised to make it four straight when he was pitted against Jens Pulver in the main event of UFC 35 at the Mohegan Sun Arena in Uncasville, Connecticut, on January 11.

BENJI RADACH
CASTLE ROCK, WA

DEBUT: UFC 37, MAY 10, 2002

Benji Radach's brief three-fight UFC stint in 2002 was characterized by bad luck. First, the former high school wrestler's TKO win over Steve Berger was overturned to a no contest. Then, after a decision win over Nick Serra a month later, Radach's third Octagon bout against Sean Sherk was stopped via cuts in the first round. Luckily, Radach found more consistent success outside of UFC. After a three-year break from 2004 to 2007 that was prompted by a broken jaw delivered by Chris Leben, Radach ran off a 5-1 stint in the IFL in which he defeated Brian Foster and Gerald Harris. He also gained recognition for foiling an armed robbery attempt in 2006.

Murilo Bustamante defeats Dave Menne to claim the UFC middleweight championship.

WESLEY CORREIRA
HILO, HI

DEBUT: UFC 39, SEPTEMBER 27, 2002

His parents named him Wesley, but to fight fans around the world, he's only known as "Cabbage." Although "Cabbage" Correira will never go down in the annals of UFC history for his technique or mastery of any particular combat sports discipline, when it came to toughness, few could match him. An unrepentant brawler, Correira was known for the granite chin that he put on display in UFC bouts against the likes of power punchers Tim Sylvia, Andrei Arlovski and Tank Abbott. But "Cabbage" went one step further, saying that his whole head was filled "with concrete and stuff." In a game full of intriguing characters, Correira holds a prominent spot near the top.

IVAN SALAVERRY
TORONTO, CANADA

DEBUT: UFC 37, MAY 10, 2002

Given his ground knowledge, along with a solid stand-up attack, Toronto native Ivan Salaverry—who has trained in the martial arts since age 13—always proved to be a rough opponent for anyone at 185 pounds. Just ask the people he defeated in the Octagon, such as Andrei Semenov, Anthony Fryklund and Joe Riggs. They will tell you that beating Salaverry is no easy task, even in the best of circumstances. But key losses against Matt Lindland and Nate Marquardt kept him from moving into title contention, and back-to-back defeats in 2007 and 2008 to Terry Martin and Rousimar Palhares forced his release from UFC.

MARK WEIR
GLOUCESTER, UNITED KINGDOM

DEBUT: UFC 38, JULY 13, 2002

There were a host of memorable moments on UFC's first UK card in 2002, but one that definitely rose to the top was Mark "The Wizard" Weir's 10-second knockout of Eugene Jackson.

Weir, who ran off eight wins after a loss in his first pro fight, was an underdog, but he delivered a spectacular finish of the veteran.

Four months later, Weir was back to face Phillip Miller. Before the fight, he said, "I want to be the first British fighter to get a title shot and then actually win the UFC middleweight title." It was not to be, however, as he lost to Miller and to David Loiseau. Missed title opportunity aside, no one can ever take away his night of UFC glory.

PETE SPRATT
DENISON, TX

DEBUT: UFC 37.5, JUNE 22, 2002

Actor, musician, former college football star—the question isn't why Pete "The Secret Weapon" Spratt fights; it's how he finds time for it.

"Fighting is first and foremost," he laughed. "That pays all the bills. It's, 'When do I find time to do all the other stuff?'"

Spratt made a splash on the UFC scene in 2003 with an upset victory over previously unbeaten Robbie Lawler at UFC 42. Unable to capitalize, Spratt went back to the local circuit. He resurfaced in a 2005 bout with Josh Koscheck and on *The Ultimate Fighter* season four. He was released after losses to Marcus Davis and Tamdan McCrory in 2007.

The fight for Pulver's UFC lightweight title marked the first time that 155-pound fighters were chosen to headline an event. While some called that a risky move, Penn had the star power to carry it. His coronation as champion was seen as a mere formality, an idea that didn't sit well with the incumbent.

"I just felt so disrespected," Pulver later said of the lead-up to the fight. "I don't know how I lost that anger when I got older; maybe it's just a young man's thing [laughs], but I felt so disrespected that I couldn't wait to get out there. When you looked at it on paper, I wasn't supposed to be anywhere near that title fight. I wasn't supposed to be the main event; I definitely wasn't supposed to beat him if you look at credentials. I probably should have just walked out there and laid it on the floor and said, 'Here ya go.' But boy, those first two rounds, it was horrible. And then something just snapped, and I started to turn it around. I was the angry little badger, I guess."

That angry little badger lost the first two rounds to Penn, and it appeared that the oddsmakers' opinions were correct. But there were still three rounds to go, and when Pulver looked across the Octagon at Penn's corner before the third round, he found his second wind.

"Somebody in his corner, one of his little entourage, was jumping up and down and doing the cut throat [gesture] at me," Pulver chuckled. "And I looked right at him and was like, 'Are you kidding me?' So because of that guy, I said, 'No way,' and he never got another takedown. That was the thing that I needed in my head. If I get beat, I get beat, but I ain't going out like this."

Pulver won the next three rounds and retained his title. It was a defining victory for Pulver and a crushing loss for Penn.

"I didn't know what I was going to do with my life or my career," Penn remembered. "Everything was in shambles. I didn't know what to think; I didn't know where to go. The only thing I was sure about was that it was a great learning experience. I didn't know what was up, what was down, what was left, what was right or what was going on."

Some say Penn didn't fully recover until he beat Matt Hughes for the welterweight title in 2004. As for Pulver, it was his last UFC fight until 2006. He soon left the promotion after a contract dispute-leaving the 155-pound title vacant in the process.

On that same UFC 35 card, the middleweight title changed hands, as Brazilian jiu-jitsu ace Murilo Bustamante showed off his striking in a second-round TKO of Dave Menne.

Another title change occurred at UFC 36 in Las Vegas two months later. Josh Barnett was too big and too strong for Randy Couture, allowing "The Babyfaced Assassin" to take the heavyweight belt via TKO in two rounds. That title soon became vacant, as Barnett failed his post-fight drug test and was stripped of it.

One championship belt that remained secure was the one owned by welterweight champion Matt Hughes. At UFC 36, he successfully defended his title for the first time with a dominant fourth-round TKO of Japanese star Hayato "Mach" Sakurai.

On May 10 in Bossier City, Louisiana, Bustamante successfully defended his title with a submission win over former Olympic silver medalist Matt Lindland at UFC 37. The card also featured the return of Penn, who stopped Paul Creighton in the second round and the debut of future welterweight champion Robbie Lawler, the latest find from the Miletich Fighting Systems camp.

Behind the scenes, the Zuffa brass continued to work tirelessly to get the sport in front of as many eyes as possible. On June 22, it was a huge hit when they were able to put a card titled UFC 37.5 on FOX Sports Net's *The Best Damn Sports Show Period*. The headline was a fight between Chuck Liddell and the returning Vitor Belfort, which introduced a national television audience to "The Iceman" (who won a three-round unanimous decision) and "The Phenom." The victory cemented Liddell's place as the No. 1 contender for Tito Ortiz' light heavyweight title, but "The Huntington Beach Bad Boy" had other plans.

On July 13, UFC made its first trip to England, with UFC 38 taking place at Royal Albert Hall in London. In the main event, Hughes defeated Carlos Newton in four rounds in their championship rematch, and England's own Ian Freeman upset rising star Frank Mir via first-round TKO.

Chuck Liddell kicks Vitor Belfort at UFC 37.5.

ROBBIE LAWLER

DEBUT: UFC 37, MAY 10, 2002
UFC WELTERWEIGHT CHAMPION

SAN DIEGO, CA

When "Ruthless" Robbie Lawler entered UFC in 2002 as a 4-0 prodigy, many expected him to be MMA's Mike Tyson—an unrepentant knockout artist who thrilled fans with each bout.

"If I play baseball, I'm going to hit home runs; if I'm playing defensive end, I'm going to get sacks, and I'm going to make it look exciting."

That's precisely what he did, defeating Aaron Riley, Steve Berger and Tiki Ghosn.

Unfortunately, Lawler was hit with some growing pains in the Octagon, losing three of his next four bouts against Pete Spratt, Nick Diaz and Evan Tanner. His only win in that stretch came against Chris Lytle in November 2003.

Released from his UFC contract, Lawler went on to fight outside UFC, but again, it was a 1-3 run. His time in STRIKEFORCE from 2011 to 2012 had fans wondering if "Ruthless," now fighting at middleweight, was still an elite fighter.

He was. Returning to UFC as a welterweight in 2013, Lawler revived his career with knockouts of Josh Koscheck and Bobby Voelker and a stirring decision win over Rory MacDonald.

Those victories earned him a shot at the UFC welterweight title vacated by Georges St-Pierre, but after five furious rounds in March 2014, Johny Hendricks ultimately took the close decision and the belt. But after wins over Jake Ellenberger and Matt Brown, Lawler got a second crack at Hendricks and the 170-pound championship at UFC 181 in December 2014. He made the most of it, defeating "Bigg Rigg" by decision to earn the title he had been seeking for years: world champion. "I'm just at the right place at the right time," Lawler said. "I'm older now, I know how to train, and I know how to take care of my body."

≡ TIM SYLVIA

DEBUT: UFC 39, SEPTEMBER 27, 2002
TWO-TIME UFC HEAVYWEIGHT CHAMPION

ELLSWORTH, ME

One of the most underrated champions in UFC history, Tim "The Maine-iac" Sylvia was initially seen as simply an imposing figure with the power that came from being 6'8" and nearly 265 pounds. By his own admission, he didn't exactly take the hard road to the title when he first held it in 2003.

He had built up a gaudy unbeaten record with just one victory in the Octagon over Wesley "Cabbage" Correira and was seen as just another faceless up-and-comer with potential when the call came for him to face Ricco Rodriguez at UFC 41.

After surviving an early triangle choke attempt by Rodriguez, Sylvia dominated, stopping the heavily favored champion with strikes at 3:09 of the first round. A new star was born, or so it seemed.

After Sylvia tested positive for an anabolic agent following a title defense win over Gan McGee in September 2003 and relinquished his belt, it was like starting over. Subsequent losses to Frank Mir and Andrei Arlovski didn't help matters.

Yet, after putting aside the demons of doubt, he came back, starting with a first-round TKO of Mike Block in an IFC show in May 2005. He then returned to the Octagon with wins over Tra Telligman and Assuerio Silva.

The only thing left was to get his redemption against Arlovski at UFC 59, and he did just that, stopping his rival in the first round. Sylvia was the UFC heavyweight champion once more. In the process, he became only the second fighter in the organization's history to wear the belt twice (with Randy Couture being the first).

After beating Arlovski in their rubber match and successfully defending the belt against Jeff Monson, Sylvia was upset by Couture at UFC 68 in 2007. Two fights later, he attempted to win the interim crown against Minotauro Nogueira, but he was submitted in what was ultimately his last UFC fight. Sylvia retired from MMA in 2015.

AARON RILEY
TELL CITY, IN

DEBUT: UFC 37, MAY 10, 2002

A respected MMA veteran whose fights against Robbie Lawler, Steve Berger and Yves Edwards are ones for the time capsule, Aaron Riley made a welcome return to UFC in November 2008 after two years away from the Octagon.

"UFC is the premier organization, the biggest and best, and it's an honor to be fighting and displaying my skills here," Riley, an iron-chinned warrior who never backed down from a fight, said at the time. "It's really exciting."

It was exciting for fight fans too. The Indiana native reintroduced himself to old fans and made new ones with a memorable war and subsequent decision win over Jorge Gurgel and victories over Shane Nelson and Joe Brammer before retiring in 2013.

Two months later, on September 27, 2002, the Octagon was back in Connecticut, and Couture was once more challenging for the heavyweight title he had won twice previously. But on this night, Ricco Rodriguez stopped Couture in the fifth round of the UFC 39 main event to become the organization's new heavyweight champion.

It was an eventful year—to say the least—but it all paled in comparison to what took place in Las Vegas' MGM Grand on November 22 That night, UFC 40: Vendetta became the biggest event in UFC history up to that time, with the rivalry between Tito Ortiz and the returning Ken Shamrock captivating an audience way beyond the hardcore MMA fan base.

Couture and Rodriguez battle against the fence at UFC 39.

Tito Ortiz and Ken Shamrock battle it out at UFC 40.

"I BRING A FEROCITY LIKE WHAT MIKE TYSON USED TO BRING TO THE RING."
—TITO ORTIZ

The bleached-blond Ortiz, UFC light heavyweight champion, was undoubtedly the promotion's biggest star at the time, but the pioneering Shamrock had an even bigger fan base thanks to his stint as a pro wrestler for WWE. It was a development that even surprised UFC President Dana White leading up to the fight.

"For this show, there's a ratio of 5 to 1 for Ken," said White regarding media requests before UFC 40. "Everybody wants Ken and not Tito. Nobody knows who Tito is, which is pretty interesting. If you look at our model and the way we've done everything in the past, Tito is our biggest guy. Now that we're going into bigger markets for this fight, going after bigger radio stations and bigger media than we ever have. They all know Ken, and nobody knows Tito."

Ortiz wanted to change that, and he was going to do it at the expense of the man he had been feuding with since his early days in UFC. "I bring a ferocity like what Mike Tyson used to bring to the ring," Ortiz said. "That's what I want to bring to the Octagon. People say that Tito Ortiz is like the Mike Tyson of UFC. Hey, I love to be called that, because each guy I take out, I'm going to show them the ferocity I bring to the ring."

As for Shamrock, his goal was simple, and it had nothing to do with winning the light heavyweight title. "I've been doing this for a long time, so I've built up quite a bit of a fan base along the way," he said. "I carry myself with a lot of pride, and I respect everybody that I've come across, except for the ones that didn't show me any respect. I'm not asking someone to respect me or even like me, but don't disrespect me. If you don't like me or don't respect me, just leave it at that."

But could Shamrock pull it off at 38? "The World's Most Dangerous Man" declared at the time "on Friday night, they're not going to question my age. They're not even going to recognize my age." As a result, more people than ever bought this UFC Pay-Per-View event. But in the fight, it was all Ortiz. If he was not a star before his bout with the MMA pioneer and former pro wrestling star, his punishing three-round stoppage victory certainly did the trick to make him one.

2002 was a good year.

GENKI SUDO
KOTO, TOKYO, JAPAN

DEBUT: UFC 38, JULY 13, 2002

A free spirit in the best sense of the word, Genki "Neo-Samurai" Sudo built a stellar reputation among hardcore fans both at home and Japan as a true showman who could still deliver the goods when the horn sounded. He even submitted Butterbean in a Japanese show in 2003. That bizarre victory aside, Sudo earned his keep in MMA because he always fought not only to win, but to entertain, a philosophy lost on many fighters. Whether it was a flying triangle, his quirky movements, or a quick flurry of fight-ending blows, Sudo always brought it. As victories over Royler Gracie, Nate Marquardt and Mike Brown showed, the Neo-Samurai could always fight at the top levels of the lightweight division.

FIGHTS OF THE YEAR

UFC 35

PULVER — W5 — PENN

UFC 37

LAWLER — W3 — RILEY

UFC 37.5

LIDDELL — W3 — BELFORT

UFC 40
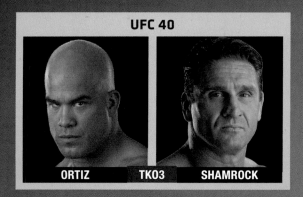
ORTIZ — TKO3 — SHAMROCK

UFC 38

FREEMAN — TKO1 — MIR

KNOCKOUTS OF THE YEAR

UFC 38

WEIR — KO1 — JACKSON

UFC 39

BARONI — KO1 — MENNE

UFC 36

RIZZO — KO3 — ARLOVSKI

UFC 37

BARONI — TKO1 — SULOEV

UFC 40
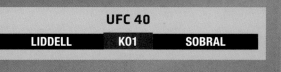
LIDDELL — KO1 — SOBRAL

SUBMISSIONS OF THE YEAR

UFC 37

BUSTAMANTE — WSUB3 — LINDLAND

UFC 36
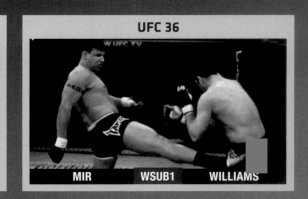
MIR — WSUB1 — WILLIAMS

UFC 38

SUDO — WSUB2 — REMEDIOS

UFC 37.5

SPRATT — WSUB1 — LIGHT

UFC 40

NEWTON — WSUB1 — SPRATT

DEBUTS

UFC 35

AMAR SULOEV

ANDREI SEMENOV

KEITH ROCKEL

UFC 36

HAYATO SAKURAI

KELLY DULLANTY

UFC 37

PAUL CREIGHTON

IVAN SALAVERRY

BENJI RADACH

ROBBIE LAWLER

AARON RILEY

UFC 37.5

JOAO PIERINI

RODRIGO RUAS

PETE SPRATT

ZACH LIGHT

NICK SERRA

UFC 38

MARK WEIR

GENKI SUDO

LEIGH REMEDIOS

JAMES ZIKIC

PHILLIP MILLER

CHRIS HASEMAN

UFC 39

WESLEY CORREIRA

TIM SYLVIA

UFC 40

TRAVIS WIUFF

KELLY DULLANTY

2003

On the heels of UFC 40—the most important and successful event in UFC history at the time—everything seemed to be coming up roses for the promotion as 2003 dawned. Its biggest star, Tito Ortiz, had just scored his biggest victory over Ken Shamrock. Welterweight champion Matt Hughes was a dominant titleholder whose work ethic and Midwestern cool appealed to hardcore fans everywhere. The heavyweight championship was now in the hands of Ricco Rodriguez, a young man who had serious crossover potential.

All that remained was for Rodriguez to get his first title defense out of the way, and for "The Prodigy," BJ Penn, to beat Caol Uno in the finals of the lightweight tournament, which was designed to fill the vacancy at the top of the 155-pound division. At least, that was the ideal scenario heading into the first event of the year, UFC 41: Onslaught, at Boardwalk Hall in Atlantic City. Well, you know that saying about the best-laid plans of mice and men...

RICH CLEMENTI
SLIDELL, LA

DEBUT: UFC 41, FEBRUARY 28, 2003

Rich "No Love" Clementi had reached a crossroads in his career in mid-2007. Despite a strong rep among his fans and peers, the *The Ultimate Fighter* season four veteran had been unable to translate his talent into success in a UFC career that had him sitting with a 1-3 record. But then something funny happened, as Clementi went on a six-fight winning streak in 2007-2008 that saw him dubbed "The Prospect Killer." He ruthlessly defeated Anthony Johnson, Melvin Guillard, Sam Stout and Terry Etim. Clementi's streak was eventually snapped by back-to-back defeats to Gray Maynard and Gleison Tibau, but for a while, "No Love" was one of the best lightweights on the UFC roster.

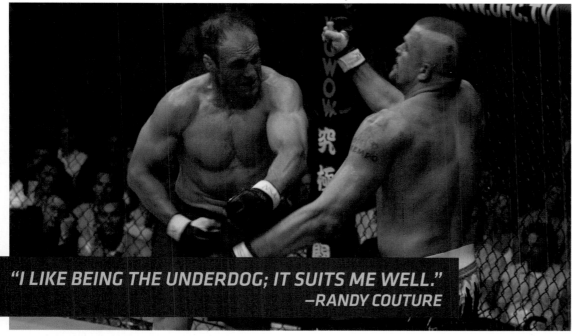

> "I LIKE BEING THE UNDERDOG; IT SUITS ME WELL."
> —RANDY COUTURE

NICK DIAZ

DEBUT: UFC 44, SEPTEMBER 26, 2003

STOCKTON, CA

There are fighters, and then there's Nick Diaz—one of the most unique figures in UFC history. Competing professionally since he was a teenager, Diaz never went into the sport for the fame, but for the fights. Within two years of his debut, he was in UFC, submitting California rival Jeremy Jackson at UFC 44 in 2003.

Seven months later, Diaz scored a monumental upset when he knocked out highly touted Robbie Lawler. While he had some peaks and valleys in the rest of his first 10-fight UFC stint, his memorable scraps with Diego Sanchez and Joe Riggs lived on.

But it was after his first stint in UFC that Diaz began to mature as a fighter. Following his memorable PRIDE bout with Takanori Gomi in 2007, the Stockton, California, native compiled an 11-1 (1 NC) record that included victories over Frank Shamrock, Scott Smith and Mach Sakurai. In 2010, he won the STRIKEFORCE welterweight title with a TKO of Marius Zaromskis.

After three successful defenses, Diaz vacated his title to return to UFC in October 2011. At UFC 137, he delivered an impressive three-round victory over BJ Penn. Diaz lost subsequent bouts to Carlos Condit and Georges St-Pierre, but in 2015, he was back in action against Brazilian icon Anderson Silva in a dream fight that fans had waited to see for years. Although Diaz lost a decision to Silva, his appeal remains untouched among his loyal followers.

Couture defeats Liddell to win the belt.

153

RICH FRANKLIN

DEBUT: UFC 42, APRIL 25, 2003
UFC MIDDLEWEIGHT CHAMPION

CINCINNATI, OH

This was it for Rich "Ace" Franklin. He gave it a good shot, but by the midway point of 2004, he had just assumed that his career as a professional fighter was nearing its end. He was respected in the sport and considered one of the top young prospects in the game, but the wisest course of action for him seemed to be returning to his full-time gig as a high school math teacher.

He would give it one more shot, though. Following wins over Jorge Rivera and Curtis Stout in 2004, he was matched with UFC Hall of Famer Ken Shamrock on an April 2005 card that wound up being the first UFC event on live cable television. He defeated Shamrock that night—and as the cliché goes—the rest is history. Franklin went on to win the UFC middleweight title, becoming a beloved fan favorite and one of the Octagon's true superstars.

A pro from 1999, Franklin made his UFC debut in April 2003 with a first-round TKO of Evan Tanner. A second Octagon victory followed five months later when he stopped Edwin Dewees. However, a December 2003 loss in Japan to future champion Lyoto Machida jeopardized his standing in UFC.

The Shamrock fight took his career and life to a whole other level. Just two months after the defining victory of his career, Franklin was given a shot at the UFC middleweight title held by former foe Tanner.

"Ace" fired on all cylinders that night, and at 3:25 of the fourth round, he was crowned 185-pound champion after a punishing TKO win.

By the end of this memorable year, Franklin defended his title with a one-punch knockout of Nate Quarry at UFC 56. He then kicked off 2006 in March with a bout against David Loiseau, a man whom many expected to give him his toughest test ever, but that turned into another clear-cut win for the champion.

Franklin lost his middleweight crown to Anderson Silva in his next bout in October 2006, but he didn't lose any prestige among his fans. He bounced back with wins over Jason MacDonald and Yushin Okami to earn a second shot at defeating "The Spider."

In their UFC 77 rematch, the result was the same: a KO win for Silva. After getting back in the win column with a UFC 83 stoppage of Travis Lutter in April 2008, Franklin moved back to the division where he first made his mark—light heavyweight.

"Ace" made an immediate impression in September 2008 with a finish of Matt Hamill. Franklin then began a string of bouts that can only be described as "dream fights," as he began matching wits and fists with fellow superstars Dan Henderson, Wanderlei Silva, Vitor Belfort, Chuck Liddell and Forrest Griffin. Along the way, he also became one of mixed martial arts' most visible ambassadors: the lead voice when it came to explaining his sport to the uninformed.

In the Octagon, Franklin defeated the aforementioned Wanderlei Silva and Chuck Liddell, the latter victory coming by knockout at UFC 115 in June 2010. What made his win even more remarkable is that Franklin knocked out Liddell after a kick had broken his arm just moments before the finish.

"You're standing in the cage, and you've got two options: you can quit, or you can continue going, and I'm not a quitter," said Franklin. That's Rich Franklin's career in a nutshell: warrior, fighter, and money player.

In the main event of UFC 41, the heavily favored Rodriguez, barely champion for six months, paid a dear price for trading punches with 6'8" challenger Tim Sylvia. A series of brutal right hands knocked Rodriguez down and out at 3:09 of the first round.

"Being the underdog 5 to 1, I was going to prove people wrong," the new champ Sylvia said. "And if I didn't win, this boy was going to be in a helluva fight, and he was gonna get hurt from it. I wasn't going out easy. I trained so hard for this fight."

As for Penn, he wasn't able to repeat his previous knockout of Uno. He wasn't even able to win the fight. The bout was declared a draw after five rounds, leaving the lightweight crown vacant.

Even the return of Tank Abbott hit the skids when he was tapped out by jiu-jitsu ace Frank Mir in a mere 46 seconds. But as the fight game adage declares, "That's why they fight the fights," and these upsets only made fans want more Octagon action.

MARVIN EASTMAN
MERCED, CA

DEBUT: UFC 43, JUNE 6, 2003

The first man to ever beat Rampage Jackson, Marvin "The Beastman" Eastman was a hard-charging fighter who was a terror at times in his career, but when it came to his battles in the Octagon, he just couldn't win the big one.

Debuting with a win over Jackson in 2000, Eastman made it to UFC in June 2003, but a nasty cut on his forehead halted his bout with Vitor Belfort. Octagon losses to Travis Lutter and Jackson (in their 2007 rematch) followed before he scored his lone victory in the organization at UFC 81, a decision over Terry Martin. After a first-round loss to Drew McFedries in 2008, Eastman was released.

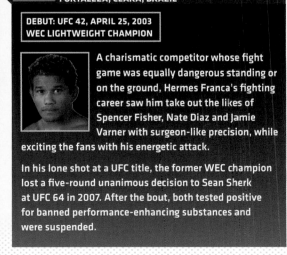

HERMES FRANCA
FORTALEZA, CEARÁ, BRAZIL

DEBUT: UFC 42, APRIL 25, 2003
WEC LIGHTWEIGHT CHAMPION

A charismatic competitor whose fight game was equally dangerous standing or on the ground, Hermes Franca's fighting career saw him take out the likes of Spencer Fisher, Nate Diaz and Jamie Varner with surgeon-like precision, while exciting the fans with his energetic attack.

In his lone shot at a UFC title, the former WEC champion lost a five-round unanimous decision to Sean Sherk at UFC 64 in 2007. After the bout, both tested positive for banned performance-enhancing substances and were suspended.

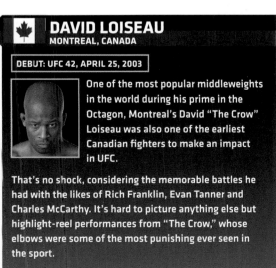

DAVID LOISEAU
MONTREAL, CANADA

DEBUT: UFC 42, APRIL 25, 2003

One of the most popular middleweights in the world during his prime in the Octagon, Montreal's David "The Crow" Loiseau was also one of the earliest Canadian fighters to make an impact in UFC.

That's no shock, considering the memorable battles he had with the likes of Rich Franklin, Evan Tanner and Charles McCarthy. It's hard to picture anything else but highlight-reel performances from "The Crow," whose elbows were some of the most punishing ever seen in the sport.

Yet, after a UFC 42 event in Florida on April 25 in which Hughes successfully defended his title with a grueling five-round decision win over Sean Sherk, and Pete Spratt upset previously unbeaten knockout artist Robbie Lawler, the biggest fight in UFC was taking place outside the Octagon. Light heavyweight champ Ortiz and number-one contender Chuck Liddell started feuding in the media.

Former training partners Ortiz and Liddell were either good friends or acquaintances, depending on which 205-pound standout you spoke to. But regardless of their previous relationship, the facts were clear: "The Iceman" had earned his shot at the belt, but Ortiz wasn't giving it to him, leading to harsh words from both sides.

"I'm a bad fight for him, a bad style," said Liddell of Ortiz. "And he knows that. I'm a really tough fight for him because I strike real well and I'm really hard to take down. When he fights someone who can strike, all he wants to do is take him down. We trained together a little bit, and he knows he'll have a hard time taking me down."

"There are so many people out there talking smack, saying I'm afraid of him and I'm a coward," Ortiz said of Liddell. "You know what, that's all hype, and people have got to stop believing in all that stuff. I'm a true champion, and I've got to stand up for what I believe in. But the next person on my mind is Chuck Liddell. I've got to shut up some people, and I've got to shut him up and get that thought out of his mind that he could ever beat me, because he never can. That's the fight I really want, and I want that fight more than Frank Shamrock because I've got a lot of people to shut up."

DUANE LUDWIG
DENVER, CO

DEBUT: UFC 42, APRIL 25, 2003

One of the most feared strikers in the sport of mixed martial arts, former kickboxer Duane "Bang" Ludwig's precision strikes turned out the lights on the likes of Jens Pulver, Jonathan Goulet and Sammy Morgan. Ludwig also holds the record for the fastest knockout in UFC history for his six-second finish of Goulet in 2006.

"I've been fighting since I was 15, doing amateur fights, and I never stepped into this for the fame," he said. "I just love training, and fighting is in my blood."

Ludwig finished his 35-fight pro career in the Octagon in 2012, going on to become a respected and successful coach.

KARO PARISYAN
YEREVAN, ARMENIA

DEBUT: UFC 44, SEPTEMBER 26, 2003

World-class judoka Karo "The Heat" Parisyan was fighting professionally from the time he was 16. While he bounced around the MMA circuit over the next few years, it wasn't until 2003 with a spectacular submission win over Dave Strasser at UFC 44, that he truly arrived as a fighter to watch.

Over the next two years, Parisyan won four out of five bouts, losing only to Georges St-Pierre and beating Matt Serra, Nick Diaz and Chris Lytle. A title shot was secured for Parisyan against then-champion Matt Hughes at UFC 56, but a hamstring tear shelved him from the bout.

JORGE RIVERA
MILFORD, MA

DEBUT: UFC 44, SEPTEMBER 26, 2003

Despite a spotty record, Jorge "El Conquistador" Rivera was always a blue-collar worker who thrived on challenges. This *The Ultimate Fighter 4* competitor faced the best over the course of his entire career, including Anderson Silva, Rich Franklin, Travis Lutter, David Loiseau, Dennis Hallman, Chris Leben, Kendall Grove and Martin Kampmann.

Yet it was a late career surge that was most memorable for the New Englander, who left on top with a January 2012 win over Eric Schafer.

"You do take your youth for granted," he admits. "I was happy just being there and saying I fight in UFC. Now I don't want to just say that—I want to say I'm one of the best there."

Soon, with Ortiz locked in heated contract negotiations with Zuffa that eventually stalled, the biggest fight that could be made didn't look like it was going to happen. But the promotion carried on, declaring that Liddell would now face former heavyweight champion Randy Couture for the interim 205-pound title in the main event of UFC 43 in Las Vegas on June 6, 2003.

Couture, fresh off back-to-back losses at heavyweight and a couple weeks shy of his 40th birthday, was expected to get run over by "The Iceman" in what appeared to be a last-ditch effort to salvage his career. It didn't happen that way, with Couture stunning the mixed martial arts world with a third-round TKO of Liddell.

"I like being the underdog; it suits me well," said Couture, who became the first man in history to win UFC titles in two weight classes. He also had a message for Ortiz: "Tito, if you want this belt, you're gonna have to come in here and take it."

The axis of the MMA world had shifted. Yet by early fall, Ortiz was ready to fight again, though it would be against Couture rather than Liddell. Despite Couture's huge upset of Liddell, most assumed lightning wasn't going to strike twice in the main event of UFC 44 in Las Vegas on September 26. Most were wrong once again, as the ageless wonder known as "The Natural" outpointed Tito Ortiz over five rounds in yet another time capsule fight.

"I guess I'm a late bloomer," Couture said. "Tito's been a great champion, and I've been honored to fight him." The loss was Ortiz' first since a 1999 defeat against Frank Shamrock, and he had few answers for Couture, who dominated from start to finish as he won via scores of 50-44 twice and 50-45. The paradigm had now shifted in UFC's glamour division. Ortiz had lost, Liddell had lost, and the man at the top of the heap was a soft-spoken 40-year-old who thrashed both of them.

The heavyweight division was similarly going to get a shakeup, but not in the Octagon. The UFC 44 co-main event saw Tim Sylvia stop 6'10" Gan McGee at 1:52 of the first round. It was the first successful title defense for "The Maine-iac," but his celebration was short-lived, as a positive post-fight drug test for steroids forced the champion to relinquish his belt. He admitted his guilt and was suspended by the Nevada State Athletic Commission, leaving the heavyweight crown vacant once more.

It had been a whirlwind year in a promotion that had gone through a tumultuous 10 years, so it was fitting that on November 21 at the Mohegan Sun Arena in Connecticut, Zuffa presented its 10th anniversary show, UFC 45: Revolution. This show used a mixture of old-school tributes and new talent to bridge the gap between past and present.

In the main event, welterweight champion Matt Hughes once again proved his superiority over the competition with a first-round submission win over Frank Trigg, a man who had been expected to give him his sternest test. In the Revolution co-feature, there was little finesse or skill shown in the heavyweight matchup between Tank Abbott and Wesley "Cabbage" Correira, but there was plenty of action and blood, at least until a crimson gash on Abbott's forehead forced a halt to the bout at 2:14 of the opening round.

It was an almost fitting bridge between old and new, with the skill and high-level athleticism exhibited by Hughes and Trigg countered by some good ol' fashioned brawling from Abbott and Correira. UFC had come a long way in a decade, and to celebrate and cap off the anniversary, it honored Royce Gracie and Ken Shamrock as the first inductees into the UFC Hall of Fame.

JOSH THOMSON
SAN JOSE, CA

DEBUT: UFC 44, SEPTEMBER 26, 2003
STRIKEFORCE LIGHTWEIGHT CHAMPION

Josh "The Punk" Thomson is a fighter whose UFC career initially could be described as a case of poor timing. His initial three-bout run in the organization coincided with the temporary hiatus of the lightweight division from 2004 to 2006.

While in UFC, "The Punk" impressed with his wins over Gerald Strebendt and Hermes Franca. Although he got knocked out by Yves Edwards at UFC 49—in what was the last 155-pound fight in UFC for nearly two years—his future was bright in the STRIKEFORCE promotion. There, he was lightweight champion from 2008 to 2009. In 2013, Thomson returned to UFC for a run highlighted by a knockout of Nate Diaz.

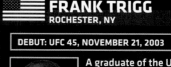

FRANK TRIGG
ROCHESTER, NY

DEBUT: UFC 45, NOVEMBER 21, 2003

A graduate of the University of Oklahoma, Frank "Twinkle Toes" Trigg was a world-class collegiate wrestler, but it was in MMA where he truly made his mark.

A pro since 1997, Trigg made appearances in PRIDE and Shooto before debuting in UFC in 2003 against welterweight champion Matt Hughes. Trigg fell short in that bout, but after wins over Dennis Hallman and Renato Verissimo, he engaged in a rematch with Hughes at UFC 52 in 2005. Despite Trigg's submission defeat to the future UFC Hall of Famer, that bout is considered one of the greatest in UFC history.

Trigg's first stint in UFC ended shortly thereafter, but he returned in 2009, losing consecutive fights against Josh Koscheck and Matt Serra.

VERNON WHITE
SPARKS, NV

DEBUT: UFC 43, JUNE 6, 2003

A quick look at Vernon "Tiger" White's record, and you may be inclined to dismiss him as a mere opponent. However, this original member of Ken Shamrock's famed Lion's Den was no pushover. Instead, he was an honest competitor who always came to fight. Although he lost bouts against the elite of the game—like Chuck Liddell, Frank Shamrock and Lyoto Machida)—when he was on, he pulled off wins over Vladimir Matyushenko, David Terrell, Sam Hoger and Marvin Eastman.

In UFC action, the Pancrase vet fought to a draw against Ian Freeman at UFC 43. He then slugged it out with Liddell at UFC 49 before being knocked out late in the first round.

FIGHTS OF THE YEAR

UFC 41

LINDLAND — W3 — BARONI

UFC 42
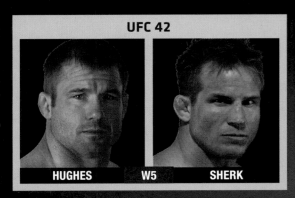
HUGHES — W5 — SHERK

UFC 43
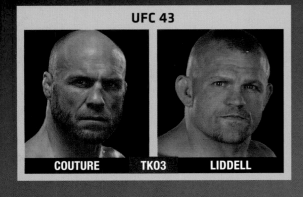
COUTURE — TKO3 — LIDDELL

UFC 44

RIVERA — W3 — LOISEAU

UFC 45
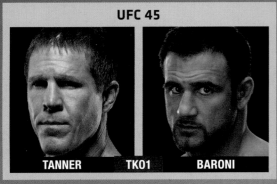
TANNER — TKO1 — BARONI

KNOCKOUTS OF THE YEAR

UFC 41
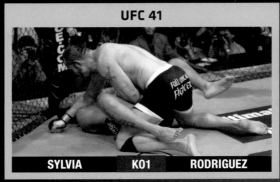
SYLVIA — KO1 — RODRIGUEZ

UFC 42
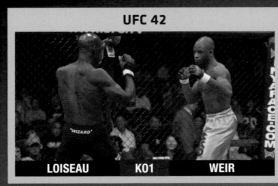
LOISEAU — KO1 — WEIR

UFC 44

FRANCA — KO2 — UNO

UFC 45

TANNER — TKO1 — BARONI

UFC 43

BELFORT — TKO1 — EASTMAN

SUBMISSIONS OF THE YEAR

UFC 44
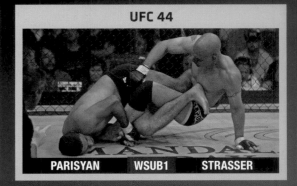
PARISYAN — WSUB1 — STRASSER

UFC 41

MIR — WSUB1 — ABBOTT

UFC 45

HUGHES — WSUB1 — TRIGG

UFC 43

LEOPOLDO — WSUB1 — ABBOTT

UFC 44

DIAZ — WSUB1 — JACKSON

DEBUTS

UFC 41

RICH CLEMENTI

UFC 42

DAVID LOISEAU	RICH FRANKLIN
HERMES FRANCA	SEAN ALVAREZ
RICHARD CRUNKILTON JR.	DAVE STRASSER
DUANE LUDWIG	ROMIE ARAM

UFC 43

MARVIN EASTMAN	VERNON WHITE
WES SIMS	FALANIKO VITALE
EDDIE RUIZ	

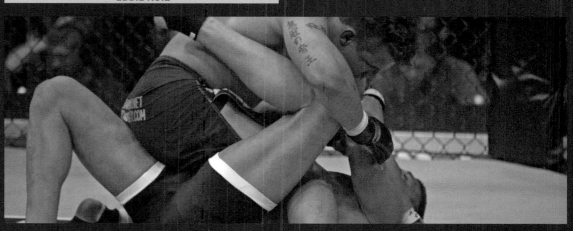

UFC 44

EDWIN DEWEES

KARO PARISYAN

JOSH THOMSON

GERALD STREBENDT

JEREMY JACKSON

NICK DIAZ

JORGE RIVERA

UFC 45

FRANK TRIGG	NICK AGALLAR
CHRIS LIGOURI	

ONE-HIT WONDERS

ART JIMMERSON

Art Jimmerson fared better in combat sports with two boxing gloves, compiling a 33-18 record as a pro boxer from 1985 to 2002. Although he never won a world title, he did face off against future champions Jeff Harding, Dennis Andries, Orlin Norris, Vassiliy Jirov and Arthur Williams.

1994
EMMANUEL YARBOROUGH

Despite only competing in one UFC match, Emmanuel Yarborough remains one of the figures fight fans just can't forget. Although he outweighed Keith Hackney by upward of 400 pounds, the sumo specialist from Rahway, New Jersey, wasn't able to secure a victory. He only fought twice more, most notably losing to Daiju Takase at PRIDE 3 in 1998.

RON VAN CLIEF

Ron Van Clief may have lost his lone UFC bout to Royce Gracie in 1994, but he holds a record that will likely never be broken. Van Clief was the oldest man to compete in the Octagon when he fought Gracie at the age of 51. A Marine Corps veteran, Van Clief is a 10th dan black belt in the style of martial arts he created, Chinese Goju.

1996
DIEUSEL BERTO

Haitian Dieusel Berto, whose MMA career finished at 0-3, may not have had the most distinguished run in the sport, but he did a fine job of producing fighters. His sons Andre and James Edson, along with his daughter Revelina, all had combat sports success. Andre was a welterweight boxing champion of the world, James Edson was a mixed martial artist who fought for the EliteXC and STRIKEFORCE organizations, and Revelina was an MMA fighter who competed for a spot on *The Ultimate Fighter: Team Rousey vs Team Tate*.

KOJI KITAO

Japan's Koji Kitao was a top-level sumo wrestler, the sport's 60th yokozuna. He fought only three times in MMA, losing his first two bouts before a submission win over Nathan Jones at PRIDE 1 in 1997.

MARK SCHULTZ

Mark Schultz was a 1984 Olympic gold medal winner in freestyle wrestling, as well as a two-time world champion on the mat. Though he was victorious at UFC 9 and probably would have been successful in MMA, he only fought once more, losing a bout in Brazil in 2003.

1998
IGOR ZINOVIEV

A talented mixed martial artist from Russia, Igor "Houdini" Zinoviev broke into the sport in 1995, winning his first four bouts and even stopping Enson Inoue in a 1996 match. After draws in his next two contests he got the call to join UFC. Unfortunately, a broken collarbone suffered during his loss to Frank Shamrock abruptly ended his career.

1999
ANDRE PEDERNEIRAS

Stopped in his lone UFC fight—a 1999 title fight against Pat Miletich—Brazil's Andre Pederneiras nevertheless remained in the fight game. In the ensuing years, he worked as the co-founder and head coach of the Nova Uniao fight team that launched the careers of such UFC stars as Jose Aldo and Renan Barão.

Coach Andre Pederneiras looks on as Tim Williams prepares for a fight during *The Ultimate Fighter* season 19.

2000
SCOTT ADAMS AND BOB COOK

Combined, Scott Adams and Bob Cook compiled a 13-1 pro mixed martial arts slate. However, both fighters, who completed their careers at UFC 24, eventually became known more for what they did outside the Octagon than in it. Adams, "The King of Leglocks," teamed up with Reed Harris to form the World Extreme Cagefighting (WEC) organization. "Crazy" Bob became one of the sport's leading managers and trainers, working with the stellar group of fighters that emerged from San Jose's American Kickboxing Academy.

Trainer Bob Cook (left) poses with Daniel Cormier and Javier Mendez at UFC 173.

IKUHISA MINOWA AND SANAE KIKUTA

With then-owners SEG finding the reality of keeping UFC afloat an almost-losing battle, the funds simply weren't there to keep solid international talent like Ikuhisa Minowa and Sanae Kikuta around. Both went on to impressive careers in their home country of Japan, with Kikuta mainly in the Pancrase organization and Minowa in Pancrase, PRIDE, Deep and Dream.

MARK HUGHES

Mark Hughes, the twin brother of UFC Hall of Famer Matt Hughes, is still inseparable from his brother's side. After a win over Leo Sylvest in 2003, he walked away from the game with a 6-2 record and no regrets.

2001
PHIL JOHNS

When it came to fighting all opponents on the Midwest circuit, Phil Johns was your man. He was a hard-nosed battler who faced Jens Pulver, Rumina Sato, Jeff Curran, Hermes Franca, and Shonie Carter over his nine-year career. Johns may not have earned a return call to UFC after UFC 30, but he could certainly fight.

JOEY GILBERT

Owner of a 2-3 pro record over the course of a career that lasted from 1998 to 2003, Gilbert's fighting legacy unfortunately has him pegged as a trivia question: who was the first pro opponent of future two-time UFC champion BJ Penn?

PAUL RODRIGUEZ

Paul Rodriguez's lone Octagon appearance was in a losing effort against Tony DeSouza, but there was no shame in his game. With a record of 10-8-2 over nine years as a pro, Rodriguez—who scored six wins by submission—never shied away from world-class competition, facing Dave Strasser, Dennis Hallman, Takanori Gomi, Tiki Ghosn and Josh Neer.

2002
NICK SERRA

The brother of former UFC welterweight champion Matt Serra, Nick Serra is a jiu-jitsu black belt under Renzo Gracie. He won three of his final five MMA bouts before leaving the sport in 2008 to focus on teaching "the gentle art" in New York.

2005
BILL MAHOOD

Despite his less-than-stellar performance against Forrest Griffin, Mahood was one of Canada's mixed martial arts pioneers. Over the course of more than a decade in the game, Mahood had nearly 20 wins, including victories over Steve Steinbeiss, Chris Haseman and Jason MacDonald.

BRIAN GASSAWAY

A long-time training partner of Shonie Carter, Brian Gassaway had already compiled 38 pro fights by the time he stepped into the Octagon against Diego Sanchez. Though he wasn't victorious in UFC, he continued to fight against quality foes like John Alessio, Jose Landi-Jons, Forrest Petz and Mike Pyle.

RON FAIRCLOTH AND SEAN GANNON

Ron Faircloth and Sean Gannon both made sizable impressions in their lone UFC bouts: Faircloth because of his low blow that ended Alessio Sakara's night, and Gannon because of his unique back story. Gannon, a Boston police officer, came to the world's attention because of an underground video that showed him being the first person to defeat a young man nicknamed Kimbo Slice. That attention got him noticed by UFC, and a contract was signed. At the time, his manager Joe Cavallaro said, "They [UFC] are always looking for big guys, and the kid is very marketable and he's got a lot of stuff going for him. He's a big, strong, very tough kid. I think anybody that watched the thing with Kimbo sees that he can fight, and ultimately, UFC is entertainment. People want to see big guys that can fight." After his lone UFC loss, Gannon never fought again.

2006
TOM MURPHY

Usually when a fighter is one-and-done in UFC he leaves with a loss. In the case of Tom Murphy, a Division III All-American wrestler and cast member on *The Ultimate Fighter* season two, he left after a win, and a TKO victory at that. Following his success at UFC 58, Murphy took two years off from the game before coming back to win a single fight each year in 2008, 2009 and 2010.

2006
RICK DAVIS

Schoolteacher Rick Davis raced out to a 3-0-1 record in his MMA career. Well, maybe "raced" isn't the right word; those four fights spanned from 2002 to 2004. In fact, when he took on Melvin Guillard at UFC 60, he hadn't fought in nearly two years, making the end result almost a foregone conclusion. After UFC 60 Davis never fought again.

2006
MARIO NETO

Though unsuccessful in the Octagon, Mario "Sukata" Neto has had an impact on UFC as the jiu-jitsu coach for England's Wolfslair team, home at one time or another to the likes of Michael Bisping, Cheick Kongo and Rampage Jackson.

2010
ROLLES GRACIE

The first Gracie to appear in the Octagon since UFC Hall of Famer Royce, Rolles Gracie couldn't match the success of his cousin. He gassed out after a strong start and was stopped in the second round; he was released from UFC after the fight.

2010
JAMES TONEY

A future boxing Hall of Famer, multi-division world champion Toney talked himself into a fight at UFC 118 despite having no previous MMA training. Give him credit for taking the plunge against Randy Couture, but it was clear from the outset that this one wasn't going to end well for him.

2004

40-year-old Randy Couture proved, as the undisputed light heavyweight champion, that age ain't nothin' but a number. UFC had a champion outside of the demographic the promotion wanted to hit, but one who captivated fans regardless. Of course, a younger, more explosive champion wouldn't be turned away, either. That's what fans got in the first event 2004, as Vitor Belfort evened the score with Couture via first-round TKO to take the 205-pound title.

The bout wasn't as dramatic as that, even though the lead-up to the January 31 event was. Fresh off dominating wins over Chuck Liddell and Tito Ortiz, Couture was once again facing a younger opponent (albeit one he already held a 1997 victory over), making the UFC 46 main event a compelling one. Adding to the drama was the fact that Belfort's sister, Priscila, had disappeared weeks before the fight, leaving "The Phenom" in a mental state of either complete focus or complete disarray.

BJ Penn reacts to his victory over Matt Hughes.

167

GEORGES ST-PIERRE

DEBUT: UFC 46, JANUARY 31, 2004
TWO-TIME UFC WELTERWEIGHT CHAMPION

SAINT-ISIDORE,
MONTÉRÉGIE, QUEBEC,

If not for his parents' intervention, we might be talking about Georges "Rush" St-Pierre as the best right wing or center to ever play for the Montreal Canadiens. But when the native of St. Isidore wanted to play hockey and begin studying karate at the age of six, he was forced to choose one or the other.

He chose karate.

In many ways, St-Pierre's choice was one of self-preservation, as he was dealing with bullies in school. Eventually, that problem went away as St-Pierre developed mentally and physically under the tutelage of his Kyokushin karate teacher, Jean Couture.

St-Pierre's parents and Jean Couture laid the groundwork for the humble warrior whom fighters have feared and fight fans have admired for years. But the mixed martial artist was just getting started on his road to the welterweight championship.

After Jean Couture's passing, St-Pierre began looking toward MMA. He won his first amateur bout at 16, and then began supplementing his knowledge of karate by studying jiu-jitsu and wrestling. He was a quick study in both disciplines—as well as boxing—and he balanced his education and combat sports studies with various odd jobs. Soon, St-Pierre was wrestling with the Canadian national team and training in Brazilian jiu-jitsu with the renowned Nova Uniao team. By 2002, the 20-year-old made his pro MMA debut with a win over Ivan Menjivar. The journey had begun.

In January 2004, St-Pierre made his UFC debut with a three-round decision win over Karo Parisyan. After a first-round TKO of Jay Hieron in the Octagon less than five months later, he was tabbed to face Matt Hughes for the vacant UFC welterweight belt in October 2004. Hughes ended St-Pierre's year on a sour note with a first-round submission win in a fight that left more questions than answers. Sure, St-Pierre was young and talented, but did he have the mental toughness to become a world champion?

Those answers came soon enough. 2005 saw St-Pierre tear through the division with extreme prejudice as he defeated Dave Strasser and Jason Miller, destroyed Frank Trigg and stopped soon-to-be lightweight king Sean Sherk. His 2006 fight with BJ Penn truly showed his progression from talent-rich athlete to true mixed martial artist. St-Pierre rebounded from a horrific first round to win the next two stanzas and gut out a three-round decision. All that was left was to beat Hughes. On November 18, 2006, he accomplished that feat with little effort. He dominated the longtime champion en route to a second-round TKO that allowed him to claim the UFC welterweight title.

But the fall—like all great falls in hindsight—seemed to be inevitable. Matt Serra, a veteran fighter whose shining attribute may be his tenacity, was waiting in the wings. On April 7, 2007, he took apart a St-Pierre who found out in Houston, Texas, that he was human just like everyone else. A maelstrom of personal issues leading up to the fight took his focus off what most believed to be a routine first title defense.

Following what may one day be deemed the "dark days" of his fighting career, St-Pierre cleaned house and became a different, and even better, fighter. A dominant decision win over Josh Koscheck in August 2007 and a submission win over Hughes in their UFC 79 rubber match served to make St-Pierre a favorite over Serra leading into their rematch at UFC 83.

On that night in his hometown of Montreal, St-Pierre destroyed Serra, regaining his title via second-round TKO at the Bell Centre. This time, he vowed not to let the belt go.

After that emotional victory, St-Pierre shut the door on all challengers at 170 pounds, defeating Jon Fitch, BJ Penn, Thiago Alves, Dan Hardy, Josh Koscheck, Jake Shields, Carlos Condit, Nick Diaz and Johny Hendricks in successive bouts before announcing that he was taking a hiatus from the sport in December 2013.

Once the bout commenced, it was over almost as soon as it began. After the two briefly sparred with each other, Belfort grazed Couture with a straight left. The competitors clinched against the fence, with Couture in obvious discomfort. Referee John McCarthy intervened, bringing in Octagonside physician Margaret Goodman to examine Couture's left eye. Goodman recommended that McCarthy call a halt to the bout at the 49-second mark, a stoppage that crowned Belfort the new champion. The culprit? A seam on Belfort's glove gashed Couture's lower left eyelid, exposing the eyeball and requiring immediate surgery. Just like that, there was a new champion at 205 pounds, shaking up the division once more.

Luckily for fight fans, there was plenty of Octagon drama in the UFC 46 co-main event. This was no surprise since the returning BJ Penn always provided compelling action. Adding to this one was the fact that after coming up short in two UFC lightweight title chances, Penn was moving 15 pounds north to face the most dominating champ in the world in welterweight king Matt Hughes. Most figured that Penn was committing athletic suicide against Hughes, who was making the sixth defense of his title. But someone forgot to tell the Hawaiian, who, in one of the sport's most memorable moments, fulfilled all of his exceptional promise in a mere four minutes and 39 seconds.

From the opening horn, Penn dictated the action and even appeared to be bigger physically than the champion. Soon, Hughes found himself on the canvas, and as the final minute of the first round got underway, a strike by Penn turned the tide of the fight. Stunned by a blow that bloodied his nose, Hughes instinctively turned to the side, giving Penn his back. With breakneck speed, Penn took the most dominant position in the sport and immediately sunk in a rear-naked choke. The tap by Hughes seconds later was a mere formality, and another new champion was crowned, proving that—like boxing— MMA is the "theater of the unexpected."

With all this happening, a quiet Canadian named Georges St-Pierre made his UFC debut with a win over Karo Parisyan. Over the next decade, the young man nicknamed "Rush" figured prominently in rivalries with Penn and Hughes as he carved out his own 170-pound legacy.

While the welterweight division was now making headlines, especially with Penn about to leave the belt and UFC behind, the light heavyweights were still the big moneymakers. There were no two 205-pounders bigger when it came to that than Ortiz and Liddell. Even though Couture had shattered each fighter's aura of invincibility, there was still no fight the fans wanted to see more than Liddell vs Ortiz.

On April 2, 2004, at the Mandalay Bay Events Center in Las Vegas, they finally got it. In many ways, Liddell-Ortiz was even bigger than Ortiz-Shamrock, simply because it was a grudge match between two fighters at the height of their prowess. At UFC 47, it was Liddell who was left standing, as he emphatically stopped the former light heavyweight champion in the second round.

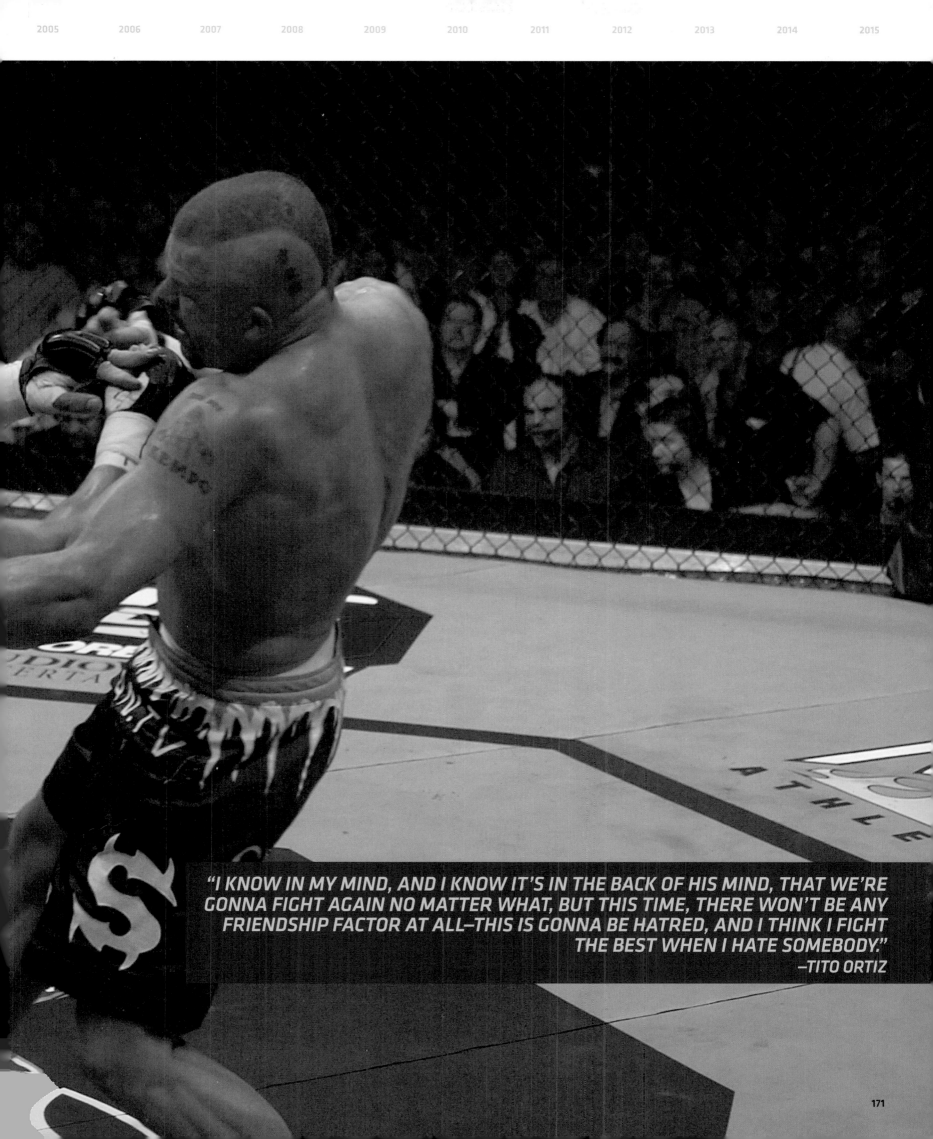

"I KNOW IN MY MIND, AND I KNOW IT'S IN THE BACK OF HIS MIND, THAT WE'RE GONNA FIGHT AGAIN NO MATTER WHAT, BUT THIS TIME, THERE WON'T BE ANY FRIENDSHIP FACTOR AT ALL—THIS IS GONNA BE HATRED, AND I THINK I FIGHT THE BEST WHEN I HATE SOMEBODY."
—TITO ORTIZ

The action didn't stray to the ground once during the match, with two Ortiz takedown attempts easily foiled by Liddell. But even though Liddell was in his element while standing, he was unable to penetrate Ortiz' tight defense for much of the opening round, as both men tentatively pawed at each other, not wanting to make a fatal mistake.

Late in the first, Liddell finally landed one of his patented bombs, exploding a right hand on Ortiz' jaw that staggered him. "The Iceman" followed with a kick to the head, and Ortiz' legs were rubbery at the horn, even as he jawed defiantly at Liddell.

Capitalizing on his good fortune, Liddell immediately moved in on Ortiz as the second round commenced. Once he landed a 1-2 combination to the jaw of "The Huntington Beach Bad Boy," the end was just moments away.

Pinned to the cage by Liddell's furious barrages, Ortiz blocked most of the punches but then got drilled with a right to the jaw, followed by a quick left that bloodied his face and put him down on the canvas. This forced referee John McCarthy to halt the bout just 38 seconds into the second round. When it was over, Liddell had the most satisfying win of his career. Ortiz, now dealing with the first two-fight losing streak of his career, was bothered by the way everything went down.

MIKE BROWN
PORTLAND, ME

DEBUT: UFC 47, APRIL 2, 2004
WEC FEATHERWEIGHT CHAMPION

It was the shot heard 'round the world as Mike Brown separated the seemingly unbeatable Urijah Faber from his WEC featherweight title in November 2008.

"I just saw him, and I threw," said Brown of the right hand that dropped Faber and set in motion the finishing sequence of one of the biggest upsets in WEC history. "Whenever I get close enough, I'm just gonna swing with all my might, and if I land, then it's gonna hurt."

For Brown, it was just years of experience coming together at the perfect time, but the hard work was just beginning. Even though he lost his crown to Jose Aldo after two successful title defenses, Brown (owner of a 2-4 UFC record) continued to compete through 2013.

PATRICK COTE
RIMOUSKI, CANADA

DEBUT: UFC 50, OCTOBER 22, 2004

Despite an impressive 5-0 start to his career, things could not have gone worse in Patrick "The Predator" Cote's early days in UFC. His first four fights in the Octagon against Tito Ortiz, Joe Doerksen, Chris Leben and Travis Lutter left the finalist of *The Ultimate Fighter* season four with a 0-4 record. "The Octagon was like a big monster for me in this sport," said Cote. With his back against the wall, he defeated Scott Smith at UFC 67, kicking off a four-fight UFC winning streak that earned him a shot at Anderson Silva's middleweight title. Unfortunately, a knee injury cut Cote's effort short in the third round. Two subsequent losses forced his release in 2010.

JOE DOERKSEN
NEW BOTHWELL, MANITOBA, CANADA

DEBUT: UFC 49, AUGUST 21, 2004

A throwback fighter who believes that the best way to get better is by actually competing, Joe "El Dirte" Doerksen's record in UFC may not stand out, but if there's one thing you could say about the Winnipeg product, it's that he always came to fight. Owner of 35 overall submission wins, it's not surprising that Doerksen's two Octagon victories over Patrick Cote and Tom Lawlor both came via rear-naked choke. Seven losses in UFC kept him from ever getting into title contention in the sport's ultimate proving ground, but the black belt's long career included bouts against Matt Hughes, Paulo Filho, Chris Leben, David Loiseau and Denis Kang.

JUSTIN EILERS
BOISE, ID

DEBUT: UFC 49, AUGUST 21, 2004

A former starting linebacker for Iowa State, Justin Eilers took off the pads and put on the gloves in 2002. Eventually, he fought his way into UFC.

Eagerly challenging the top fighters, Eilers knocked out Mike Kyle at UFC 49, but was victim of a first-round finish himself six months later against Paul Buentello.

Eilers received a title shot in his next bout, but against Andrei Arlovski, his body gave out on him as he tore his ACL en route to a first-round loss. After recovering, Eilers fought just once more in the Octagon, getting knocked out by Brandon Vera at UFC 57.

With a 10-2 record in his final 12, Eilers was making a name for himself in mixed martial arts. Sadly, he was shot and killed by his stepfather during a domestic dispute on December 25, 2008. He was only 30.

TRAVIS LUTTER
CHAMBERLAIN, SD

DEBUT: UFC 50, OCTOBER 22, 2004
THE ULTIMATE FIGHTER 4 WINNER

After his first-round dismantling of dangerous striker Patrick Cote in November 2006 to win the series finale of *The Ultimate Fighter* season four and earn a world title shot, soft-spoken Travis Lutter was confident about his chances against world champion Anderson Silva. The Brazilian jiu-jitsu black belt backed up those words by giving "The Spider" one of his toughest fights ever—despite not making weight for the championship bout.

In the end, Silva prevailed via submission in the second round. But after an injury-induced layoff, Lutter—who holds victories over Marvin Eastman, Jose Landi-Jons and Pete Sell—got back in the saddle against middleweight star Rich Franklin at UFC 83, only to lose that bout and his UFC contract.

IVAN MENJIVAR
LA PAZ DEPARTMENT, EL SALVADOR

DEBUT: UFC 48, JUNE 19, 2004

With a professional record that includes bouts against Georges St-Pierre, Matt Serra, Joe Lauzon, Caol Uno and Urijah Faber, it's safe to say that Ivan "The Pride of El Salvador" Menjivar has never ducked a challenge during his 13-year long stint in mixed martial arts.

Owner of impressive UFC wins over veteran Charlie Valencia and 135-pound prospects Nick Pace and John Albert, the fighting "Pride of El Salvador" has always been a throwback warrior.

As for his motivation for fighting, it was one close to his heart: "The people I have met, the great challenges that have faced me, and the opportunity to perform at a high level in what I love to do."

Frank Mir performs a bout-stopping armbar on Tim Sylvia at UFC 48.

"Liddell's his own man now, and for him to say that we were never friends, that's just BS, and he knows the truth," Ortiz said. "And when we fought, that was one of the reasons why I couldn't compete on the level that I usually did. It really hurt me a lot at that time, but now it's all hard feelings. We're acquaintances, no longer friends. When I see him, I say, 'Hey Chuck, what's up?' and that's as far as the conversation ever goes. I know in my mind, and I know it's in the back of his mind, that we're gonna fight again no matter what, but this time, there won't be any friendship factor at all—this is gonna be hatred, and I think I fight the best when I hate somebody."

In 2006, the two met once more, with the same result: Liddell winning by knockout.

At UFC 48 in Las Vegas on June 19, Shamrock knocked out Kimo Leopoldo in the first round of their main event rematch, but the most notable action took place midway through the main card. There, Frank Mir executed a frightening armbar that caused referee Herb Dean to halt the bout and Tim Sylvia to make his way to the disabled list with two broken bones in his arm. Mir won the UFC heavyweight title most had designated for him since his debut in 2001. Born and raised in Las Vegas, the marketable Mir had everything in his favor in terms of being UFC's golden boy in a division that normally ruled combat sports.

Three months later, on September 16, 2004, it all came to a screeching halt after Mir was blindsided by a car while riding his motorcycle. Thrown at least 70 feet from his bike, Mir's left femur broke, requiring four hours of surgery and forcing a titanium rod to be placed in his leg permanently. He didn't fight again until 2006, and he didn't regain championship form until 2008.

🏴 LEE MURRAY
LONDON, UNITED KINGDOM

DEBUT: UFC 46, JANUARY 31, 2004

In normal circumstances, a fighter with one UFC appearance wouldn't warrant a mention, even if that one bout were a win. But for right or wrong, "Lightning" Lee Murray remains one of the most fascinating characters to ever set foot in the organization, and it has nothing to do with his upset submission win over Jorge Rivera at UFC 46 in 2004. A brawler who once extended Anderson Silva the full distance, Murray first came to the attention of fans for a post-UFC 38 brawl with then-champion Tito Ortiz. His later notoriety was more ominous, though, as he participated in a 2006 robbery that netted more than 53 million pounds (approximately $81 million USD), making it the largest cash robbery in British history. He is currently incarcerated in Morocco.

🏴 TREVOR PRANGLEY
CAPE TOWN, SOUTH AFRICA

DEBUT: UFC 48, JUNE 19, 2004

An ultra-tough warrior who relocated to the United States from South Africa, Trevor Prangley was the type of fighter opponents never wanted to see across from them on fight night. They knew that unless they could submit him on the canvas, odds are that they were in for a long, grueling battle.

Prangley's toughness served him well as a two-time All-American wrestler for North Idaho, and as a mixed martial artist. He scored UFC victories over Curtis Stout and Travis Lutter during a four-fight stint in the promotion from 2004 to 2006.

On August 21, it was an eventful night at the MGM Grand, as Randy Couture settled his score with Vitor Belfort in the main event of UFC 49. He halted "The Phenom" in three rounds of their rubber match, regaining the UFC light heavyweight title in the process. It was Couture's record fourth title-winning effort.

In the UFC 49 co-feature, Liddell earned another shot at Couture's crown with an exciting first-round stoppage of a game Vernon White. White continually battled back from teeth-rattling blows early on to give Liddell hell, only to be sent to defeat with a big right hand that ended matters conclusively at the 4:05 mark.

Also victorious was middleweight contender David Terrell, who shocked fans and his peers in the division with a 24-second knockout of former world title challenger Matt Lindland.

Yves Edwards and Josh Thomson showed why the lightweight division was the destination for fast-paced, high-quality action in a bout where Edwards pulled a right high kick out of a comic book frame and sent Thomson crashing to defeat at the 4:32 mark of the first round. However, this bout was unfortunately the last 155-pound matchup in UFC until the division was reinstated at UFC 58 in 2006.

JOE RIGGS
PHOENIX, AZ

DEBUT: UFC 49, AUGUST 21, 2004

Owner of some of the heaviest hands in all of mixed martial arts, Joe Riggs has had quite a journey through the sport since his debut in 2001.

Starting off his career as a 300-pound heavyweight, Riggs fought anyone and everyone. Along the way, he kept shedding the pounds as he looked for his true weight class. Four years later, he found himself as a 170-pound contender, but he blew his biggest chance when he couldn't make weight for a title fight against Matt Hughes in 2005. Submitted that night by the champion, Riggs bounced back with a win over Nick Diaz, but losses in two of his next three fights forced him to fight elsewhere. He returned to UFC in 2014.

DAVID TERRELL
SACRAMENTO, CA

DEBUT: UFC 49, AUGUST 21, 2004

A gifted jiu-jitsu fighter who was pegged for greatness, Cesar Gracie black belt David "The Soul Assassin" Terrell instead saw his mixed martial arts career fall short of expectations due to repeated bouts with debilitating injuries.

An IFC and Grapplers Quest champion, Terrell debuted in the Octagon at UFC 49 with a stunning 24-second knockout of top contender Matt Lindland in August 2004. That victory propelled him into a title shot against Evan Tanner at UFC 51, but the veteran Tanner pulled off the victory in a significant upset. After being sidelined for over a year, Terrell returned at UFC 59 with a first-round submission of Scott Smith in 2006, but injuries ultimately kept him from competition.

RENATO VERISSIMO
RIO DE JANEIRO, RIO DE JANEIRO, BRAZIL

DEBUT: UFC 46, JANUARY 31, 2004

If you take a glance at Renato "Charuto" Verissimo's UFC record of 1-2, you will undoubtedly wonder what the big deal was. But during 2004 in UFC, he was one of the welterweight division's toughest contenders, one who might have challenged for world title honors if not for a close decision loss to Matt Hughes at UFC 48.

That defeat, and a subsequent one to Frank Trigg, forced his release from the organization. Nevertheless, hardcore fans will always refer to his dominant win over Carlos Newton at UFC 46, his pre-UFC victory over Gil Castillo and his long association with BJ Penn in Hawaii when discussing the talented Brazilian jiu-jitsu black belt.

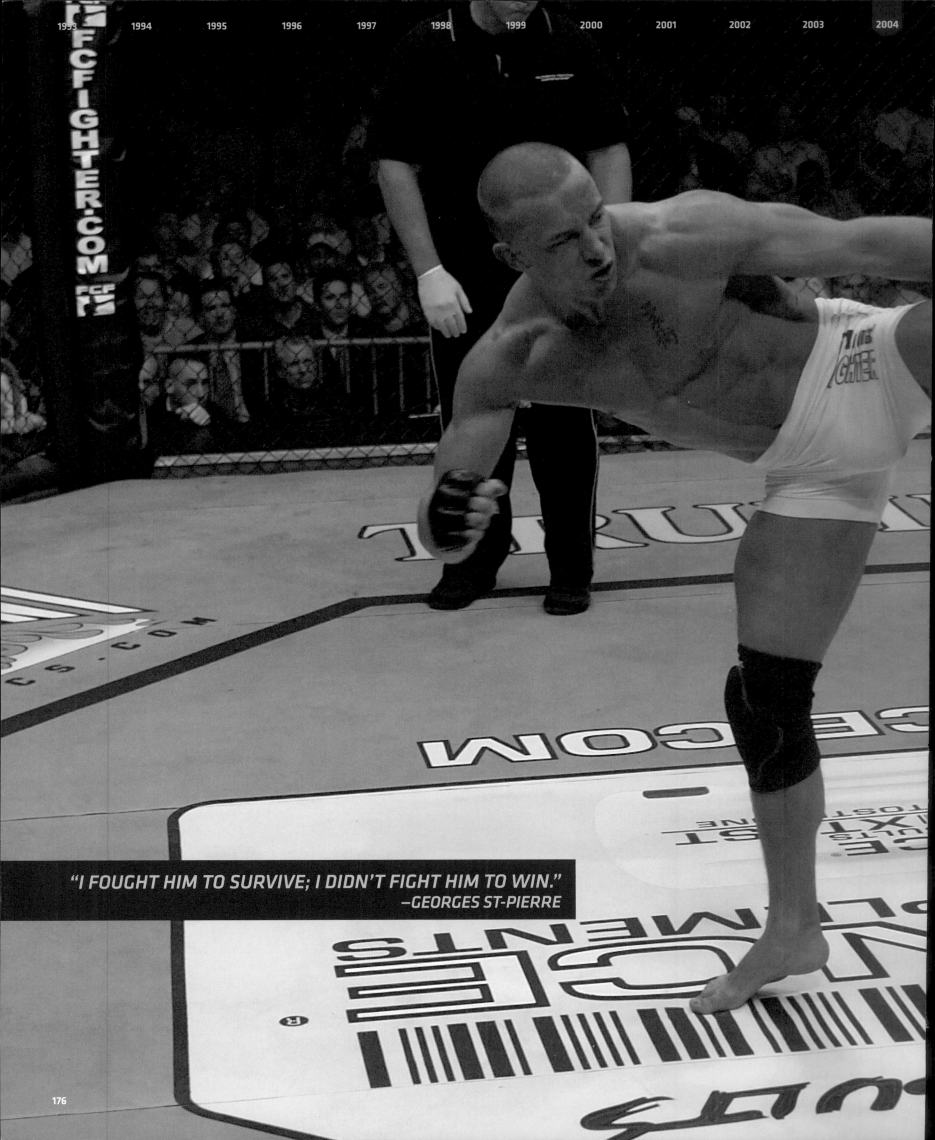

"I FOUGHT HIM TO SURVIVE; I DIDN'T FIGHT HIM TO WIN."
—GEORGES ST-PIERRE

Heading back east, UFC 50 took place at Boardwalk Hall in Atlantic City, New Jersey, and saw Ortiz break his two-fight losing streak with a lopsided unanimous decision win over late replacement Patrick Cote of Canada.

In the co-feature, Matt Hughes reigned once again, regaining the UFC welterweight crown vacated by BJ Penn by showing a new tool in his arsenal. He submitted a game Georges St-Pierre with an armbar at 4:59 of the first round. After setting things up with a good jab, St-Pierre used an effective single-leg takedown to put Hughes to the canvas seconds into the fight. Both quickly stood, and it was Hughes who used his left hand to work his opponent to the fence. Of course, moments later, Hughes lifted St-Pierre and dropped him to the canvas. St-Pierre worked his way out of trouble and used a left kick to the midsection to stun the former champion.

With a little over a minute to go, Hughes was able to take St-Pierre down, and he tried to work his ground-and-pound from the Canadian's guard. Suddenly, though, with the round ticking away, Hughes swung into an armbar. Just when an upset seemed possible by the 23-year-old, the veteran won the bout via tapout with a single second to go in the opening round.

"When I fought Hughes, I was afraid of him," St-Pierre later said. "I fought him to survive; I didn't fight him to win. I wasn't aggressive like I am usually, and I gave him too much respect. Every time I was going for something, I hesitated, and usually when I fight someone, I don't do this; I act instinctively." It was the last time GSP dealt with such issues against Matt Hughes.

FIGHTS OF THE YEAR

UFC 47

| LIDDELL | KO2 | ORTIZ |

UFC 49

| LIDDELL | KO1 | WHITE |

UFC 48

| TANNER | W3 | BARONI |

UFC 46

| ST-PIERRE | W3 | PARISYAN |

UFC 50
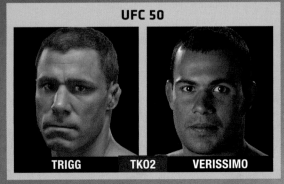

| TRIGG | TKO2 | VERISSIMO |

KNOCKOUTS OF THE YEAR

UFC 47
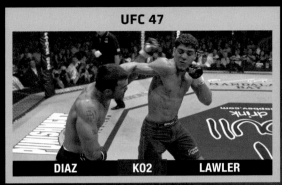

| DIAZ | KO2 | LAWLER |

UFC 49

| EDWARDS | KO1 | THOMPSON |

UFC 50

| LUTTER | KO2 | EASTMAN |

UFC 46

| MIR | KO2 | SIMS |

UFC 48
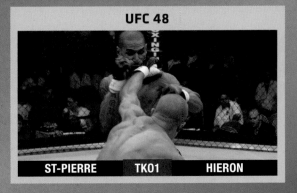

| ST-PIERRE | TKO1 | HIERON |

SUBMISSIONS OF THE YEAR

UFC 46

| PENN | WSUB1 | HUGHES |

UFC 48

| MIR | WSUB1 | SYLVIA |

UFC 50

| HUGHES | WSUB1 | ST-PIERRE |

UFC 47

| SUDO | WSUB1 | BROWN |

UFC 49

| LYTLE | WSUB2 | JHUN |

DEBUTS

UFC 46
- JEFF CURRAN
- GEORGES ST-PIERRE
- LEE MURRAY
- RENATO VERISSIMO

UFC 47
- MIKE BROWN
- JONATHAN WIEZOREK
- WADE SHIPP
- MIKE KYLE

UFC 48
- IVAN MENJIVAR
- TREVOR PRANGLEY
- JAY HIERON

UFC 49
- JOE DOERKSEN
- JOE RIGGS
- DAVID TERRELL
- JUSTIN EILERS
- RONALD JHUN

UFC 50
- TRAVIS LUTTER
- PATRICK COTE

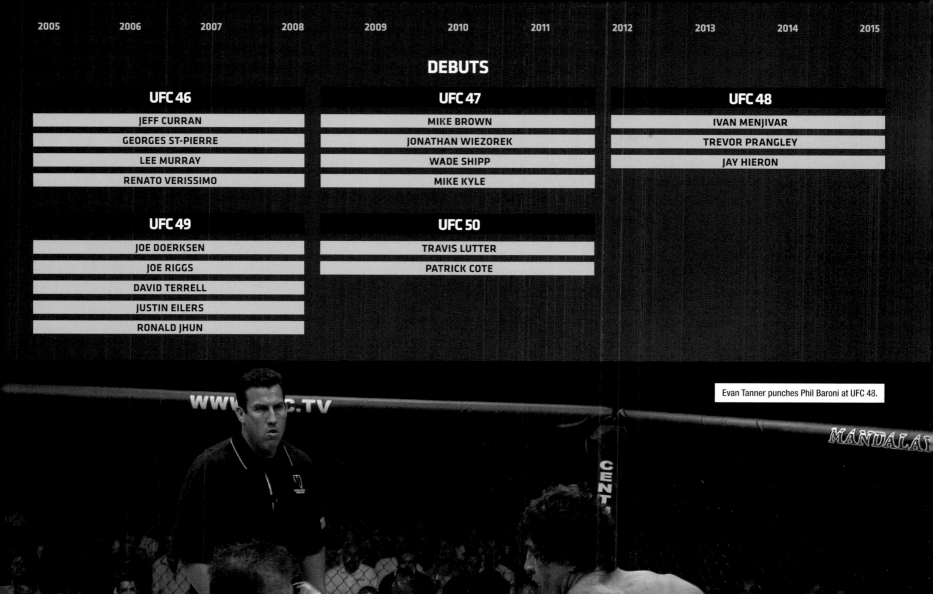

Evan Tanner punches Phil Baroni at UFC 48.

179

Today, UFC President Dana White calls *The Ultimate Fighter* the promotion's Trojan horse. Back in 2005, it was all that stood between UFC sticking around or going out of business.

The Zuffa ownership team of Frank Fertitta III, Lorenzo Fertitta, and Dana White bought the dying UFC brand in 2001. The team brought it to a place where the fights were great, the fans were happy, the sport was being sanctioned in states with major athletic commissions—like Nevada and New Jersey—and UFC was back on easily accessible Pay-Per-View. But it all came at a heavy price, somewhere around $44 million, and the end seemed near.

"It was brutal," White said. "We were waiting any day for the plug to be pulled. We felt like we were getting momentum and getting traction, but it wasn't enough to dig us out of the hole that we were in, and it didn't look like there was any light at the end of the tunnel. When was this gonna turn? Then, boom, *The Ultimate Fighter*."

"IT WAS BRUTAL. WE WERE WAITING ANY DAY FOR THE PLUG TO BE PULLED."
–UFC PRESIDENT, DANA WHITE

The Ultimate Fighter, a reality show that introduced viewers to the personalities behind those who fought in the Octagon while awarding a six-figure UFC contract to the winner of the season's elimination tournament, was a stroke of genius. As White said, it was a Trojan horse. Viewers tuned in for either reality show drama or the fights themselves. Subsequently, viewers built an emotional attachment with the athletes that kept them interested in the sport and those athletes long after the final episode aired. It was brilliant, but also risky. No network wanted to take that risk, so the UFC brass put up the money to produce the first season and bought airtime on the Spike TV cable network.

It was a success. The roll of the dice worked, but not until the season finale, which was the first full UFC card airing live on free national cable television. That night, UFC superstar Ken Shamrock headlined against up-and-comer Rich Franklin. But it was one of two *The Ultimate Fighter* final bouts that stole the show and kicked off the mixed martial arts explosion. Forrest Griffin and Stephan Bonnar engaged in what many still regard as the most important fight in UFC history.

Their three-round bout was a back-and-forth, action-packed, drama-filled war. It was one of those fights you can watch over and over and not grow tired of. It was worthy of being called great. While the fight was one to remember, the men who fought in it were what fans latched onto, and that's why people stuck around and wanted to see what happened next.

"People could relate to us," Bonnar said. "We were just regular guys, and we didn't take ourselves too seriously, and people like that."

Griffin compared the two to the cartoon characters Ralph Wolf and Sam Sheepdog. "They would clock in and beat each other up, then clock out and have their lunch," he said.

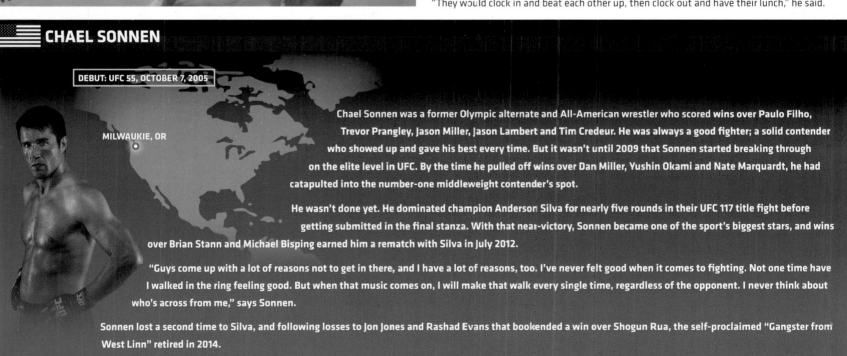

CHAEL SONNEN

DEBUT: UFC 55, OCTOBER 7, 2005

MILWAUKIE, OR

Chael Sonnen was a former Olympic alternate and All-American wrestler who scored wins over Paulo Filho, Trevor Prangley, Jason Miller, Jason Lambert and Tim Credeur. He was always a good fighter; a solid contender who showed up and gave his best every time. But it wasn't until 2009 that Sonnen started breaking through on the elite level in UFC. By the time he pulled off wins over Dan Miller, Yushin Okami and Nate Marquardt, he had catapulted into the number-one middleweight contender's spot.

He wasn't done yet. He dominated champion Anderson Silva for nearly five rounds in their UFC 117 title fight before getting submitted in the final stanza. With that near-victory, Sonnen became one of the sport's biggest stars, and wins over Brian Stann and Michael Bisping earned him a rematch with Silva in July 2012.

"Guys come up with a lot of reasons not to get in there, and I have a lot of reasons, too. I've never felt good when it comes to fighting. Not one time have I walked in the ring feeling good. But when that music comes on, I will make that walk every single time, regardless of the opponent. I never think about who's across from me," says Sonnen.

Sonnen lost a second time to Silva, and following losses to Jon Jones and Rashad Evans that bookended a win over Shogun Rua, the self-proclaimed "Gangster from West Linn" retired in 2014.

RASHAD EVANS

DEBUT: THE ULTIMATE FIGHTER 2 FINALE, NOVEMBER 5, 2005
THE ULTIMATE FIGHTER 2 WINNER
UFC LIGHT HEAVYWEIGHT CHAMPION

NIAGARA FALLS, NY

If you listened to the critics, "Suga" Rashad Evans never should have been here. Supposedly too small for heavyweight and not dynamic enough for light heavyweight, the former Michigan State University wrestler instead went on to become a UFC superstar. He won the title on *The Ultimate Fighter* season two at heavyweight before winning the UFC world title at 205 pounds.

Not that he's going to say, "I told you so."

"I surprised a lot of people, including [UFC president] Dana White," said Evans. "A lot of people thought that I didn't have any talent at all. See, I always had confidence in myself, but the better I did, people would say, 'Wow,' and they just couldn't believe it. I knew my own potential, but they didn't know, so it was a big surprise to them."

Following his graduation from MSU, Evans found a new calling in the sport of mixed martial arts. His wrestling acumen from a Division I career, and being a junior college national champion for Niagara Community College, served him well as he built an unbeaten record on the local circuit.

In 2005, he got his big break when he was selected to compete on *The Ultimate Fighter* season two. But at 5'11" and 220 pounds, he was a significant underdog going up against a host of heavyweights. Four wins later, though, he had a UFC contract in hand. As the winner of *The Ultimate Fighter*, a bright future was ahead, albeit in his natural weight class at 205 pounds.

The road wasn't easy, though, as wins over Sam Hoger and Stephan Bonnar weren't exactly met with great fanfare. Undeterred, Evans began showing off the new elements of his game in subsequent bouts; namely, a frightening ability to mix speed and power to produce highlight-reel knockouts.

Jason Lambert and Sean Salmon were both victims of Evans' striking ability. After a draw against Tito Ortiz and a decision win over Michael Bisping, "Suga" made his biggest statement at UFC 88 in 2008 with a one-punch right-hand knockout of future UFC Hall of Famer Chuck Liddell.

Next up after that defining win was a UFC light heavyweight championship bout against Forrest Griffin on December 27, 2008. At 2:46 of the third round, Evans became only the third man to win *The Ultimate Fighter* and UFC title when he stopped the second man to do it, Griffin.

Evans' reign and his unbeaten streak both came to a halt four months later when he was knocked out in the second round by Lyoto Machida. Fortunately, a stint as a coach on *The Ultimate Fighter* season 10 and back-to-back wins over Thiago Silva and Rampage Jackson in 2010 put him back on top. After scoring subsequent victories over Tito Ortiz, Dan Henderson and Chael Sonnen, he hopes that he will be wearing the gold belt around his waist once again—sooner rather than later.

That was the difference between perception and reality in a sport that got an undeserved and inaccurate rap from the start. To most non-fight fans back then, the idea of two men fighting in an Octagon meant that those two men were Neanderthals who hated each other and wanted nothing more than complete annihilation on fight night. You couldn't put them near each other before or after the fight because they were seemingly hard-wired to destroy and nothing else. Ignorant? Yes, but it wasn't an uncommon feeling among the uninformed.

The Ultimate Fighter helped chip away at some of those misconceptions, but Griffin and Bonnar tore them down completely. Griffin was a former police officer with a BA degree in political science from the University of Georgia; Bonnar was a Purdue University grad with a degree in sports medicine. They were educated, witty and affable. They also liked getting into sanctioned fistfights, and at the time of *The Ultimate Fighter* season one, the two were prospects in a sport where being a newcomer meant you weren't making any money. *The Ultimate Fighter* was the way out for the winner because victory in the tournament meant a six-figure contract with UFC.

Griffin won the fight and the contract that night, with the bout being so good that White and the Fertittas decided to give Bonnar a contract, too.

"It was a good fight," Griffin said in typical understatement. "I don't try to fix anything or think about what I should have done when I watch it. I do remember how exhausted I was. But it was what it was, and it worked out the way it needed to. Sometimes when you do things wrong, it still works out."

"I knew it was a good fight during the fight," Bonnar adds. "It hit me when everyone started stomping their feet and it felt like the whole place was shaking. And that was in the second round. I was like, 'Oooh, this must be good.'"

It was better than that; it was the rare moment where everybody won. That night behind the venue after the fight, UFC and Spike TV agreed on a deal to keep *The Ultimate Fighter* going. History was made, and UFC would not only survive, but also thrive.

The monumental event that was *The Ultimate Fighter* dominated 2005, but plenty of action was going on elsewhere in UFC that year. A highlight of the year began with a dream fight that finally came to fruition at UFC 51 on February 5. That night, former world champions Tito Ortiz and Vitor Belfort met in a bout that was originally supposed to take place at UFC 33 in 2001. While there was nothing on the line this time but bragging rights, the two light heavyweights fought as if that were all that mattered. Ortiz fought his way back into the 205-pound title picture with an exciting three-round split decision victory.

Arlovski submits Syliva for the interim UFC heavyweight crown at UFC 51.

THIAGO ALVES
FORTALEZA, CEARÁ, BRAZIL

DEBUT: ULTIMATE FIGHT NIGHT 2, OCTOBER 3, 2005

Given Thiago "Pitbull" Alves' ever-present smile and laidback demeanor, you wouldn't expect him to live up to his nickname in the Octagon. But when the bell rings on fight night, you won't find any welterweight more feared than the native of Fortaleza, Brazil.

That's now. In the early stages of Alves' UFC career, which began with a submission loss to Spencer Fisher on October 3, 2005, his reputation was that of an ultra-talented rising star who wasn't devoting the proper time to his chosen craft in the gym. That meant that when he was on, he gave anyone at 170 pounds fits. When he wasn't, he was merely average.

After the loss to Jon Fitch in June 2006, though, Alves realized that he would never reach the next level if he didn't train as hard as he fought. The transformation was amazing, and from October 2006 to October 2008, he was unstoppable. Alves won seven fights in a row, including TKO victories over Chris Lytle and Karo Parisyan, a knockout of Matt Hughes and a decision win over Josh Koscheck.

The 7-0 run earned him a shot at Georges St-Pierre's welterweight title at UFC 100 on July 11, 2009, but he lost a lopsided five-round unanimous decision. He hasn't abandoned his dream of championship gold, though, and he is still chasing glory in the Octagon.

JOE STEVENSON
TORRANCE, CA

DEBUT: THE ULTIMATE FIGHTER 2 FINALE, NOVEMBER 5, 2005
THE ULTIMATE FIGHTER 2 WINNER

Joe "Daddy" Stevenson was done. After fighting professionally since the age of 16, he compiled an impressive mixed martial arts record in more than 30 fights. Basically, he did whatever was asked of him as a fighter without reaping the benefits of such dedication. It was time to move on; time to think about doing something else for a living. Then he received a phone call that changed his life as he was asked to compete in Spike TV's *The Ultimate Fighter*. The reality series saved the career of Forrest Griffin in its first season, and in its second, Stevenson got a new lease on his career after he beat Luke Cummo in the welterweight finale in 2006.

From there, the popular Joe "Daddy" dropped down to the lightweight division, squaring off with the best in the game. After a four-fight winning streak in 2006-2007, he was pegged to face BJ Penn for the vacant UFC lightweight title.

Sometimes, you learn more about a fighter in defeat than you do in victory. That was the case when Stevenson fell short to Penn at UFC 80; he showed both his prodigious talent and the heart of a champion as he battled through a bad cut.

MIKE SWICK
HOUSTON, TX

DEBUT: THE ULTIMATE FIGHTER 1 FINALE, APRIL 9, 2005

A cast member of *The Ultimate Fighter* season one, Houston native Mike "Quick" Swick certainly lived up to his nickname "Quick" in his first four UFC bouts. It only took him a combined five minutes and 10 seconds to take out Alex Schoenauer, Gideon Ray, Steve Vigneault and Joe Riggs in spectacular fashion.

But after defeating David Loiseau, Swick hit the middleweight wall in April 2007 as he lost to Yushin Okami. The defeat gave him the opening he needed to make a move down to welterweight, and he went on to score victories over Josh Burkman, Marcus Davis, Jonathan Goulet, DaMarques Johnson and Ben Saunders. Losses to Paulo Thiago, Dan Hardy and Matt Brown held him back, but after a long break in which he spent time with his family and opened a gym in Thailand, he expects to make a return to the top when he comes back to the Octagon in 2015.

In undercard action, the long and frustrating wait for Belarus bomber Andrei Arlovski was over, as he finally got his title shot and made the most of it. He submitted former champ Tim Sylvia to earn the interim UFC heavyweight crown made available when champion Frank Mir was injured in a motorcycle accident in September 2004. Following a long dry period, UFC finally got a middleweight champion after veteran Evan Tanner stopped David Terrell in the first round of a scheduled five-round title bout.

PAUL BUENTELLO
AMARILLO, TX

DEBUT: UFC 51, FEBRUARY 5, 2005

An old-school brawler with dynamite in his fists, Paul "The Headhunter" Buentello wasn't fancy, but he was effective. Winner of nearly 20 bouts before he even engaged in a UFC match, Buentello finished off Justin Eilers and Kevin Jordan in back-to-back Octagon contests in 2005. This earned him a shot at heavyweight champion Andrei Arlovski at UFC 55 on October 7, 2005. In this battle of gunslingers, Arlovski drew first, halting Buentello in 15 seconds. "The Headhunter" rebounded with a win over Gilbert Aldana, but he wouldn't return to UFC for nearly four years as he fought in other organizations. When he came back, he lost consecutive bouts to Stefan Struve and Cheick Kongo.

JOSH BURKMAN
SALT LAKE CITY, UT

DEBUT: THE ULTIMATE FIGHTER 2 FINALE, NOVEMBER 5, 2005

Football was Josh "The People's Warrior" Burkman's first love, but when the JUCO All-American running back discovered mixed martial arts, he turned down a scholarship to the University of Utah to pursue a career in the fight game. Two years into his new endeavor, he was chosen to compete on season two of The Ultimate Fighter. After defeating Melvin Guillard, a broken hand eliminated him from the show. From there, the well-rounded Burkman went on to win five of seven UFC bouts against the likes of Sam Morgan, Drew Fickett, Josh Neer and Forrest Petz. A three-bout losing streak against Mike Swick, Dustin Hazelett and Pete Sell in 2008 forced his absence from the organization for nearly seven years.

MARCIO CRUZ
RIO DE JANEIRO, BRAZIL

DEBUT: UFC 55, OCTOBER 7, 2005

One of the rare fighters to make his MMA debut inside the UFC Octagon, Marcio "Pe de Pano" Cruz wasn't a mere rookie when he opened his career in October 2005 with a submission win over Keigo Kunihara. In fact, he was one of the game's most decorated grapplers—a six-time Brazilian jiu-jitsu world champion and five-time national champion. But it was his striking that garnered him his biggest win when he spoiled the comeback of former UFC champion Frank Mir at UFC 57, stopping him in the first round. That win was the highlight of "Pe de Pano's" UFC stay, which saw him drop his last two bouts in the organization to Jeff Monson and Andrei Arlovski.

Tanner is victorious against Terrell, becoming the middleweight champion.

Following the first card in *The Ultimate Fighter*'s finale, which also saw Diego Sanchez crowned the season's middleweight winner thanks to a TKO win over Kenny Florian, UFC was back in Vegas seven days later for UFC 52. The rematch between Randy Couture and Chuck Liddell headlined this event. This time, Liddell evened the score with "The Natural," obtaining a first-round knockout win. It had been a long time coming for "The Iceman"—seven years to be exact—but despite this stirring win, it was Matt Hughes and Frank Trigg who stole the show on April 16.

🇺🇸 DIEGO SANCHEZ

DEBUT: THE ULTIMATE FIGHTER 1 FINALE, APRIL 9, 2005
***THE ULTIMATE FIGHTER 1* WINNER**

ALBUQUERQUE, NM

Diego "The Nightmare" Sanchez is one of the most popular stars in mixed martial arts, but he hasn't been handed anything on his way to the top.

A native of Albuquerque, New Mexico, Sanchez first rose to prominence when he won the first season of the reality show *The Ultimate Fighter* by defeating Kenny Florian. He subsequently built a stellar pro record 19-0 that included UFC wins over Karo Parisyan, Nick Diaz and Joe Riggs.

But in 2007, Sanchez hit a wall, losing back-to-back decisions to Josh Koscheck and Jon Fitch while also going through the transition of changing his training team and relocating to California.

In 2008, Sanchez returned with an unyielding vengeance, scoring a submission win over David Bielkheden and then stopping Luigi Fioravanti to improve to 21-2. The win over Fioravanti was particularly revealing for the groundfighting ace as he showed off an ever-improving standup game.

Sanchez made his move in 2009, dropping to the 155-pound weight class and quickly defeating respected contenders Joe Stevenson and Clay Guida to earn a title shot against 155-pound champion BJ Penn. But in their UFC 107 bout, "The Prodigy" was too much for Sanchez, and he stopped him in the fifth round.

In 2010, Sanchez suffered a second consecutive loss when he was upset by John Hathaway, but this time, he knew what was missing: a return to his roots and his original trainer, Greg Jackson. The reunion was a success, as Sanchez went on to thrill fans with Fight of the Night battles against Paulo Thiago, Martin Kampmann, Jake Ellenberger and Gilbert Melendez, proving himself as one of UFC's most reliable action heroes.

JON FITCH

DEBUT: ULTIMATE FIGHT NIGHT 2, OCTOBER 3, 2005

FORT WAYNE, IN

In the American Kickboxing Academy gym in San Jose, California, the first man to earn the title "Captain" was welterweight standout Jon Fitch.

"Jon wasn't the greatest athlete when he came here," said Javier Mendez, founder of AKA. "What he had was the greatest mind and determination." Those traits carried the Fort Wayne, Indiana, native through high school and college wrestling, and he capped off his amateur career as a four-year letterman and team captain for the Purdue Boilermakers.

With his assistant coach at Purdue, Tom Erikson, being a former PRIDE star, it wasn't surprising that Fitch decided to give MMA a go after graduation. His early days in the game saw him struggle to a 2-2 record that included losses to future UFC fighters Mike Pyle and Wilson Gouveia.

Undeterred, Fitch ran off a seven-fight winning streak, and in October 2005, he received his shot in the Octagon. He made the most of it by defeating Brock Larson via decision, the first of eight victories that tied Royce Gracie for most consecutive wins in UFC history—a record since broken by Anderson Silva. Fitch's defeats of Thiago Alves and Diego Sanchez earned him a shot at Georges St-Pierre's welterweight title at UFC 87 in August 2008.

That night in Minnesota, Fitch showed the heart of a lion in what St-Pierre has called his toughest fight ever. Although he lost a five-round decision to the champion that night, he left a lasting impression with fight fans. Fitch fought in UFC until 2013.

KEITH JARDINE
BUTTE, MT

DEBUT: THE ULTIMATE FIGHTER 2 FINALE, NOVEMBER 5, 2005

Make no mistake about it: Keith "The Dean of Mean" Jardine likes the underdog role. "I love that role," he said. "All I've got to do is go out and be my best, and that's my goal."

But there's a fine line between being the underdog and being underestimated. Jardine wants to make it clear that the real "Dean of Mean" was the one who scored monumental wins over Forrest Griffin, Brandon Vera and Chuck Liddell, not the one who fell short against Wanderlei Silva and Thiago Silva. Win or lose, Jardine is respected by his peers and loved by his fans.

TERRY MARTIN
CHICAGO, IL

DEBUT: UFC 54, AUGUST 20, 2005

With a Master's degree in psychology to accompany his knockout punch, Terry Martin was one of UFC's most intriguing fighters. But after losses to James Irvin and Jason Lambert in the light heavyweight division, the Chicago native was in danger of never reaching a mainstream audience.

With his career on the line, Martin dropped down to 185 pounds and took on Jorge Rivera at UFC 67. The change couldn't have been more dramatic, as Martin knocked Rivera out in just 14 spectacular seconds, proving that he had found a new home. The glory was short-lived, though, as a knockout of Ivan Salaverry came before consecutive defeats to Chris Leben and Marvin Eastman. Martin was released in 2008.

In the evening's second title bout, the UFC welterweight champ made it two in a row over Trigg, sending "Twinkle Toes" to defeat via a rear-naked choke in a rematch that packed more drama into 4:05 than most do in five rounds.

After an opening stare down, the two combatants met at the center of the cage and traded punches until a lock-up. While against the cage, Trigg caught Hughes with a low knee that referee Mario Yamasaki didn't catch. As Hughes retreated and tried to regain his bearings, Trigg pounced and sent Hughes to the canvas with a left to the jaw.

STEPHAN BONNAR

DEBUT: THE ULTIMATE FIGHTER 1 FINALE, APRIL 9, 2005
UFC HALL OF FAME (2013)

HAMMOND, IN

One half of what many consider the greatest UFC fight of all time, Stephan "The American Psycho" Bonnar still remains humble after putting mixed martial arts on the map with Forrest Griffin in 2005. In fact, he admits that he just happened to stumble on the sport that became his vocation in life.

"I did it kind of as a hobby," Bonnar explains. "I always loved fighting, and I did wrestling and taekwondo growing up and got into jiu-jitsu and boxing. And I really just wanted to get better, so what's the best way to get better? Enter a competition and see where you're at. Then you enter another one. Then with boxing, it's like, 'Let me enter the Golden Gloves and see how good I am.' It just keeps escalating. Each time you win or each tournament you do, you get a little better. And then with the mixed martial arts, why not try it? I won some fights and got some bigger fights, and it pretty much just snowballed. And it wasn't something that I really planned on doing— it was something I always wanted to, and I'm really thankful to find myself here."

A pro since 2001 whose only early loss came via cuts to Lyoto Machida in 2003, Bonnar was part of the grand experiment in 2005 known as *The Ultimate Fighter*. "I remember [UFC president] Dana White being worried that the show wasn't even gonna make it to TV, and I could tell he was worried that it wouldn't be a success," Bonnar recalled.

"For some reason, in my mind, I was like, 'What, are you kidding me? This thing's gonna be a hit, and we're gonna have a bunch of seasons like this.' I always thought it was gonna be the coolest show ever."

After beating Bobby Southworth and Mike Swick, Bonnar made it to the season finale against Griffin, and what happened next was nothing short of amazing. For three rounds, Bonnar and Griffin threw caution to the wind and engaged in a fight for the ages. When it was over, Griffin had won the razor-thin unanimous decision.

Dana White was so impressed with Bonnar's effort that he awarded him a UFC contract on the spot. After three straight wins over Sam Hoger, James Irvin and Keith Jardine, Bonnar proved that decision was the correct one.

Two decision losses followed, one to Rashad Evans and the second to Griffin in their long-awaited rematch. However, worse news came when Bonnar was suspended for nine months after a positive test for the banned substance Boldenone following the Griffin bout.

After his suspension was up, Bonnar was back in form with finishes of Mike Nickels and Eric Schafer. However, disaster struck again from a knee injury that required reconstructive surgery. When Bonnar returned 15 months later, he was defeated via decision by young phenom Jon Jones at UFC 94, and then by UFC Hall of Famer Mark Coleman at UFC 100.

"When you're fighting a lot, you're not that worried about it because you know you're in shape," said Bonnar. "There were like six months when I just couldn't do anything in terms of training, and once I did start, it was a real gradual process. So in my mind, I said, 'I gotta keep pushing more, gotta keep training harder,' and looking back now, I see that it was a mistake."

Down but not out, Bonnar entered 2010 with his career on the line. While he lost an exciting war with Krzysztof Soszynski at UFC 110, he avenged the loss by TKO five months later in another instant classic. He finished the year by defeating Croatia's Igor Pokrajac via decision, proving that "The American Psycho" was back. Bonnar's last UFC bout was a 2012 loss to Anderson Silva. He was inducted into the UFC Hall of Fame on July 6, 2013.

> "I REALLY JUST WANTED TO GET BETTER, SO WHAT'S THE BEST WAY TO GET BETTER? ENTER A COMPETITION AND SEE WHERE YOU'RE AT."
> —STEPHAN BONNAR

LUKE CUMMO
NEW HYDE PARK, NY

DEBUT: THE ULTIMATE FIGHTER 2 FINALE, NOVEMBER 5, 2005

If you were building the stereotype of a fighter, he wouldn't look like Luke "The Silent Assassin" Cummo, and that's just fine with the New Yorker. "I'm probably always going to be the underdog just because I'm skinny," he said. "I like proving people wrong." And beginning with his time on season two of *The Ultimate Fighter*, he did just that, defeating Anthony Torres and Sammy Morgan to shock the field and earn a place in the finals. On that night in 2005, Cummo lost a hard-fought three-round decision to Joe Stevenson. He went on to defeat Jason Von Flue, Josh Haynes and Edilberto Crocota before a two-fight losing streak prompted his release.

MARCUS DAVIS
HOULTON, ME

DEBUT: THE ULTIMATE FIGHTER 2 FINALE, NOVEMBER 5, 2005

After a successful 17-1-2 boxing career, Marcus "The Irish Hand Grenade" Davis believed the conventional wisdom that a legit pro boxer would have no problem knocking out anyone in his path in mixed martial arts. He was wrong. Davis learned the hard way as he lost three of his first six bouts, including a TKO defeat against *The Ultimate Fighter* season two castmate Melvin Guillard in 2005. But then Davis flipped the script, learned the ground game and ran off an 11-fight winning streak that featured six submission wins and six UFC victories. The ultra-popular "Irish Hand Grenade" eventually hit some landmines, though, losing four of his last five Octagon bouts before being released in 2011.

DREW FICKETT
TAMPA, FL

DEBUT: UFC 51, FEBRUARY 5, 2005

A seasoned veteran, Arizona-born Drew "The Master" Fickett's reputation as a gifted gatekeeper for rising stars earned him respect from his peers and fans. Fickett used submission wins over young guns Josh Koscheck, Kurt Pellegrino and Josh Neer to cement his role as a tough opponent for anyone at 170 pounds.

He explained, "Once I get hit one time, I'm all about strategy; I'm all about how can I win. If I'm fighting, I'm going to fight until the very end. There's always a way to pull it out and always a way to get that victory."

Fickett finished up his UFC career in 2007 with a decision win over Keita Nakamura.

SPENCER FISHER
CASHIERS, NC

DEBUT: ULTIMATE FIGHT NIGHT 2, OCTOBER 3, 2005

Spencer "The King" Fisher was an exciting slugger who proved himself over the years as a fighter who never rested on his laurels. He has wins over highly regarded contenders Thiago Alves and Matt Wiman, and was also a participant in three classics with Sam Stout.

"I don't focus on anything else outside of my own fight," said Fisher. "Those guys were all tough and they deserve to be there, but my opinion is, you're only as good as your last fight."

Well, if his subsequent UFC wins against Caol Uno, Jeremy Stephens, Shannon Gugerty and Curt Warburton are any indication, "The King" has been pretty damn good.

GABRIEL GONZAGA
RIO DE JANEIRO, BRAZIL

DEBUT: UFC 56, NOVEMBER 19, 2005

Gabriel "Napao" Gonzaga's rise up the heavyweight ranks in 2005-2007 was nothing short of spectacular. His wins over Kevin Jordan, Fabiano Scherner and Carmelo Marrero, along with an unforgettable highlight-reel knockout of Mirko Cro Cop at UFC 70, put the Brazilian jiu-jitsu black belt on the world map as a top contender.

In August 2007, his well-deserved title shot arrived, but Randy Couture halted him in three rounds at UFC 74. Over the ensuing years, Gonzaga became a popular gatekeeper for the division, fighting the best of the best at every turn.

MELVIN GUILLARD
NEW ORLEANS, LA

DEBUT: THE ULTIMATE FIGHTER 2 FINALE, NOVEMBER 5, 2005

The life of Melvin "The Young Assassin" Guillard had seen its share of ups and downs, from surviving Hurricane Katrina and the death of his father a couple years later, to other, out of the ring, issues that threatened his career. But the resilient veteran of *The Ultimate Fighter* season two was not about to let his talent go to waste.

After a 3-3 start to his UFC career, Guillard bounced back. With a renewed focus, he won nine bouts over the likes of Mac Danzig, Evan Dunham, Jeremy Stephens, Gleison Tibau and Ronys Torres before being released in 2014.

In serious trouble, Hughes caught a flurry of blows on the ground as Trigg worked his way into the mounted position. Hughes tried to escape the bottom but wound up giving Trigg his back at the three-minute mark. The challenger quickly capitalized with a rear-naked choke. Hughes' face turned crimson, but amazingly, he escaped. He then followed up this good fortune by picking his foe up and carrying him across the cage before dropping him on his back with a trademark slam.

Now it was Hughes in control, and in full mount, he opened up on Trigg with both hands. With the packed house going wild, Trigg then turned, and it was Hughes sinking in a rear-naked choke. That choke produced a tapout at the 4:05 mark, ending one of the greatest fights of all time.

On June 4, UFC's middleweight title changed hands once again. Former high school math teacher Rich Franklin followed up his April win over Ken Shamrock with a fourth-round stoppage of Evan Tanner at UFC 53 in Atlantic City. In the main event, Arlovski successfully defended his interim heavyweight title with a first-round stoppage of Justin Eilers.

In August, Liddell got some more payback in defense of his title, as he halted Jeremy Horn, the first man to beat him in UFC, in four rounds. In October, newly elevated heavyweight champion Arlovski celebrated shaking the interim tag by knocking out Paul Buentello in 15 seconds.

November saw two more *The Ultimate Fighter* champions crowned, as Rashad Evans defeated Brad Imes and Joe Stevenson beat Luke Cummo to earn season two titles. Two weeks later, on November 19, one of the most pivotal years in UFC history came to a close. Franklin knocked out Nate Quarry in defense of his middleweight crown, and Hughes submitted Joe Riggs in what turned into a non-title bout when Riggs failed to make weight.

JASON MILLER
FAYETTEVILLE, NC

DEBUT: UFC 52, APRIL 16, 2005

One of MMA's most intriguing figures, Jason "Mayhem" Miller came back to UFC in 2011 after a six-year absence where he fought the likes of Jake Shields, Robbie Lawler, Tim Kennedy and Ronaldo Souza. He also gained worldwide fame for his stint as the host of MTV's *Bully Beatdown*.

He lost his return bouts to Michael "The Count" Bisping—his opposing coach on *The Ultimate Fighter* season 14—as well as to CB Dollaway. He was subsequently cut from the promotion.

JOSH NEER
DES MOINES, IA

DEBUT: ULTIMATE FIGHT NIGHT 1, AUGUST 6, 2005

A three-sport athlete in high school, Josh "The Dentist" Neer found his true calling in the sport of mixed martial arts, where he scored six UFC wins in a career that began in 2003.

"I just love going in there and getting in a war," he said. "It's the best thing in the world; it's just me against the other guy, and I don't want to be the guy who falls first."

Known as "The Dentist" for his tendency to rearrange his opponents' teeth, Neer has long been one of the sport's most rugged warriors. He put that attribute to good use in Octagon victories against Din Thomas, Mac Danzig, Melvin Guillard and Joe Stevenson.

NATE QUARRY
ARCATA, CA

DEBUT: THE ULTIMATE FIGHTER 1 FINALE, APRIL 9, 2005

A member of *The Ultimate Fighter* season one's cast, Nate "Rock" Quarry roared up the middleweight ranks with unbelievable speed, scoring knockouts of Lodune Sincaid, Shonie Carter and Pete Sell to earn a 185-pound title shot in 2005 against Rich Franklin. Franklin turned him back that night via first-round knockout. After surgery for a serious back injury, some thought Quarry would never fight again.

But fighters like the "Rock" don't quit that easily. After an exhaustive rehab, he came back with wins over Pete Sell, Kalib Starnes, Jason MacDonald and Tim Credeur. Only losses against Demian Maia and Jorge Rivera kept him from a perfect comeback record.

KENNY FLORIAN

DEBUT: THE ULTIMATE FIGHTER 1 FINALE, APRIL 9, 2005

WESTWOOD, MA

As a senior project manager for a translation firm following his graduation from Boston College, where he was also a Division I soccer player, Kenny "KenFlo" Florian's post-graduate life appeared pretty well set.

It wasn't, at least not in the eyes of the competitive Florian, who was soon testing his jiu-jitsu black belt in local mixed martial arts shows in Massachusetts. In one of those shows, he caught the eye of UFC president, Dana White. By 2005, he was in America's living rooms as a member of *The Ultimate Fighter* season one's cast.

Following that life-altering moment, his road to respect took him from the first season finale of *The Ultimate Fighter* and the 185-pound weight class all the way down to the 145-pound featherweight division.

In between 185 and 145, Florian was virtually unstoppable. Among his 12 Octagon wins were victories over Din Thomas, Joe Lauzon, Roger Huerta, Joe Stevenson, Clay Guida, Takanori Gomi, Sam Stout and Alex Karalexis. His only losses came against top contenders Diego Sanchez and Gray Maynard, and in title bouts against Sean Sherk, BJ Penn and Jose Aldo.

All the while, all that mattered for "KenFlo" was making good on his potential while still chasing that elusive goal of perfection. "Every single day is to get better to the point where it's perfection. I know it's an impossibility, but that's my goal every single day, to have flawless technique, and in everything I do, I want it to be perfect. If I have that in my mind but never get down because it's not perfect, then I'll have the perfect mindset."

ALESSIO SAKARA
ROME, ITALY

DEBUT: UFC 55, OCTOBER 7, 2005

After building a reputation as a fighter to watch in UFC from his fights against Ron Faircloth and Elvis Sinosic, Alessio "Legionarius" Sakara hit a wall in his MMA career with losses to Dean Lister, Drew McFedries and Houston Alexander. But beginning with UFC 80 in January 2008, this former pro boxer showed his resilience and style. He stopped James Lee in the first round, engaged in a memorable scrap with Chris Leben and then added a highlight-reel knockout to his resume with his KO of Joe Vedepo in September 2009. "Legionarius" wasn't through yet; he defeated Thales Leites and James Irvin before seeing his winning streak end in 2011 at the hands of Chris Weidman.

BRANDON VERA
NORFOLK, VA

DEBUT: ULTIMATE FIGHT NIGHT 2, OCTOBER 3, 2005

Brandon "The Truth" Vera's talent was always undeniable. Whether fighting at heavyweight or light heavyweight, "The Truth" was seemingly just a win or two away from competing for a UFC title shot. But despite his often stirring wins over Frank Mir, Justin Eilers and Michael Patt, losses in his biggest bouts against the likes of Randy Couture, Jon Jones, Tim Sylvia and Shogun Rua kept him from glory in the Octagon, prompting his release from the promotion in 2014.

Stevenson vs Cummo, The Ultimate Fighter 2 Finale

🇺🇸 JOSH KOSCHECK

DEBUT: THE ULTIMATE FIGHTER 1 FINALE, APRIL 9, 2005

WAYNESBURG, PA

Josh Koscheck, a four-time All-American wrestler and 2001 NCAA champion for Edinboro University, knows all about pressure. He was 37-0 entering the 2001 NCAA championships, and one wrong move could have kept him from finishing his dream season undefeated. But that was the kind of pressure he enjoyed, and he took that attitude with him into UFC.

No ordinary fighter, Koscheck turned from a dominant yet one-dimensional wrestler on *The Ultimate Fighter* season one into the type of well-rounded fighter who could give anyone fits wherever the bout goes. He was especially devastating was his right hand, a weapon that led him to victory over Dustin Hazelett, Yoshiyuki Yoshida and Frank Trigg.

Along the way, Koscheck also became a polarizing figure thanks to his bold statements and occasional trash talk, which was on full display when he returned to *The Ultimate Fighter* as a coach for season twelve.

Koscheck experienced his share of highs and lows, including a five-round decision loss at UFC 124 to the only man to beat him twice: then-UFC welterweight champion Georges St-Pierre. Nevertheless, he was always determined to show the world just what he could do when he was firing on all cylinders.

"At this level, you're gonna get to see a lot of speed, a lot of power, a lot of technique and a lot of skill. So now it's a question of who's going to have the mental edge. Who's gonna break first, and who's gonna impose their will on the other person?"

🇺🇸 CHRIS LEBEN

DEBUT: THE ULTIMATE FIGHTER 1 FINALE, APRIL 9, 2005

PORTLAND, OR

This sparkplug from *The Ultimate Fighter* season one used his aggressive style and brash personality to gain a legion of fans while building an unbeaten 5-0 Octagon record that included wins over Patrick Cote, Edwin Dewees, Jorge Rivera and Luigi Fioravanti. Chris "The Crippler" Leben then hit hard times over a 12-month period in 2006-2007 as he was beaten by soon-to-be UFC middleweight champion Anderson Silva, as well as Jason MacDonald and Kalib Starnes. He only managed one knockout win over Jorge Santiago.

But "The Crippler" was not one to give up on his dream of a world championship. He got back to business in September 2007 with a spectacular knockout of Terry Martin, and he followed that win up with an even more impressive victory over Alessio Sakara.

After two losses against Michael Bisping and Jake Rosholt, the Portland native truly showed that he was back in middleweight title contention with a trifecta 2010 wins over Jay Silva, Aaron Simpson and Yoshihiro Akiyama, the latter two victories coming just two weeks apart.

Despite a subsequent loss to Brian Stann at UFC 125, a 27-second knockout over Wanderlei Silva in July 2011 was a career-defining one, showing just how far he had come since his days on reality television.

"My career's definitely been through a lot of ups and downs since then, and I'd like to think I've improved quite a bit and gained a lot of experience both inside and outside the ring." Leben retired in January 2014.

🇺🇸 NATE MARQUARDT
LANDER, WY

DEBUT: ULTIMATE FIGHT NIGHT 1, AUGUST 6, 2005
STRIKEFORCE WELTERWEIGHT CHAMPION

There are plenty of class acts in the world of MMA, and one of those people you will never hear a bad word about is middleweight contender and former STRIKEFORCE welterweight champion Nate "The Great" Marquardt.

That type of class is a great attribute to have, but when you're a fighter in a business where the squeaky wheel is often the one that gets oiled, it can be a problem. It's been a particular issue with Marquardt, whose talent in the sport is matched by his previous accomplishments, which include recognition as a seven-time King of Pancrase while competing in Japan.

But beginning with his UFC debut in 2005, Marquardt still brought the "nice guy" into the Octagon with him. While he won his first four fights, he lost the fifth, a UFC title fight against Anderson Silva in 2007. In 2008, he added a new mindset to his arsenal: strike first; ask questions later. The results have amazed fight fans, as several of his wins over Martin Kampmann, Wilson Gouveia, Demian Maia, Tyron Woodley and Rousimar Palhares have come by knockout.

He's still a nice guy and a class act, but not when the horn sounds.

FORREST GRIFFIN

DEBUT: THE ULTIMATE FIGHTER 1 FINALE, APRIL 9, 2005
THE ULTIMATE FIGHTER 1 WINNER
UFC LIGHT HEAVYWEIGHT CHAMPION
UFC HALL OF FAME (2013)

COLUMBUS, OH

In 2005, shortly after winning , the idea of stardom hadn't set in for Forrest Griffin. Forget that he almost single-handedly put mixed martial arts on the mainstream map with his stirring three-round victory over Stephan Bonnar on April 16, 2005, and captivated a nation with his self-effacing humor and ability to smile through a mask of blood. He was just another guy taking out his stitches with an X-Acto knife nine days after the biggest fight of his life.

He remained the same guy, and celebrity sat unsteadily on his head. He'd rather have a good book (particularly one of the two New York Times bestsellers that he's written) in his hands than do the rounds of the hottest clubs. Life was always fairly simple: train, eat, train, sleep, train, fight. Throw in the usual media obligations, and you've got the picture.

But as the years went by, the Georgia product was no longer an unknown brawler looking to make a name for himself while trying to earn a spot in UFC. Instead, he was a former world champion and one of the seminal figures in the rise of the sport.

By staying humble and grounded, he's been able to keep himself on an even keel. In this game, more than in any other, there are no guarantees, and Griffin's career is a case study.

On top of the world after beating Bonnar in April 2005, Griffin won his next two bouts over Bill Mahood and Elvis Sinosic before a high-profile clash with former UFC light heavyweight boss Tito Ortiz in April 2006. On a UFC 59 card aptly titled "Reality Check," Griffin survived a frightful first-round beating to come back and arguably win the next two rounds. He lost a close decision to Ortiz, but his stock may have risen even higher in defeat.

That wasn't the case two fights later, when Keith Jardine halted him in the first round in December 2006. Unable to accept simply getting caught and stopped, Griffin questioned himself incessantly after the bout's conclusion, wondering if he could compete with the best in the division.

In his return against Hector Ramirez at UFC 72, Griffin showed a different side of his fight game as he picked his foe apart methodically and with a discipline he sorely needed. No longer was it "hit Forrest and watch him put his head down and swing away." He looked like a contender.

On September 22, 2007, most questions about Forrest Griffin disappeared in 14 minutes and 45 seconds, the time it took him to dominate and then submit Shogun Rua, the PRIDE star with a reputation as one of the top 205-pounders in the world. Griffin made him look like he shouldn't even have showed up for the fight, and when it was over, the idea of Griffin as light heavyweight champion wasn't so far-fetched anymore.

But it was on July 5, 2008, that he fulfilled all his promise with a fight for the ages against Rampage Jackson. For five rounds, the two battled tooth and nail in search of victory, and it was Griffin who got it with a unanimous decision.

He lost his crown five months later to Rashad Evans, and at UFC 101 in August 2009, he got knocked out by Anderson Silva. But after dealing with a myriad of injuries, Griffin won three of his last four bouts, capping off a career that earned him a place in the UFC Hall of Fame on July 6, 2013.

FIGHTS OF THE YEAR

THE ULTIMATE FIGHTER 1 FINALE

GRIFFIN   W3   BONNAR

UFC 52

HUGHES   WSUB1   TRIGG

THE ULTIMATE FIGHTER 2 FINALE

EVANS   W3   IMES

UFC 51

ORTIZ   WSD3   BELFORT

UFC 53
FRANKLIN   TKO4   TANNER

KNOCKOUTS OF THE YEAR

UFC 56

FRANKLIN   KO1   QUARRY

UFC 54

IRVIN   KO2   MARTIN

UFC 52

LIDDELL   KO1   COUTURE

ULTIMATE FIGHT NIGHT

SWICK   TKO1   RAY

UFC 53
LOISEAU   TKO2   MCCARTHY

SUBMISSIONS OF THE YEAR

UFC 52

HUGHES   WSUB1   TRIGG

UFC 53
ARLOVSKI   WSUB1   SYLVIA

ULTIMATE FIGHT NIGHT 2
FICKETT   WSUB3   KOSCHECK

THE ULTIMATE FIGHTER 2 FINALE
FLORIAN   WSUB2   COPE

UFC 55
SOBRAL   WSUB2   SONNEN

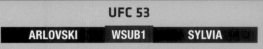

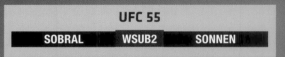

DEBUTS

UFC 51

PETE SELL

PAUL BUENTELLO

JAMES IRVIN

GIDEON RAY

DREW FICKETT

UFC 53

CHARLES MCCARTHY

KEVIN JORDAN

BILL MAHOOD

ULTIMATE FIGHT NIGHT 2

BRANDON VERA

FABIANO SCHERNER

THIAGO ALVES

SPENCER FISHER

BROCK LARSON

JON FITCH

JONATHAN GOULET

UFC 56

NICK THOMPSON

KEITH WISNIEWSKI

ANSAR CHALANGOV

JEFF NEWTON

GABRIEL GONZAGA

THE ULTIMATE FIGHTER 1 FINALE

ALEX KARALEXIS

JOSH RAFFERTY

MIKE SWICK

ALEX SCHOENAUER

NATE QUARRY

LODUNE SINCAID

JOSH KOSCHECK

CHRIS SANFORD

CHRIS LEBEN

JASON THACKER

SAM HOGER

BOBBY SOUTHWORTH

DIEGO SANCHEZ

KENNY FLORIAN

FORREST GRIFFIN

STEPHAN BONNAR

ULTIMATE FIGHT NIGHT 1

NATE MARQUARDT

JOSH NEER

UFC 55

ALESSIO SAKARA

RON FAIRCLOTH

MARCIO CRUZ

KEIGO KUNIHARA

CHAEL SONNEN

BRANDEN LEE HINKLE

SEAN GANNON

UFC 52

JASON MILLER

JOHN MARSH

UFC 54

TERRY MARTIN

BRIAN GASSAWAY

THE ULTIMATE FIGHTER 2 FINALE

RASHAD EVANS

BRAD IMES

JOE STEVENSON

LUKE CUMMO

KIT COPE

JOSH BURKMAN

SAM MORGAN

MELVIN GUILLARD

MARCUS DAVIS

KEITH JARDINE

KERRY SCHALL

THE ULTIMATE FIGHTER

2005
THE ULTIMATE FIGHTER SEASON ONE

UFC president Dana White called it "UFC's Trojan horse," a reality show that both entertained viewers on a weekly basis and introduced them to the sport of mixed martial arts and the athletes who competed in it. But the Spike TV show was also a risky endeavor. If it didn't hit on all cylinders, the sport would have been in serious jeopardy.

We'll never know what that doomsday scenario would have been like. Audiences were captivated by the antics in and out of the Octagon of future standouts such as Forrest Griffin, Stephan Bonnar, Kenny Florian, Josh Koscheck, Mike Swick, Chris Leben and Diego Sanchez—all of whom were competing for a UFC contract.

Starring superstar coaches Chuck Liddell and Randy Couture, as well as UFC president Dana White and host Willa Ford, the first season saw the teams compete in various challenges to determine who would fight in the elimination bouts. The season made an immediate impression: from its gripping fights, Bobby Southworth's battle with making weight, Chris Leben's feud with Southworth and Josh Koscheck and White's unforgettable "Do you want to be a fighter?" speech. But no reality show drama could match the drama in the light heavyweight final, as Forrest Griffin and Stephan Bonnar delivered one of the greatest fights of all time. This three-round war not only earned both fighters UFC contracts, it also kicked off the mixed martial arts explosion.

PREMIERE DATE	
January 17, 2005	
COACHES	
Chuck Liddell	
Randy Couture	
TEAM LIDDELL	**TEAM COUTURE**
Bobby Southworth	Stephan Bonnar
Sam Hoger	Mike Swick
Forrest Griffin	Lodune Sincaid
Alex Schoenauer	Jason Thacker
Josh Koscheck	Nate Quarry
Diego Sanchez	Chris Leben
Kenny Florian	Alex Karalexis
Josh Rafferty	Chris Sanford
WINNERS	
Light Heavyweight—Forrest Griffin over Stephan Bonnar	
Middleweight—Diego Sanchez over Kenny Florian	

THE ULTIMATE FIGHTER SEASON TWO: TEAM HUGHES VS TEAM FRANKLIN

Hoping to catch lightning in a bottle, *The Ultimate Fighter* season two returned to the Spike TV airwaves four months after the groundbreaking first season. With another world-class set of competitors, the train kept rollin' with UFC welterweight champion Matt Hughes and his middleweight counterpart Rich Franklin at the helm.

This season gave the audience a glimpse of what can happen to a fighter whose life is thrust into the reality TV fishbowl. Eli Joslin left the show on the first episode, unable to deal with life under the bright lights. Kenny Stevens left as well, unable to make weight for his fight.

Those who did stay were some of the best up-and-coming fighters in the game. However, two surprises in particular stunned viewers: Undersized heavyweight Rashad Evans and quirky New York welterweight Luke Cummo. Both made it to the finals of their respective divisions. In the end, though, Cummo was defeated by Joe Stevenson in the welterweight final. Only Evans walked away with the season title after his war with Brad Imes.

PREMIERE DATE	
August 22, 2005	
COACHES	
Matt Hughes	
Rich Franklin	
TEAM HUGHES	**TEAM FRANKLIN**
Joe Stevenson	Marcus Davis
Luke Cummo	Jorge Gurgel
Josh Burkman	Anthony Torres
Sammy Morgan	Melvin Guillard
Jason Von Flue (replaced Burkman)	Keith Jardine
Mike Whitehead	Seth Petruzelli
Dan Christison	Rashad Evans
Rob MacDonald	Brad Imes
Tom Murphy	
ALSO APPEARING	
Kenny Stevens	
Eli Joslin	
Kerry Schall	
WINNERS	
Heavyweight—Rashad Evans over Brad Imes	
Welterweight—Joe Stevenson over Luke Cummo	

2006

THE ULTIMATE FIGHTER SEASON THREE: TEAM ORTIZ vs TEAM SHAMROCK

The first two seasons of *The Ultimate Fighter* featured coaches who were friendly rivals (Liddell and Couture) or simply friends (Hughes and Franklin). The third season turned things upside down when former light heavyweight champion Tito Ortiz returned to the UFC fold for the first time in over a year to coach against his hated rival, Ken Shamrock.

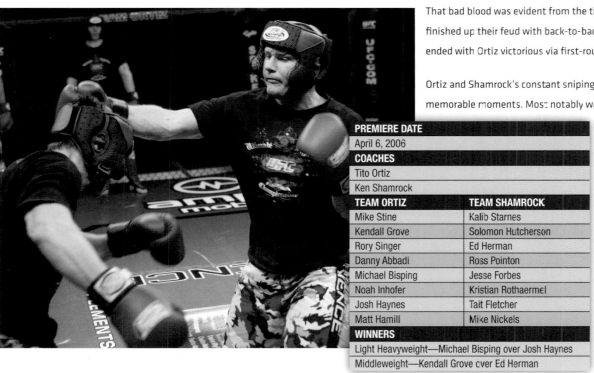

That bad blood was evident from the time the show aired in early 2006 until Ortiz and Shamrock finished up their feud with back-to-back fights in the summer and fall of 2006. Both battles ended with Ortiz victorious via first-round knockout.

Ortiz and Shamrock's constant sniping was the talk of the MMA world, but there were other memorable moments. Most notably was a change to the rules that required each competitor to fight before earning a semifinal bid, as well as a move from three rounds to two with a sudden victory elimination round in the event of a tie. Viewers also remember Ortiz' impressive coaching and the emergence of future UFC stars Michael Bisping, Kendall Grove, Ed Herman and Matt Hamill. And, of course, who could forget Noah Inhofer leaving the house because he couldn't make a phone call to his girlfriend?

PREMIERE DATE	
April 6, 2006	
COACHES	
Tito Ortiz	
Ken Shamrock	
TEAM ORTIZ	**TEAM SHAMROCK**
Mike Stine	Kalib Starnes
Kendall Grove	Solomon Hutcherson
Rory Singer	Ed Herman
Danny Abbadi	Ross Pointon
Michael Bisping	Jesse Forbes
Noah Inhofer	Kristian Rothaermel
Josh Haynes	Tait Fletcher
Matt Hamill	Mike Nickels
WINNERS	
Light Heavyweight—Michael Bisping over Josh Haynes	
Middleweight—Kendall Grove over Ed Herman	

THE ULTIMATE FIGHTER SEASON FOUR: THE COMEBACK

In a twist on its usual concept of bringing the best MMA prospects together to compete for a UFC contract, *The Ultimate Fighter* season four brought in 16 UFC veterans looking for one last shot at the top. The winners of the middleweight and welterweight divisions would be skyrocketed into a title shot. Though this concept was controversial among fans at the time, it proved to be a brilliant move. This was especially true when one of the winners, Matt Serra, made good on the title shot he won on the show by knocking out Georges St-Pierre in one of the biggest upsets in UFC history. The other winner, Travis Lutter, wasn't so lucky. Lutter had more than a few barbs thrown at him for not even making weight for the biggest fight of his career. His subsequent non-title loss to Anderson Silva was just the topper on a bad week.

PREMIERE DATE	
August 17, 2006	
COACHES	
Randy Couture	
Georges St-Pierre	
Mark DellaGrotte	
Marc Laimon	
Rich Franklin	
Chuck Liddell	
Matt Hughes	
TEAM NO LOVE	**TEAM MOJO**
Travis Lutter	Pete Sell
Charles McCarthy	Scott Smith
Gideon Ray	Patrick Cote
Jorge Rivera	Edwin Dewees
Rich Clementi	Shonie Carter
Mikey Burnett	Chris Lytle
Jeremy Jackson	Matt Serra
Pete Spratt	Din Thomas
WINNERS	
Middleweight—Travis Lutter over Patrick Cote	
Welterweight—Matt Serra over Chris Lytle	

PREMIERE DATE	
April 5, 2007	
COACHES	
Jens Pulver	
BJ Penn	
TEAM PENN	**TEAM PULVER**
Gray Maynard	Corey Hill
Matt Wiman	Nate Diaz
Gabe Ruediger	Brandon Melendez
Joe Lauzon	Marlon Sims
Rob Emerson	Manny Gamburyan
Andy Wang	Cole Miller
Allen Berube	Brian Geraghty
Noah Thomas	Wayne Weems
WINNER	
Lightweight—Nate Diaz over Manny Gamburyan	

2007

THE ULTIMATE FIGHTER SEASON FIVE

For years, BJ Penn seethed, hoping for the opportunity to avenge the first loss of his career to Jens Pulver. Five years after their UFC 35 bout, the two met again as coaches on *The Ultimate Fighter* season five. The revival of this heated feud was reason enough to tune in, but even more compelling was the fact that the field consisted of perhaps the best young talent ever assembled for the show. Sure, some stragglers were weeded out, but Gray Maynard, Matt Wiman, Joe Lauzon, Manny Gamburyan, Cole Miller and season winner Nate Diaz are all still UFC fighters—with some of them even boasting Top 20 or higher in the world status. That's an impressive lineup, even if viewers mostly remember the outside brawl that got Noah Thomas, Marlon Sims and Allen Berube ousted from the house, or Gabe Ruediger's battles with cake and the scale.

Keeping with the "coaches not wanting to be in the same room with each other" theme, newly crowned UFC welterweight champion Matt Serra battled former two-time champ Matt Hughes as coaches on *The Ultimate Fighter: Team Hughes vs Team Serra*. You couldn't find more opposite personalities than the brash New Yorker and the no-nonsense country boy, and the contrast made for compelling viewing—as did the emergence of a few diamonds in the rough like George Sotiropoulos and Ben Saunders. Everyone gravitated to the drama of Joe Scarola leaving the house after his loss to Mac Danzig, severing his friendship with Serra in the process. As for the fights, the veteran Danzig was a heavy favorite going in, and he didn't disappoint in winning the season title.

PREMIERE DATE	
September 19, 2007	
COACHES	
Matt Hughes	
Matt Serra	
TEAM HUGHES	**TEAM SERRA**
Dan Barrera	Matt Arroyo
Blake Bowman	Richie Hightower
Mac Danzig	John Kolosci
Paul Georgieff	Troy Mandaloniz
Billy Miles	Roman Mitichyan
Dorian Price	Jon Koppenhaver (replaced Roman Mitichyan)
Jared Rollins	Ben Saunders
Tommy Speer	Joe Scarola
	George Sotiropoulos
WINNER	
Welterweight—Mac Danzig over Tommy Speer	

PREMIERE DATE	
April 2, 2008	
COACHES	
Rampage Jackson	
Forrest Griffin	
TEAM RAMPAGE	**TEAM FORREST**
CB Dollaway	Tim Credeur
Matthew Riddle	Amir Sadollah
Patrick Schultz	Jesse Taylor
Dan Cramer	Matt Brown
Gerald Harris	Cale Yarbrough
Mike Dolce	Dante Rivera
Jeremy May	Nick Klein
Brandon Sene	Luke Zachrich
Paul Bradley	
WINNER	
Middleweight—Amir Sadollah over CB Dollaway	

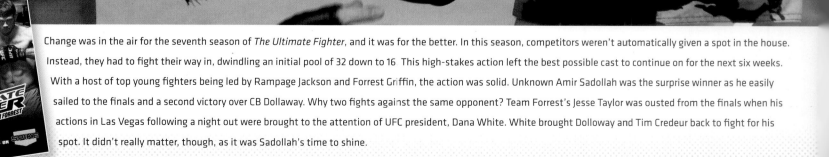

Change was in the air for the seventh season of *The Ultimate Fighter*, and it was for the better. In this season, competitors weren't automatically given a spot in the house. Instead, they had to fight their way in, dwindling an initial pool of 32 down to 16. This high-stakes action left the best possible cast to continue on for the next six weeks. With a host of top young fighters being led by Rampage Jackson and Forrest Griffin, the action was solid. Unknown Amir Sadollah was the surprise winner as he easily sailed to the finals and a second victory over CB Dollaway. Why two fights against the same opponent? Team Forrest's Jesse Taylor was ousted from the finals when his actions in Las Vegas following a night out were brought to the attention of UFC president, Dana White. White brought Dolloway and Tim Credeur back to fight for his spot. It didn't really matter, though, as it was Sadollah's time to shine.

PREMIERE DATE	
September 17, 2008	
COACHES	
Minotauro Nogueira	
Frank Mir	
TEAM NOGUEIRA	**TEAM MIR**
Rolando Delgado	Junie Browning
Efrain Escudero	Dave Kaplan
Phillipe Nover	Shane Nelson
John Polakowski	George Roop
Ryan Bader	Tom Lawlor
Jules Bruchez	Vinny Magalhaes
Kyle Kingsbury	Eliot Marshall
Shane Primm	Krzysztof Soszynski
WINNERS	
Light Heavyweight—Ryan Bader over Vinny Magalhaes	
Lightweight—Efrain Escudero over Phillipe Nover	

When you talk about the eighth season of *The Ultimate Fighter*, you can discuss multiple different storylines: The introduction of heavyweight legend Minotauro Nogueira to an entirely new television audience; the performances of season winners Ryan Bader and Efrain Escudero; the seemingly limitless talent of Phillipe Nover; and the bizarre comments of Team Nogueira assistant coach Al Stankie are just a few highlights. Still, it's likely that the first thing that comes to mind are the antics of Junie Browning. A raw talent with an appetite for destruction, Browning polarized a nation during this season for his ability to pick fights, lose his temper and just generally be a lightning bolt for controversy on one of the craziest seasons in *The Ultimate Fighter* history.

THE ULTIMATE FIGHTER: UNITED STATES VS UNITED KINGDOM

Nothing gets the blood flowing like a little nation vs. nation action. On this season of *The Ultimate Fighter*, Dan Henderson (United States) and Michael Bisping (United Kingdom) gladly led their nations into a fistic battle over six weeks in Las Vegas. A tight-knit group whose members embraced their underdog status, Bisping's team was a destructive unit. The more free-wheeling U.S. group proved to be even more self-destructive, never quite getting on track against the battling Brits. Not surprisingly, three of the four final spots were filled by Team U.K., with James Wilks and Ross Pearson winning contracts and giving Bisping bragging rights. Henderson would get the last word on "The Count," though, knocking him out in their UFC 100 bout.

PREMIERE DATE	
April 1, 2009	
COACHES	
Dan Henderson	
Michael Bisping	
TEAM UNITED STATES	**TEAM UNITED KINGDOM**
Santino DeFranco	Jeff Lawson
Jason Dent	Ross Pearson
Cameron Dollar	Martin Stapleton
Richie Whitson	Andre Winner
DaMarques Johnson	Dean Amasinger
Frank Lester	David Faulkner
Mark Miller	Nick Osipczak
Jason Pierce	James Wilks
WINNERS	
Welterweight—James Wilks over DaMarques Johnson	
Lightweight—Ross Pearson over Andre Winner	

THE ULTIMATE FIGHTER: HEAVYWEIGHTS

A blockbuster season in terms of both media attention and ratings, *The Ultimate Fighter: Heavyweights* not only featured street-fighting legend Kimbo Slice in his attempt to earn a UFC contract, but also veteran standout—and eventual winner—Roy Nelson. There were even four former football players, including NFL vets Matt Mitrione and Marcus Jones, and University of Colorado fullback Brendan Schaub. That could have been enough to ensure that everyone tuned in each week. But when you threw the growing rivalry between former light heavyweight champs Rampage Jackson and Rashad Evans into the mix, it was television gold. When the dust settled, Kimbo was eliminated in his first fight by Nelson; Mitrione emerged as a charismatic presence with potential; Nelson knocked out Schaub for the season title; and Evans and Jackson hated each other a lot more at the end of the season than they did at the beginning.

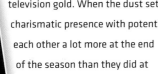

PREMIERE DATE	
September 16, 2009	
COACHES	
Rampage Jackson	
Rashad Evans	
TEAM RAMPAGE	**TEAM RASHAD**
Kimbo Slice	James McSweeney
Abe Wagner	Brendan Schaub
Demico Rogers	Justin Wren
Wes Sims	Jon Madsen
Scott Junk	Roy Nelson
Wes Shivers	Darrill Schoonover
Marcus Jones	Matt Mitrione
Zak Jensen	Mike Wessel
WINNERS	
Heavyweight—Roy Nelson over Brendan Schaub	

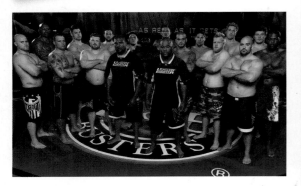

2010
THE ULTIMATE FIGHTER: TEAM LIDDELL vs TEAM ORTIZ

After the fireworks of season 10, UFC and Spike TV had to come up with something big for the next season of *The Ultimate Fighter*. You couldn't get bigger than reigniting the rivalry between UFC Hall of Famer Chuck Liddell and former light heavyweight boss Tito Ortiz, with the two set to fight at the end of the season. Unfortunately, after some early fireworks, an injury scrapped Ortiz from the fight, and surgery forced his ouster from the show. Replacing him as coach late in the season was Rich Franklin, who also wound up taking Ortiz' place in the Liddell fight at UFC 115.

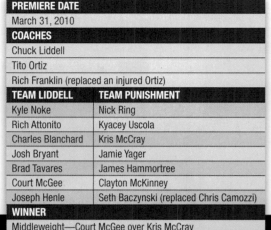

PREMIERE DATE	
March 31, 2010	
COACHES	
Chuck Liddell	
Tito Ortiz	
Rich Franklin (replaced an injured Ortiz)	
TEAM LIDDELL	**TEAM PUNISHMENT**
Kyle Noke	Nick Ring
Rich Attonito	Kyacey Uscola
Charles Blanchard	Kris McCray
Josh Bryant	Jamie Yager
Brad Tavares	James Hammortree
Court McGee	Clayton McKinney
Joseph Henle	Seth Baczynski (replaced Chris Camozzi)
WINNER	
Middleweight—Court McGee over Kris McCray	

In the UFC training center this time around, a "wild card" bout was added to the mix. This bout allowed two fighters who had lost earlier in the competition to earn a quarterfinal berth by fighting one more time. In the first season of this new addition, Kris McCray won his "wild card" fight and made it all the way to the finals before losing to Court McGee.

THE ULTIMATE FIGHTER: TEAM GSP vs. TEAM KOSCHECK

With a December 2010 showdown looming at UFC 124, what better way for old rivals Georges St-Pierre and Josh Koscheck to get reacquainted than through six weeks as coaches on *The Ultimate Fighter*? Surprisingly, the expected fireworks between the standout welterweights never materialized. St-Pierre refused to engage in Koscheck's verbal warfare, instead choosing to focus strictly on the development of his team. This was a good thing for pure fight fans, as the show turned the spotlight on the fighters. Winner Jonathan Brookins, along with Michael Johnson, Cody McKenzie and Nam Phan, all showed particular promise when it came to the idea of them transitioning from reality television to the UFC Octagon.

PREMIERE DATE	
September 15, 2010	
COACHES	
Georges St-Pierre	
Josh Koscheck	
TEAM GSP	**TEAM KOSCHECK**
Michael Johnson	Marc Stevens
Jonathan Brookins	Sevak Magakian
Spencer Paige	Sako Chivitchian
Alex Caceres	Andy Main
Kyle Watson	Nam Phan
Cody McKenzie	Aaron Wilkinson
Dane Sayers	Jeff Lentz
WINNER	
Lightweight—Jonathan Brookins over Michael Johnson	

THE ULTIMATE FIGHTER: TEAM LESNAR VS TEAM DOS SANTOS

PREMIERE DATE	
March 30, 2011	
COACHES	
Brock Lesnar	
Junior Dos Santos	
TEAM LESNAR	**TEAM DOS SANTOS**
Len Bentley	Shamar Bailey
Charlie Rader	Ryan McGilivray
Tony Ferguson	Javier Torres
Clay Harvison	Ramsey Nijem
Chris Cope	Zachary Davis
Nordin Asrih	Mick Bowman
Chuck O'Neil (replaced Myles Jury)	Justin Edwards (replaced Keon Caldwell)
WINNERS	
Lightweight—Tony Ferguson over Ramsey Nijem	

It was literally the biggest fight to be made in the heavyweight division. Former world champion Brock Lesnar prepared to face off with top contender Junior Dos Santos in a battle to determine a challenger for newly crowned champion Cain Velasquez. However, it wasn't meant to be; a bout with diverticulitis struck Lesnar from the matchup. Before this happened, though, Lesnar did meet up with "Cigano" as coaching rivals on *The Ultimate Fighter* season 13. With no initial elimination round to get into the house, it was just 16 top welterweight prospects fighting it out for the season title. Tony Ferguson survived the drama of the house to beat Ramsey Nijem in the finale. He then moved back to the lightweight division and has since become a top contender at 155 pounds.

THE ULTIMATE FIGHTER: TEAM BISPING VS TEAM MILLER

You had to know that any season with Michael Bisping and Jason "Mayhem" Miller would produce its share of entertaining antics and trash talk, and the two certainly didn't disappoint. In the end, however, the biggest takeaway from *The Ultimate Fighter* season 14 was the level of talent on display. Diego Brandão and John Dodson were the winners, but Louis Gaudinot, Dennis Bermudez and Bryan Caraway also emerged from *The Ultimate Fighter* to become legitimate contenders in UFC. The show even produced *The Ultimate Fighter*'s fourth world champion. Finalist TJ Dillashaw won the UFC bantamweight title in 2014, putting him in the select company of Rashad Evans, Forrest Griffin and Matt Serra as the only *The Ultimate Fighter* alums to become UFC champions.

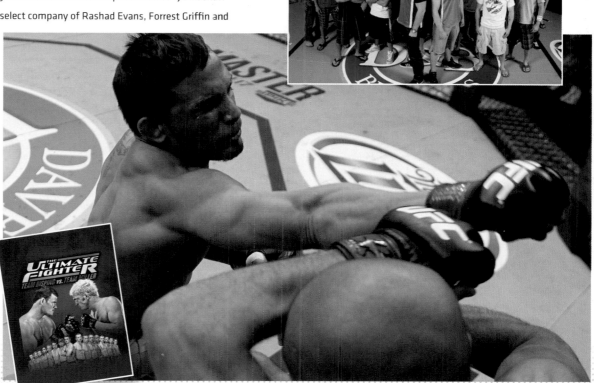

PREMIERE DATE	
September 21, 2011	
COACHES	
Michael Bisping	
Jason "Mayhem" Miller	
TEAM BISPING	**TEAM MILLER**
Louis Gaudinot	John Dodson
TJ Dillashaw	Johnny Bedford
John Albert	Dustin Pague
Josh Ferguson	Roland Delorme
Diego Brandão	Dennis Bermudez
Akira Corassani	Bryan Caraway
Marcus Brimage	Dustin Neace
Stephen Bass	Steven Siler
WINNERS	
Featherweight—Diego Brandão over Dennis Bermudez	
Bantamweight—John Dodson over TJ Dillashaw	

2012

THE ULTIMATE FIGHTER: LIVE

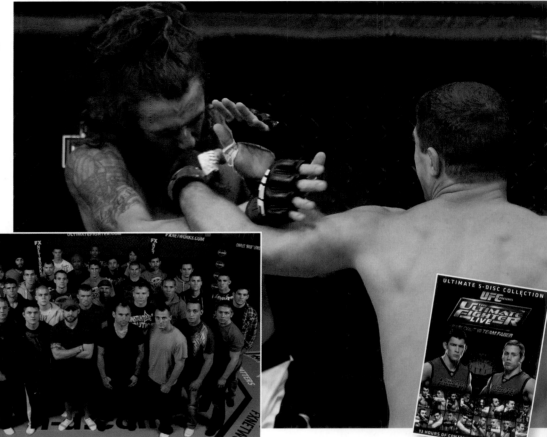

Following UFC's landmark deal with FOX in 2012, things were immediately shaken up *as The Ultimate Fighter* shifted to the FX channel. It was announced that the fights on the show would air live each week, transforming the season from a six-week competition to a 13-week one. It was a war of attrition as coaches Dominick Cruz and Urijah Faber led their fighters through the grueling process. Despite losing his father to leukemia early on, Michael Chiesa stayed on the show and defeated everyone in his path, finishing the process with a victory over Al Iaquinta that earned him the title on *The Ultimate Fighter: Live.*

PREMIERE DATE	
March 9, 2012	
COACHES	
Dominick Cruz	
Urijah Faber	
TEAM CRUZ	**TEAM FABER**
Justin Lawrence	Al Iaquinta
Sam Sicilia	Cristiano Marcello
Myles Jury	Daron Cruickshank
Mike Rio	Joe Proctor
James Vick	Michael Chiesa
Vinc Pichel	John Cofer
Chris Tickle	Andy Ogle
Jeremy Larsen	Chris Saunders
WINNER	
Lightweight—Michael Chiesa over Al Iaquinta	

THE ULTIMATE FIGHTER: BRAZIL

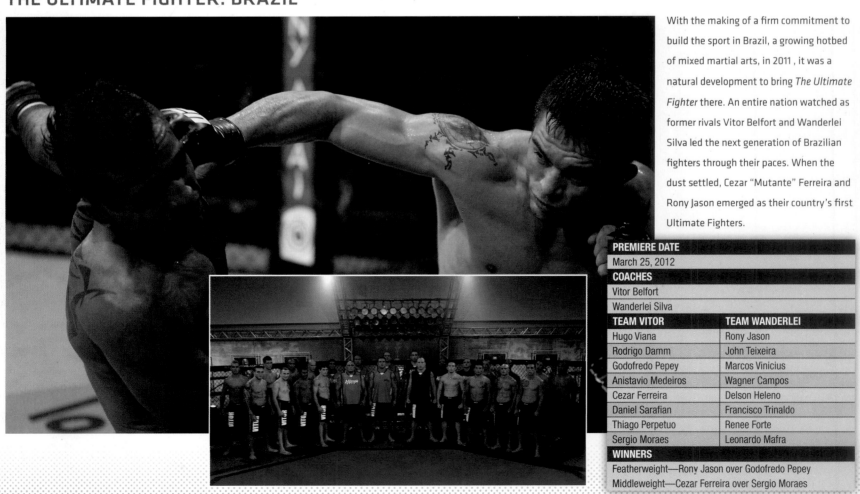

With the making of a firm commitment to build the sport in Brazil, a growing hotbed of mixed martial arts, in 2011 , it was a natural development to bring *The Ultimate Fighter* there. An entire nation watched as former rivals Vitor Belfort and Wanderlei Silva led the next generation of Brazilian fighters through their paces. When the dust settled, Cezar "Mutante" Ferreira and Rony Jason emerged as their country's first Ultimate Fighters.

PREMIERE DATE	
March 25, 2012	
COACHES	
Vitor Belfort	
Wanderlei Silva	
TEAM VITOR	**TEAM WANDERLEI**
Hugo Viana	Rony Jason
Rodrigo Damm	John Teixeira
Godofredo Pepey	Marcos Vinicius
Anistavio Medeiros	Wagner Campos
Cezar Ferreira	Delson Heleno
Daniel Sarafian	Francisco Trinaldo
Thiago Perpetuo	Renee Forte
Sergio Moraes	Leonardo Mafra
WINNERS	
Featherweight—Rony Jason over Godofredo Pepey	
Middleweight—Cezar Ferreira over Sergio Moraes	

THE ULTIMATE FIGHTER: TEAM CARWIN VS TEAM NELSON

After going live for season 15, *The Ultimate Fighter,* led by coaches Shane Carwin and Roy Nelson, returned to the usual six-week taped process for season sixteen. For the most part, the fights on the show were lackluster, a development reflected in the fact that the only competitors included on the season finale fight card were finalists Colton Smith and Mike Ricci, with Smith taking the title via decision. Eventually, Sam Alvey, Bristol Marunde, Neil Magny, Jon Manley and Igor Araujo were brought back for UFC bouts, though only Alvey, Magny and Araujo remain on the roster heading into 2015.

PREMIERE DATE	
September 14, 2012	
COACHES	
Shane Carwin	
Roy Nelson	
TEAM CARWIN	**TEAM NELSON**
Sam Alvey	Dom Waters
Bristol Marunde	Michael Hill
Mike Ricci	Cameron Diffley
Neil Magny	Colton Smith
James Chaney	Jon Manley
Eddy Ellis	Nic Herron-Webb
Igor Araujo	Joey Rivera
Matt Secor	Julian Lane
WINNER	
Welterweight—Colton Smith over Mike Ricci	

THE ULTIMATE FIGHTER: THE SMASHES

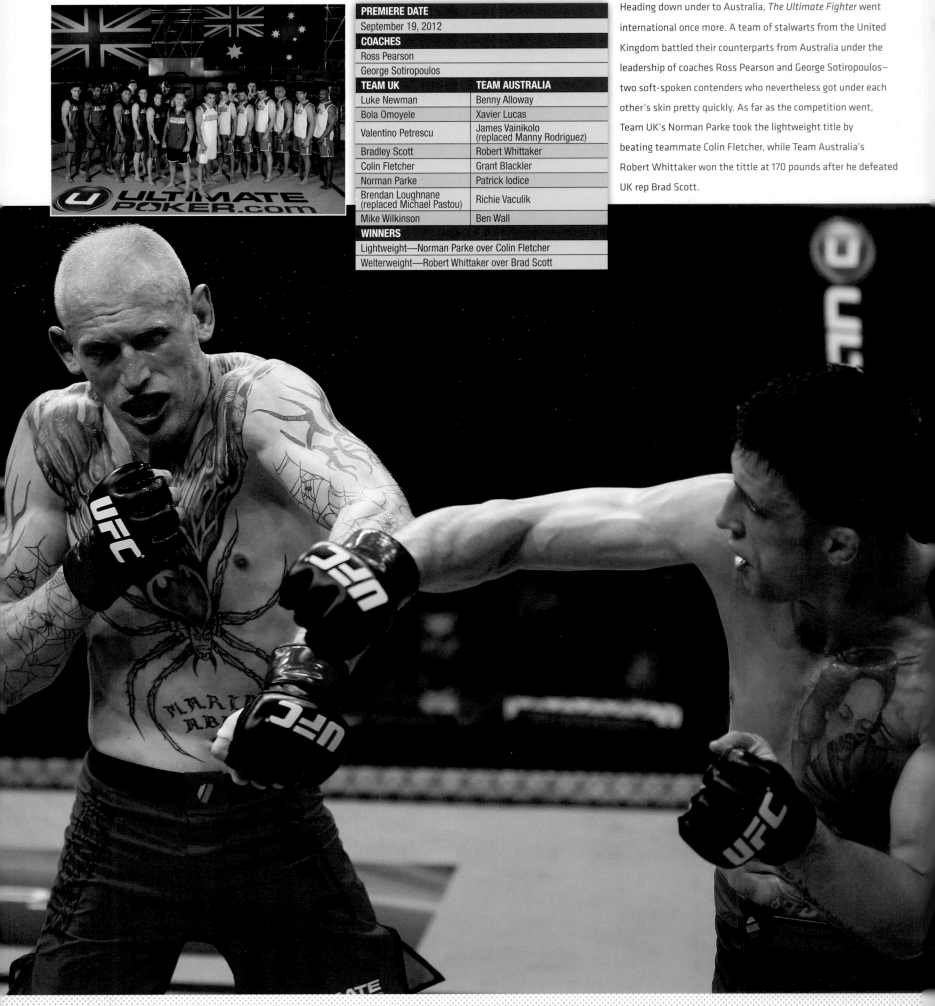

PREMIERE DATE	
September 19, 2012	
COACHES	
Ross Pearson	
George Sotiropoulos	
TEAM UK	**TEAM AUSTRALIA**
Luke Newman	Benny Alloway
Bola Omoyele	Xavier Lucas
Valentino Petrescu	James Vainikolo (replaced Manny Rodriguez)
Bradley Scott	Robert Whittaker
Colin Fletcher	Grant Blackler
Norman Parke	Patrick Iodice
Brendan Loughnane (replaced Michael Pastou)	Richie Vaculik
Mike Wilkinson	Ben Wall
WINNERS	
Lightweight—Norman Parke over Colin Fletcher	
Welterweight—Robert Whittaker over Brad Scott	

Heading down under to Australia, *The Ultimate Fighter* went international once more. A team of stalwarts from the United Kingdom battled their counterparts from Australia under the leadership of coaches Ross Pearson and George Sotiropoulos—two soft-spoken contenders who nevertheless got under each other's skin pretty quickly. As far as the competition went, Team UK's Norman Parke took the lightweight title by beating teammate Colin Fletcher, while Team Australia's Robert Whittaker won the tittle at 170 pounds after he defeated UK rep Brad Scott.

2013

THE ULTIMATE FIGHTER: TEAM JONES VS TEAM SONNEN

PREMIERE DATE	
January 22, 2013	
COACHES	
Jon Jones	
Chael Sonnen	
TEAM JONES	**TEAM SONNEN**
Luke Barnatt	Clint Hester
Uriah Hall	Josh Samman
Zak Cummings	Bubba McDaniel
Tor Troeng	Gilbert Smith
Jimmy Quinlan	Collin Hart
Kevin Casey	Adam Cella
Kelvin Gastelum	Dylan Andrews
WINNER	
Middleweight—Kelvin Gastelum over Uriah Hall	

The sport's greatest fighter took on the sport's greatest trash talker on season 17 of *The Ultimate Fighter*, with Jon Jones pitted against Chael Sonnen. While the light heavyweight champ thrashed Sonnen, it was Sonnen who put two fighters in the finale. Uriah Hall, who had delivered a series of highlight-reel finishes on the show, including a frightening knockout of Adam Cella, was a huge favorite to win the finale over unheralded Kelvin Gastelum. However, Gastelum ultimately continued his habit of upsets by defeating Hall for the season crown.

THE ULTIMATE FIGHTER: BRAZIL 2

More than 300 hopefuls showed for tryouts for the second season of *The Ultimate Fighter: Brazil*, but only 16 made it to the house to be coached by heavyweight legend Minotauro Nogueira and top contender Fabricio Werdum. While young gun William "Patolino" Macario and Argentina native Santiago Ponzinibbio ultimately made it to the finals, an injury to Ponzinibbio took him out of his match on the finale card. This allowed veteran competitor Leonardo Santos, who had lost to the Argentinean in the semifinals, to swoop in and win the season title by submitting Macario.

PREMIERE DATE	
March 17, 2013	
COACHES	
Minotauro Nogueira	
Fabricio Werdum	
TEAM NOGUEIRA	**TEAM WERDUM**
Luiz Dutra	Pedro Irie
Santiago Ponzinibbio	Tiago Alves
Leonardo Santos	Viscardi Andrade
David Vieira	Marcio Santos
William Macario	Juliano Wandalen
Cleiton Duarte	Thiago de Lima Santos
Thiago Goncalves (replaced Neilson Gomes)	Daniel Oliveira (replaced Yan Cabral)
WINNER	
Welterweight—Leonardo Santos over William Macario	

THE ULTIMATE FIGHTER: TEAM ROUSEY VS TEAM TATE

Moving to FOX Sports 1, *The Ultimate Fighter* gave its new network plenty of drama, and it wasn't necessarily between the fighters. Originally scheduled to coach against number-one contender Cat Zingano, UFC women's bantamweight champion Ronda Rousey had a wrench thrown into the works when Zingano was forced from the competition due to a knee injury. In stepped Rousey's nemesis, Miesha Tate, and the two butted heads all season long. In the Octagon, the show featured women for the first time, with Julianna Pena winning the season title. On the male side of the equation, Team Alpha Male's Chris Holdsworth emerged victorious, defeating Davey Grant.

PREMIERE DATE	
September 4, 2013	
COACHES	
Ronda Rousey	
Miesha Tate	
TEAM ROUSEY	**TEAM TATE**
Shayna Baszler	Julianna Pena
Jessamyn Duke	Sarah Moras
Peggy Morgan	Raquel Pennington
Jessica Rakoczy	Roxanne Modafferi
Chris Beal	Cody Bollinger
Davey Grant	Chris Holdsworth
Anthony Gutierrez	Joshua Hill
Michael Wootten	Louis Fisette (replaced Tim Gorman)
WINNERS	
Men's bantamweight—Chris Holdsworth over Davey Grant	
Women's bantamweight—Julianna Pena over Jessica Rakoczy	

THE ULTIMATE FIGHTER: CHINA

PREMIERE DATE	
December 7, 2013	
COACHES	
Tiequan Zhang	
Ao Hailin	
Cung Le	
TEAM SKY DRAGONS	**TEAM FLYING LIONS**
Ning Guangyou	Jianping Yang
Fu Chang Xin	Rocky Lee
Yao Zhikui	Allen Chong
He Jianwei	Shih Liang
Zhang Lipeng	Wang Sai
Albert Cheng	Wang Anying
Wu Qi Ze	Zhu Qing Xiang
Fu Ziyi (replaced Li Jin Ying)	Yong Shun (replaced Dong Xin)
WINNERS	
Featherweight—Ning Guangyou over Jianping Yang	
Welterweight—Zhang Lipeng over Wang Sai	

With Asia a high priority for UFC, the quest to find the top talent from the region kicked into high gear with *The Ultimate Fighter: China*. Aiding with the process was UFC veteran Cung Le, who served as a mentor and head coach overseeing the entire season, as well as individual team coaches Tiequan Zhang and Ao Hailin. While the talent was raw, there was plenty of it on display during the competition, which saw Zhang Lipeng and Ning Guangyou emerge victorious with *The Ultimate Fighter* titles and UFC contracts.

2014
THE ULTIMATE FIGHTER NATIONS: CANADA VS AUSTRALIA

It was country against country once more on *The Ultimate Fighter* in 2014, as Canada and Australia's best prospects met in the first *Ultimate Fighter Nations* series. Coached by UFC (and *The Ultimate Fighter*) vets Patrick Cote from Canada and Kyle Noke from Australia, the experience of the Canadian team proved too much for the Aussies. The gentlemen from the Great White North closed the brackets at welterweight and middleweight, with Chad Laprise and Elias Theodorou defeating their countrymen Olivier Aubin-Mercier and Sheldon Westcott, respectively, for the season titles.

PREMIERE DATE	
January 15, 2014	
COACHES	
Patrick Cote	
Kyle Noke	
TEAM CANADA	**TEAM AUSTRALIA**
Olivier Aubin-Mercier	Chris Indich
Matthew DesRoches	Jake Matthews
Kajan Johnson	Brendan O'Reilly
Chad Laprise	Richard Walsh
Luke Harris	Vik Grujic
Nordine Taleb	Dan Kelly
Elias Theodorou	Tyler Manawaroa
Sheldon Westcott	Zein Saliba
WINNERS	
Welterweight—Chad Laprise over Olivier Aubin-Mercier	
Middleweight—Elias Theodorou over Sheldon Westcott	

THE ULTIMATE FIGHTER: BRAZIL 3

A war in the gym was expected for *The Ultimate Fighter: Brazil* season three, and it did get heated between Wanderlei Silva and Chael Sonnen. Silva even took down his rival coach after one particular argument. The oddest part of the whole scenario is that Sonnen actually became a favorite of his Brazilian team and fans during the show. In terms of coaching, the "Gangster from West Linn" proved his magic touch, as his team produced three of the four finalists. Winners of the show were Team Sonnen's Warlley Alves (middleweight) and Team Wanderlei's Antonio Carlos Junior (heavyweight).

PREMIERE DATE	
March 9, 2014	
COACHES	
Wanderlei Silva	
Chael Sonnen	
TEAM WANDERLEI	**TEAM SONNEN**
Paulo Costa	Joilton Santos
Wagner Silva	Guilherme Vasconcelos
Ricardo Abreu	Warlley Alves
Ismael de Jesus	Marcio Alexandre Junior
Jollyson Francisco	Job Kleber Melo
Antonio Carlos Junior	Edgar Castaldelli Filho
Richardson Moreira	Marcos Rogerio de Lima
Antonio Branjao	Vitor Miranda
WINNERS	
Middleweight—Warlley Alves over Marcio Alexandre Junior	
Heavyweight—Antonio Carlos Junior over Vitor Miranda	

THE ULTIMATE FIGHTER: TEAM EDGAR VS TEAM PENN

They had fought twice before and were going to meet once again at the end of the season, but coaches Frankie Edgar and BJ Penn put any personal heat to the side, allowing their fighters to take center stage during season 19 of *The Ultimate Fighter*. Although the majority of the fights on the show weren't overly compelling, when it came to the finale show in Las Vegas, Corey Anderson and Eddie Gordon blasted out opponents Matt Van Buren and Dhiego Lima in rapid-fire fashion, making statements that they were here to stay in the Octagon.

PREMIERE DATE	
April 16, 2014	
COACHES	
Frankie Edgar	
BJ Penn	
TEAM EDGAR	**TEAM PENN**
Hector Urbina	Cathal Pendred
Ian Stephens	Roger Zapata
Eddie Gordon	Tim Williams
Dhiego Lima	Mike King
Todd Monaghan	Daniel Spohn
Patrick Walsh	Chris Fields
Matt Van Buren	Anton Berzin
Corey Anderson	Josh Clark
WINNERS	
Middleweight—Eddie Gordon over Dhiego Lima	
Light Heavyweight—Corey Anderson over Matt Van Buren	

THE ULTIMATE FIGHTER: LATIN AMERICA

PREMIERE DATE	
August 20, 2014	
COACHES	
Cain Velasquez	
Fabricio Werdum	
TEAM VELASQUEZ	**TEAM WERDUM**
Enrique Briones	Marlon Vera
Jose Quinonez	Bentley Syler
Alejandro Perez	Guido Cannetti
Marco Beltran	Fredy Serrano
Gabriel Benitez	Alexander Torres
Yair Rodriguez	Diego Rivas
Rodolfo Rubio	Leonardo Morales
Masio Fullen	Humberto Brown
WINNERS	
Bantamweight—Alejandro Perez over Jose Alberto Quinonez	
Featherweight—Yair Rodriguez over Leonardo Morales	

The perfect lead-in to UFC's first visit to Mexico for UFC 180 on November 15, 2014, was the inaugural season of *The Ultimate Fighter: Latin America*. Featuring a team of Mexican prospects led by UFC heavyweight champion Cain Velasquez against a squad of Latin American up-and-comers coached by Fabricio Werdum, the season showed off plenty of heart and potential from both sides. A heated pair of final bouts saw Yair Rodriguez defeat Leonardo Morales and Alejandro Perez outlast Jose Quinonez, giving Team Velasquez both season titles.

THE ULTIMATE FIGHTER: A CHAMPION WILL BE CROWNED

Coached by lightweight champion Anthony "Showtime" Pettis and top contender Gilbert "El N no" Melendez, the 20th season of *The Ultimate Fighter* was the first to feature an all-female cast. If that was not historic enough, UFC also announced in this landmark season that the winner would not just earn a UFC contract. Rather, the winner of the show, Carla Esparza, was crowned UFC's first strawweight champion in the finale with her win over Rose Namajunas. These 16 competitors weren't just prospects but were the best 115-pound female fighters in the world, which made it must-see TV from start to finish.

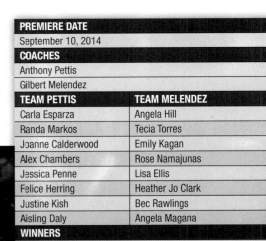

PREMIERE DATE	
September 10, 2014	
COACHES	
Anthony Pettis	
Gilbert Melendez	
TEAM PETTIS	**TEAM MELENDEZ**
Carla Esparza	Angela Hill
Randa Markos	Tecia Torres
Joanne Calderwood	Emily Kagan
Alex Chambers	Rose Namajunas
Jessica Penne	Lisa Ellis
Felice Herring	Heather Jo Clark
Justine Kish	Bec Rawlings
Aisling Daly	Angela Magana
WINNERS	
Women's Strawweight—Carla Esparza over Rose Namajunas	

GRIFFIN VS BONNAR

On April 9, 2005, light heavyweight hopefuls Forrest Griffin and Stephan Bonnar had survived six weeks in the fishbowl of reality television; now they were one win away from glory,

a UFC contract and a life-altering change to everything they had known previously.

That's plenty to fight hard for, but Griffin and Bonnar went beyond that in the finale of *The Ultimate Fighter's* first season. The ensuing 15 minutes encapsulated the best of what this sport has to offer, and these two warriors fought as if their lives were at stake. If you didn't walk away from your television set a fan that night, check your pulse. About the only person disappointed with the three-round war was the winner.

"I only watched it once," admitted Griffin. "I guess I kinda had to. It was a hard, a lot of missed opportunities, and a lot of things where you know better. You know you can do this or do that, but you don't. But the bottom line is I felt like I fought a great first round. I felt like I came out and just started going at it."

Bonnar eagerly accepted Griffin's willingness to scrap, and the pattern and pace rarely changed throughout the bout. Griffin took the first round, but Bonnar rebounded in the second, leaving his foe bloodied from a cut on the bridge of his nose.

> "BUT THE BOTTOM LINE IS I FELT LIKE I FOUGHT A GREAT FIRST ROUND. I FELT LIKE I CAME OUT AND JUST STARTED GOING AT IT."
> —FORREST GRIFFIN

"I don't know, man," he chuckled. "You need to get popped; you need to get a little bit of something. It helps if you get backed into a corner."

Backed into a corner by Bonnar's attack and exhausted by the furious pace of the first 10 minutes, Griffin's chest visibly heaved for any air it could get. Nevertheless, he continued to fight, and the third round became as memorable as the first two, with fans in attendance on their feet screaming and a national television audience growing with each punch and kick.

"I knew it was a good fight when the final bell rang and the crowd was going nuts and yelling for another round," said Bonnar. "Just looking into the crowd and at everyone's face, the energy level was so high, I said, 'It must have been a good one.'"

In the end, even though Griffin got the decision, both he and Bonnar received UFC contracts, and a sport was given the jolt it needed. To this day, UFC president Dana White calls the bout the most important in UFC history. To prove it, both Griffin and Bonnar are now members of the UFC Hall of Fame, inducted together in 2013.

"I KNEW IT WAS A GOOD FIGHT WHEN THE FINAL BELL RANG AND THE CROWD WAS GOING NUTS AND YELLING FOR ANOTHER ROUND."
—STEPHAN BONNAR

2006

In countless ways, the success of *The Ultimate Fighter* saved UFC. With the collaboration of Zuffa and producer Craig Piligian, fans got a look at mixed martial arts and its athletes that they had never seen before.

"We kept this thing raw," UFC president Dana White said. "Originally, they wanted to edit the fights, too. They're television people. And the difference is that we're in the fight business; this is what we do for a living. Craig Piligian and his people are in the reality TV show business, and that's what they do. So we got together and worked together to make a great show. They handled the reality, and we handled the fights and how we wanted them done."

Two seasons in, and the series was a hit for the network. It was also an opportunity for Zuffa to continue the work it started in 2001 to bring the sport to the masses both in the United States and abroad.

"We're running our business the best we can right now, putting on fights where we've already gotten it worked out and it is sanctioned," White said in 2005. "But eventually, not only do I want this to be sanctioned in all the states, but the unified set of rules we use here in the United States, I would like to see all over the world. To really make this a sport, it's gotta be like basketball, baseball, soccer—the same game we play over here is the same game they play in England, Brazil, Japan, and that's the way it needs to be." It was a lofty goal, but if White and the Fertitta brothers had proven one thing, it's that their tenacity knew no bounds.

Meanwhile, it was time to take advantage of the sport's increased popularity in the United States. What better way to do that than with a rubber match between UFC's two biggest superstars, Chuck Liddell and Randy Couture, in the first Pay-Per-View event of the year?

So at UFC 57 on February 4, the two met up again, and Liddell won the battle and the war. Before a sold-out Mandalay Bay Events Center crowd, "The Iceman" retained his UFC light heavyweight crown with a second-round TKO of Couture, giving him the final 2-1 edge in the trilogy between the light heavyweight greats. After the bout, the 42-year-old Couture—the only fighter in UFC history to win the heavyweight and light heavyweight titles—announced his retirement, though he returned at UFC 68 a year later.

As for Liddell-Couture 3, the two future UFC Hall of Famers circled each other warily early on, looking for openings as the crowd alternately cheered for their favorite fighter. Couture stalked behind a high guard, and his sporadic strikes seemed to take Liddell out of his rhythm. Liddell quickly recovered, rocking Couture briefly with a right to the head. But as Liddell moved in for the kill, Couture, his nose now bloodied, was able to recover and take the champion to the canvas for the remainder of the round.

Couture refused to deviate from his fight plan in the second round, following Liddell around the Octagon while throwing in the occasional counter. But Couture's luck soon ran out, and as he shot in with a left hand, Liddell landed the same short right hand that ended the pair's second fight. Couture again fell to the canvas, and referee John McCarthy called a stop to the bout at 1:28 of the second stanza. The victory established Liddell as the biggest star in the sport—not a bad gig for someone who used fighting as a way to get out of having to get a "real job."

"I loved fighting, and it was a way to keep away from getting a real job," Liddell said. "To be honest, when I was a kid, I dreamt of having a karate gym. I wanted to be a martial artist for the rest of my life. That's what I loved, I had been doing it since I was 12, and that seemed like the dream job to me anyway. I took accounting in college because my grandmother didn't consider PE a real major. So I ended up doing it, and it was something that came easy to me. But I always thought of that as my fallback plan."

He didn't need to use that accounting degree to make a living, only to help manage his growing paychecks. And what fans didn't realize at the time was that they were in the middle of watching one of the most dominant runs in UFC history. Liddell's seven-fight streak went unbeaten—with every victory ending via knockout—most of those coming by way of his devastating right hand.

"I threw from a lot of different angles; I threw a lot of different right hands and I threw them hard," he explains. "Jeremy Horn was looking for all the looping punches, and he didn't know I had a straight right. And that's what I dropped him with. They just forget that you have a straight right. They're expecting the other stuff, and that straight right slips right in. Or I'm throwing it over, over, over, and now I come up and through the middle. Like with Guy Mezger, I was throwing over and over, and I just came up through the middle and changed it. It was a lot of precision timing, accuracy and angles. I throw that punch hard from a lot of different directions. And you're never sure where it's coming from."

 ## ALAN BELCHER
JONESBORO, AR

DEBUT: UFC 62, AUGUST 26, 2006

The moments before the opening horn can be the scariest for even the toughest fighters. Alan "The Talent" Belcher described it as "a bungee jump. Because you have to get yourself ready, and there's no turning back." That's an accurate statement in the career of this middleweight, who took fans on an unpredictable ride from the time of his UFC debut in 2006. "The Talent" consistently brought excitement such as: a front flip against Yushin Okami; a single-kick knockout of Jorge Santiago; a three-round war with Yoshihiro Akiyama; and a submission of Patrick Cote.

 ## WILSON GOUVEIA
FORTALEZA, CEARÁ, BRAZIL

DEBUT: THE ULTIMATE FIGHTER 3 FINALE, JUNE 24, 2006

Wilson Gouveia came into UFC with an unimpressive 6-3 record and few expectations from fight fans. But then came a hard-fought loss to Keith Jardine at The Ultimate Fighter Finale in 2006, and the MMA world started to pay attention to the exciting jiu-jitsu black belt.

Three consecutive wins continued building Gouveia's reputation, but it was after a fourth straight victory over Jason Lambert via knockout that he became a player in the Octagon. A move to middleweight after a UFC 84 loss to Goran Reljic followed, but victories over Ryan Jensen and Jason MacDonald were tempered by back-to-back KO defeats against Nate Marquardt and Alan Belcher, forcing his release after UFC 107.

 ## TYSON GRIFFIN
SACRAMENTO, CA

DEBUT: UFC 63, SEPTEMBER 23, 2006

A relentless force who took down Urijah Faber, Clay Guida, Thiago Tavares and Marcus Aurelio, Las Vegas' Tyson Griffin was on the fast track to a world championship fight, especially when he took on former lightweight title challenger Hermes Franca at UFC 103. Griffin put on a spectacular performance that resulted in a second-round knockout win; his first knockout or submission win since he tapped out David Lee in his Octagon debut in September 2006.

But a trio of losses against Evan Dunham, Takanori Gomi and Nik Lentz sent the talented Griffin back to the drawing board. After going 1-1 as a featherweight in 2011, he was released.

While knockouts and his imposing look brought people in the door, what kept him there was Liddell's willingness to face all opponents at a moment's notice.

"I always felt that way, and I always thought I was the best in the world and could beat anybody," he said. "And I wanted to go and prove it every time I came out."

One standout from the early Zuffa era wasn't as fortunate at UFC 57. Former heavyweight champion Frank Mir didn't get the welcome back he expected after a 20-month absence due to injury. Instead, Brazil's Marcio "Pe de Pano" Cruz stopped him in the first round. It was a stunning upset, prompting many to wonder if Mir would ever be the same fighter he was before the 2004 motorcycle accident that cost him his title.

Such is the nature of combat sports. You can be on top of the world one minute and forgotten the next, with one punch or injury being the difference between feast and famine. On the feast side of the equation, UFC returned with a March 4 show in Las Vegas where Rich Franklin retained his middleweight title for the second time with a hard-fought but clear-cut decision win over David Loiseau. Also victorious that night was Canada's Georges St-Pierre, who began the biggest year of his career to date with a three-round split decision win over BJ Penn. Penn was making his first UFC appearance since 2004, and despite the loss, "The Prodigy" was going to stick around awhile this time.

St-Pierre defeats Penn via split decision at UFC 58.

ED HERMAN
VANCOUVER, WA

DEBUT: THE ULTIMATE FIGHTER 3 FINALE, JUNE 24, 2006

If history has proven anything in the career of Ed "Short Fuse" Herman, it's that he's most dangerous when his back is against the wall. For proof of that, look at the three-fight unbeaten streak that saw the finalist of *The Ultimate Fighter* season three submit Chris Price and Scott Smith and knock out Joe Doerksen after he dropped a 2006 bout to Jason MacDonald.

However, hard times hit again when he lost back-to-back bouts to Demian Maia and Alan Belcher in 2008. After spoiling the return of former world title challenger David "The Crow" Loiseau at UFC 97, Herman injured his knee in a defeat to Aaron Simpson. He was forced to the sidelines for nearly two years before making a triumphant return in 2011.

KENDALL GROVE
WAILUKU, HI

DEBUT: THE ULTIMATE FIGHTER 3 FINALE, JUNE 24, 2006 • *THE ULTIMATE FIGHTER 3* WINNER

Confidence is a necessary element in any top-level fighter's arsenal; whereas overconfidence can be a killer. Yet Kendall "Da Spyder" Grove walked the line between confidence and cockiness better than almost anyone.

The middleweight winner of *The Ultimate Fighter* season three, Hawaii's Grove started his UFC career off with a nice winning streak as he won a classic battle with Ed Herman to win *The Ultimate Fighter* before submitting Chris Price and Alan Belcher.

From there, big wins over Evan Tanner, Jason Day, Jake Rosholt and Goran Reljic were evened out by a host of losses against 185-pound standouts Patrick Cote, Mark Munoz, Demian Maia and Tim Boetsch. But when his back was against the wall, the 6'6" Grove was always at his best, and his resilience made him a favorite among fans who respect his talent, style and will to win.

MARK HOMINICK
ZORRA, CANADA

DEBUT: UFC 58, MARCH 4, 2006

Mark "The Machine" Hominick was always known as one of the best conditioned fighters in the game, hence his nickname. But in addition to his limitless gas tank, he also made his mark in the fight game with a ferocious striking attack that saw him end several fights via knockout.

In March 2006, the Canadian standout made his UFC debut, shocking fight fans with a submission win over Yves Edwards. Later, Hominick walked away from UFC to compete in the WEC's featherweight division.

At 145 pounds, Hominick was nearly unstoppable, earning a title shot when he returned to the Octagon. Though he fell short of victory in his challenge for Jose Aldo's 145-pound crown, his gritty effort earned him Fight of the Night honors at UFC 129.

UFC 58 also marked the welcome return of the lightweight division; Canadian teammates Mark Hominick and Sam Stout scored exciting upsets over Yves Edwards and Spencer Fisher, respectively.

With the popularity of *The Ultimate Fighter* increasing demand for more UFC shows on cable television, the promotion responded with the launch of the UFC Fight Night series in 2005. The series provided a mix of *The Ultimate Fighter* alumni, rising stars and seasoned veterans, putting them in competitive bouts that set the stage for future Pay-Per-View appearances.

On April 15, UFC made its first appearance in California—a state that had recently legalized the sport—and UFC 59 took place

at the Arrowhead Pond in Anaheim. Headlined by the rematch between heavyweight champion Andrei Arlovski and Tim Sylvia, the bout between the big men was an exciting (albeit short) one. Sylvia regained his title with a TKO in less than three minutes. But to many, Sylvia-Arlovski 2 was the walkout bout to the "real" main event, a bout between former light heavyweight champion Tito Ortiz and Forrest Griffin, one of those aforementioned fighters who emerged from *The Ultimate Fighter* ready for prime time.

What turned into an epic three-round battle didn't look like one after the first five minutes, as Ortiz dominated the Georgia upstart.

"I knew I was better than what I was showing, and I knew I was falling apart in front of a lot of people—my family and friends—and I was letting my team down," Griffin said. "I was disgusted with myself for it. It's like when a bully pushes you at school and you don't do anything about it—you let it sink in, and you just get angry and then do something about it, hopefully."

Griffin did, roaring back over the next two rounds to make a fight out of it. Ortiz got the split decision win, but Griffin earned his respect as a legit contender and not just a reality television star.

Later that spring, another match fans had dreamt about came to fruition when it was announced that Royce Gracie would come back to UFC to face welterweight champion Matt Hughes in a non-title bout on May 27 at STAPLES Center in Los Angeles.

On the night the bout was made official, Gracie had one comment to make: "This is my house, I built it." Hughes, respectful of his foe but a heavy favorite, was asked how he was going to avoid being overconfident.

"I'll keep saying his last name," Hughes said. "He's a Gracie. You've got to respect the name, and anytime that I make a mistake, he can catch me in a submission, so that's motivation enough."

It was a motivated Hughes who showed up to fight in the main event of UFC 60, as he scored a one-sided first-round stoppage win.

A month later, two new winners were crowned on *The Ultimate Fighter*, with Michael Bisping and Kendall Grove both earning UFC contracts. On that same June card at the Hard Rock in Las Vegas, the recently retired Couture was inducted into the UFC Hall of Fame. It was also announced that Jens Pulver would be returning to the Octagon later that year. Just four days later, the most important news for the promotion took place under the radar with the arrival of Brazilian middleweight Anderson Silva.

A veteran of the sport who had competed around the world, UFC signed "The Spider" and put him in a UFC Fight Night main event against *The Ultimate Fighter* alum Chris Leben. Those who had never seen Silva fight were in for a treat, as he needed just 49 seconds to knock out the steel-chinned Leben. What Silva brought to the Octagon was striking so advanced and dynamic that it was unlike anything ever seen in the eight-sided cage. He was something special. And if the world didn't know it yet, they were about to.

Anderson Silva vs Chris Leben at Ultimate Fight Night 5

There was other business to tend to before the next Silva sighting, though. Tim Sylvia concluded his UFC trilogy with Andrei Arlovski victoriously via five-round decision in the main event of UFC 61 in July, and Tito Ortiz scored a controversial 78-second TKO win over Ken Shamrock in their rematch on the same card.

ANDERSON SILVA

DEBUT: ULTIMATE FIGHT NIGHT 5, JUNE 28, 2006
UFC MIDDLEWEIGHT CHAMPION

SÃO PAULO, BRAZIL

Deadly in the Octagon, but light-hearted and quick with a smile or a joke outside of it, Anderson "The Spider" Silva dominated UFC for nearly a decade, earning accolades as perhaps the greatest fighter of all time.

But there was work to be done before he ruled UFC. A taekwondo practitioner from age 14, the lanky, yet graceful, Silva came up the hard way in life and in the fight game. He eventually turned to mixed martial arts, making his debut at home in Curitiba in 2000.

By 2001, after introducing himself on the Vale Tudo circuit, he began making inroads in Japan. A year later, he began what turned into a five-fight stint in PRIDE. While in the Land of the Rising Sun's premier organization, he defeated Alex Stiebling, Alexander Otuska and Carlos Newton, but got submitted by Daiju Takase and Ryo Chonan.

The still-raw talent also became a world traveler of sorts: he defeated Jeremy Horn in South Korea; beat Lee Murray, Jorge Rivera, Curtis Stout and Anthony Fryklund in England; and lost via disqualification due to an illegal upkick to Yushin Okami in Hawaii.

The Okami defeat proved to be his last until 2013, and after he knocked out Fryklund with a spectacular elbow to the head in April 2006, he got the call to compete in UFC.

At the time, UFC was just taking off with mainstream sports fans, and many fans of this fast-growing sport had no exposure to the mysterious young man known as "The Spider." But to diehard aficionados, he was both the real deal and a fighter entering his prime who was about to shake up UFC's middleweight division.

He made an immediate impression, blitzing and finishing Chris Leben in less than a minute. But the real shock was to come on October 14, 2006.

Given an immediate title shot after the win over Leben, Silva was pitted against popular champion Rich Franklin in the main event of UFC 64 in Las Vegas. The card was dubbed "Unstoppable," and Silva was. At two minutes and 59 seconds of the first round, Anderson Silva was crowned the champion.

The early days of Silva's reign at 185 pounds were filled with spectacular win after spectacular win. But his second-round submission of Dan Henderson in a UFC/PRIDE middleweight unification bout at UFC 82 in March 2008 saw people putting him on top of the mythical pound-for-pound list and talking about him reigning for as long as he wanted.

In July 2008, he moved up to the light heavyweight division for a one-shot bout against knockout artist James Irvin. He needed just 61 seconds to end the night of "The Sandman."

Even as he defended his crown with wins over Patrick Cote (TKO3) and Thales Leites (W5), Silva appeared bored at 185 pounds, and his lackluster (though dominating) performances showed it. In response, UFC president Dana White decided to test his champion at 205 pounds again, setting up an August 2009 bout against former UFC light heavyweight titleholder Forrest Griffin. But this UFC 101 bout quickly got ugly for Griffin when Silva displayed amazing offensive and defensive wizardry, knocking him out in just 3:23.

But another disappointing showing followed at UFC 112 with a lopsided five-round decision win against Demian Maia. After a prolonged trash-talking attack from Chael Sonnen, Silva was on the receiving end of a thrashing from the number-one contender in their August 2010 bout. But just as he was on the verge of losing his title to Sonnen, Silva (nursing a pre-fight rib injury) sprang into action in the fifth round, submitting his foe at the 3:10 mark to cap off perhaps the most spectacular comeback in UFC history.

"The Spider" was back, and if there were any doubters, he silenced them at UFC 126 in February 2011. His first-round knockout of Vitor Belfort began with an indescribably devastating front kick to the jaw.

Following the Belfort win, Silva successfully defended his title twice more before losing it to Chris Weidman in July 2013. A horrific leg break ended their rematch five months later, but the resilient Brazilian returned in January 2015 with a win over Nick Diaz.

At UFC 62 in August, Liddell successfully defended his crown with a 95-second finish of Renato "Babalu" Sobral, and Forrest Griffin repeated his decision win over Stephan Bonnar, albeit in a less frantic fashion than he did the first time.

The fall was a busy one, beginning with Hughes' rematch win over Penn at UFC 63 in September, and Ortiz and Shamrock doing it one more time in Florida in October with the same result: a first-round win for "The Huntington Beach Bad Boy."

But the real history took place in Las Vegas on October 14, 2006. In the co-main event, a lightweight champion was crowned for the first time since Jens Pulver held the belt, as Sean Sherk pounded out a five-round decision win over *The Ultimate Fighter* season one finalist Kenny Florian. In the UFC 64 main event, Silva proved that he was for real, destroying Franklin in less than a round to win the UFC middleweight title—a crown he held until 2013.

A new champion also emerged in November, as St-Pierre capped off his year with a first-round TKO of Hughes that earned him the welterweight belt.

By now, it was clear that a new breed of stars was emerging in UFC, with Silva and St-Pierre leading the way. But the "old" guard still packed a punch (literally and figuratively), with the final event of the year, UFC 66 on December 30, proving that fans still wanted to see Liddell and Ortiz, especially if they were punching each other.

Make no mistake about it: Ortiz came to fight in the UFC 66 main event, and as he admitted afterward, he brought his "A game." But when you're facing the best light heavyweight on the planet, sometimes that's just not enough. Liddell defended his UFC crown for the fourth time with a third-round TKO of Ortiz before a sold-out crowd of 14,607 at the MGM Grand Garden Arena in Las Vegas.

It was the "Year of the Iceman," but also so much more. As 2006 drew to a close, UFC had not just presented top card after top card, but it had made moves outside the Octagon, as well. In December, the organization purchased select assets of the WFA promotion that included the contracts of fighters like Rampage Jackson and Lyoto Machida. Also that month, Zuffa purchased the WEC organization, a popular local promotion that would continue to run shows under the auspices of its new owners. And there were even more deals to come.

MICHAEL BISPING

DEBUT: THE ULTIMATE FIGHTER 3 FINALE, JUNE 24, 2006
THE ULTIMATE FIGHTER 3 WINNER

NICOSIA, CYPRUS

Before Michael "The Count" Bisping arrived, the track record of fighters from the United Kingdom in UFC was spotty at best. Fighters like Mark Weir and Ian Freeman only showed flashes of their potential, but "The Count" established himself as one of the game's top 185-pounders, regardless of nationality.

A martial artist since age 8, Bisping turned to MMA in 2003. With his kickboxing and jiu-jitsu background, he was a quick study, running through the local ranks to build an impressive unbeaten record. His obvious talent earned him a spot on *The Ultimate Fighter* season three, and to no one's surprise, he ran the table, winning three straight fights to take the season title.

Not skipping a beat, Bisping maintained his winning streak with a win against Eric Schafer and a UFC 70 stoppage of Elvis Sinosic in the organization's return to the UK. Those wins made Bisping a star in his home country. But after a controversial decision win over Matt Hamill at UFC 75, the outspoken Brit started to become a villain everywhere else.

"I am who I am," he said. "I speak my mind, but a lot of what I say sometimes is tongue in cheek, and I think sometimes people don't get that and they just think I'm being arrogant and cocky."Embracing the attention, Bisping headlined UFC 78 in a losing effort against Rashad Evans. He then dropped to 185 pounds and started a new winning streak with victories over Charles McCarthy, Jason Day and Chris Leben. Next up was another stint on *The Ultimate Fighter*, this time as a coach against Dan Henderson on season nine. Although his team won both season titles, Coach Bisping got knocked out by Henderson at UFC 100.

Undeterred, Bisping showed what he was made of: he bounced back with a TKO of Denis Kang at UFC 105 in November 2009. He continued to test himself consistently against the best at 185 pounds, proving that this UK standout was here to stay.

JOE LAUZON

DEBUT: UFC 63, SEPTEMBER 23, 2006

BROCKTON, MA

Joe Lauzon has been on the UFC scene for nearly a decade. First as the man who knocked out Jens Pulver in 2006, then as a cast member of *The Ultimate Fighter* season five, and now as one of the top lightweights in the sport.

"I didn't imagine when I took the Pulver fight that I'd be where I am right now," Lauzon said. "As a fighter, as a person, my whole life has been completely changed and flipped on its head."

During this journey, the New Englander has compiled several impressive Octagon victories. After back-to-back finishes of Kyle Bradley and Jeremy Stephens, Lauzon seemed poised for his leap to the next level, but a knee injury sidelined him for much 2009.

Since his 2010 return, Lauzon continued to impress with his technical acumen, but his penchant for engaging in entertaining fights and providing highlight-reel finishes has established him as the leading post-fight bonus award recipient in UFC history; a title he holds in high regard.

"I don't start counting the money, but it's gonna be sad when I have a fight and I don't get a bonus," he laughs. "But I'm more focused on putting a good fight and winning than I am about saying, 'Oh, I'm definitely gonna try and get a bonus.' And the way I fight brings lots of bonuses my way, so I don't think about it too much."

MATT WIMAN
DENVER, CO

DEBUT: UFC 60, MAY 27, 2006

After battling through ups and downs for much of his career, *The Ultimate Fighter* season five's Matt Wiman had the breakthrough year he was looking for in 2008. He submitted Justin Buchholz and knocked out Thiago Tavares before finishing up in December with a Fight of the Night against Jim Miller.

Always exciting, Wiman made his Octagon debut before his stint on *The Ultimate Fighter* season five, losing a memorable UFC 60 bout to Spencer Fisher in 2006. He is known for his dynamic and gritty style and ability to be a tough opponent for anyone he faces on fight night.

CHEICK KONGO
PARIS, FRANCE

DEBUT: UFC 61, JULY 8, 2006

Not much was known of France's Cheick Kongo when he made his UFC debut in July 2006 against Gilbert Aldana. He answered that question quickly and emphatically as he halted his rugged foe in a little over four minutes of the first round.

But not everyone was sold on the dynamic striker, so Kongo jumped back in the Octagon a month later to defeat Christian Wellisch. After a temporary setback against Carmelo Marrero, he impressively defeated Assuerio Silva and PRIDE superstar Mirko Cro Cop in successive bouts.

A three-fight winning streak that began in 2008 inched him closer to a title shot, but losses against Cain Velasquez, Frank Mir, Mark Hunt and Roy Nelson helped end his UFC stint.

THALES LEITES
RIO DE JANEIRO, BRAZIL

DEBUT: THE ULTIMATE FIGHTER 4 FINALE, NOVEMBER 11, 2006

A fighter who made his bones as a professional on the tough Brazilian fight circuit, Thales Leites' grappling pedigree was evident as he built an impressive unbeaten record against standouts like Ronald Jhun and Jose Landi-Jons. In his UFC debut against Martin Kampmann in 2006, Leites faced defeat for the first time, losing a three-round decision. Yet in that defeat, he displayed the qualities of heart and determination that all elite fighters possess.

Leites rebounded with a five-fight winning streak—including wins over Nate Marquardt and Drew McFedries—that led to a title shot in 2009. Even though he fell short against Anderson Silva, he returned in 2013, fighting better than ever.

JASON MACDONALD
NEW GLASGOW, CANADA

DEBUT: ORTIZ VS SHAMROCK 3, OCTOBER 10, 2006

It took Jason "The Athlete" MacDonald close to seven years to get to UFC, but once he arrived with a first-round win over Ed Herman in 2006, he made it clear that he belonged in the world's premier mixed martial arts organization.

Following that bout, "The Athlete" weathered some rocky moments, but he also won more fights in the Octagon during his time there than any Canadian fighter besides Georges St-Pierre. He defeated Chris Leben, Rory Singer, Jason Lambert and old nemesis Joe Doerksen.

At UFC 129, he was expected to be pushed by fellow vet Ryan Jensen. Instead, he kept the fireworks all to himself as he submitted his foe in the first round.

SCOTT SMITH
RENO, NV

DEBUT: UFC 59, APRIL 15, 2006

The Ultimate Fighter season four's Scott "Hands of Steel" Smith knew he only had one punch left in him after getting badly hurt with a body shot from Pete Sell in their November 2006 fight in Las Vegas. If he landed, he had a chance; if he didn't, he was probably going to get knocked out. Sell rushed in, Smith timed his delivery, and BOOM, the fight was over as he knocked his opponent out in one of the most spectacular finishes ever seen in mixed martial arts history.

But for the exciting Californian, it was just another day at the office in a career that saw his "Hands of Steel" produce a lot of memorable endings, even though losses against David Terrell, Patrick Cote and Ed Herman shortened his UFC career.

CLAY GUIDA
ROUND LAKE, IL

DEBUT: UFC 64, OCTOBER 14, 2006
STRIKEFORCE LIGHTWEIGHT CHAMPION

It's hard to believe that you can fit such unbelievable amounts of energy into a 155-pound body, but with each UFC fight, Clay Guida showed that it's not only possible, but that he could put on action-packed bouts night in and night out.

After a solid career on the Midwest circuit, Guida debuted in UFC with a win over Justin James at UFC 64, followed by razor-thin decision defeats to Din Thomas and Tyson Griffin in 2007. Each fight had fans on their feet, and he went on to become one-half of the best fight 2007 when he faced Roger Huerta in December of that year. But after the heartbreaking third-round defeat, Guida did some soul-searching and realized that being exciting wasn't enough in UFC.

In 2008, Guida upped his game in a big way, defeating Samy Schiavo and Mac Danzig as he made himself as effective in the Octagon as he is entertaining. Guida went on to deliver wins over Nate Diaz, Shannon Gugerty, Rafael dos Anjos and Takanori Gomi before landing in the featherweight division.

ROGER HUERTA
LOS ANGELES, CA

DEBUT: UFC 63, SEPTEMBER 23, 2006

One of the most charismatic young stars in UFC during an eight-fight stint from 2006 to 2009, Roger "El Matador" Huerta announced his arrival as a serious threat to the lightweight title with an unforgettable win over Leonard Garcia in April 2007. The victory even landed him the cover of *Sports Illustrated*—making him the first MMA fighter to ever be so honored.

Huerta refused to rest on his laurels, jumping right back into the Octagon to stop tough newcomers Doug Evans and Alberto Crane. But none of those victories compared to his stirring tide-turning win in December 2007 over Clay Guida in what was widely acknowledged as one of the best fights of the year. It was the perfect end to an amazing year.

MARTIN KAMPMANN
AARHUS, DENMARK

DEBUT: UFC FIGHT NIGHT 6, AUGUST 17, 2006

Martin "Hitman" Kampmann came to UFC in 2006 with a reputation as a fierce stand-up fighter. But in his first Octagon bout against Crafton Wallace, Kampmann displayed his all-around MMA game as he quickly took Wallace down and submitted him.

Unfortunately, after a submission of Drew McFedries at UFC 68, a knee injury put him on the shelf. But after a year away, he returned with a win over Jorge Rivera, and after dropping to 170 pounds, "The Hitman" made an impact at welterweight. His victories over Alexandre Barros, Carlos Condit, Jacob Volkmann and Paulo Thiago consistently showed the effortless cool that became his trademark.

YUSHIN OKAMI

DEBUT: UFC 62, AUGUST 26, 2006

KANAGAWA PREFECTURE, JAPAN

After arriving in UFC in 2006, Yushin "Thunder" Okami ripped through the middleweight ranks, defeating Mike Swick, Alan Belcher, Kalib Starnes and Rory Singer along the way.

But it was in a close decision loss to Rich Franklin in June 2007 that Okami truly showed he belonged among the elite at 185 pounds. He pushed the former UFC champion to the limit and almost submitted him in the final round of a closely contested bout.

The powerful Okami then got back in the win column with consecutive victories over former middleweight champ Evan Tanner, Jason MacDonald and Dean Lister. While he lost a decision to Chael Sonnen at UFC 104 in October 2009, Okami showed off his "Thunder." In 2010 with an ultra-impressive TKO of Lucio Linhares in March 2010 and a hard-fought three-round win over Mark Munoz five months later.

Next up was a pivotal battle against Nate Marquardt at UFC 122. With a title shot on the line, Okami was at his best as he pounded out a three-round decision win to achieve his longtime goal: an August 2011 rematch with UFC middleweight champion Anderson Silva—the man Okami held a 2006 disqualification win over. Okami was stopped by Silva in his lone UFC title fight, and after going 3-2 in his next five bouts, he was released by UFC in 2013.

ANTHONY PEROSH
SYDNEY, AUSTRALIA

DEBUT: UFC 61, JULY 8, 2006

Anthony "The Hippo" Perosh is a Brazilian jiu-jitsu black belt and 10-time Australian jiu-jitsu champion who finally scored his long-awaited first Octagon win in 2011 when he submitted Tom Blackledge at UFC 127.

It was a great moment for the native of Sydney, Australia. Once the former heavyweight dropped to his optimum weight 205 pounds, Perosh found the secret to UFC success, winning bouts over Cyrille Diabate, Nick Penner, Vinny Magalhaes and Guto Inocente in the division.

JAMIE VARNER
PHOENIX, AZ

DEBUT: UFC 62, AUGUST 26, 2006 • WEC LIGHTWEIGHT CHAMPION

Jamie Varner burst on the world scene for the first time with two exciting UFC fights in 2006-2007, defeating Jason Gilliam and losing to Hermes Franca. His success attracted the WEC, who brought him to the organization in 2007.

By February 2008, Varner had become the WEC lightweight champion after his third-round TKO of Rob McCullough. Next up were wins over Marcus Hicks and Donald Cerrone in defense of his crown, and suddenly, it looked like Varner was settling in for a long reign at the top. But after a long layoff due to a hand injury, Varner fell short of victory against Benson Henderson in 2010, and he didn't show his old form until a 2012 return to UFC. After a seven-fight second stint in the Octagon, Varner retired in 2014.

SAM STOUT

DEBUT: UFC 58, MARCH 4, 2006

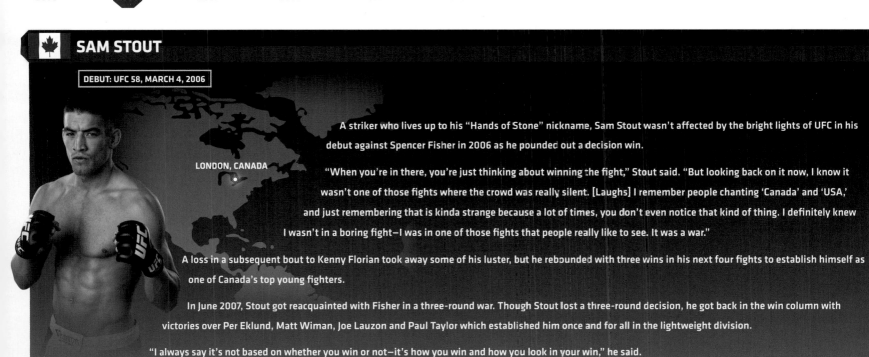

LONDON, CANADA

A striker who lives up to his "Hands of Stone" nickname, Sam Stout wasn't affected by the bright lights of UFC in his debut against Spencer Fisher in 2006 as he pounded out a decision win.

"When you're in there, you're just thinking about winning the fight," Stout said. "But looking back on it now, I know it wasn't one of those fights where the crowd was really silent. [Laughs] I remember people chanting 'Canada' and 'USA,' and just remembering that is kinda strange because a lot of times, you don't even notice that kind of thing. I definitely knew I wasn't in a boring fight—I was in one of those fights that people really like to see. It was a war."

A loss in a subsequent bout to Kenny Florian took away some of his luster, but he rebounded with three wins in his next four fights to establish himself as one of Canada's top young fighters.

In June 2007, Stout got reacquainted with Fisher in a three-round war. Though Stout lost a three-round decision, he got back in the win column with victories over Per Eklund, Matt Wiman, Joe Lauzon and Paul Taylor which established him once and for all in the lightweight division.

"I always say it's not based on whether you win or not—it's how you win and how you look in your win," he said.

MATT HAMILL
LOVELAND, OH

DEBUT: THE ULTIMATE FIGHTER 3 FINALE, JUNE 24, 2006

As one of the contenders in UFC's most high-profile division, light heavyweight star Matt "The Hammer" Hamill proved that being deaf wasn't a handicap, but instead, a mere obstacle to be overcome on the way to bigger and better things. This was never more evident than in his 2008 wins over Tim Boetsch and Reese Andy, in which he took out each of his foes with strikes in the second round. But this was just a taste of what "The Hammer" could do in the Octagon.

A two-time world champion wrestler, Hamill first made his mark in UFC on *The Ultimate Fighter* season three. He has since shown off his improving MMA game as he bounced back from defeats to Michael Bisping (via controversial decision) and Rich Franklin (via knockout), as well as a disappointing disqualification win over Jon Jones. Hamill finished Mark Munoz with a highlight-reel head-kick knockout and outlasted longtime contender Keith Jardine in a classic three-round battle that earned Fight of the Night honors back in June 2010.

But at UFC 121 in October 2010, Hamill showed just how far he had come in the sport with his three-round unanimous decision victory over his former *The Ultimate Fighter* coach, Tito Ortiz. He dominated his mentor for 15 minutes en route to what remains the most important win of his career.

KURT PELLEGRINO
POINT PLEASANT, NJ

DEBUT: UFC 61, JULY 8, 2006

An energetic fighter who participated in some of the most exciting lightweight bouts of the current era against George Sotiropoulos, Nate Diaz and Thiago Tavares, Kurt "Batman" Pellegrino was someone who always gave fans their money's worth.

His reasoning was simple: "I'm not fighting because I think it's cool. I'm fighting because this is the only thing I can do with my life."

With a 7-5 record in UFC from 2006 to 2011, Pellegrino won a Fight of the Night award for his 2008 victory over Thiago Tavares and a Submission of the Night award for his finish of Fabricio Camoes in 2010. Following back-to-back losses to George Sotiropoulos and Gleison Tibau, both by decision, the New Jersey native decided to take a hiatus from the sport.

GLEISON TIBAU
RIO GRANDE DO NORTE, BRAZIL

DEBUT: UFC 65, NOVEMBER 18, 2006

Gleison Tibau showed he belonged in UFC in 2006 as he put forth a courageous effort against Nick Diaz at UFC 65. Displaying stellar jiu-jitsu techniques that had Diaz in trouble, Tibau was eventually overpowered by the bigger fighter and stopped in the second round.

But with the knowledge gained from that loss and a drop to the 155-pound weight class, Tibau got back in the Octagon and showed what he could truly do when he was on a level playing field. He scored notable victories over Kurt Pellegrino, Josh Neer, Terry Etim, Rich Clementi, Caol Uno and Jeremy Stephens while only suffering a handful of defeats against elite-level opponents.

FIGHTS OF THE YEAR

UFC 58
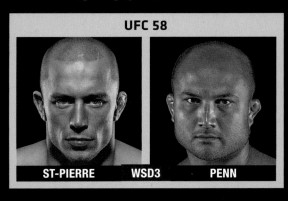
ST-PIERRE | WSD3 | PENN

ULTIMATE FIGHT NIGHT 6

SANCHEZ | W3 | PARISYAN

UFC 63
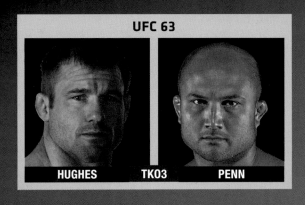
HUGHES | TKO3 | PENN

UFC 59

ORTIZ | W3 | GRIFFIN

THE ULTIMATE FIGHTER 4 FINALE

SMITH | KO2 | SELL

KNOCKOUTS OF THE YEAR

ULTIMATE FIGHT NIGHT 3

LUDWIG | TKO1 | GOULET

UFC 57

LIDDELL | KO2 | COUTURE

ULTIMATE FIGHT NIGHT 5

SILVA | KO1 | LEBEN

UFC 63

LAUZON | KO1 | PULVER

UFC 64

SILVA | TKO1 | FRANKLIN

SUBMISSIONS OF THE YEAR

ORTIZ VS SHAMROCK 3

MACDONALD | WSUB1 | HERMAN

UFC 62
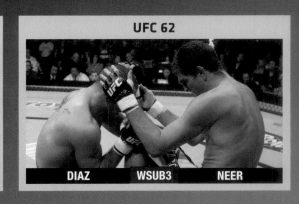
DIAZ | WSUB3 | NEER

ULTIMATE FIGHT NIGHT 6

KAMPMANN | WSUB1 | WALLACE

ULTIMATE FIGHT NIGHT 3

VON FLUE | WSUB3 | KARALEXIS

UFC 58
HOMINICK | WSUB2 | EDWARDS

DEBUTS

ULTIMATE FIGHT NIGHT 3

ASSUERIO SILVA

JASON VON FLUE

UFC 57

GILBERT ALDANA

MIKE WHITEHEAD

UFC 58

STEVE VIGNEAULT

MARK HOMINICK

SAM STOUT

ROB MACDONALD

JASON LAMBERT

TOM MURPHY

ULTIMATE FIGHT NIGHT 4

DAN CHRISTISON

LUIGI FIORAVANTI

UFC 59

JUSTIN LEVENS

SCOTT SMITH

DERRICK NOBLE

UFC 60

RICK DAVIS

DEAN LISTER

MATT WIMAN

THE ULTIMATE FIGHTER 3 FINALE

MICHAEL BISPING

JOSH HAYNES

KENDALL GROVE

ED HERMAN

WILSON GOUVEIA

RORY SINGER

ROSS POINTON

KALIB STARNES

DANNY ABBADI

SOLOMON HUTCHERSON

MATT HAMILL

JESSE FORBES

WES COMBS

MIKE NICKELS

ULTIMATE FIGHT NIGHT 5

JORGE SANTIAGO

KRISTIAN ROTHAERMEL

JORGE GURGEL

ANDERSON SILVA

UFC 61

JOE JORDAN

ANTHONY PEROSH

CHEICK KONGO

KURT PELLEGRINO

UFC FIGHT NIGHT 6

PAT HEALY

ANTHONY TORRES

FORREST PETZ

KRISTOF MIDOUX

JAKE O'BRIEN

MARTIN KAMPMANN

CRAFTON WALLACE

YUKI SASAKI

UFC 62

CHRISTIAN WELLISCH

JAMIE VARNER

ERIC SCHAFER

DAVID HEATH

CORY WALMSLEY

YUSHIN OKAMI

ALAN BELCHER

UFC 63

TYSON GRIFFIN

DAVID LEE

MARIO NETO

EDDIE SANCHEZ

ROGER HUERTA

JASON DENT

JOE LAUZON

GABE RUEDIGER

ORTIZ VS SHAMROCK 3

CHRIS PRICE

JASON MACDONALD

SETH PETRUZELLI

DUSTIN HAZELETT

UFC 64

KUNIYOSHI HIRONAKA

CARMELO MARRERO

DAN LAUZON

JUSTIN JAMES

CLAY GUIDA

JUNIOR ASSUNCAO

THE ULTIMATE FIGHTER 4 FINALE

THALES LEITES

UFC 65

JOSH SCHOCKMAN

HECTOR RAMIREZ

ANTONI HARDONK

SHERMAN PENDERGARST

GLEISON TIBAU

DOKONJONOSUKE MISHIMA

DREW MCFEDRIES

UFC FIGHT NIGHT: SANCHEZ VS RIGGS

STEVE BYRNES

LOGAN CLARK

KEITA NAKAMURA

VICTOR VALIMAKI

UFC president Dana White laughs about it now, but in 2011, he was adamant that women would never fight in the Octagon. It wasn't necessarily a sexist comment; it was one based on the realities of the female mixed martial arts scene at the time. Yes, there was a host of talented athletes competing, but the gap between the haves and have-nots in terms of talent was wide, leading to several notable mismatches.

White, however, has always led UFC with a "never say never" attitude. When an Olympic bronze medalist in judo named Ronda Rousey began competing for the Zuffa-owned STRIKEFORCE promotion, he had to reconsider his original position.

Rousey was a different breed, not just in women's MMA, but also in MMA as a whole. She was a talented, hard-working, and determined force of destruction on fight night, as well as a striking, quotable, and charismatic figure outside of competition. Add in her Olympic pedigree and compelling backstory, and White was intrigued. So much so that after Rousey's STRIKEFORCE bout with Miesha Tate was over, he seriously considered bringing the women's bantamweight division to UFC. In late 2012, he announced that it was time to make it happen. Rousey, UFC's first female champion, was slated to defend her new title against Liz Carmouche in the main event of UFC 157 on February 23, 2013.

"Ronda is the real deal," White said at the time. "She's nasty. She's mean. She's like Chuck Liddell. She goes out there and tries to finish her opponents. And Carmouche is tough as nails, too. She was a Marine, and she's got great ground-and-pound. I look forward to having the women join the UFC."

At the Honda Center in Anaheim, California, Rousey and Carmouche delivered. The champion survived a spirited effort by her challenger before submitting her toward the end of the very first round.

The revolution had begun.

Soon, the best female bantamweights in the world began fighting under the UFC banner, thrilling fans around the globe. Leading the way was Rousey, a dominant champion who was the perfect ambassador for the sport. She drew praise from all quarters, including female fighting pioneer Gina Carano.

"Going to the UFC fights, I remember sitting up in the last row and thinking, 'Someday, someday,'" she said. "And being able to watch other women experience that and doing it with such confidence, it's really changed a lot. At one point, it was bad to be female and walk in a gym, and people don't understand that. But now, they're all looking for the next female fighter that's going to make it. When I was training, it was a lot harder. Now little girls can put on gis at whatever age, and not having to see them struggle through what I kind of went through really has an emotional impact on me."

In 2013, *The Ultimate Fighter* introduced women to the series, with Julianna Pena winning the season eighteen title. In 2014, UFC brought in a second women's division, featuring the 115-pound strawweights on *The Ultimate Fighter: A Champion Will Be Crowned*. When the dust settled on that season, Carla Esparza emerged not just as the winner, but also as UFC's first women's strawweight champion.

It has been quite a whirlwind journey, but one Rousey and her peers are enjoying as they pave the way for a new generation of female mixed martial artists who can compete on the sport's premier stage and gain the respect they have deserved for so many years.

Ronda Rousey and Liz Carmouche

243

Miesha Tate kicks Ronda Rousey during a 2012 STRIKEFORCE bout.

"It's extremely satisfying because that was my goal from the very beginning," Rousey said. "I wanted to gain the respect of people that I respected, and I knew that I was capable. It's funny, but you can see on some old interviews that I did where I said, 'I'm gonna make these people love me, I'm gonna make these people respect me and all I have to do is win and win impressively.' It's not like they're gonna put me in the middle of an arena and be like, 'Okay, here's a model airplane, put it together in 60 seconds.' [Laughs] I have no idea how to do that. But my mom was making me drill judo and armbars and being a fighter and an athlete ever since I can remember. I can't remember not being an athlete. It's just doing what comes natural, and I feel like I've always been deserving of that respect, but I have to do things to earn it."

Sarah Kaufman enters the arena in preparation for her STRIKEFORCE bout against Ronda Rousey.

During *The Ultimate Fighter* season 18, Julianna Pena punches Gina Mazany in their elimination bout.

Carla Esparza attempts a submission on Angela Hill during *The Ultimate Fighter: A Champion Will Be Crowned*.

2007

As 2007 dawned, UFC ruled the mixed martial arts world. *The Ultimate Fighter* reality TV series was a hit; events were sanctioned in MMA hotbeds like Nevada, California and New Jersey; and stars old and new ruled the roost.

As fighters like Chuck Liddell, Anderson Silva and Georges St-Pierre dominated their respective divisions, a segment of the hardcore fan base loudly demanded to know how the elite of UFC would fare against those from PRIDE. Japan's leading MMA promotion was home to standouts such as Minotauro Nogueira, Wanderlei Silva and Takanori Gomi.

On March 27, 2007, those fans didn't need to wonder any longer. It was announced that the majority owners of UFC had formed a new company and purchased PRIDE from Dream Stage Entertainment, essentially combining the forces of the two premier MMA organizations.

"While we have certainly been fierce competitors, at the same time, we have respected each other as the premier organizations in the world for mixed martial arts," owner Lorenzo Fertitta said at the time. "About 10 months ago, we started talking about some type of strategic alliance that we could put together that would ensure the future of MMA. There are a lot of newfound competitors with really no experience and no history that are trying to jump into this sport. UFC and PRIDE are really the foundation of the sport, and we believe that by entering this transaction and coming together that there really is no number three, four or five. These are clearly the two best organizations in the world, and we're going to put on mega fights that will take mixed martial arts to the next level."

"When fighters fight, money's great, as well as the fame and everything that goes along with it," UFC president Dana White added. "But at the end of the day, it's about their legacy. PRIDE and UFC have the best fighters in the world in all the different weight classes. Finally, we're going to be able to find out who the best fighter in the world is. The fans win, both of the organizations win and the fighters win."

"THESE ARE CLEARLY THE TWO BEST ORGANIZATIONS IN THE WORLD, AND WE'RE GOING TO PUT ON MEGA FIGHTS THAT WILL TAKE MIXED MARTIAL ARTS TO THE NEXT LEVEL."
—LORENZO FERTITTA

Anderson Silva submits Travis Lutter with a triangle choke at UFC 67.

Couture defeats Sylvia by unanimous decision at UFC 68.

The announcement sent shockwaves throughout the mixed martial arts world, but it also showed the commitment of UFC brass to give the fans what they want. Plenty of that happened in 2007. If there was a recurring theme throughout the year, it was that no one was safe when the horn sounded. This 12-month period went down as the "Year of the Upset," beginning early on January 25 with the debut of former PRIDE star Heath Herring. Herring's UFC debut was marred by unbeaten but unheralded prospect Jake O'Brien. And it only got crazier from there.

UFC's first Pay-Per-View event 2007 took place on February 3 in Las Vegas, headlined by what should have been Anderson Silva's first middleweight title defense against Travis Lutter. Both Lutter and welterweight Matt Serra had earned title shots in their respective divisions with victories in 2006 on a unique season of *The Ultimate Fighter* entitled *The Comeback*. The series featured UFC veterans looking for a second chance at glory, and the winners received a world title shot instead of a six-figure contract. Lutter's opportunity fell by the wayside when he didn't make weight for the biggest fight of his career. Silva was Silva regardless, submitting his opponent in the second round.

RAMPAGE JACKSON

DEBUT: UFC 67, FEBRUARY 3, 2007
UFC LIGHT HEAVYWEIGHT CHAMPION

MEMPHIS, TN

What's in a nickname? Well, if you go by the moniker "Rampage," you'd better not lay and pray, jab and grab or practice any other less than scintillating technique in search of victory in the mixed martial arts arena. Luckily, Rampage Jackson has only one speed in competition and life: it's all out.

"It's a fight; you win some and you lose some, but you have to give the fans what they want, what they paid for," said Jackson. "They're the most important ones in the sport, and there's no sport without them. I really love my fans, and I really try to give them what they want. And I really don't call them fans, I call them friends."

Born and raised in Memphis, Tennessee, Jackson came up hard in life. To get past the fact that he didn't have the same clothes and things that more fortunate kids had in school, he quickly learned how to use his fists. But eventually, the young Rampage got a strong lecture from an uncle. Coupled with his own mental fortitude and a move to a more stable environment, Jackson suddenly had reason to leave the dead-end life behind.

A few years after his first exposure to organized wrestling, his friend and former wrestling rival Dave Roberts introduced him to MMA. Jackson fell in love, and after a loss to Marvin Eastman in his pro debut in June 2000, he proceeded to win eight in a row before getting the call to be the sacrificial lamb to Japanese superstar Kazushi Sakuraba in the PRIDE organization.

Jackson was submitted by Sakuraba in that July 2001 bout, but he made enough of an impression that he kept getting called back. He soon became a fan favorite, known for his charisma and the trademark heavy chain he wore around his neck. Over the next two years in PRIDE, he only lost once (via a controversial disqualification to Daijiro Matsui) while beating the likes of Ricardo Arona, Igor Vovchanchyn, Kevin Randleman, Murilo Bustamante and UFC star Chuck Liddell. But from the tail end of 2003, Jackson started becoming a bit disillusioned with fighting in Japan, and the idea of coming home to the states to reap the rewards of his hard work began to take shape.

Jackson left PRIDE after his February 2006 win over Dong Sik Yoon. After a brief stay in the now-defunct WFA for a win over Matt Lindland, Rampage finally arrived in the world-famous Octagon in 2007. After avenging his loss to Eastman at UFC 67, he won the UFC light heavyweight championship in May of that year by knocking out Liddell—for a second time.

Now a star in his own country, Jackson became the first man to unify the UFC and PRIDE titles when he won by decision over Dan Henderson at UFC 75. However, he lost his belt in July 2008 via a razor-thin decision to Forrest Griffin.

Despite going 4-4 in his next eight UFC bouts, Jackson always showed up to fight, win or lose, and the fans stayed by his side throughout.

Rampage defeats Marvin Eastman via KO at UFC 67.

UFC 67's lack of a title fight didn't dilute its star power, though, not by a long shot. The card featured the UFC debuts of former PRIDE stars Rampage Jackson and Mirko Cro Cop, as well as international star Lyoto Machida, all of who emerged victorious. Also debuting was an unknown lightweight prospect from New Jersey named Frankie Edgar. By the end of the night, everyone knew who Edgar was; he picked up Fight of the Night honors for his win over Tyson Griffin.

Yet, all the good vibes from the event turned into something different over the next couple of weeks. Many concerned fight fans thought that 43-year-old Randy Couture was going to get seriously injured in his UFC 68 main event bout against heavyweight champion Tim Sylvia on March 3. Simply put, after losing two out of three fights to UFC light heavyweight champion Chuck Liddell, and a tearful retirement in 2006, most believed that Couture had run out of miracles. His last two fights at heavyweight saw him stopped by Josh Barnett and Ricco Rodriguez. But before a packed house at the Nationwide Arena, the UFC Hall of Famer shocked the world once again, dominating Tim Sylvia for five rounds en route to a shutout five-round decision that earned him a third UFC heavyweight championship. "Not bad for an old man," said Couture after the bout.

The victory was an inspiring one, but still a major upset. However, it was surpassed a month later in Houston, as Matt Serra got his crack at the welterweight title that came along with his win on *The Ultimate Fighter* season four. Like Couture against Sylvia, Serra was a prohibitive underdog against Georges St-Pierre on April 7, but odds mean nothing in mixed martial arts. What matters is what happens when the horn sounds, and when it sounded at the Toyota Center, Serra came to fight. When you do that, good things can happen. They certainly did for the Long Island native. Serra stunned the world with a first-round TKO win over St-Pierre to win the UFC welterweight championship.

"Tonight, I got beat by a better fighter than myself," said a gracious St-Pierre after the bout. "He beat me fair and square. I'm very sad right now, but I will come back."

Only four months into the year, and UFC had already been thrown into upheaval. But the show must go on. Two weeks after Serra-St-Pierre, the promotion's international expansion kicked into gear with UFC 70 in Manchester, England. Featuring *The Ultimate Fighter* season three winner Michael Bisping, who scored a Fight of the Night win over Elvis Sinosic in his hometown, the card was headlined by European star Mirko Cro Cop. Cro Cop looked to secure a shot at Couture with a win over Brazil's Gabriel Gonzaga, a sizeable underdog.

By this point, you know what underdog meant in 2007, and Cro Cop was the next victim of the upset bug. For years, the Croatian had knocked opponents out in devastating fashion with fearsome kicks to the head. On April 21, before a packed house at the M.E.N. Arena, Gonzaga gave Cro Cop a taste of his own medicine at UFC's first event in England since UFC 38. He sent Cro Cop crashing to defeat with a single right kick to the head that earned him a shot at UFC heavyweight champion Couture.

After all the madness, the MMA world was expected to get back to normal in Las Vegas on May 26, as Liddell defended his title against Rampage Jackson. The bout was a rematch of a 2003 PRIDE matchup won by Jackson. At the time, there was no bigger match to be made in the sport, with mainstream coverage of the UFC 71 event hitting an all-time high. Yet, at the MGM Grand Garden Arena, it was Jackson—still relatively unknown in the United States despite his track record in Japan—who ended Liddell's title reign and seven-fight winning streak with a stunning first-round TKO.

Gonzaga defeats Cro Cop via a first round KO at UFC 70.

FABRICIO WERDUM

DEBUT: UFC 70, APRIL 21, 2007
INTERIM UFC HEAVYWEIGHT CHAMPION

PORTO ALEGRE, BRAZIL

Fabricio "Vai Cavalo" Werdum turned to Brazilian jiu-jitsu after falling victim to a triangle choke in a fight with his girlfriend's ex-boyfriend. Embarrassed by this turn of events, he began training fanatically, eventually earning his black belt and becoming one of the world's top jiu-jitsu practitioners.

"He finished the fight in five seconds with a triangle choke; it was amazing," recalled Werdum, able to laugh about it now. "The next day, I decided to know more about jiu-jitsu and started to train a lot to be a world champion."

In 2002, Werdum looked for a new challenge and found it in MMA. He established himself as a top heavyweight contender in PRIDE and UFC by beating the likes of Tom Erikson, Alistair Overeem, Gabriel Gonzaga and Brandon Vera.

Following a UFC 90 loss to Junior Dos Santos, Werdum moved on to STRIKEFORCE. There, he stunned the world in June 2010 with a 69-second submission win over former PRIDE heavyweight champion Fedor Emelianenko.

Werdum returned to UFC in 2012 and was better than ever, running off a five-fight winning streak. That streak culminated in a second-round knockout of Mark Hunt at UFC 180 on November 15, 2014, awarding Werdum the interim UFC heavyweight championship belt.

"It's the result of years of hard work," said Werdum. "In my life, I always set goals, and luckily, I always achieved them. When I started training in Brazilian jiu-jitsu, I wanted to become world champion, and I did it three times. I wanted to become ADCC world champion; I did it two times. And now, my main goal is to be the best UFC heavyweight in the world."

MANNY GAMBURYAN
GYUMRI, ARMENIA

DEBUT: THE ULTIMATE FIGHTER 5 FINALE, JUNE 23, 2007

Manny "The Anvil" Gamburyan has made a career of upsetting the odds. Just 5'5", the man dubbed "The Anvil" has battled the best in the world over the course of a career that began in 1999, including Sean Sherk, Jorge Santiago and Nate Diaz. What made *The Ultimate Fighter* season five finalist's accomplishments even more impressive is that he made it to the upper reaches of the lightweight division while giving up size to his opponents every time out.

But in 2009, Gamburyan found a place to call home in the 145-pound featherweight division. After making his mark there, he moved to bantamweight, where he looks better than ever.

LEONARD GARCIA
PLAINVIEW, TX

DEBUT: UFC 69, APRIL 7, 2007

Leonard "Bad Boy" Garcia's fighting journey has seen him stop the legendary Jens Pulver in just 72 seconds, fight in a three-round WEC classic that saw him emerge victorious over "The Korean Zombie" Chan Sung Jung and win several Fight of the Night awards. All the while, the Texan with the wild swinging style endeared himself to fans around the world with his affable personality and desire to always deliver the action-packed fights they want, whether he emerges victorious or not. For him, it's all about the battle.

AKIHIRO GONO
HIGASHIKURUME, TOKYO, JAPAN

DEBUT: UFC 78, NOVEMBER 17, 2007

Charismatic Akihiro "The Japanese Sensation" Gono has been competing in mixed martial arts since 1994, compiling more than 30 wins. Along the way, he faced a Who's Who of the sport from welterweight to light heavyweight—including former UFC champions Matt Hughes and Shogun Rua, UFC and PRIDE vet Yuki Kondo and two-division PRIDE champion Dan Henderson. He made a name for himself in the PRIDE, Pancrase and Shooto organizations for his aggressive style and well-rounded attacks, along with his memorable ring entrances.

In UFC, Gono's résumé included a win over Tamdan McCrory in his UFC debut in November 2007 and hard-fought decision losses against Dan Hardy and Jon Fitch.

LYOTO MACHIDA

DEBUT: UFC 67, FEBRUARY 3, 2007
UFC LIGHT HEAVYWEIGHT CHAMPION

SALVADOR, BAHIA,
BRAZIL

The son never had a chance.

There would be no soccer fields or jiu-jitsu canvases for Lyoto "The Dragon" Machida, at least not if his father had a say in the matter. As the head of the family, Yoshizo Machida did have the last word, so when his son was three, he began training in the family business—not as a banker, a farmer, a storekeeper or a craftsman, but as a martial artist.

As he grew older, Machida found time for the usual pursuits of youth, but he never strayed far away from a gym or dojo, whether it was to study and compete in karate, sumo wrestling or jiu-jitsu, an art usually associated with Brazil. There was no doubt that young Machida was going to be a fighter.

Preparing to fight for a living would be anything but easy, though. His true graduation day didn't come until May 2, 2003, when he made his professional MMA debut with a decision over Kengo Watanabe. Four months later, Machida took just 4:21 to stop future UFC Hall of Famer Stephan Bonnar, and suddenly, fight industry insiders began noticing the son of the karate master.

Fight fans soon jumped on the bandwagon that New Year's Eve in Japan, when unbeaten rising star Rich Franklin stepped into battle with Machida and left with his first loss via TKO. Now, things were about to get interesting.

Machida began fighting for the K-1 organization in 2004. 2005 saw another high-profile name fall to defeat at Machida's hands, as BJ Penn rose up in weight to fight the then-heavyweight and lost a three-round decision. Then it was off to UFC, where Machida debuted in 2007 with a win over Sam Hoger at UFC 67.

In his early days in the organization, Machida was criticized for his methodical and unorthodox style, but you couldn't argue with the results. He accrued two more victories over David Heath and Kazuhiro Nakamura.

But when he submitted Rameau Sokoudjou, defeated Tito Ortiz via decision and knocked out Thiago Silva, he made believers out of even the harshest critics. Next up was a world title shot, and with a second-round knockout of Rashad Evans at UFC 98 in May 2009, he announced to the world "karate is back."

A two-fight series with countryman Shogun Rua was the first order of business for the new champion. But after winning the first bout via controversial decision, he was knocked out in the rematch at UFC 113 in 2010, costing him his belt and his unbeaten record.

Machida's journey was far from over, though. After six more bouts at 205 pounds, he made the move to middleweight. He is now a top candidate to become only the third man in UFC history to win titles in two weight classes.

The tension was thick before the bout, as camera flashes were seen throughout the arena. The action didn't match the atmosphere in the opening minute, though, bringing a look of disdain and a wave-in from Jackson to engage. Liddell obliged, but after Jackson absorbed a left hook from "The Iceman," he came back immediately with a right hook that dropped Liddell to the canvas hard. Rampage immediately pounced on the soon-to-be ex-champion, and after four unanswered blows, referee John McCarthy halted the bout at the 1:53 mark, and a new king was crowned at 205 pounds.

That wasn't the only UFC 71 upset: Octagon newcomer Houston Alexander made quite an impression in his debut, stunning 205-pound contender Keith Jardine via a devastating first-round knockout.

Things finally calmed down for a bit over the next few months. UFC continued staging Fight Night events, traveled to Belfast, Northern Ireland for the first time for UFC 72 and crowned a new *The Ultimate Fighter* champion in Nate Diaz, winner of season five. The upset bug even stayed away for July 7th's UFC 73 event, as Anderson Silva and Sean Sherk successfully defended their titles against challengers Nate Marquardt and Hermes Franca. Also in action on that card in Sacramento, California, was former PRIDE heavyweight champion Minotauro Nogueira, who made his long-awaited UFC debut with a decision win over Heath Herring.

At UFC 74 on August 25, Gonzaga cashed in his title fight ticket to face Couture at the Mandalay Bay Events Center in Las Vegas, but he got stopped in the third round. The co-main event saw the return of Georges St-Pierre, who got back on the winning track with a decision victory over Josh Koscheck.

In September, UFC returned to England for its first show in London, which was a historic event in several ways: Jackson retained his UFC light heavyweight title and became the first fighter to unify UFC and PRIDE championships. He defeated two-division PRIDE champ Dan Henderson in Hendo's first Octagon bout since 1998.

With the PRIDE purchase, there was one fight that fans wanted more than any other: a showdown between Liddell and "The Axe Murderer" Wanderlei Silva. On September 22, 2007, the only thing holding the fight back was Liddell beating Keith Jardine in the UFC 76 main event. Before the fight, Silva was asked if he felt nervous.

"Nervous?" asked Silva. "Of course. I want to fight him [Liddell]. I've waited so long for this fight, and everyone wants to see it. But a fight is a fight, and this guy [Jardine] is a strong guy. But they have a movie out now, I see it many times on the TV, it says, 'Good Luck Chuck.' [Laughs] That's the message I give for him: good luck, Chuck."

Liddell needed luck but didn't get it, as Jardine upset the former light heavyweight champ on a card that also saw former PRIDE Grand Prix champion Shogun Rua lose his highly anticipated UFC debut to Forrest Griffin.

As the year wound down, Anderson Silva proved his dominance over the middleweight division once more by knocking out Rich Franklin in their UFC 77 rematch. Also, Rashad Evans outpointed Bisping in a meeting of former *The Ultimate Fighter* winners who headlined UFC 78, and Mac Danzig was crowned the winner of *The Ultimate Fighter* season six.

All that was left was the big year-end show in Las Vegas on December 29. The headline bout was St-Pierre's win of the interim UFC welterweight title in his rubber match against Matt Hughes. But the fans' main event was the long-awaited Liddell vs Silva bout—set by UFC despite Liddell's loss to Jardine—proving that there is a Santa Claus.

And though Mr. Claus came six years and four days late, he finally showed up with a fight between Liddell and Silva, the two most dominant light heavyweights in history. The ensuing three-round war lived up to all expectations, with Liddell emerging victorious via a three-round unanimous decision.

"It would have been a travesty if we wouldn't have fought because it's a great fight for the fans," said Liddell in the understatement of the year. "I knew it was a big fight for everybody, especially for me to get back on track."

"I gave my best," said Silva. "Win or lose, I like to give to my fans." Both fighters truly did that, and more.

SHOGUN RUA

DEBUT: UFC 76, SEPTEMBER 22, 2007
UFC LIGHT HEAVYWEIGHT CHAMPION
2005 PRIDE MIDDLEWEIGHT (205 POUND) GRAND PRIX CHAMPION

CURITIBA, PARANÁ, BRAZIL

When he was a child just getting into combat sports, one of Shogun Rua's first heroes was former heavyweight boxing champion Mike Tyson. As he got older and began his own journey through the world of mixed martial arts, his idols included his older brother Murilo and his Chute Boxe teammate Wanderlei Silva. Silva was obviously the PRIDE wrecking machine and MMA's most feared competitor, while "Ninja" could do no wrong in or out of the ring just by virtue of being Shogun's brother.

"I started out because of my brother and could train and watch him and Wanderlei train every day, and this gave me great models to look after and made me believe I could achieve something," said Shogun.

As Shogun progressed through the sport, he was soon awarded (or some would say burdened with) the tag of "invincible" as he won 12 of 13 fights in PRIDE. His only loss to Mark Coleman was the result of a freak arm injury. It was a remarkable string of excellence highlighted by a four-fight streak in 2005 that saw him defeat Rampage Jackson, Minotauro Nogueira, Alistair Overeem and Ricardo Arona. This earned him the 2005 PRIDE middleweight Grand Prix title and recognition as one of the top 205-pound fighters on the planet.

"I remember that training every day at my academy was tougher than anything else," he said when asked about winning the prestigious Grand Prix. "Back in those days at Chute Boxe, there were a lot of tough fighters, and usually, you would get a tougher time in the gym. My coaches always made me believe in myself, and I felt I was capable of beating anyone. I entered the PRIDE Grand Prix considered the least favorite out of 16 to win the whole thing. That really motivated me a lot, as I don't mind when people doubt me; it just motivates me to work harder."

Shogun's hard work allowed him to skyrocket to the top. His eventual arrival in UFC in September 2007 was greeted with great fanfare, as Shogun finally had the opportunity to address all the questions that fans wanted answered. It didn't work out as planned, though. Shogun lost his Octagon debut to Forrest Griffin and subsequently underwent the first of multiple knee surgeries.

Following his second surgery and the entire rehabilitation process, Shogun returned to the Octagon in January 2009 against his old nemesis, Mark Coleman, at UFC 93. Although the bout was awarded Fight of the Night honors, it was far from a stellar performance from Shogun, who nonetheless stopped "The Hammer" with 24 seconds left in the fight. Again, many wondered whether his best days were behind him, and Shogun heard all the criticism.

But three months later at UFC 97 in April 2009, the critics were silenced. Shogun finally delivered the UFC performance that fans had been waiting to see, knocking out Chuck Liddell in the first round. That victory propelled him into a title shot against UFC light heavyweight champion Lyoto Machida. After their 25-minute war of attrition at UFC 104, most observers believed that a new king was about to be crowned. The three judges disagreed, awarding the highly controversial verdict to Machida.

Disappointed but undeterred, Shogun went back to the gym to devise a strategy to crack the Machida riddle at their May 2010 rematch. At UFC 113, he did just that, knocking out the previously unbeaten "Dragon" in the first round to win UFC's 205-pound title.

Shogun's reign lasted less than a year, as he was stopped in the third round by Jon Jones at UFC 128 on March 19, 2011. But Shogun continues to fight the best in the world, as he pursues another championship.

MIRKO CRO COP
VINKOVCI, CROATIA

DEBUT: UFC 67, FEBRUARY 3, 2007
PRIDE GRAND PRIX OPEN WEIGHT CHAMPION

"Right leg hospital, left leg cemetery." It's the line that made feared Croatian striker Mirko Cro Cop a legend, and when he landed one of his trademark kicks to the head or body, that was usually all she wrote for opponents.

A former kickboxer who began training to compete in the K-1 organization back in 1994, Cro Cop made his pro debut in 1996 at age 21. Over the next seven years, he fought the elite of the sport. If that weren't impressive enough, when he wasn't training or fighting, he was a member of the Croatian anti-terrorist unit ATJ Lucko and then later served on Croatia's Parliament.

In 2001, Cro Cop made his first inroads into MMA when he stopped Kazuyuki Fujita. Later that year, he entered the PRIDE organization in Japan and started a reign that saw him compile a 21-4-2 MMA record. Cro Cop ultimately fell short of the PRIDE heavyweight title when Fedor Emelianenko defeated him via decision in 2005. His last stop in Japan saw him win the organization's open weight Grand Prix tournament.

How do you top that? You come to UFC and try to repeat your success there. Unfortunately, Cro Cop's time in the Octagon was epitomized by more stops than starts, disappointing the competitive veteran. A 2015 return saw him stop Gabriel Gonzaga, though, pumping new life into this superstar's career.

NATE DIAZ
STOCKTON, CA

DEBUT: THE ULTIMATE FIGHTER 5 FINALE, JUNE 23, 2007
THE ULTIMATE FIGHTER 5 WINNER

If you ever read an interview with Nate Diaz or see him fight, there will never be a question about where he comes from, as few athletes rep their hometown quite like Diaz does. "Stockton's where I live, where I come from," he said. "All my family and friends are here, and I just put it out there because I remember where I came from."

A pro since age 19, Diaz followed his older brother, UFC veteran Nick Diaz, into the world of mixed martial arts. By 2006, he had already fought in Japan and battled for the WEC lightweight title held by Hermes Franca. But there were bigger things ahead, and in 2007, he made it through perhaps the most talent-rich cast in *The Ultimate Fighter* history to win the season five title and earn a UFC contract.

Through his first four fights in the Octagon, the Cesar Gracie jiu-jitsu black belt was unstoppable as he submitted Junior Assuncao, Alvin Robinson and Kurt Pellegrino, and defeated Josh Neer by decision. Razor-thin decision losses to Clay Guida, Joe Stevenson and Gray Maynard sandwiched a finish of Melvin Guillard in 2009 and slowed his progress. A jump to welterweight kick-started his career again as he took out veterans Rory Markham and Marcus Davis before two losses brought him back to the lightweight division in 2011.

DEMIAN MAIA
SAO PAULO, BRAZIL

DEBUT: UFC 77, OCTOBER 20, 2007

When a world-class grappler enters the MMA world, there is always a little skepticism, but Demian Maia impressed from the moment he put on the gloves. He was the winner of a seemingly endless array of grappling tournaments, including the world championships, Abu Dhabi and Pan Ams.

In 2007, he made his UFC debut with a first-round submission win over Ryan Jensen. In subsequent bouts, he submitted Ed Herman, Jason MacDonald, Nate Quarry and Chael Sonnen before a knockout loss to Nate Marquardt.

At UFC 112, Maia fought Anderson Silva for the middleweight title. Despite losing a five-round decision, he was praised for his toughness, which he continues to show in his run toward a title in a new division: welterweight.

"I'm feeling good at welterweight," he said. "At middleweight, I barely had to cut weight, and I would actually make an effort to get bigger and heavier to not give away too much power to my opponents. Fighting as a welterweight, I'm feeling at least closer in size and strength to most of the other fighters, and this has been helping me to perform better. Both weight classes have top fighters, and there are no easy paths, but I think that for my genetics and frame, welterweight seems more equal."

HOUSTON ALEXANDER
EAST ST. LOUIS, IL

DEBUT: UFC 71, MAY 26, 2007

For a brief spell in 2007, the talk of the mixed martial arts world was Houston "The Assassin" Alexander, an exciting knockout artist with a heart of gold who went from obscurity to stardom thanks to a compelling backstory and a 48-second finish of Keith Jardine at UFC 71. A single father raising six children, Alexander even donated one of his kidneys to his daughter in 2000. In the Octagon, Alexander's ferocious first-round knockout wins over Jardine and Alessio Sakara put him on the light heavyweight map. But a four-fight losing streak capped by a dismal decision loss to Kimbo Slice in 2009 prompted his release from UFC.

RYO CHONAN
TSURUOKA, YAMAGATA PREFECTURE, JAPAN

DEBUT: UFC 78, NOVEMBER 17, 2007

You wouldn't know it by walking around Tokyo, but many of the buildings in the Japanese city bear the fingerprints of former construction worker Ryo "Piranha" Chonan. Similarly, you wouldn't know how good a fighter Chonan was by looking at his UFC record, but fans that followed him during his time in the PRIDE and DEEP organizations know that he has earned his place in MMA lore. One of the few to finish Anderson Silva, Chonan did it in their 2004 PRIDE bout with one of the greatest submissions ever: a flying scissor heel hook. Chonan also defeated Carlos Newton and Hayato Sakurai, but never seemed to catch a rhythm in his four-fight UFC stint.

MARCUS AURELIO
FORTALEZA, CEARÁ, BRAZIL

DEBUT: UFC 74, AUGUST 25, 2007

A pro fighter since 2002, Brazilian jiu-jitsu black belt Marcus "Maximus" Aurelio's ground game first made an international impact in April 2006, when he handed Japanese superstar Takanori Gomi his first defeat in the PRIDE organization. Seven months later, Gomi got even via split decision, but following the bout, Aurelio received a UFC contract. Aurelio sometimes struggled, with stellar finishes of Luke Caudillo and Ryan Roberts overshadowed by his losses—including a decision defeat against his hometown rival Hermes Franca at UFC 90 that doubled as a Fortaleza turf war. After the loss to Franca, Aurelio was brought back one more time at UFC 102, but he was dropped following a close decision to Evan Dunham.

  MARK BOCEK
TORONTO, CANADA

DEBUT: UFC 73, JULY 7, 2007

In 1994, everything changed for 12-year-old Mark Bocek when he watched Royce Gracie submit foe after foe at UFC 2. "Once I started learning it [jiu-jitsu], it was this new profound experience. It was something you could feel was working." Bocek subsequently became one of the world's finest practitioners of the art. The black belt used his talent on the canvas to win eight UFC bouts, including four by submission over Alvin Robinson, David Bielkheden, Joe Brammer and Dustin Hazelett. His only Octagon losses came against fellow standouts Frankie Edgar, Mac Danzig, Benson Henderson, Rafael dos Anjos and Jim Miller. Bocek retired in 2014.

  ROAN CARNEIRO
RIO DE JANEIRO, BRAZIL

DEBUT: UFC FIGHT NIGHT: STEVENSON VS GUILLARD, APRIL 5, 2007

How's this for a welcome to the world of professional fighting? After losing his debut in 2000 to Marcelo Belmiro, Roan "Jucao" Carneiro got matched up with none other than future UFC superstar Anderson Silva. "Nobody really wanted to fight him, but I decided I had nothing to lose, so I stepped up, and I'm glad I did," said Carneiro years later. Luckily, after losing to Silva, things got better for "Jucao," who went on to win 10 of his next 13 fights, earning him a shot in UFC.

 **MAC DANZIG**
CLEVELAND, OH

DEBUT: THE ULTIMATE FIGHTER: TEAM HUGHES VS TEAM SERRA FINALE, DECEMBER 8, 2007
THE ULTIMATE FIGHTER 6 WINNER

When it was announced that six-year MMA veteran Mac Danzig had been selected to compete on the sixth season of *The Ultimate Fighter*, most assumed that the Ohio native was going to romp over his castmates on the way to the season title. They were right, as Danzig submitted all four of his foes in the first round to earn a UFC contract. Then, things got tricky for the most notable vegan in the sport, as an opening post-*The Ultimate Fighter* victory over Mark Bocek was followed by three consecutive losses. But after a change of scenery for training camp and wins over Justin Buchholz and Joe Stevenson, Danzig showed his potential once more. He retired in 2014.

UFC FIGHTERS 2005-06

HEATH HERRING
FORT WORTH, TX

DEBUT: UFC FIGHT NIGHT: EVANS VS SALMON, JANUARY 25, 2007

A true Texan from the top of his 10-gallon hat to the bottom of his cowboy boots, Waco-born Heath "The Texas Crazy Horse" Herring made his state proud with his aggressive style and world-class MMA game. While that was good news for people in the Lone Star State, it was even better for fight fans around the globe. When "The Texas Crazy Horse" was on his game and matched with a fighter as eager to throw down as he was, it always made for a memorable night.

With a record of 28-14 with one no contest, Herring, a PRIDE vet, is the owner of standout wins over Mark Kerr, Igor Vovchanchyn, Gary Goodridge and Cheick Kongo. However, his rocky ascension up the UFC ranks hit a roadblock when he lost to Brock Lesnar in August 2008. It was his last bout in the organization.

ANTHONY JOHNSON
DUBLIN, GA

DEBUT: UFC FIGHT NIGHT: STOUT VS FISHER, JUNE 12, 2007

Anthony "Rumble" Johnson is one of those "can't miss" fighters, the type who gets better with each passing win. But despite the success that saw the former junior college national wrestling champion score UFC victories over Chad Reiner, Tommy Speer, Kevin Burns, Luigi Fioravanti, Yoshiyuki Yoshida, Phil Davis, Rogerio Nogueira and Alexander Gustafsson, Johnson remained grounded.

This attitude helped him deal with a string of UFC losses, as well as battles with the scale. When the former welterweight returned to the Octagon in 2014 as a light heavyweight, he rapidly shot to the top of the division.

COLE MILLER
AUGUSTA, GA

DEBUT: THE ULTIMATE FIGHTER 5 FINALE, JUNE 23, 2007

A talented ground fighter and submission artist with a finisher's mentality, Georgia native Cole Miller first burst onto the national scene during his stint on *The Ultimate Fighter* season five, where he made it to the show's quarterfinals. But after notching impressive post-show wins over Andy Wang and Leonard Garcia, "Magrinho" furthered his reputation as one of UFC's top up-and-comers even more. Although he hit bumps in the road over the years, his victories over Jorge Gurgel, Junie Browning, Dan Lauzon and Ross Pearson have kept him in the hunt for world title honors.

MINOTAURO NOGUEIRA

DEBUT: UFC 73, JULY 7, 2007
INTERIM UFC HEAVYWEIGHT CHAMPION
PRIDE HEAVYWEIGHT CHAMPION

VITÓRIA DA CONQUISTA,
BAHIA, BRAZIL

November 9, 2003. For almost 10 minutes at the Tokyo Dome, Minotauro Nogueira went through hell. In a battle for the PRIDE heavyweight championship, feared striker Mirko Cro Cop battered the Brazilian. When the round was over, Nogueira may have thought about what just happened. Most likely, though, he thought about Bahia, the city where his life almost ended at 10 years old.

At a neighborhood party, Nogueira and his friends were playing in the street. But soon, everything changed when a truck began to move and backed up and over Minotauro.

He remained in a coma for four days and in the hospital for almost 11 months with broken legs and internal injuries. After finally being released from the hospital, Nogueira still couldn't walk for two more months. If anyone had told his family that this child would someday be one of the greatest heavyweights of all time, they would have been smacked for telling such a cruel joke—but they would have been right.

"I think that time makes me strong. I feel when I fight that nothing's gonna be worse than that," says Noguiera.

By age 19, Minotauro was making his professional debut. From there, he established himself as the best heavyweight in the business, a fact born from his reign as PRIDE heavyweight champion and his victories over Dan Henderson, Jeremy Horn, Ricco Rodriguez, Josh Barnett, Mark Coleman, Heath Herring...and Mirko Cro Cop.

When the horn sounded for the second round, Nogueira showed his unbreakable spirit by taking Cro Cop to the canvas and securing an armbar for the submission victory. It was the sweetest and most memorable win of his PRIDE career, but there were new mountains to climb in UFC.

At UFC 73 in July 2007, he faced a familiar foe in Herring. In typical Nogueira style, he rose from the canvas to defeat his opponent by decision over three rounds. More of the same occurred in his next bout at UFC 81 in 2008. For two rounds, he took a horrific pounding from Tim Sylvia before winning the interim UFC heavyweight title with a guillotine choke in the third. As Nogueira said after becoming the first man to win UFC and PRIDE heavyweight titles, "I played his game for almost three rounds. He played my game for two minutes, and I won the fight."

Following the victory, Nogueira and former UFC heavyweight champion Frank Mir squared off as coaches on The Ultimate Fighter season eight. After the season, the two met in the Octagon at UFC 92. But there were no miracles this time, as Nogueira was knocked out for the first time in his career by Mir.

Despite Nogueira entering the Mir bout with a knee injury and a recent staph infection, many fans believed he was done as a top-level heavyweight. But the great ones don't fade away that easily, and he received a shot at redemption at UFC 102 in August 2009. Facing Randy Couture in Oregon, a place "The Natural" had called home for years, Nogueira was going to be fighting a UFC Hall of Famer. The crowd and the doubts were coming from scores of fight fans, but he liked those odds.

That night was a vintage Nogueira performance. For three action-packed rounds, he went to war with Couture. Despite the competitive nature of the bout, there was no doubt who had won when the fight was all over: Minotauro Nogueira was back.

In February 2010, Nogueira was back in action against unbeaten rising star Cain Velasquez, but there was no stopping the man who would soon be heavyweight champion. Velasquez knocked Nogueira out in the first round.

Injuries hampered the Brazilian over the next several years, but don't count him out yet. There is no more resilient fighter on the planet than Minotauro Nogueira.

FRANKIE EDGAR

DEBUT: UFC 67, FEBRUARY 3, 2007
UFC LIGHTWEIGHT CHAMPION

TOMS RIVER, NJ

April 10, 2010. Frankie "The Answer" Edgar had been in this position before: on the wrestling mats for Toms River High School East and Clarion University, and now, thousands of miles away in Abu Dhabi.

He had just given everything he had in 25 minutes against the best lightweight fighter ever, BJ Penn. Now, he just had to wait for Octagon announcer Bruce Buffer to announce the decision that determined whether he would have to settle for second (as he did in high school and college) or if he would finally have the spotlight all to himself at the top.

50-45 was the first score, one met with "oohs" and "aahs" from Yas Island to Hilo and the Jersey Shore, mainly because in a fight as close as this one was, it was shocking that someone saw it as a shutout. Score number two: 48-47. Score number three: 49-46.

"For the winner," bellowed Buffer, "annnnnnnnnnnnnnnnnnnd NEW!!!!"

For Frankie Edgar, UFC lightweight champion of the world, everything went blank. "I've been there so many times that this was just unbelievable—I didn't know how to feel," he said. "I had been there so many times and disappointed so many times."

Not this time. While Edgar's win over Penn was rightfully seen as an upset considering the dominance of "The Prodigy" over the division since 2008, it came as no surprise to Team Edgar. The team had approached the entire fight and the training camp leading up to it with calm and confidence that made it look like Edgar had been in 10 championship fights before.

Continually elevating his game has been Edgar's MO throughout his UFC career. He came into UFC in 2007 as a scrappy wrestler with a lot of heart. By the time his 2009 bout with Sean Sherk arrived, he had developed a refined standup game that opened plenty of eyes around the MMA world.

The Penn win was icing on the cake, but instead of resting on his laurels, Edgar returned to the Octagon in August 2010 to defeat Penn again. In January 2011, he faced off against the first man to beat him, Gray Maynard, in the main event of UFC 125. After surviving a horrific first round, Edgar roared back to earn a five-round draw with "The Bully," setting up a third bout in late 2011 that he won by knockout.

Edgar lost the title to Benson Henderson in 2012, but "The Answer" kept moving. He took himself to the featherweight division in 2013 to chase after another crown—one he is determined to take back home to New Jersey with him.

GRAY MAYNARD
PHOENIX, AZ

DEBUT: THE ULTIMATE FIGHTER 5 FINALE, JUNE 23, 2007

An undefeated record can be a burden for many fighters, making them fight not to lose as opposed to fighting to win. Gray Maynard, who was unbeaten in 13 pro MMA bouts before losing for the first time to Frankie Edgar in their third bout in 2011, was not one of those fighters.

"I get asked what my record is, and I couldn't even tell you," he laughs. "I just expect to win."

As Kenny Florian, Rich Clementi, Frankie Edgar, Jim Miller, Roger Huerta and Nate Diaz will tell you, when the former NCAA Division I All-American from Michigan State and *The Ultimate Fighter* season five alumnus was on, beating him was a near-impossible task.

THIAGO SILVA
SÃO CARLOS, SÃO PAULO, BRAZIL

DEBUT: UFC 71, MAY 26, 2007

Houston Alexander was everywhere in the weeks leading up to his UFC 78 bout against Thiago Silva, with newspapers and websites telling his story with a fervor. But when the two 205-pounders stepped into the Octagon, it was Silva who carved his own name into the headlines as he stopped the knockout artist in the first round.

Now everyone knew the Brazilian, who scored notable UFC victories over Alexander, Antonio Mendes, Tomasz Drwal, James Irvin and Keith Jardine. Unfortunately, issues outside of the Octagon hampered Silva more than his opponents did, shortening a UFC career that ended in 2014.

DENNIS SIVER
OMSK, RUSSIA

DEBUT: UFC 70, APRIL 21, 2007

With victories like those over rising stars George Sotiropoulos and Andre Winner, Russia's Dennis Siver gathered more and more fans with each bout. But if you asked him about his crowd-pleasing style, he just smiled, saying that it's just luck that he happens to be in more than his share of exciting bouts.

Since debuting in UFC in 2007, Siver has earned two Knockout of the Night awards, four Fight of the Night awards and one Submission of the Night award, making the master of the spinning back kick a must-see whenever he steps into the Octagon.

GEORGE SOTIROPOULOS
GEELONG, AUSTRALIA

DEBUT: THE ULTIMATE FIGHTER: TEAM HUGHES VS TEAM SERRA FINALE, DECEMBER 8, 2007

George Sotiropoulos came to *The Ultimate Fighter* in 2007 as a virtual unknown, despite his solid 7-2 record. But after two big wins on the show and spectacular victories over Billy Miles, Roman Mitichyan, George Roop and Jason Dent, the native of Geelong, Australia proved that he had what it takes to carve out a place for himself in UFC.

A Brazilian jiu-jitsu black belt with an impressive standup game, as well, Sotiropoulos honed his skills in the United States. His progress was never more evident than when he defeated lightweight contenders Joe Stevenson, Kurt Pellegrino and Joe Lauzon in succession. A four-fight losing streak prompted his release in 2013.

JEREMY STEPHENS
DES MOINES, IA

DEBUT: UFC 71, MAY 26, 2007

A stellar example of the kind of fighters that the state of Iowa produces, Jeremy "Lil' Heathen" Stephens is as tough as they come. "I've been a fighter all my life," he said. "I fought through some difficult times in my life, and I feel like fighting's just for me. I was born a fighter, and I want to be made into a champion."

Besides toughness, Stephens also has the skill and power to succeed in the Octagon, and that's garnered him a reputation as a top competitor in both the lightweight and featherweight divisions.

THIAGO TAVARES
FLORIANÓPOLIS, BRAZIL

DEBUT: UFC FIGHT NIGHT: STEVENSON VS GUILLARD, APRIL 5, 2007

A proud native of Florianopolis, Brazil, Thiago Tavares was first exposed to mixed martial arts while watching the UFC exploits of the legendary Royce Gracie on television.

Aiming to emulate the success of his countryman, Tavares earned black belts in jiu-jitsu and judo. He showed flashes of brilliance in his UFC wins over Naoyuki Kotani, Jason Black, Michihiro Omigawa and Manny Gamburyan, as well as in spectacular (yet losing) efforts against Matt Wiman and Kurt Pellegrino. Now competing in the featherweight division, the former lightweight contender has a title shot in his sights.

FIGHTS OF THE YEAR   KNOCKOUTS OF THE YEAR   SUBMISSIONS OF THE YEAR

THE ULTIMATE FIGHTER: TEAM HUGHES VS TEAM SERRA FINALE

HUERTA   WSUB3   GUIDA

UFC 70

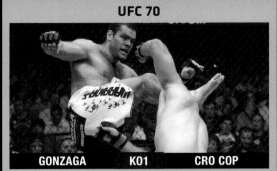

GONZAGA   KO1   CRO COP

UFC 76

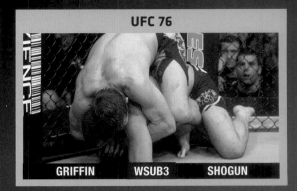

GRIFFIN   WSUB3   SHOGUN

UFC 67

EDGAR   W3   GRIFFIN

UFC 71

JACKSON   TKO1   LIDDELL

UFC 73

LYTLE   WSUB1   GILLIAM

UFC 79

LIDDELL   W3   SILVA

UFC 71

ALEXANDER   TKO1   JARDINE

UFC 75

DAVIS   WSUB1   TAYLOR

THE ULTIMATE FIGHTER: TEAM HUGHES VS TEAM SERRA FINALE

KOPPENHAVER   TKO3   ROLLINS

UFC FIGHT NIGHT: EVANS VS SALMON

EVANS   KO2   SALMON

UFC 79

ST-PIERRE   WSUB2   HUGHES

UFC FIGHT NIGHT: STOUT VS FISHER

FISHER   W3   STOUT

UFC 69

SERRA   TKO1   ST-PIERRE

DEBUTS

UFC FIGHT NIGHT: EVANS VS SALMON

- CHAD REINER
- HEATH HERRING
- SEAN SALMON

UFC 67

- MIRKO CRO COP
- JOHN HALVERSON
- RAMPAGE JACKSON
- FRANKIE EDGAR
- LYOTO MACHIDA
- DIEGO SARAIVA

UFC 68

- REX HOLMAN
- JASON GILLIAM

UFC FIGHT NIGHT: STEVENSON VS GUILLARD

- THIAGO TAVARES
- NAOYUKI KOTANI
- ROAN CARNEIRO
- NATE MOHR
- JUSTIN McCULLY

UFC 69

- LEONARD GARCIA

UFC 70

- FABRICIO WERDUM
- TERRY ETIM
- MATT GRICE
- JESS LIAUDIN
- DENNIS SIVER
- PAUL TAYLOR
- EDILBERTO CROCOTA

UFC 71

- HOUSTON ALEXANDER
- THIAGO SILVA
- JEREMY STEPHENS

UFC FIGHT NIGHT: STOUT VS FISHER

- LUKE CAUDILLO
- ANTHONY JOHNSON
- JEFF COX
- TAMDAN McCRORY
- JASON BLACK
- JORDAN RADEV

UFC 72

- COLIN ROBINSON
- STEVE LYNCH
- JASON TAN

THE ULTIMATE FIGHTER 5 FINALE

- BRIAN GERAGHTY
- ALLEN BERUBE
- ROB EMERSON
- GRAY MAYNARD
- COLE MILLER
- ANDY WANG
- BRANDON MELENDEZ
- DOUG EVANS
- FLOYD SWORD
- NATE DIAZ
- MANNY GAMBURYAN

UFC 73

- ALVIN ROBINSON
- MINOTAURO NOGUEIRA
- MARK BOCEK

UFC 74

- MARCUS AURELIO
- RYAN JENSEN
- ALBERTO CRANE

UFC 75

- TOMASZ DRWAL

UFC FIGHT NIGHT: THOMAS VS FLORIAN

- JOE VERES

UFC 76

- SHOGUN RUA
- KAZUHIRO NAKAMURA
- SCOTT JUNK

UFC 77

- DEMIAN MAIA

UFC 78

- RYO CHONAN
- JASON REINHARDT
- AKIHIRO GONO

THE ULTIMATE FIGHTER: TEAM HUGHES VS TEAM SERRA FINALE

- TROY MANDALONIZ
- RICHIE HIGHTOWER
- ROMAN MITICHYAN
- DORIAN PRICE
- PAUL GEORGIEFF
- MATT ARROYO
- JOHN KOLOSCI
- BEN SAUNDERS
- DAN BARRERA
- GEORGE SOTIROPOULOS
- BILLY MILES
- JARED ROLLINS
- JON KOPPENHAVER
- MAC DANZIG
- TOMMY SPEER

UFC 79

- SOA PALELEI
- RAMEAU SOKOUDJOU
- LUIZ CANE

PRIDE

Launched in 1997, PRIDE Fighting Championships quickly became the gold standard for mixed martial arts in Japan. Through the years, the organization was the only serious competition for the United States-based UFC in terms of winning over the loyalties of fight fans.

Home to such superstars as Wanderlei Silva, Kazushi Sakuraba, Minotauro Nogueira, Shogun Rua, Fedor Emelianenko, Takanori Gomi, Mirko Cro Cop and Rampage Jackson, PRIDE fights matched spectacle with sport to create a phenomenon in the Land of the Rising Sun.

In the early days, the promotion relied on the star power of fighters like Rickson and Renzo Gracie and former UFC stars Kimo Leopoldo, Dan Severn, Gary Goodridge and Oleg Taktarov to sell its product in Asia. But as the shows progressed, new stars emerged.

The first great star to make his name in PRIDE was the homegrown Kazushi Sakuraba, who scored victories over UFC vets Carlos Newton and Vitor Belfort before earning the nickname "The Gracie Hunter" for his wins against Royler, Royce, Renzo and Ryan. His 90-minute epic showdown with Royce Gracie in the opening round of the 2000 PRIDE Openweight Grand Prix is consistently mentioned as one of the greatest fights of all time.

His wars with Rampage Jackson and Wanderlei Silva are also key parts of his legacy.

In that 2000 Grand Prix, it was an old pro, Mark Coleman, who scored four emotional victories to win the title and resurrect a career that had gone sour in the United States. The win by "The Hammer" opened the door for more veterans to make their way to Japan. However, a new breed was emerging, and soon it was Minotauro Nogueira, Wanderlei Silva, Ricardo Arona, Murilo Bustamante, Shogun Rua and his brother Murilo "Ninja" Rua who were dominating the circuit.

In the heavyweight ranks, the resilient Nogueira became the first PRIDE heavyweight champion in 2001. He would hold the belt until Russian powerhouse Fedor Emelianenko seized the throne in 2003.

Some of the organization's best fights were taking place at 205 pounds, as a heated rivalry erupted between Wanderlei Silva and Rampage Jackson. They would fight twice in PRIDE, with Silva winning both matches. UFC star Chuck Liddell also got into the act, as he was sent to Japan three times to fight in PRIDE bouts.

In 2003, the PRIDE Bushido series was launched, and with it came star-making turns by Shogun Rua, Takanori Gomi and former UFC lightweight champion Jens Pulver.

With all this action erupting, fight fans quickly grasped on to anything and everything involving PRIDE. Since the rules varied from UFC matches, it gave aficionados a different look than what they were used to. First, PRIDE matches took place in a ring, as opposed to the Octagon. The rounds system was different, head stomps and soccer kicks were legal, and a unique yellow card system allowed referees to penalize a fighter for a lack of action, causing him to lose 10 percent of his purse.

Despite PRIDE's significant run of success—including two events in the United States in 2006 and 2007—the company was eventually sold in March 2007. Luckily, it fell into good hands in the form of UFC majority owners Frank Fertitta III and Lorenzo Fertitta, two fans who vowed that the legacy of PRIDE would not be forgotten.

And as the likes of Nogueira, Cro Cop, Silva, Gomi, Shogun and Rampage made their way into the UFC Octagon, fans finally got to see the dream fights they had been waiting for. But PRIDE is not gone. In fact, it's still alive through the UFC's streaming service UFC FIGHT PASS, where fans old and new can relive the greatest MMA fights ever seen in the ring.

PRIDE CHAMPIONSHIP ROSTER

HEAVYWEIGHT

MINOTAURO NOGUEIRA

FEDOR EMELIANENKO

MIDDLEWEIGHT
205 pounds, equivalent to UFC light heavyweight

WANDERLEI SILVA

DAN HENDERSON

Ricardo Arona and Wanderlei Silva compete in the PRIDE Grand Prix 2005.

WELTERWEIGHT
183 pounds, roughly equivalent to UFC middleweight

DAN HENDERSON

LIGHTWEIGHT
161 pounds, roughly equivalent to UFC lightweight

TAKANORI GOMI

Fedor Emelianenko wins PRIDE heavyweight title match, 2005.

GRAND PRIX CHAMPIONS

MARK COLEMAN

DAN HENDERSON

MIRKO CRO COP

KAZUO MISAKI

FEDOR EMELIANENKO

SHOGUN RUA

TAKANORI GOMI

WANDERLEI SILVA

UFC CHAMPIONS WHO HAVE FOUGHT IN PRIDE

JOSH BARNETT

CARLOS NEWTON

VITOR BELFORT

MINOTAURO NOGUEIRA

MURILO BUSTAMANTE

JENS PULVER

MARK COLEMAN

KEVIN RANDLEMAN

RAMPAGE JACKSON

RICCO RODRIGUEZ

ROBBIE LAWLER

ANDERSON SILVA

CHUCK LIDDELL

MAURICE SMITH

2008

BJ Penn defeats Joe Stevenson at UFC 80.

BJ Penn was always one of the most fascinating figures in the sport of mixed martial arts. Inside or outside of the Octagon, "The Prodigy" always moved to the beat of his own drummer, even when it was to his own detriment.

But as 2008 began, he wasn't a kid anymore. He was going to turn 30 that year, and even though he returned to his winning ways with a 2007 victory over old rival Jens Pulver, fans wanted to see more. They wanted to see if Penn was serious, and he was going to get his chance on January 19 in Newcastle, England. He faced *The Ultimate Fighter* winner Joe Stevenson for the UFC lightweight title, which was vacated when Sean Sherk was stripped of it after testing positive for the anabolic steroid Nandrolone following his UFC 73 win over Hermes Franca.

You could say that the fight might have been Penn's last stand, and he took it seriously. "Something just awoke inside of me where I said, 'What are you doing? You can beat every one of these people. You've been doing it half-assed all this time, and it's time to finally step up and let's see it,'" Penn said. "If you can't, you can't, but at least you know you tried. Words can't explain how pumped I am about fighting right now. It's what I am, it's who I am and it's what I want to be.

"You want to be categorized in a league of your own, like Randy [Couture] is," he continued. "You don't want to be in the mix with everybody else. When they talk about you, you want them to say something special, like a Joe Frazier or [Muhammad] Ali, those kinds of people. You want to be extraordinary. You want to shoot for greatness, and I think every fighter should."

The Stevenson fight was the first step, and Penn delivered, halting "Joe Daddy" in two rounds to win the lightweight crown he had twice failed to capture. Along with Randy Couture, he was now one of the only two fighters to win UFC titles in two weight classes. It was the perfect start to the year, but a month later, things would get bigger—literally.

Late in 2007, before the Anderson Silva-Rich Franklin rematch in Cincinnati, UFC signed a former NCAA champion and WWE wrestler named Brock Lesnar. Lesnar, with just a 1-0 pro MMA record, looked like he was being fed to the wolves. But that's just how the Minnesotan wanted it.

"A lot of people say, 'Well, he was just doing that to get attention.' Well, I got some attention, so I got what I wanted," Lesnar said. "Now, the bottom line is, I want to fight, and I want some credible people and I want to beat them. What that does for me is it makes me very credible. That's why I did it; I want to fight good people. If you want to go with the NFL of the fighting game, it's UFC. It was an easy choice for me, and I'm glad things worked out."

"From the first conversation I had with Brock Lesnar, I was confident that he was gonna fight in UFC," UFC president Dana White added. "He had fought in another show, and after he fought in that show, he realized what it was like to fight in a rinky-dink organization. Fighters and athletes of that caliber want to come to UFC because this is the place to be. It's the most professional, it's got the best fighters in the world and if you want to make your name and cement your legacy, UFC is the only place to do it."

At UFC 81 in Las Vegas on February 2, Lesnar made his debut against none other than former heavyweight champion Frank Mir. It was a gutsy move, but Lesnar soon became known throughout MMA for backing up his talk every step of the way. For a little over a minute, the highly touted newcomer looked like he was going to have his way with Mir. But at this level of the game, it only takes one mistake to end up on the losing end of the equation. Mir proved it by submitting Lesnar 90 seconds into the opening round.

The end was a controversial one, with referee Steve Mazzagatti stopping the fight earlier to talk to Lesnar about blows to the back of the head, giving Mir precious time to regroup and land the fight-ending kneebar.

There was no such controversy in the UFC 81 main event. Minotauro Nogueira took a pounding from Tim Sylvia for 10 minutes of their bout before finally finding the opening he needed in the third round. He submitted Sylvia and won the interim UFC heavyweight championship. In the process, he became the first man in history to hold both the UFC and PRIDE heavyweight championship belts.

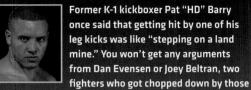
PAT BARRY
NEW ORLEANS, LA

DEBUT: UFC 92, DECEMBER 27, 2008

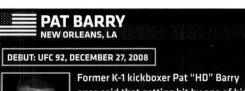
Former K-1 kickboxer Pat "HD" Barry once said that getting hit by one of his leg kicks was like "stepping on a land mine." You won't get any arguments from Dan Evensen or Joey Beltran, two fighters who got chopped down by those kicks. Fellow kickboxer Antoni Hardonk also got finished by the big man from the Big Easy. These devastating performances, paired with his gregarious personality, rapidly made Barry a fan favorite.

TIM BOETSCH
LINCOLNVILLE, ME

DEBUT: UFC 81, FEBRUARY 2, 2008

A former wrestler for Lock Haven University, Tim "The Barbarian" Boetsch brought some different tricks to the table in his UFC debut against David Heath at UFC 81. Boetsch threw his opponent to the canvas and finished him off with strikes to become an overnight sensation in the Octagon. But he wasn't able to keep that momentum going, as his UFC 88 win over Michael Patt was sandwiched by defeats to Matt Hamill and Jason Brilz. The jeet kune do practitioner then ran off a three-fight winning streak that earned him a return call to UFC in 2010. He has since maintained his roster spot with his trademark tenacity.

JUNIE BROWNING
LEXINGTON, KY

DEBUT: THE ULTIMATE FIGHTER: TEAM NOGUEIRA VS TEAM MIR FINALE, DECEMBER 13, 2008

For a brief spell in 2008-2009, no mixed martial artist received more attention and was more of a polarizing figure than a young man from Lexington, Kentucky, named Junie Allen "The Lunatic" Browning. Perhaps the most controversial figure in *The Ultimate Fighter* history, the brash Browning got into a number of incidents with his castmates during season eight before getting submitted and eliminated by eventual winner Efrain Escudero. Following the show, Browning was brought back to the Octagon, defeating Dave Kaplan. But in his second UFC bout, he was submitted in less than two minutes by Cole Miller and subsequently released.

JON JONES

ROCHESTER, NY

DEBUT: UFC 87, AUGUST 9, 2008

Before he was called "NBT" (next big thing), Jon "Bones" Jones was a 21-year-old armed with talent, desire and the dreams of every young fighter in MMA: to be in UFC.

Despite a spotless 6-0 record, when he set foot inside the Octagon for the first time to face Andre Gusmao in 2008, it was more than just another fight. "Being an MMA fighter, you put UFC on such a high pedestal, and you look at these guys like they're superheroes and unbeatable," said Jones. Since that night in Minnesota, Jones himself has been either blessed or cursed with the words "superhero" and "unbeatable" in many circles.

Jones scored a unanimous decision win over Gusmao that night, showing glimpses of the unorthodox and dynamic techniques that have become his trademark. When his hand was raised, he knew his time has come.

"Once I got my very first win, and I heard, 'The winner is Jonny "Bones" Jones,' a level of 'Yes, I can' came across me, and it made me believe from that point on," said the New Yorker.

Five months later, he defeated Stephan Bonnar at UFC 100. Victories over Jake O'Brien, Brandon Vera, Vladimir Matyushenko and Ryan Bader (which were sandwiched around a controversial disqualification defeat to Matt Hamill) followed quickly after that, earning him a shot at Shogun Rua after his then-teammate Rashad Evans became injured.

At UFC 128 on March 19, Jones tore through Shogun in fewer than three rounds. What made the feat even more amazing was that the fight was the capper on a day that began with Jones and coaches Greg Jackson and Mike Winklejohn foiling a robbery in a park in Paterson, New Jersey.

Jones went on to defeat Rampage Jackson, Lyoto Machida, Rashad Evans, Vitor Belfort, Chael Sonnen, Alexander Gustafsson, Glover Teixeira and Daniel Cormier. Jones was stripped of his belt in 2015, but he is determined to get back on track, and his goals have nothing to do with fame or money.

"I think it's really important to have goals that have nothing to do with the financial side of things," he said. "I don't necessarily do this because of the money. I do it because of the way it makes me feel, to be the best in the world at something and to be able to pursue excellence and be a better version of yourself.
Things like that make you feel good and always give you a reason to improve in life.
That's what fighting's done for me; it's given me a way to be better."

Silva defeats Jardine in Round 1 at UFC 84.

At UFC 86, Griffin wins a unanimous decision against Jackson.

Liddell lands a solid blow against Evans at UFC 88.

The frantic start to the year didn't let up in March, when Anderson Silva submitted former PRIDE two-division champion Dan Henderson in the second round of their UFC 82 main event—a card highlighted by the induction of Mark Coleman into the UFC Hall of Fame.

By April, though, all eyes were on Montreal's Bell Centre as UFC presented its first event in Canada. The fans (all 21,390 of them) responded, breaking the previous attendance record set by UFC 68 the year before. While those who packed the venue were happy to see a UFC event, what they really wanted to see was their hometown hero, Georges St-Pierre, regain his welterweight title from Matt Serra, who had beaten him a year earlier.

The fans were loud at the Bell Centre on April 19: chair-shaking, eardrum-breaking, can't-hear-ring-announcer-Bruce-Buffer loud. Just when you thought the decibels couldn't go higher, they did when St-Pierre regained his title with a second-round TKO, putting a fitting cap on UFC 83. That event also saw the debut of Cain Velasquez, a young man from California with world heavyweight title aspirations.

At UFC 84 in May, the stars kept shining. Penn defeated the returning Sherk to retain his lightweight title, Wanderlei Silva knocked out Keith Jardine in 36 seconds and Lyoto Machida sent Tito Ortiz packing from the organization temporarily with a shutout decision win.

The buzz from the card kept fans happy for a while, through an injury-plagued UFC 85 event in London and a June *The Ultimate Fighter* season seven finale event that crowned Amir Sadollah as the latest Ultimate Fighter.

That late-spring lull came to an end on July 5, though, as Rampage Jackson defended his light heavyweight title against the man he had coached against on *The Ultimate Fighter* season seven, Forrest Griffin. In the days leading up to the bout, fans and pundits almost unanimously agreed that, on paper, champion Jackson should win. Yet those comments were always followed by the word "but" and some way of describing how you could never count Griffin out.

At the sold-out Mandalay Bay Events Center, Griffin took all the "buts" out of the equation, overturning the odds and pounding out a thrilling unanimous five-round decision win over Jackson to win the 205-pound world championship and etch his name in the history books. "This is the greatest night of my life," said Griffin, the first winner of *The Ultimate Fighter* and the second show winner to earn a world title, following former welterweight boss Serra.

It was the feel-good story of the year. A month later in Minnesota, it was followed by another Fight of the Year candidate as St-Pierre scored a hard-fought five-round decision win over No. 1 contender Jon Fitch. On the same UFC 87 card, Lesnar picked up his first UFC win, running over Heath Herring en route to a three-round unanimous decision victory.

Placed in the UFC 88 main event against Chuck Liddell, Rashad Evans finally had the chance to get in the spotlight and fulfill the promise he showed ever since winning *The Ultimate Fighter* season two. He was not about to let it go, even against a legend like "The Iceman." So he took his time and made Liddell chase him, and after frustrating the veteran and forcing him to lead, Evans unleashed a right hand for the ages that ended the September 6 bout in the second round.

"My intention when I threw the punch was to throw it as fast as I can," Evans recalled. "And I threw it, it went through, and I was going to follow up with the left hook, but he was already going down. And after the left hook went by, I was like, 'Oh no, he fell down. I've gotta hurry up and finish him.' But it seemed like it took forever for me to come out of that left hook to turn around and get on him."

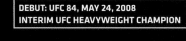

SHANE CARWIN

DEBUT: UFC 84, MAY 24, 2008
INTERIM UFC HEAVYWEIGHT CHAMPION

GREELEY, CO

Shane Carwin has been an interim UFC heavyweight champion and an NCAA Division II wrestling champion. He has earned recognition as a two-time All-American in football and garnered a tryout with the Philadelphia Eagles. He has degrees in mechanical engineering and environmental technology, and he still works full time as an engineer. That's enough of a résumé for anyone to settle into civilian life and breathe a satisfied sigh of accomplishment—but not this heavyweight.

"Everybody has hobbies in their life, and competing just happens to be mine," said Carwin. "I enjoy it, and I've been blessed with the gifts God has given me, and I'll continue this stuff as long as it allows." That was a good thing for fight fans, as Carwin was a thrilling knockout artist ever since entering the Octagon in 2008.

Carwin blitzed Christian Wellisch, Neil Wain and Gabriel Gonzaga, knocking each of them out in the first round. When he did the same thing to Frank Mir at UFC 111 to win the interim heavyweight title, it looked like a long reign at the top was a done deal—and it almost was. Carwin battered Brock Lesnar for nearly five minutes in their 2010 bout for the undisputed heavyweight crown. But when the round was finished, so was Carwin's gas tank, and he was submitted in the second stanza.

Following an injury-induced layoff, Carwin returned against Junior Dos Santos at UFC 131 in 2011, but after a decision loss to "Cigano," he announced his retirement.

RYAN BADER
RENO, NV

DEBUT: THE ULTIMATE FIGHTER: TEAM NOGUEIRA VS TEAM MIR FINALE, DECEMBER 13, 2008
THE ULTIMATE FIGHTER 8 WINNER

An imposing physical force with the size, strength and athleticism to give any opponent a tough time in the Octagon, Ryan "Darth" Bader has been one of the top prospects for world title honors in the ultra-competitive 205-pound weight class.

A lifelong athlete, Bader was a two-time state high school champion in Nevada, throwing in recognition as the state's 2001 Defensive Player of the Year in football for good measure. In college, Bader's excellence continued. By the time he graduated from Arizona State University, he had achieved All-American status twice and was a three-time Pac-10 champion.

Missing competition after college, Bader and college teammate CB Dollaway began training in mixed martial arts. By 2007, he made his pro debut, and after compiling a 7-0 record, he was brought to Las Vegas to compete as a cast member of *The Ultimate Fighter* season eight.

Bader tore through his three opponents on the show before capping off his run with a TKO of Vinny Magalhaes that earned him the season title. Bader's stellar wrestling carried him through early on, but he then began showing the evolution of his all-around fight game as he knocked out Keith Jardine and defeated veteran contender Minotauro Nogueira via decision. Today, he remains one of the division's top competitors.

MATT BROWN
XENIA, OH

DEBUT: THE ULTIMATE FIGHTER: TEAM RAMPAGE VS TEAM FORREST FINALE, JUNE 21, 2008

A gritty battler who is as tough as they come, Ohio's Matt "The Immortal" Brown survived some rough years and a mediocre 7-6 start to his pro MMA career. However, he was given a new start when he was picked to compete on *The Ultimate Fighter* season seven.

Brown didn't win a UFC contract then, but he went on to earn one as he won four of his first five Octagon bouts. He finished Matt Arroyo, Ryan Thomas, Pete "Drago" Sell and James Wilks, with his only loss coming via split decision to Dong Hyun Kim.

A losing skid slowed Brown's momentum, but it was unwise to count out "The Immortal." A 2012 knockout of Chris Cope kicked off a seven-fight winning streak that included wins over Mike Swick, Jordan Mein, Mike Pyle and Erick Silva, turning Brown into a top welterweight contender. Close decision losses to Robbie Lawler and Johny Hendricks have been the only setbacks since 2011 for Brown, whose goal isn't to stay in UFC, but to win the promotion's world championship belt.

It didn't matter, as the fight was stopped and Evans became the top contender to face his fellow *The Ultimate Fighter* winner, Forrest Griffin, for the 205-pound title. That bout took place in December, but first, there was a title fight taking place in November. Randy Couture returned from a contract dispute to defend his heavyweight title against none other than Brock Lesnar. There was plenty of criticism about the fight, considering Lesnar's lack of UFC experience, but even with just two Octagon bouts, he didn't care what people thought.

"I'm not here to shut people's mouths," Lesnar said. "I'm in a spot where there might be the toughest [guy] out there, but nobody knows his name and he's climbing the ranks, and here you've got a guy like myself, who is a household name all across the world. From the business side of things, I've got to make the right business decisions, and at the same time on the fighting side of things, I don't want any tomato cans, either."

He was making the right business decision, and Couture was no tomato can. By the end of less than two rounds at UFC 91 on November 15, "The Natural" was a champion no longer. Lesnar stopped him to win the title, becoming only the second man to win the heavyweight title in his fourth pro fight. The first? Randy Couture.

After Ryan Bader and Efrain Escudero won their respective divisions on *The Ultimate Fighter* season eight, season coaches Nogueira and Mir met on December 27 as a featured bout on a card entitled The Ultimate 2008. It was pretty special: recently dethroned Rampage Jackson avenged two losses to Wanderlei Silva with a first-round knockout; Mir upset Nogueira to win the interim heavyweight title and complete a comeback four years in the making; and Evans stopping Griffin in three rounds to win the UFC light heavyweight belt. Ultimate, indeed.

CB DOLLAWAY
BATTLE CREEK, MI

DEBUT: THE ULTIMATE FIGHTER: TEAM RAMPAGE VS TEAM FORREST FINALE, JUNE 21, 2008

An amateur wrestling standout that won a junior college national championship for Colby Community College and then earned All-American honors at Arizona State, CB "The Doberman" Dollaway followed his college teammates Ryan Bader and Cain Velasquez into mixed martial arts. The finalist on season seven of *The Ultimate Fighter* has since become a middleweight contender and quite the submission artist, earning two Submission of the Night awards thus far in his UFC career while reintroducing fight fans to the deadly wonders of the "Peruvian Necktie" finishing hold.

EFRAIN ESCUDERO
SONORA, MEXICO

DEBUT: THE ULTIMATE FIGHTER: TEAM NOGUEIRA VS TEAM MIR FINALE, DECEMBER 13, 2008
THE ULTIMATE FIGHTER 8 WINNER

Efrain "Hecho en Mexico" Escudero may not have been the loudest talker on *The Ultimate Fighter* season eight, but he certainly carried the biggest stick as he submitted three opponents en route to the lightweight finals and a win over the favored Phillipe Nover.

Unfortunately, injuries kept Escudero sidelined after the finale. But in September 2009, he finally got his chance to compete again, responding with a first-round TKO over Cole Miller. An unsteady UFC career followed, but in his third stint in the promotion, he seems to have found his groove. He has even earned a spot as coach on *The Ultimate Fighter Latin America*.

JUNIOR DOS SANTOS

DEBUT: UFC 90, OCTOBER 25, 2008
UFC HEAVYWEIGHT CHAMPION

As a stablemate of fighters like Anderson Silva, Lyoto Machida and Minotauro Nogueira early in his career, heavyweight Junior "Cigano" Dos Santos received almost daily reminders of the tradition he was expected to carry on after reaching the heights of the sport. But instead of being daunted by this prospect, he embraced it.

CAÇADOR, CURITIBA, BRAZIL

"The great Brazilian fighters inspire me," said Dos Santos. "I try to do my work as well as possible because I believe I can follow the same path and one day become a great champion."

He's certainly on his way to being one of the South American nation's best of all time. Entering the Octagon at UFC 90 in 2008 as a virtual unknown, Dos Santos stunned the MMA world with a one-punch knockout of top contender Fabricio Werdum. But this win was no fluke, as "Cigano" went on to finish Stefan Struve, Mirko Cro Cop, Gilbert Yvel and Gabriel Gonzaga before scoring a punishing three-round decision win over Roy Nelson at UFC 117 in August 2010.

The best was yet to come, though. Dos Santos won the UFC heavyweight title in emphatic fashion in November 2011 when he knocked out Cain Velasquez in 64 seconds. Following that victory, JDS successfully defended his title against Frank Mir before Velasquez regained the belt with a decision win over the Brazilian at UFC 155 in December 2012.

Dos Santos won two of his next three bouts over Mark Hunt and Stipe Miocic, with the only loss coming in his 2013 rubber match against Velasquez. He continues chasing after his title, and expects to get another shot at the belt very soon.

RAFAEL DOS ANJOS

DEBUT: UFC 91, NOVEMBER 15, 2008
UFC LIGHTWEIGHT CHAMPION

Rafael dos Anjos is a Brazilian jiu-jitsu champion and a protégé of former UFC contender Marcio Cruz. In 2008, he came to UFC with the intention of making not only a positive impression, but also a statement that he was a fighter to watch in the coming years.

RIO DE JANEIRO, BRAZIL

He achieved those goals, winning 12 of 15 fights to earn a shot at the UFC lightweight championship belt held by Anthony Pettis. But it was only after a loss to Khabib Nurmagomedov in April 2014 that Dos Anjos was able to turn up the volume on his promising career.

"You can't think too much about the belt," dos Anjos said. "The belt will come naturally. So my focus right now is to keep fighting, to keep good health with no injuries and to keep doing my job, which I love. I learned a lot in that fight [with Nurmagomedov] because I was too worried about losing the fight. I had five wins in a row, and I was thinking, 'If I lose, I go to the back of the line.'"

In March 2015, he was at the front of the line. In the main event of UFC 185, he made his championship dreams come true with a dominant five-round unanimous decision over Pettis to earn the 155-pound title and begin a new chapter in his life and career at the top of the MMA world.

DAN HARDY

NOTTINGHAM, UNITED KINGDOM

DEBUT: UFC 89, OCTOBER 18, 2008

Part of the United Kingdom's first wave of contenders who made their mark in the world of MMA, Nottingham's Dan "The Outlaw" Hardy has been training in martial arts since age 6, even spending time with the famed Shaolin monks in China.

In October 2008, this exciting battler with the red Mohawk and confident manner began his journey in the Octagon with a three-round win over Akihiro Gono. Following a knockout of Rory Markham and upset victories over Marcus Davis and Mike Swick, he became the first British fighter to contend for a UFC title when he fought Georges St-Pierre in 2010. His gritty five-round loss to GSP kicked off a four-fight losing streak that he reversed with two wins in 2012.

BROCK LESNAR

DEBUT: UFC 81, FEBRUARY 2, 2008
UFC HEAVYWEIGHT CHAMPION

WEBSTER, SD

When the news hit the street that former WWE superstar Brock Lesnar was about to embark on a career in mixed martial arts, many snickered. Sure, he had legit physical talent that saw him win an NCAA Division I National Championship in wrestling for the University of Minnesota and then earn a tryout with the NFL's Minnesota Vikings, but this was different.

Actually, it wasn't for Lesnar, who drew raves for his MMA potential and showed some of it in his debut win over Min-Soo Kim in 2007. Of course, after such an explosive first performance, the question everyone had was, "What's next?" In Lesnar's eyes, the next step had to take place in UFC, and he wasn't shy about calling out the top heavyweights in the organization.

He got his wish, and in his first Octagon bout at UFC 81 in February 2008, Lesnar was paired with none other than former world champion Frank Mir. Yet after a strong start and a controversial restart from the referee, Lesnar was caught in a kneebar. Though he won the first 1:20 of the fight, the last 10 seconds and the victory went to Mir.

Picking himself up and dusting himself off, Lesnar's next bout went much better as he dominated former PRIDE star Heath Herring over three rounds at UFC 87. Three months later, on November 15, 2008, he become only the second man in history to win a UFC title in just his fourth professional fight as he stopped the first man to do it, UFC Hall of Famer Randy Couture, in the second round at UFC 91.

But the Lesnar story was far from finished. After he got his revenge on Mir at UFC 100 in July 2009, halting him in the second round, the big man from Minnesota was stricken in October of that year with diverticulitis, an intestinal ailment. Put on antibiotics and pain medication, Lesnar fortunately avoided initial surgery as his body began to heal itself. But after 11 days in the hospital, he had lost 40 pounds.

Doctors at the Mayo Clinic recommended surgery to remove his colon, but Lesnar still held out hope to avoid the procedure. After returning to the gym and gaining 30 pounds, a January 2010 checkup and CT scan revealed that, amazingly, the champion was back to full strength.

To top this news, Lesnar put on the performance of his career in his return against Shane Carwin at UFC 116 in July 2010. He survived a hellacious first-round beating to roar back and submit Carwin with an arm triangle in the second round.

The big man lost his crown later in 2010, as he was TKOed by Cain Velasquez at UFC 121 in October. But after a stint as a coach on *The Ultimate Fighter* season 13, Lesnar was prepared to face number-one contender Junior Dos Santos in July 2011 before another bout with diverticulitis sidelined him. Following surgery, Lesnar fought for the last time in December 2011, losing to Alistair Overeem.

JIM MILLER

DEBUT: UFC 89, OCTOBER 18, 2008

SPARTA, NJ

A former Virginia Tech wrestler who turned to MMA in 2005, Jim Miller came to the Octagon in 2008 with a stellar reputation as a fighter to watch after winning numerous titles on the East Coast circuit. That reputation was spot-on, as the Brazilian jiu-jitsu black belt became one of the lightweight division's top competitors, a tenacious battler who always looks to end a fight before the judges get involved.

"I go out there and just try to let it all out," Miller said. "I'm not one of those guys that can sit there and say that they fight because of the money. I fight because I love to fight and I love to win. I get a rush from submitting guys, and if there's time on the clock, I'm trying to finish the fight." Owner of nearly 15 UFC victories, the New Jersey contender has sent competitors like Duane Ludwig, Mark Bocek, Charles Oliveira, Melvin Guillard, Joe Lauzon and Yancy Medeiros down to defeat, and he's a tough opponent for anyone at 155 pounds.

"I'm not afraid of getting knocked out, I'm not afraid of getting hit," he said, "But I'd rather be known as good than be known as being tough. Anybody that says, 'Aw, I like getting hit,' or any of that stuff, I gotta say, 'Come on, really?' Nobody wants to get hit. But there are some guys that just don't let it bother them. I try not to let it bother me. It's part of the game. You're going to get hit."

AMIR SADOLLAH
NEW YORK CITY, NY

DEBUT: THE ULTIMATE FIGHTER: TEAM RAMPAGE VS TEAM FORREST FINALE, JUNE 21, 2008 • *THE ULTIMATE FIGHTER 7* WINNER

Amir Sadollah's emergence on the mixed martial arts scene in 2008 as the winner of *The Ultimate Fighter* season seven was one of the year's great stories. But there were more chapters to be written in a pro career that saw him develop into a welterweight talent after arriving simply as a raw and gutsy prospect.

"One thing I took from the show is that I saw it as a microcosm of everything that's hard about fighting, and I looked at it as my grad school," he said. "All the little things and little pressures: interviews, seeing your opponent, not seeing your opponent, injuries, last-minute fights. Every little scenario that happens on the show, whether it was purposely built or not, I think prepares you to be a fighter."

On *The Ultimate Fighter*, Sadollah stunned Steve Byrnes, Gerald Harris, Matt Brown and CB Dollaway (twice). Yet even after going from unknown to star at breakneck speed, he remained refreshingly humble. "The only thing I've got figured out is that I'll never have it figured out," he said.

In his first post-*The Ultimate Fighter* bout, Sadollah was the victim of a controversial TKO at the hands of Johny Hendricks at UFC 101. However, he went on to win five bouts in the Octagon.

DONG HYUN KIM
SUWON, SOUTH KOREA

DEBUT: UFC 84, MAY 24, 2008

One of South Korea's fighting pioneers, Dong Hyun "Stun Gun" Kim became only the second fighter from his country to compete in UFC when he made his debut in May 2008.

"It's an honor for me to fight in the UFC, the world's best fight event," he said before his bout with Jason Tan. "It will be a big opportunity for me to show my fighting style to MMA fans around the world."

But just showing up wasn't enough for this talented judo black belt, and he scored a stirring TKO victory over Tan. He followed it up with several more wins over the likes of Matt Brown, TJ Grant, Amir Sadollah and Nate Diaz, marking him as an exciting contender in the 170-pound shark tank.

"I am at the most important time of my career. I could choose to be either one of those seasoned fighters who win some and lose some, or gamble and fight aggressively to gain the title shot. I'd rather venture to be aggressive. There is no opportunity for boring fighters."

KRZYSZTOF SOSZYNSKI
STALOWA WOLA, POLAND

DEBUT: THE ULTIMATE FIGHTER: TEAM NOGUEIRA VS TEAM MIR FINALE, DECEMBER 13, 2008

One of *The Ultimate Fighter* season eight's most successful veterans, Krzysztof "The Polish Experiment" Soszynski logged a slew of UFC wins. After a heated two-fight series against Stephan Bonnar and a win against Goran Reljic, he has added "most exciting" to his list of accolades, despite 12 pro losses. In boxing, a glossy unbeaten record is the only way to sail to the top. But in mixed martial arts, the top fighters in the sport wear their defeats as painful badges of honor that taught them the lessons they needed to learn to move forward, and Soszynski was no exception.

ROUSIMAR PALHARES
DORES DO INDAIÁ, MINAS GERAIS, BRAZIL

DEBUT: UFC 84, MAY 24, 2008

Rousimar "Toquinho" Palhares entered the Octagon in May 2008 with a well-deserved reputation as one of the premier submission artists in the game, having won his previous four bouts via first-round tapouts. But virtually no one expected the decorated jiu-jitsu black belt to submit seasoned veteran Ivan Salaverry in just over two minutes the way he did at UFC 84 in May 2008.

A protégé of former middleweight champ Murilo Bustamante, the heel hook master also scored UFC wins over the likes of Jeremy Horn, Lucio Linhares, Tomasz Drwal and Dave Branch before being released in 2013.

CAIN VELASQUEZ

DEBUT: UFC 83, APRIL 19, 2008
TWO-TIME UFC HEAVYWEIGHT CHAMPION

SALINAS, CA

A member of the world-renowned AKA camp that produced such UFC standouts as Luke Rockhold and Daniel Cormier, Cain Velasquez came to the Octagon in April 2008 with only two pro fights, but the buzz around the two-time All-American wrestler from Arizona State University was deafening. His approach to fighting was just one reason.

"I'm non-stop, I don't get tired out there, my game is good all around, and I want people to see that I'm going to be the next big thing. That's what I want people to keep thinking about, that they can't wait to see me fight again."

The other reason was that Velasquez' respected coach, Javier Mendez, told anyone and everyone who would listen that the young man training at his gym was going to be the next world champion of UFC. That could have been unbearable pressure on Velasquez, but there was a method to his madness.

"He [Mendez] said, 'I'm saying this kind of stuff now to get you prepared so when it all comes down to it, you'll be ready,'" recalled Velasquez. "He's prepared me ever since I got here, and he's talked me up."

It wasn't mere talk, though, and Velasquez proved his mentor right as soon as the horn sounded for his first UFC fight. After wins over Brad Morris and Jake O'Brien in 2008, Velasquez blazed through 2009 with TKOs of Denis Stojnic and Ben Rothwell. A stirring three-round decision win over Cheick Kongo showed off even more of his ever-improving fight game. And while his fan base continued to grow as he upped his stellar pro record to 7-0, Velasquez wasn't letting the attention get to his head.

"I'm a perfectionist in the gym," he said. "I know my skills all aren't where they're supposed to be or where I want them to be. I need everything to be perfect."

His skills were perfect at UFC 110 in Australia, though. Velasquez made himself the No. 1 contender to Brock Lesnar's title with a first-round knockout of heavyweight superstar Minotauro Nogueira in the biggest fight of his young career.

The stage was now set for Velasquez to not only win his first title at UFC 121 in October 2010, but to also become the first fighter of Mexican descent to win a major combat sports heavyweight title. Again, he took the pressure and attention in stride, and when fight night arrived in Anaheim, he wasn't intimidated; he was ready to take his belt home.

At the sound of the horn, Lesnar, a nearly 300-pound Mack truck with no brakes, charged at Velasquez, intent on taking out his most dangerous challenger before he could even get a shot off. It certainly wasn't what Velasquez and his coaches expected, but he got back into the fight in a big way. He rose quickly from two Lesnar takedowns to score his own before finishing off the giant with a crushing series of ground strikes that brought a halt to the bout at 4:12 of the opening round. Cain Velasquez was the new UFC heavyweight champion, and now he belonged to the world.

Yet despite his quiet nature, he embraced his newfound fame. To celebrate his win and introduce him to anyone who hadn't met him already, Velasquez went coast to coast and to Mexico to meet with the media and fans. It was a well-deserved victory tour, but it was soon time to get back to work.

In November 2011, Velasquez was stopped in the first round by Junior Dos Santos, losing his title. But after a comeback win over Antonio Silva, he regained the belt from "Cigano" at UFC 155 in December 2012. He has since successfully defended his crown twice against Silva and Dos Santos.

FIGHTS OF THE YEAR

UFC 86

GRIFFIN   **W5**   **JACKSON**

UFC 87

ST-PIERRE   **W5**   **FITCH**

UFC 92

EVANS   **TKO3**   **GRIFFIN**

UFC 85
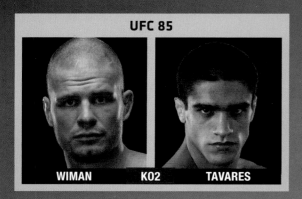
WIMAN   **KO2**   **TAVARES**

UFC 88
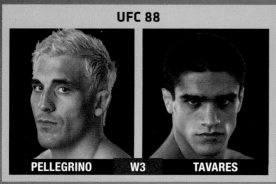
PELLEGRINO   **W3**   **TAVARES**

KNOCKOUTS OF THE YEAR

UFC 88

EVANS   **KO2**   **LIDDELL**

UFC 92

JACKSON   **KO1**   **SILVA**

UFC 90

DOS SANTOS   **KO1**   **WERDUM**

UFC FIGHT FOR THE TROOPS
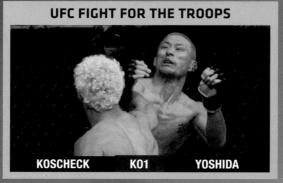
KOSCHECK   **KO1**   **YOSHIDA**

UFC 91

STEPHENS   **KO3**   **DOS ANJOS**

SUBMISSIONS OF THE YEAR

UFC 81
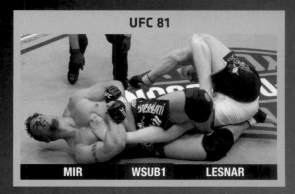
MIR   **WSUB1**   **LESNAR**

UFC 82

SILVA   **WSUB2**   **HENDERSON**

UFC FIGHT NIGHT: FLORIAN VS LAUZON

DIAZ   **WSUB2**   **PELLEGRINO**

UFC 86

MILLER   **WSUB3**   **GURGEL**

UFC: SILVA VS IRVIN

DOLLAWAY   **WSUB1**   **TAYLOR**

DEBUTS

UFC 80
- JAMES LEE
- PER EKLUND
- PAUL KELLY

UFC FIGHT NIGHT: SWICK VS BURKMAN
- JUSTIN BUCHHOLZ
- COREY HILL

UFC 81
- BROCK LESNAR
- ROB YUNDT
- KYLE BRADLEY
- TIM BOETSCH

UFC 82
- CHRIS WILSON
- DAVID BIELKHEDEN

UFC FIGHT NIGHT: FLORIAN VS LAUZON
- SAMY SCHIAVO
- RYAN ROBERTS

UFC 83
- JASON DAY
- CAIN VELASQUEZ
- BRAD MORRIS

UFC 84
- GORAN RELJIC
- ANTONIO MENDES
- YOSHIYUKI YOSHIDA
- ROUSIMAR PALHARES
- DONG HYUN KIM
- SHANE CARWIN

UFC 85
- KEVIN BURNS

THE ULTIMATE FIGHTER: TEAM RAMPAGE VS TEAM FORREST FINALE
- ROB KIMMONS
- MATT BROWN
- MATTHEW RIDDLE
- DANTE RIVERA
- AMIR SADOLLAH
- CB DOLLAWAY

UFC: SILVA VS IRVIN
- BRAD BLACKBURN
- JAMES GIBOO
- RORY MARKHAM
- BRODIE FARBER
- DALE HARTT
- SHANNON GUGERTY
- NATE LOUGHRAN
- JOHNNY REES
- TIM CREDEUR
- CALE YARBROUGH
- JESSE TAYLOR
- REESE ANDY

UFC 87
- DAN EVENSEN
- JON JONES
- ANDRE GUSMAO
- STEVE BRUNO
- RYAN THOMAS

UFC 88
- MICHAEL PATT

UFC FIGHT NIGHT: DIAZ VS NEER
- DAN MILLER
- MIKE MASSENZIO
- JASON BRILZ
- JOE VEDEPO

UFC 89
- NEIL WAIN
- DAN HARDY
- JIM MILLER
- DAVID BARON

UFC 90
- JUNIOR DOS SANTOS
- MATT HORWICH

UFC 91
- JOSH HENDRICKS
- RAFAEL DOS ANJOS

UFC FIGHT FOR THE TROOPS
- BRANDON WOLFF
- STEVE CANTWELL
- RAZAK AL-HASSAN

THE ULTIMATE FIGHTER: TEAM NOGUEIRA VS TEAM MIR FINALE
- ROLANDO DELGADO
- JOHN POLAKOWSKI
- SHANE NELSON
- GEORGE ROOP
- KYLE KINGSBURY
- TOM LAWLOR
- ELIOT MARSHALL
- JULES BRUCHEZ
- KRZYSZTOF SOSZYNSKI
- SHANE PRIMM
- JUNIE BROWNING
- DAVE KAPLAN
- RYAN BADER
- VINNY MAGALHAES
- PHILLIPE NOVER
- EFRAIN ESCUDERO

UFC 92
- MOSTAPHA AL-TURK
- MIKE WESSEL
- PAT BARRY

UFC began its most ambitious international year to date with a trip to Dublin, Ireland, on January 17 headlined by Dan Henderson's split decision win over Rich Franklin. In 2009 the UFC held five international events, taking place in Ireland, England, Canada and Germany. Each show garnered plenty of media attention, and the brand continued to grow each step of the way.

But as the year commenced, the only thing most fight fans were thinking about was UFC 94 on January 31, where a superfight between welterweight champion Georges St-Pierre and lightweight titleholder BJ Penn would take place in Las Vegas . The rematch of their 2006 matchup was the most highly anticipated fight in years, by fans and fighters alike.

"The shape I'm gonna be in, it's gonna be a thing of who wants it more," said Penn. "He's this good, I'm this good [holds both hands up to the same level]. I feel I'm better technically, but when you're such a great athlete, you have no choice but to always use your athleticism when you cannot do the technique right. You can make things work just because you're a great athlete. I'm an athlete, but I wouldn't say I'm a gifted athlete. He is. I'm gifted up here [points to his temple]. I'm not gifted throughout my body. I'm flexible and a strong guy. But this is the greatest athlete in the world against the greatest fighting mind in the world. That's what you've got right here."

"I think if you ask somebody who's the best pound-for-pound in the world, a lot of people would say it's BJ Penn, so for me, it's a great challenge," St-Pierre added. "When you're a UFC world champion, you have to fix your goals even higher. I don't want to fight to be champion anymore because I'm already the champion. I want to fight to become a legend in the sport, and that's what this fight will give me."

Everything was there: high stakes, history, a storyline and two of the best ever to set foot in the Octagon. Yet when the horn sounded for the biggest fight of St-Pierre's career, the welterweight champion delivered a clinic, shutting down the lightweight champion completely before forcing a stoppage at the end of the fourth round.

Georges St-Pierre defeats BJ Penn at UFC 94.

Carlos Condit kicks Martin Kampmann during UFC Fight Night Condit vs Kampmann.

The fight may have been anti-climactic, but the momentum from UFC 94 kept fight fans tuning in to every event, eager to see both established names and rising stars battle it out in the Octagon. In April, UFC followers got their first look at Carlos Condit, a former WEC welterweight champion who came to the Octagon after Zuffa eliminated the heavyweight, light heavyweight, middleweight and welterweight divisions from the home of the blue cage. Even though he lost a split decision to Martin Kampmann in Nashville, he made enough of an impression that you knew you were going to see him back in action soon enough.

Later that month, UFC was back in Montreal's Bell Centre for a UFC 97 card that saw Anderson Silva successfully defend his middleweight title with a decision win over countryman Thales Leites. It was Silva's second straight less-than-thrilling win, and UFC brass was starting to get concerned.

MIKE PIERCE
PORTLAND, OR

DEBUT: UFC FIGHT NIGHT: DIAZ VS GUILLARD, SEPTEMBER 16, 2009

A standout wrestler for Portland State University who finished fourth in the Pac-10 as a true freshman, Mike Pierce isn't used to doing anything at half speed, and his promising mixed martial arts career has proven that.

"I hope people see that I've got heart and that I'm ready to throw down with anybody," said Pierce.

A tenacious battler always looking for a spectacular finish, the Portland, Oregon, native has won several bouts in UFC, with only a handful of defeats.

MIKE PYLE
DRESDEN, TN

DEBUT: UFC 98, MAY 23, 2009

A brown belt in Brazilian jiu-jitsu, Mike "Quicksand" Pyle was one of those fighters about whom fans would always say, "I can't wait until he comes to UFC."

The Tennessee native felt the same way as he battled up the ranks, defeating UFC vets such as Jon Fitch, Brian Gassaway and Shonie Carter. He even made his pro debut against former light heavyweight champion Rampage Jackson.

In 2009, Pyle finally got the call to the Octagon, and more than six years later, he's still a respected member of the welterweight roster.

BEN ROTHWELL
KENOSHA, WI

DEBUT: UFC 104, OCTOBER 24, 2009

Despite a decade and 30 professional mixed martial arts wins in the fight game, Ben Rothwell regarded his UFC debut in October 2009 against Cain Velasquez as the beginning of his career.

"I've been doing this for 10 years, and it's always been about being in the UFC. It sounds like I've done some things, but to me, it's all been training for this."

Although Rothwell fell short of victory against Velasquez, he got back in the win column at UFC 115 with a win over Gilbert Yvel, showing fans the mixture of technique and tenacity that made him one of the most frequently discussed big men in the game.

At UFC 97, Thales Leites connects with Anderson Silva.

283

JOHNY HENDRICKS

DEBUT: UFC 101, AUGUST 8, 2009
UFC WELTERWEIGHT CHAMPION

ADA, OK

Charismatic and talented, two-time NCAA Division I wrestling champion Johny "Bigg Rigg" Hendricks was always seen by fight insiders as a possible future titleholder in UFC's welterweight division. This possibility became a reality in March 2014 when he defeated Robbie Lawler for the vacant title.

The Ada, Oklahoma, native agreed with that early assessment, claiming that the only reason he began training in mixed martial arts in June 2007 was a simple but definitive one: "To be the world champion."

And he did it against Lawler after winning all but two of his first 17 professional bouts, with Knockout of the Night victories over TJ Waldburger, Jon Fitch and Martin Kampmann. His Fight of the Night win against Carlos Condit solidified his place as the number-one contender at 170 pounds. Yet it was a crushing and controversial decision loss to Georges St-Pierre in their 2013 title fight that really lit a fire under Hendricks to succeed.

"You never really get over it," said Hendricks of the GSP fight, which many observers believed he had won. "You just learn to live with it. But you can't just dwell on it; you've got to try to move forward and learn from it."

So what did Hendricks learn from his first five-round championship fight?

"You learn 1) you can go the distance, and 2) that you did prepare yourself the right way," he said. "Those are two important things: that your camp went well and you were able to go five rounds. That's huge. And not only that, but confidence-wise that you were able to go in there with a guy that hasn't lost in a long time and make him look like he's never looked after a fight before. Those are the things that you can just take as positives."

One fight later, he put it all together, defeating Lawler in the 2014 Fight of the Year. He wasn't content, though.

"I'm never satisfied," he said. "And that's one thing that not only wrestling, but my dad and [OSU] Coach [John] Smith and all my coaches have taught me. Once you hit something, you can never be satisfied. You always have to strive to be better. Now it's, 'How many times can I defend it, how can I do this, how can I do that?' That's my mindset. Now I know that I'm going to get the best out of everybody, and that's what I've been waiting for and striving for—to have the target on my back. This is where it starts making it fun for me. It's gonna be kill or get killed, in a sense, and I've got to make sure I train the hardest that I can and do the right things so I can avoid [losing] at all costs."

Hendricks lost his title in a UFC 181 rematch with Lawler by way of another razor-thin decision, but he bounced back in March 2015 with a win over Matt Brown, setting the stage for another title run.

MATT MITRIONE
SPRINGFIELD, IL

DEBUT: THE ULTIMATE FIGHTER: HEAVYWEIGHTS FINALE, DECEMBER 5, 2009

A four-year NFL veteran, Matt Mitrione turned to mixed martial arts as a way to keep his competitive spirit satisfied. With his win over UFC vet Scott Junk on the 10th season of *The Ultimate Fighter*, the entertaining heavyweight made it clear that he was going to keep his name in the headlines for a long time. It was his performance on the season finale card that really turned heads, though. Mitrione showed that he could deliver big hits, even without his helmet and pads, by knocking out Marcus Jones in devastating fashion. He then topped that victory with a host of knockout wins, confirming him as one of the most unlikely heavyweight contenders ever.

DAMARQUES JOHNSON
WEST JORDAN, UT

DEBUT: THE ULTIMATE FIGHTER: UNITED STATES VS UNITED KINGDOM FINALE, JUNE 20, 2009

DaMarques "Darkness" Johnson first made waves on *The Ultimate Fighter* nine for his trash talk about Team UK coach Michael Bisping. However, it was his fighting that got him to the season's final match. Although he fell short in his attempt to add James Wilks to the names of opponents he sent packing, there was no question that we had not heard the last of Johnson.

That fact was evident in wins over Edgar Garcia and Brad Blackburn that both earned him post-fight bonus awards. Whether he was beating vets like Mike Guymon or falling short of victory against Matthew Riddle and Amir Sadollah, you could always expect a fight out of the Utah native.

ROGÉRIO NOGUEIRA
VITÓRIA DA CONQUISTA, BAHIA, BRAZIL

DEBUT: UFC 106, NOVEMBER 21, 2009

The twin brother of heavyweight legend Minotauro Nogueira, Rogerio Nogueira remains on a quest to join his sibling in the history books as a world champion.

A Brazilian jiu-jitsu black belt whose boxing talent earned him a bronze medal in the 2007 Pan American Games, Nogueira entered the world of MMA in 2001. He made his mark with wins over Kazushi Sakuraba, Dan Henderson, Vladimir Matyushenko and Alistair Overeem, as well as in a classic war with Shogun Rua in 2005.

In November 2009, Nogueira made a spectacular UFC debut against Luiz Cane, earning Knockout of the Night honors.

Shogun Rua defeats Chuck Liddell at UFC 97.

There were no complaints about the co-main event, as former PRIDE star Mauricio "Shogun" Rua scored a devastating first-round stoppage of Chuck Liddell. Many considered this the end of the road for "The Iceman," who was now 1-4 in his last five fights.

One fighter whose career at the top was just beginning was unbeaten Brazilian Lyoto Machida. When the unorthodox striker shouted, "Karate's back," it was hard to argue with him after the words "UFC light heavyweight champion" began preceding his name. Machida performed a spectacular second-round knockout of Rashad Evans in the main event of UFC 98 on May 23 to win the light heavyweight crown.

Lyoto Machida punches Rashad Evans during their bout at UFC 98.

CARLOS CONDIT

**DEBUT: UFC FIGHT NIGHT: CONDIT VS KAMPMANN, APRIL 1, 2009
INTERIM UFC WELTERWEIGHT CHAMPION
WEC WELTERWEIGHT CHAMPION**

ALBUQUERQUE, NM

After a 5-0 run in the WEC that saw him become the last man to hold the organization's welterweight title, Carlos "The Natural Born Killer" Condit knew that he would be starting over when he came to UFC in 2009. That was just fine with the Albuquerque native.

"For me, it's more motivation," he said. "I feel like I have to climb back up the ladder. UFC welterweight division is one of the toughest, if not the toughest, divisions in the whole sport, and I feel honored to be competing with some of the best guys in the world, and I'm excited to make my mark and hopefully make a big splash in the UFC."

A few years later, with action-packed bouts in UFC against Martin Kampmann and Jake Ellenberger, a stirring Fight of the Night win over Rory MacDonald, Knockout of the Night victories against Dan Hardy and Dong Hyun Kim and an interim title-winning effort against Nick Diaz in the bank, "The Natural Born Killer" earned his undisputed title shot against Georges St-Pierre.

Confident and ready, Condit embraced his moment in the sun at UFC 154 in November 2012. Despite knocking St-Pierre down and nearly out, he lost a five-round decision to the Canadian star.

Undeterred, Condit nearly earned another title shot four months later when he engaged in a Fight of the Night war with Johny Hendricks at UFC 158 in March 2013. Hendricks took the decision in the close match, but Condit bounced right back in August 2013. His Fight of the Night knockout win over Kampmann avenged his 2009 loss to "The Hitman."

In March 2014, a knee injury forced a TKO loss to Tyron Woodley, but Condit plans to return in 2015 to battle the welterweight division's best once more.

Brock Lesnar defeats Frank Mir via TKO at UFC 100.

ALEXANDER GUSTAFSSON

DEBUT: UFC 105, NOVEMBER 14, 2009

ARBOGA, SWEDEN

In 2006, 19-year-old Alexander "The Mauler" Gustafsson decided that he wasn't going to follow the conventional path chosen by his friends when it came to a career. Instead, he was going to blaze his own trail as a professional mixed martial artist.

"I just trained boxing because my friends did it and I thought it was a cool thing to do," he recalled. "I was a young kid. I trained for a while, and then I stopped for a year. I didn't know what to do, so I moved to another city with a friend and I was just hanging out. But then I trained the first session [in MMA], and after that, I started looking at all these YouTube clips of old PRIDE with Cro Cop, Wanderlei Silva and all these guys, and I got hooked. Since then, I've been doing it."

In November 2009, Gustafsson made his highly anticipated UFC debut and impressed fight fans with a blistering 41-second knockout of Jared Hamman.

"The Mauler" was just getting started. After a tough loss against fellow prospect Phil Davis, Gustafsson won three times before announcing his arrival to the elite level of the 205-pound weight class with wins over Vladimir Matyushenko and Thiago Silva. His biggest win was yet to come, though, as he defeated Shogun Rua in December 2012.

Following that bout, Gustafsson fought Jon Jones in a 2013 title fight that is seen as one of the best championship bouts ever. Gustafsson lost a close decision to Jones, but after a win over Jimi Manuwa, he was back on track for another crack at UFC gold before getting temporarily derailed by Anthony "Rumble" Johnson in 2015.

Following the wild series of light heavyweight bouts shaking up the division, there was a brief calm in the storm. Rich Franklin and Cain Velasquez emerged victorious over Wanderlei Silva and Cheick Kongo, respectively, at UFC 99 in Cologne, Germany. England's own James Wilks and Ross Pearson picked up *Ultimate Fighter* titles in the series' first United States vs United Kingdom edition.

All of it led up to UFC 100 on July 11, an event widely considered to be the biggest of all time, which was self-evident from looking at the card: the headlining fight was the heavyweight unification bout and rematch between Brock Lesnar and Frank Mir. The welterweight title fight between Georges St-Pierre and Thiago Alves and the middleweight grudge match, which preceded the heavyweight battle, was between *The Ultimate Fighter* season nine coaches Dan Henderson and Michael Bisping. Even better than the lineup was the fact that when the horn sounded, the card delivered.

In the main event, Lesnar may not have made many fans in the Mandalay Bay Events Center by stopping local hero Frank Mir in the second round of their long-awaited rematch, but he did make it clear that he was the real deal as a world champion. Welterweight champion St-Pierre made fighting look easy in the UFC 100 co-feature, but it was far from that. His five-round unanimous decision win over number-one contender Alves was beleaguered by a gritty challenger who refused to go away without a fight, as well as a third-round groin injury that forced the Canadian superstar to dig deep in order to finish off the championship rounds. Although Bisping had the right stick-and-move plan heading into his bout with Henderson, when you're dealing with the former two-division PRIDE champion it only takes one wrong move and one right hand to end matters. That's precisely what happened, as Henderson knocked out "The Count" in the second round with the "H-Bomb."

287

After such a massive event, it would have been understandable if UFC took their foot off the gas for their next card in Philadelphia on August 8. However, with BJ Penn and Anderson Silva fighting in the co-featured bouts of UFC 101, there was no chance of that.

Written off by many after his failed quest for the welterweight title against St-Pierre in January, Penn returned to the lightweight division and showed why he was still the best 155-pounder in the world. He submitted number-one contender Kenny Florian in the fourth round of their main event bout.

In the co-feature, it was clear that middleweight champion Silva heard the boos, and he knew what the fans thought of his previous two bouts against Patrick Cote and Thales Leites. So what did the best pound-for-pound fighter in the world do? He put on one of the most spectacular striking displays ever seen in the Octagon, knocking out former UFC light heavyweight champion Forrest Griffin in less than four minutes of the first round. When it was over, all he heard were cheers.

 **ROY NELSON**
LAS VEGAS, NV

DEBUT: THE ULTIMATE FIGHTER: HEAVYWEIGHTS FINALE, DECEMBER 5, 2009
THE ULTIMATE FIGHTER 10 WINNER

 A favorite of hardcore fight fans, Roy "Big Country" Nelson may not have a typical fighter's physique, but it's hard to argue with the success of the big-bellied man known as "Big Country."

Owner of a black belt in Brazilian jiu-jitsu from Renzo Gracie, Nelson competed successfully in a number of grappling tournaments before turning his eye to MMA in 2004. Having won his first six bouts, Nelson soon signed with the now-defunct IFL in 2007, and within five fights, he was the promotion's heavyweight champion.

Following two successful title defenses and then two non-IFL losses to Andrei Arlovski and Jeff Monson, he finally hit the big time in 2009 as he defeated Kimbo Slice, Justin Wren and James McSweeney on *The Ultimate Fighter* season ten. He closed out the series in spectacular fashion in the finale by knocking out Brendan Schaub and winning *The Ultimate Fighter* season ten title.

Nelson's journey was just beginning. In UFC, he has scored each of his victories by knockout, and although he has had his setbacks over the years, the man with the most potent right hand in the division is always one swing away from another big win.

Anderson Silva is victorious over Forrest Griffin at UFC 101.

ROSS PEARSON
SUNDERLAND, UNITED KINGDOM

DEBUT: THE ULTIMATE FIGHTER: UNITED STATES VS UNITED KINGDOM FINALE, JUNE 20, 2009
THE ULTIMATE FIGHTER 9 WINNER

Sunderland, England's Ross "The Real Deal" Pearson was an early favorite on *The Ultimate Fighter* season nine, and he lived up to all expectations with his wins over Richie Whitson and Jason Dent. However, there was still one more mountain to climb for Pearson, and in June 2009, he reached the summit when he defeated his UK teammate Andre Winner to earn *The Ultimate Fighter* season nine's lightweight title. It was a dream win for "The Real Deal," who, despite his star status, may still be UFC's ultimate fan.

"I'm a crazy fan myself," he said. "I get excited before each UFC fight comes on, and I still watch all of them. I watch so many fights that I pick up other guys' stuff because I'm a fan and I try things out. I think that's why I'm improving so much, because I still am a fan of the sport. I love going to the UFC events, I love cornering my teammates and I just love it."

The journey's not over yet for Pearson. The former bricklayer is eager to put on his hard hat, pack a lunch and go to work to prepare for the coming years and his road to a world title shot.

In August, the Octagon landed in Portland for the first time, and while it wasn't Manila, UFC had its "Thrilla" as veteran heavyweight legends Minotauro Nogueira and Randy Couture turned back the clock like Muhammad Ali and Joe Frazier did in 1975. In the main event of UFC 102, they reminded fight fans just what greatness is in a three-round war that Nogueira won. September also saw the return of one of MMA's seminal figures, as Vitor Belfort made his first Octagon appearance since 2005, knocking out Rich Franklin in the first round of Dallas' UFC 103 main event.

The first light heavyweight title defense of Lyoto Machida pitted the karate master against fellow countryman Mauricio Rua in the featured bout of UFC 104 at Los Angeles' STAPLES Center on October 24. It was an intriguing matchup on paper that continued to be one in reality. When the final scorecards were tallied, Machida's razor-thin unanimous decision win sparked controversy throughout the MMA world, prompting a call for a rematch that followed in 2010. There was no controversy in the co-main event, with rising heavyweight star Cain Velasquez moving one step closer to a title shot with a second-round TKO of Ben Rothwell.

Minotauro Nogueira defeats Randy Couture via unanimous decision.

Injuries plagued the November 21 card in Las Vegas, with myriad changes occurring before Forrest Griffin and Tito Ortiz finally settled into the UFC 106 main event for a rematch of their UFC 59 bout. This fight didn't match the drama of the first one, but Griffin did get a measure of revenge in this clash of the former 205-pound champions, outpointing Ortiz over three rounds.

The Ultimate Fighter season ten came to a close on December 5, with Roy Nelson knocking out Brendan Schaub for the series title. The undercard made plenty of noise, as well. Streetfighting sensation Kimbo Slice defeated Houston Alexander by decision in his debut, and Matt Hamill pulled off a bizarre win over previously unbeaten Jon Jones.

For much of the fight, it looked like Jones was sailing to maintain his unblemished recorded with his 10th consecutive victory, but it was not to be. An illegal elbow from Jones prompted a controversial first-round disqualification from referee Steve Mazzagatti at The Pearl at The Palms.

"They say that after you lose, you become a better, stronger person," said Jones. "Everything happens for a reason."

BJ Penn would agree with that notion. After a crushing loss to St-Pierre that began 2009, he ended the year in Memphis on December 12 with his second consecutive win. This time, his fifth-round stoppage of Diego Sanchez saw him frustrate, punish, and dominate a talented challenger en route to his record third successful title defense in the main event of UFC 107. The victory established "The Prodigy" as the greatest lightweight of all time, but there was a hungry challenger in Frankie Edgar waiting in the wings.

EVAN DUNHAM
EUGENE, OR

DEBUT: UFC 95, FEBRUARY 21, 2009

Though you'll never hear an ounce of trash talk coming from the mouth of soft-spoken Evan Dunham, when the Octagon door closes, you won't find a fiercer competitor. Quietly entering UFC in early 2009, Dunham made his intentions known immediately with a TKO of Per Eklund. The Brazilian jiu-jitsu black belt continued to turn heads with upset wins over Marcus Aurelio, Efrain Escudero and Tyson Griffin. By the time he lost his first bout, a highly controversial split decision to former world champion Sean Sherk at UFC 119 in 2010, everyone knew Dunham's name.

JAKE ELLENBERGER
OMAHA, NE

DEBUT: UFC FIGHT NIGHT: DIAZ VS GUILLARD, SEPTEMBER 16, 2009

Despite a solid early career that saw him take on and beat a series of established foes over his first four years, Nebraska native Jake "The Juggernaut" Ellenberger wasn't going to make his move toward UFC until he felt the time was right.

Well, "The Juggernaut" proved to the world that his attitude was correct in his UFC debut in September 2009. He engaged in a three-round war with Carlos Condit that saw him take the former WEC welterweight champion to the brink of defeat before he lost a controversial split decision. Ellenberger rebounded with a series of emphatic wins, establishing himself as a 170-pound title threat.

TJ GRANT
COLE HARBOUR, CANADA

DEBUT: UFC 97, APRIL 18, 2009

One of Canada's top imports, Nova Scotia's TJ Grant made a loud statement to the 170-pound division in 2009 with his wins over veteran competitors Ryo Chonan and Kevin Burns, the latter earning him UFC 107's Knockout of the Night award.

However, the Brazilian jiu-jitsu brown belt and underrated striker is far from finished when it comes to making an impact in the Octagon. Despite being momentarily sidelined by injury, he is prepared for big things in the future.

During UFC 107 BJ Penn triumphs over Diego Sanchez.

 **JOHN HATHAWAY**
BRIGHTON, UNITED KINGDOM

DEBUT: UFC 93, JANUARY 17, 2009

 One of the UK's brightest talents, Brighton's John "The Hitman" Hathaway cut an impressive figure in his home country ever since he turned pro with a first-round submission victory over Jim Morris in June 2006.

From there, he continued to dominate his opposition Perhaps no win was bigger than his TKO of Tom Egan in January 2009 in his UFC debut. But there was more to come, as he delivered subsequent wins over Rick Story, Paul Taylor, Kris McCray and Diego Sanchez.

 YOSHIHIRO AKIYAMA
OSAKA, OSAKA PREFECTURE, JAPAN

DEBUT: UFC 100, JULY 11, 2009

 A judo black belt who earned All-Asia and All-Japan titles, Yoshihiro Akiyama is a certified star in Japan, dubbed "Sexyama" for his appearances on television and on fashion show catwalks. How big is he at home? "Like Chuck Liddell in the U.S.," he said. Thankfully, he could also fight. After a stellar stint in Asia, he brought his immense talents to UFC in 2009. He entered the record books as the first competitor to win Fight of the Night awards in each of his first three UFC bouts.

 NIK LENTZ
EL PASO, TX

DEBUT: UFC 103, SEPTEMBER 19, 2009

 Former University of Minnesota wrestler Nik "The Carny" Lentz has been one of the most active young fighters in the lightweight division, with nearly 40 fights since he turned pro in 2005. But he isn't just showing up for these bouts; he's winning them. Most notably, his UFC victories over Tyson Griffin, Rafaello Oliveira, Rob Emerson and Andre Winner have justified all his hard work.

"Even though it took a while, it's been for the best, because now when I go to the UFC, I feel I can really compete, and I'll be at the same level as everyone else," said Lentz.

MARK MUÑOZ
YOKOSUKA, KANAGAWA PREFECTURE, JAPAN

DEBUT: UFC 96, MARCH 7, 2009

Winner of the 2001 NCAA Division I national wrestling championship for Oklahoma State, two-time All-American Mark "The Filipino Wrecking Machine" Munoz finally listened to the prodding of former WEC featherweight champ Urijah Faber in 2007 and began training in mixed martial arts.

From there, the Filipino sensation thrilled fans and struck fear into opponents. In August 2009 at UFC 102, he added another accolade to his résumé as he bounced back from a knockout loss to Matt Hamill to pound out a decision over Nick Catone for his first UFC win.

Following stoppages of CB Dollaway, Ryan Jensen and Kendall Grove, a hard-fought scrap with Yushin Okami and a decision win over Aaron Simpson, Munoz established himself as one of the best middleweights in the game.

KIMBO SLICE
NASSAU, BAHAMAS

DEBUT: THE ULTIMATE FIGHTER: HEAVYWEIGHTS FINALE, DECEMBER 5, 2009

One of the most unlikely sports success stories of recent years is that of Kimbo Slice, a former streetfighter turned MMA athlete and worldwide sensation who set viewing records after his stint on *The Ultimate Fighter* season 10.

So what was it about the Miami resident that has captivated millions around the world?

"I keep it real in every way whatsoever," he said. "I'm the same guy as the guy that shops at K-Mart. Then they see me on TV, and it's like, 'There's that guy again,' and they feel like they can relate to that. I'm one of theirs."

In the Octagon, Slice outpointed Houston Alexander in December 2009 before getting cut after a UFC 113 loss to his *The Ultimate Fighter* season 10 castmate Matt Mitrione.

BRIAN STANN
TOKYO, JAPAN

**DEBUT: UFC 97, APRIL 18, 2009
WEC LIGHT HEAVYWEIGHT CHAMPION**

As a former WEC light heavyweight champion, Brian "All American" Stann knows how to handle himself in a fight. It's a trait he picked up as a captain in the United States Marine Corps who was awarded the prestigious Silver Star for his valor in combat.

After completing his active duty, Stann began focusing on his fight career. He compiled a 2-2 record in UFC at 205 pounds before deciding to try his hand at competing in the middleweight division.

The positive results were immediate. He scored the first submission win of his career, finishing Mike Massenzio with a triangle choke. He followed that up with 2011 knockout victories over steel-chinned Chris Leben and top contender Jorge Santiago. Stann retired in 2013 but remains involved in MMA as a commentator for the UFC.

BRENDAN SCHAUB
AURORA, CO

DEBUT: THE ULTIMATE FIGHTER: HEAVYWEIGHTS FINALE, DECEMBER 5, 2009

With size, speed and a Spartan work ethic, former college football standout Brendan "Big Brown" Schaub joined the talent-rich UFC heavyweight division after making it to the finale of *The Ultimate Fighter* season 10 with wins over Demico Rogers, Jon Madsen and Marcus Jones.

It was the Coloradan's impressive first-round knockouts of Chase Gormley and Chris Tuchscherer that really opened eyes. After he defeated former world title challenger Gabriel Gonzaga via decision and knocked out PRIDE legend Mirko Cro Cop, a star was born in one of the sport's most talent-rich weight classes.

RICK STORY
TACOMA, WA

DEBUT: UFC 99, JUNE 13, 2009

The rise of Washington's Rick "The Horror" Story up the welterweight ranks happened with the speed of a runaway train. That's not surprising, given the fact that Story's intention every time out is to keep moving forward until he's broken his opponent's will.

Although he only started training in mixed martial arts in 2004, he came a long way in a short time, truly hitting his stride in 2008 when he earned a call from UFC after winning six straight bouts. He hasn't regretted a moment since, as he continues to battle UFC's best.

STEFAN STRUVE
BEVERWIJK, NETHERLANDS

DEBUT: UFC 95, FEBRUARY 21, 2009

At 6'11½", Stefan "Skyscraper" Struve may be the most imposing heavyweight in UFC. His ability to intimidate doesn't stop with his height, as Struve's ferocious attack saw him defeat UFC veterans Colin Robinson, Stipe Miocic, Mario Neto, Paul Buentello, Denis Stojnic and Chase Gormley.

Winner of nearly 10 UFC bouts, with setbacks coming only against elite-level foes like Mark Hunt, Alistair Overeem, Junior Dos Santos, Roy Nelson and Travis Browne, Struve is confident of his future, but also patient about getting there.

FIGHTS OF THE YEAR

THE ULTIMATE FIGHTER SEASON 9 FINALE

SANCHEZ   **W3**   **GUIDA**

UFC 102

NOGUEIRA   **W3**   **COUTURE**

UFC FIGHT NIGHT: DIAZ VS GUILLARD

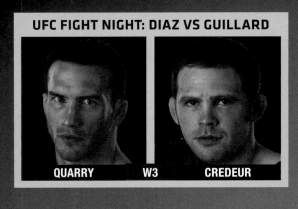

QUARRY   **W3**   **CREDEUR**

UFC 99

FRANKLIN   **W3**   **SILVA**

UFC FIGHT NIGHT: DIAZ VS GUILLARD

CONDIT   **W3**   **ELLENBERGER**

KNOCKOUTS OF THE YEAR

UFC 101

SILVA   **KO1**   **GRIFFIN**

UFC 98

MACHIDA   **KO2**   **EVANS**

UFC 96

HAMILL   **KO1**   **MUNOZ**

UFC 100

HENDERSON   **KO2**   **BISPING**

UFC 102

MARQUARDT   **KO1**   **MAIA**

SUBMISSIONS OF THE YEAR

UFC 99

ETIM   **WSUB2**   **BUCHHOLZ**

UFC 95

MAIA   **WSUB1**   **SONNEN**

UFC 107

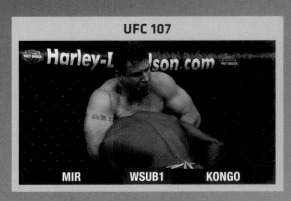

MIR   **WSUB1**   **KONGO**

UFC 107

JOHNSON   **WSUB1**   **GARCIA**

UFC FIGHT NIGHT: LAUZON VS STEPHENS

LAUZON   **WSUB2**   **STEPHENS**

DEBUTS

UFC 93

DENIS KANG

TOM EGAN

JOHN HATHAWAY

ALEXANDRE BARROS

IVAN SERATI

UFC 94

JOHN HOWARD

DAN CRAMER

UFC 95

PAULO THIAGO

BRIAN COBB

STEFAN STRUVE

EVAN DUNHAM

MIKE CIESNOLEVICZ

NEIL GROVE

UFC 96

MARK MUNOZ

RYAN MADIGAN

UFC 97

BRIAN STANN

XAVIER FOUPA-POKAM

TJ GRANT

UFC 98

MIKE PYLE

TIM HAGUE

UFC 99

PETER SOBOTTA

RICK STORY

UFC 100

YOSHIHIRO AKIYAMA

UFC 101

JOHNY HENDRICKS

DANILLO VILLEFORT

JESSE LENNOX

UFC 102

CHRIS TUCHSCHERER

MIKE RUSSOW

TODD DUFFEE

UFC 103

PAUL DALEY

STEVE LOPEZ

RAFAELLO OLIVEIRA

NIK LENTZ

BRIAN FOSTER

IGOR POKRAJAC

UFC 104

BEN ROTHWELL

CHASE GORMLEY

UFC 105

ALEXANDER GUSTAFSSON

JARED HAMMAN

UFC 106

JACOB VOLKMANN

ANTONIO ROGERIO NOGUEIRA

FABRICIO CAMOES

UFC 107

RICARDO FUNCH

LUCIO LINHARES

UFC FIGHT NIGHT: LAUZON VS STEPHENS

DENIS STOJNIC

JAKE ROSHOLT

MATT VEACH

DEREK DOWNEY

NICK CATONE

UFC FIGHT NIGHT: CONDIT VS KAMPMANN

CARLOS CONDIT

JESSE SANDERS

NISSEN OSTERNECK

TIM MCKENZIE

AARON SIMPSON

UFC FIGHT NIGHT: DIAZ VS GUILLARD

JAKE ELLENBERGER

JAY SILVA

MIKE PIERCE

STEVE STEINBEISS

THE ULTIMATE FIGHTER: UNITED STATES VS UNITED KINGDOM FINALE

DAMARQUES JOHNSON

JAMES WILKS

ANDRE WINNER

ROSS PEARSON

EDGAR GARCIA

FRANK LESTER

NICK OSIPCZAK

CAMERON DOLLAR

THE ULTIMATE FIGHTER: HEAVYWEIGHTS FINALE

JOE BRAMMER

RODNEY WALLACE

JON MADSEN

JUSTIN WREN

DARRILL SCHOONOVER

JAMES McSWEENEY

MARCUS JONES

MATT MITRIONE

KIMBO SLICE

BRENDAN SCHAUB

ROY NELSON

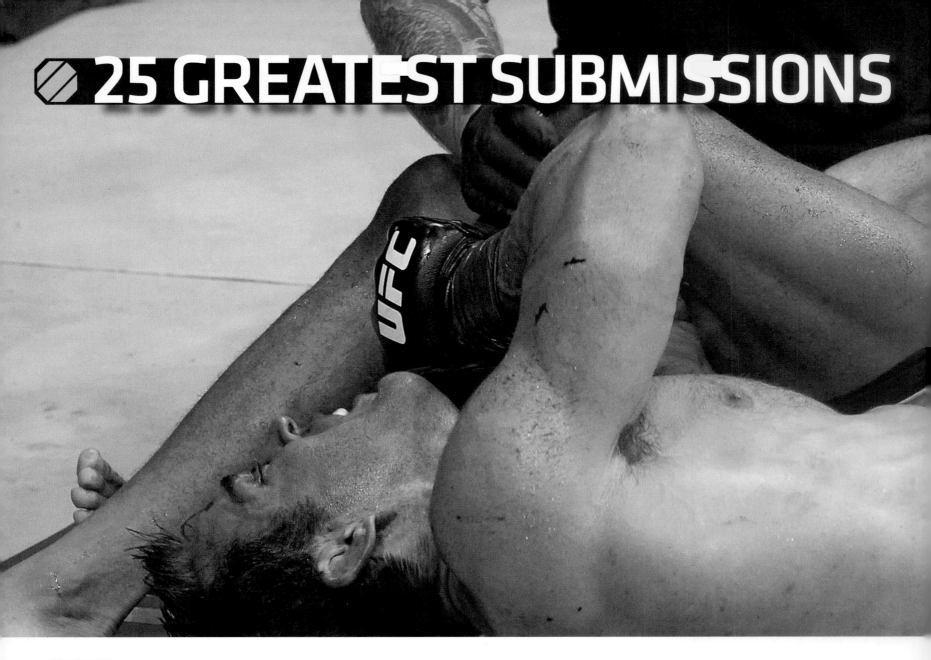

25 GREATEST SUBMISSIONS

UFC 1

ROYCE GRACIE vs KEN SHAMROCK I

When Royce Gracie submitted Art Jimmerson in the first UFC tournament in 1993, observers were confused. When the skinny, gi-wearing Brazilian did the same thing to the imposing Ken Shamrock—this time by rear-naked choke in just under a minute—a sport was born. Suddenly, every martial artist wanted to learn jiu-jitsu. This is where it all began.

UFC 3

ROYCE GRACIE vs KIMO LEOPOLDO

Royce Gracie is rightfully revered for his technical acumen and impact on the sport of mixed martial arts, but what sometimes gets lost is that he is also one of the toughest and most determined fighters ever. Kimo, whose shocking beat down of Gracie turned into a defeat in mere seconds, thanks to a tight armbar, won't dispute this fact.

UFC 4

ROYCE GRACIE vs DAN SEVERN

After winning two of the first three UFC tournaments, Royce Gracie was the undisputed king of MMA. But after two big wins at UFC 4, Dan Severn was a serious threat to the crown. He looked to be putting the finishing touches on his coup d'etat before Gracie pulled off a triangle choke that turned the tables after nearly 16 minutes of combat.

UFC 37

MURILO BUSTAMANTE vs MATT LINDLAND

We should probably give Murilo Bustamante two spots on this list, considering that he submitted Matt Lindland twice in the same bout. When Bustamante's armbar finish was disallowed because Lindland claimed that he didn't tap, the middleweight champ finally ended things definitively in the third round with a guillotine choke.

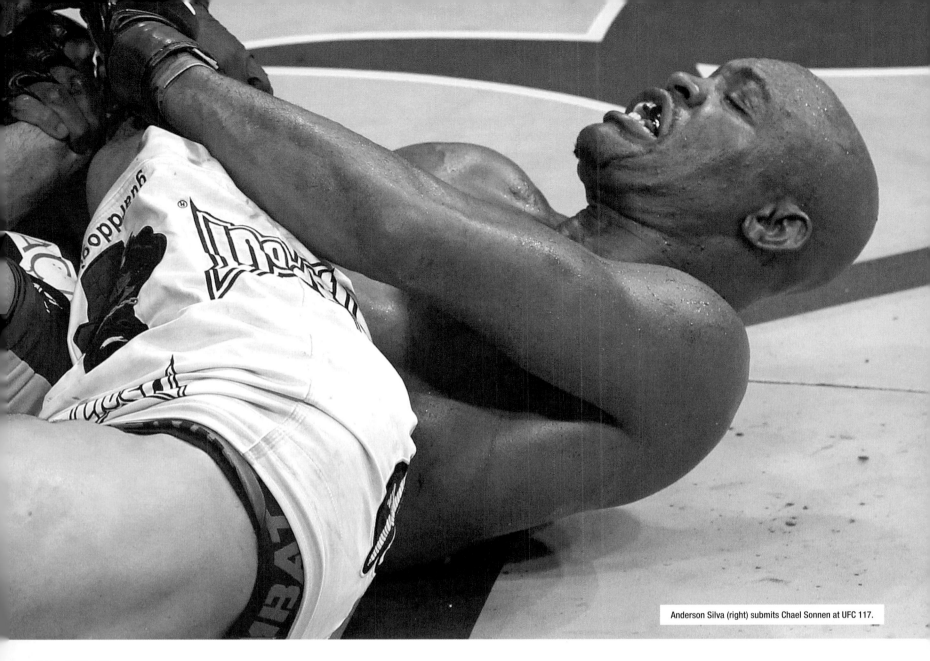

Anderson Silva (right) submits Chael Sonnen at UFC 117.

UFC 44

KARO PARISYAN vs DAVE STRASSER

Shocking those who didn't believe that judo had a place in mixed martial arts, Karo "The Heat" Parisyan put those critics on notice as he gave a clinic against veteran Dave Strasser at UFC 44. He finished matters less than four minutes into the first round with a rare rolling kimura.

UFC 46

MATT HUGHES vs BJ PENN I

Riding a 13-fight winning streak that included six victories in UFC title fights, welterweight champion Matt Hughes was understandably being dubbed "invincible." But former lightweight BJ Penn wasn't called "The Prodigy" for no reason. The confident Hawaiian shocked the world with a rear-naked choke submission of Hughes at UFC 46.

UFC 48
FRANK MIR vs TIM SYLVIA

Remember the way Mike Tyson approached his fights when he was the heavyweight boxing champion? Well, Frank Mir attacked submissions the way Tyson sought knockouts: he wanted to take an arm or a leg home. He almost got his wish against Tim Sylvia when he broke his opponent's arm with an armbar to earn the vacant UFC heavyweight crown in 2004.

UFC 50
MATT HUGHES vs GEORGES ST-PIERRE I

Nine months after losing his welterweight title to BJ Penn, Matt Hughes got the opportunity to wear gold around his waist once again when he took on Canadian phenom Georges St-Pierre for the vacant belt. Although GSP soon became the future of the division, on that night, Hughes was the present as he sunk in an armbar that made St-Pierre tap with just one second left in the first round.

UFC 52
MATT HUGHES vs FRANK TRIGG II

After taking an inadvertent low blow and almost getting choked out by Frank Trigg, Matt Hughes not only broke free from the choke hold, but he picked Trigg up, carried him across the Octagon, and slammed him before sinking in a fight-ending rear-naked choke. This wasn't just one of the greatest submissions in UFC history; it was one of the greatest fights.

UFC 73
CHRIS LYTLE vs JASON GILLIAM

At this level, if you have stellar technique and can capitalize on a well-trained opponent's mistake and submit him, it's safe to say that you're a pretty good fighter. But locking your opponent up in two submission holds at once? That's what Chris Lytle did in his win over Jason Gilliam, catching his foe in a triangle choke and an armlock to get the tapout.

UFC 81
FRANK MIR vs BROCK LESNAR I

For a little more than a minute, UFC newcomer Brock Lesnar was well on his way to one of the most impressive debuts of all time. But against a crafty veteran like Frank Mir, all it takes is one slip-up. That's just what happened to the overaggressive Lesnar, who got caught in a kneebar that resurrected Mir's career in emphatic fashion.

UFC 117
ANDERSON SILVA vs CHAEL SONNEN I

Great champions aren't defined by their dominance; they are defined by how they react to adversity. Anderson Silva got nearly five rounds' worth of punishment from trash-talking Chael Sonnen. But just when it appeared that the UFC middleweight champion's title was slipping away, he pulled off a final-round submission of Sonnen that forever etched his name in the record books as one of the sport's best ever.

THE ULTIMATE FIGHTER: TEAM RAMPAGE VS TEAM FORREST FINALE
JOSH BURKMAN vs DUSTIN HAZELETT

Just 22 years old at the time, Dustin Hazelett quickly earned a reputation as one of UFC's most impressive ground fighters thanks to wins like this one over the perpetually tough Josh Burkman. This fight was ended by what Joe Rogan described as "probably the sweetest armbar I have ever seen in mixed martial arts."

UFC 95
DEMIAN MAIA vs CHAEL SONNEN

It's hard not to be impressed with Brazilian jiu-jitsu black belt Demian Maia. It's not just his technique; it's the fact that every time he steps into the Octagon his opponent knows what he's going to do, and most of the time they still can't stop it. In this fight, it was a beautiful takedown right into a triangle choke that spelled doom for Chael Sonnen and gave Maia another submission win.

UFC 76
SHOGUN RUA vs FORREST GRIFFIN I

Sometimes the best submissions aren't ones that are memorable for spectacular technique or the "wow" factor, but ones that live on for what they meant at that particular moment in time. When Forrest Griffin closed the show on the heavily favored PRIDE import Shogun Rua with a rear-naked choke in the final minute, it was an exclamation mark on a result no one saw coming, especially the Brazilian jiu-jitsu black belt Rua.

UFC 81
TIM SYLVIA vs MINOTAURO NOGUEIRA

One of the sport's most talented and toughest fighters, PRIDE legend Minotauro Nogueira's quest for a UFC heavyweight title against Tim Sylvia wasn't going too well early on. But as Nogueira explained his eventual win by guillotine choke, "I played his game for almost three rounds. He played my game for two minutes, and I won the fight."

UFC 82
ANDERSON SILVA vs DAN HENDERSON

Anderson Silva has scored highlight-reel-worthy knockouts, is a jiu-jitsu black belt and is universally recognized as a state-of-the-art mixed martial artist. So how does he top that? He rebounds from a shaky first round against Dan Henderson to win by submission in the second stanza of a historic UFC/PRIDE unification bout.

UFC FIGHT NIGHT 13: FLORIAN VS LAUZON
NATE DIAZ vs KURT PELLEGRINO

A lot of fighters are great at being the hammer, but not many can come back after being the nail. After a rough first round, Nate Diaz proved that he can talk tough and walk tough as he roared back and caught Kurt Pellegrino in a fight-ending triangle choke in the second while thrusting his fists in the air in triumph.

UFC 51
ANDREI ARLOVSKI vs TIM SYLVIA I

Andrei "The Pitbull" Arlovski showed just how well rounded a fighter he had become in this 2005 battle for the interim UFC heavyweight title. He not only knocked 6'8" Tim Sylvia to the mat, but he then landed an ankle lock that forced "The Maine-iac" to tap out less than a minute into the bout.

UFC 157
KENNY ROBERTSON vs BROCK JARDINE

The move Kenny Robertson used to get his first UFC win in February 2013 didn't even have a name. Commentator Joe Rogan called it a form of leglock, but it's listed as a kneebar on the online fight databases. While both are correct, it was a move never executed in UFC the way the former Eastern Illinois University wrestler did on Brock Jardine. Suffice it to say that it was one of the most painful-looking submissions ever. As far as descriptions go, let's stick with Robertson's own name for it: the kickstand.

THE ULTIMATE FIGHTER: TEAM HUGHES VS TEAM SERRA FINALE
ROGER HUERTA vs CLAY GUIDA

Down on all three scorecards entering the final round, Roger Huerta turned the tables on Clay Guida in an amazing show of heart, as well as skill. He initially hurt his foe with a knee and then finished him off with an improbable rear-naked choke that made the fans at The Palms in Las Vegas erupt.

UFC 157
RONDA ROUSEY VS LIZ CARMOUCHE

Ever since Ronda Rousey turned pro, every opponent she faced knew that they were going to have to deal with an armbar attempt sooner or later (usually sooner). Liz Carmouche was no different, and part of her preparation for the UFC 157 bout against the women's bantamweight champ involved defending random armbar attempts by her teammates at every possible moment. Yet when Rousey made her move on Carmouche after surviving a rear-naked choke attempt moments earlier, the Marine Corps veteran got caught and was finished by the armbar. If there's a better finishing move in all of combat sports, we'd like to know about it.

UFC FIGHT NIGHT: TEHUNA VS MARQUARDT
CHARLES OLIVEIRA VS HATSU HIOKI

There are certain bouts that you show to folks who say they like fighting, but just not ground-and-pound. The June 2014 matchup between jiu-jitsu black belts Charles Oliveira and Hatsu Hioki is one of those bouts. Compelling and action-packed from start to finish, this was high-level MMA grappling at its finest. When it was over, Oliveira became the first man to submit Hioki. Whether you call it a guillotine, an anaconda, a D'Arce, or any variation of those, it was a thing of beauty.

UFC FIGHT NIGHT NOGUEIRA VS DAVIES
LEONARD GARCIA VS CHAN SUNG JUNG

Before Chan Sung Jung's March rematch with Leonard Garcia, you might have assumed that the fight game of "The Korean Zombie" started and finished with his ability to brawl. Perhaps Garcia, who defeated Jung in their classic 2010 WEC bout, figured the same thing. He might have even thought that he was safe as the seconds wound down in round two in Louisville in 2011. But that's when Jung struck with Eddie Bravo's "Twister," a painful maneuver that had never finished a fight in UFC—up until Garcia's tapout at 4:59 of the second round. It was a beautifully executed move, and a historic one.

UFC 140
FRANK MIR VS MINOTAURO NOGUEIRA II

There is a small school of believers who think that a knockout is more devastating than a submission. Frank Mir does not attend that school. In December 2011, he proved it again, becoming the first man to submit former PRIDE/UFC champ Minotauro Nogueira. To do that during a fight is impressive; to do it after getting buzzed and almost finished by one of the greatest heavyweights of all time takes it to another level.

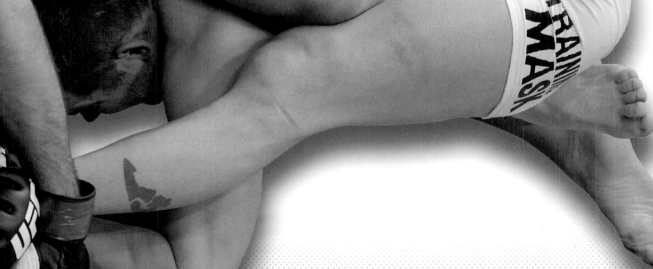

2010

Couture strikes Coleman at UFC 109

In the first year of Zuffa's ownership of UFC, the promotion presented fight fans with five events. Nine years later, 2010 featured 24 events, an average of two per month, proving that the company was not simply meeting worldwide demand, it was running like a well-oiled machine. Seven international events took place, with Australia and Abu Dhabi being added to the worldwide mix that already included Europe and Canada.

At last, MMA was a worldwide phenomenon. UFC fighters were not just based in the United States; champions hailed from the U.S., Brazil and Canada. Those champions who began the year (Brock Lesnar, Lyoto Machida, Anderson Silva, Georges St-Pierre and BJ Penn) were pushed to the limit over the next 12 months. All entered 2010 as champions, but were no longer champions heading into 2011.

2010 started off relatively slow in terms of high-profile championship matchups, with UFC 108 featuring a win by former titleholder Rashad Evans over Thiago Silva and UFC 109 headlined by Randy Couture's victory over fellow UFC Hall of Famer Mark Coleman. The promotion's first visit to Australia for UFC 110 starred Cain Velasquez, who scored the biggest win of his career over Minotauro Nogueira.

At UFC 111 in Newark, New Jersey, on March 27, the championship drought ended. Georges St-Pierre successfully defended his welterweight title with a decision win over gutsy challenger Dan Hardy. Shane Carwin stopped Frank Mir to win the interim UFC heavyweight title created by the bout with diverticulitis that sidelined Brock Lesnar.

Later that month, lightweight contender Kenny Florian looked like a southpaw Larry Holmes as he peppered former PRIDE star Takanori Gomi with jab after jab for two rounds. In the third, however, Florian took the fight to the canvas and finished it there, spoiling Gomi's long-awaited UFC debut via submission in Charlotte, North Carolina.

Kenny Florian and Takanori Gomi battle at UFC Fight Night: Florian vs Gomi.

TAKANORI GOMI
AIKAWA, KANAGAWA PREFECTURE, JAPAN

> **DEBUT: UFC FIGHT NIGHT: FLORIAN VS GOMI, MARCH 31, 2010**
> **PRIDE LIGHTWEIGHT CHAMPION**
> **2005 PRIDE GRAND PRIX CHAMPION**

A former PRIDE lightweight and Shooto welterweight champion from Kanagawa, Japan, Takanori "The Fireball Kid" Gomi has faced the top international competition for more than 11 years. He first made an impact in mixed martial arts circles when he defeated the legendary Rumina Sato for the Shooto title in 2001.

From there, it was practically one big fight after another for Gomi, whose stellar wrestling ability and two-fisted knockout power thrilled fight fans. In 2004, he made his debut in PRIDE with a first-round TKO of Jadson Costa that kicked off one of the greatest runs in the organization's history. From 2004 to 2007, Gomi went 13-1 with 1 no contest, defeating Ralph Gracie (with a PRIDE record six-second KO), Jens Pulver, Tatsuya Kawajiri, Luiz Azeredo and David Baron, among others. He also won the 2005 lightweight Grand Prix that earned him the first PRIDE lightweight championship.

A 2007 no contest against Nick Diaz ended his PRIDE run, and Gomi went on to win four of his next six bouts before deciding that the time was right to test himself in UFC.

Gomi stumbled in UFC bouts against Kenny Florian and Clay Guida, but a one-punch knockout of Tyson Griffin in August 2010 reminded fight fans why "The Fireball Kid" was still one of the most dangerous lightweights in the sport.

Florian takes down Gomi at UFC Fight Night: Florian vs Gomi.

Yas Island in Abu Dhabi on April 10 was the next international stop for the UFC juggernaut and it was an event to remember for multiple reasons—good and bad. On the positive side of the ledger, fans got to see a thrilling five-round title fight. Heavy underdog Frankie Edgar used a solid standup attack to score a five-round unanimous decision victory over BJ Penn and win the UFC lightweight championship.

On a less satisfying note, UFC middleweight champion Anderson Silva's return to the Octagon after an eight-month absence wasn't nearly as explosive as his previous battle with Forrest Griffin—not even close.

Though he retained his belt with a five-round unanimous decision victory over Demian Maia in the UFC 112 main event at Yas Island in Abu Dhabi, it was a bout filled with more stalemates than submissions and more posing than punching. The match forced Silva to apologize rather than celebrate after the final horn sounded.

Frankie Edgar triumphs over BJ Penn to win the UFC lightweight championship.

"Demian actually surprised me with some of his punches," said Silva. "I apologize to everybody; I don't know what got into me. I wasn't as humble as I should have been. It was just the ring rust and a little bit of everything. I can guarantee that next time it won't happen."

UFC President Dana White was furious with Silva's performance and was not shy about letting the world know. One of those listening was a middleweight contender from West Linn, Oregon, named Chael Sonnen.

After the Silva debacle at UFC 112, UFC management hoped that there would be no controversy in the May 8 rematch between Lyoto Machida and challenger Shogun Rua. Just like their first fight, there wasn't, as Rua became the UFC light heavyweight champion of the world after a stunning first-round knockout of the previously unbeaten Machida in the main event of UFC 113 in Montreal.

The decisive finish of Rua-Machida II brought positive vibes back to the organization, and it was perfect timing for the UFC 114 headliner between Rampage Jackson and Rashad Evans.

Shogun Rua celebrates his victory over Lyoto Machida at UFC 113.

Although the long-awaited grudge match between the former light heavyweight champions occasionally looked like the calm after the storm of trash talk and bad blood, an action-packed third round and a solidly executed game plan from Evans remained in fight fans' minds as he pounded out a three-round unanimous decision win over Rampage.

The focus remained on the 205-pounders in June, as UFC 115 featured an all-star matchup between former world champions Chuck Liddell and Rich Franklin. For "The Iceman," it was a last stand. Franklin scored his most important victory since he took the middleweight title in 2005. He knocked out the returning UFC Hall of Famer in devastating fashion in the first round, remarkably while fighting with a broken arm.

"I broke my hand before and didn't quit," Franklin said with a smile after the bout. The injury occurred earlier in the first round from a Liddell kick, but Franklin both soldiered on and knocked out one of the sport's most feared strikers. This was a bittersweet victory for fans of Liddell, who saw the 40-year-old light heavyweight legend lose his third straight fight by knockout.

MARK HUNT
SOUTH AUCKLAND

DEBUT: UFC 119, SEPTEMBER 25, 2010

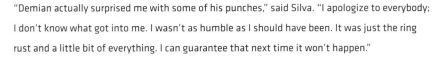

A legend of the K-1 kickboxing circuit having scored 30 wins against the likes of Stefan Leko, Jerome LeBanner, and Gary Goodridge, Australia's Mark "Super Samoan" Hunt turned to MMA in 2004, quickly becoming a star in Japan's PRIDE organization.

There were still mountains to climb, however. After UFC wins over Ben Rothwell, Roy Nelson, and Stefan Struve, he became a top heavyweight contender and one of the most popular fighters in the sport.

"I think people like the underdog story, but I'm a real fighter," Hunt said when asked about his appeal to the fans. "I'm a fighter for over half my life. 24 years of fighting in two different sports, and I'm still banging. I'm here trying to take these guys out. I haven't got a martial arts pedigree or background; I didn't even know I was going to be a fighter for all my life, but this is God's will and this is what God wants me to do. This is the way I look at things, and I think that's why people get excited. They want to see someone like myself, that's overcome all sorts of obstacles and he's still here."

Rich Franklin defeats Chuck Liddell via knockout at UFC 115.

A somber mood hovered over the fight world after Liddell's final bout, but the show must go on. After the finale of *The Ultimate Fighter* season 11 saw Court McGee crowned as the series' latest winner, a ray of light showed up in the form of UFC 116 on July 3 in Las Vegas. Without exaggeration, when it came to action fights and high drama, this may have been one of the greatest cards in UFC history.

RORY MacDONALD
QUESNEL, CANADA

DEBUT: UFC FIGHT NIGHT: MAYNARD VS DIAZ, JANUARY 11, 2010

Rory "Red King" MacDonald entered UFC at 21 years old with plenty of hype behind him, and he kept the buzz going with a first-round submission victory against veteran Mike Guymon in January 2010.

The kid from Kelowna made believers out of the staunchest skeptics in June 2010 when he battled tooth and nail with Carlos Condit, a longtime contender with whom no 21-year-old should be holding his own. MacDonald, however, is far from your typical fighter, and though he got stopped in the third round of UFC 115's Fight of the Night, he returned from his first pro loss better than ever at UFC 129, where he defeated Nate Diaz via decision.

"After every fight, there's a change," he said. "There's a learning experience in every fight, so I definitely feel different from when I first started, and I've gained so much more experience and I'm so much more comfortable in the UFC under the lights in the cage and stuff like that. It's definitely changed."

Following that bout, MacDonald's stock rose as the wins piled up. Victories over BJ Penn, Jake Ellenberger, Demian Maia, Tyron Woodley and Tarec Saffiedine had him knocking on the door of a world championship.

For a few minutes in the first round of the UFC 116 main event, it looked like the heavy hands of Shane Carwin were going to forcibly remove the UFC heavyweight title from Brock Lesnar's grasp. But with an amazing show of heart and resilience and a chin of steel, Lesnar survived the first round and then closed the show in the second with a submission victory that kept the belt around the Minnesotan's waist.

Brock Lesnar and Shane Carwin during the UFC 116 weigh-in.

Lesnar gains a second round submission victory over Carwin at UFC 116.

EDSON BARBOZA
NOVA FRIBURGO, RIO DE JANEIRO, BRAZIL

DEBUT: UFC 123, NOVEMBER 20, 2010

A native of Rio de Janeiro, Brazil, Edson "Junior" Barboza may not have entered UFC with as much professional MMA experience as his peers, but he was far from inexperienced. His résumé included 28 Muay Thai bouts that saw him compile a 25-3 record with 22 knockouts, 17 of them in the first round. His devastating striking attack continued to pay dividends in the MMA world, with his 2012 head kick knockout of Terry Etim a staple on UFC highlight-reels forever.

TRAVIS BROWNE
OAHU, HI

DEBUT: THE ULTIMATE FIGHTER: TEAM LIDDELL VS TEAM ORTIZ FINALE, JUNE 19, 2010

Hawaii native Travis "Hapa" Browne represents everything that fans love in heavyweights: he is 6'7", he comes to fight, and his opponents usually end up getting knocked out. After sending his previous nine opponents to defeat, he delivered the same sentence to veteran James McSweeney in his UFC debut in June 2010, halting him in the first round. Several more wins over Stefan Struve, Alistair Overeem, Josh Barnett and Brendan Schaub established him as a serious title threat.

MICHAEL JOHNSON
ST. LOUIS, MO

DEBUT: THE ULTIMATE FIGHTER: TEAM GSP VS TEAM KOSCHECK FINALE, DECEMBER 4, 2010

Michael "The Menace" Johnson was the one fighter both Georges St-Pierre and Josh Koscheck wanted on their teams on The Ultimate Fighter season 12 in 2010. The talented Missouri native did not disappoint, racing to the finals, and losing a close decision to Jonathan Brookins. Since then, Johnson has won several Octagon bouts over Tony Ferguson, Joe Lauzon, Melvin Guillard and Edson Barboza, establishing himself as a legitimate lightweight contender.

SETH BACZYNSKI
HONOLULU, HI

DEBUT: THE ULTIMATE FIGHTER: TEAM LIDDELL VS TEAM ORTIZ FINALE, JUNE 19, 2010

A gritty battler with tons of heart, Seth "Polish Pistola" Baczynski had a wild introduction to UFC fans in 2010 as a member of *The Ultimate Fighter* season eleven. Two fights with Brad Tavares followed: one on the show, and one on the season 11 finale card. Although he lost both, Baczynski returned to UFC in 2011 with a vengeance, winning four straight matches between 2011 and 2012.

PHIL DAVIS
HARRISBURG, PA

DEBUT: UFC 109, FEBRUARY 6, 2010

One of the new breed of mixed martial artists who combined athleticism, technique, and a Spartan work ethic to dominate their opponents, Phil "Mr. Wonderful" Davis impressed UFC fans with a host of significant wins. A four-time All-American wrestler from Penn State who won the 2008 NCAA National championship, Davis came to UFC in 2010 after going 3-0 on the local circuit. He showed improvement each step of the way, defeating Brian Stann, Alexander Gustafsson, Rodney Wallace, Tim Boetsch, Lyoto Machida and Rogerio Nogueira.

"This isn't about me tonight," said Lesnar, who was forced to the sidelines for nearly a year due to his bout with diverticulitis. "This is about my family. This is about my doctors. This is about my training partners. This is about my training staff. I am blessed by God. Ladies and Gentlemen, I stand before you a humble champion, and I'm still the toughest SOB around."

There were a few tough competitors on the undercard, as well. The co-main event featured the conclusion to one of the most amazing stretches in UFC history, and middleweight Chris Leben pulled it off. He won his second fight in two weeks by taking an action-packed war against Japanese contender Yoshihiro Akiyama via third-round submission. Leben, who replaced the injured Wanderlei Silva in the UFC 116 bout, was coming off a knockout victory over Aaron Simpson on June 19, 2010.

RENZO GRACIE
RIO DE JANEIRO, BRAZIL

DEBUT: UFC 112, APRIL 10, 2010

With a lifetime of memories in and out of the ring, including victories over four former UFC champions, Renzo Gracie could have chosen just about any snapshot to frame and post in his New York jiu-jitsu academy.

But the one picture adorning the walls that he sees every time he walks through the door is of perhaps his most notable loss—the technical submission defeat to Kazushi Sakuraba in their 2000 PRIDE bout in Japan.

"Technical" is the key word here, because Gracie did not tap out that night, despite a severely dislocated elbow. In a nutshell, that is who Renzo Gracie is: a warrior.

In 2010, Gracie made his long-awaited UFC debut against Matt Hughes. Although he lost that night at UFC 112 in Abu Dhabi, the ultra-popular Gracie still is, and will always remain, a fighter.

After three straight losses, including a defeat against the man facing him at UFC 116, Krzysztof Soszynski, light heavyweight Stephan Bonnar needed a win in the worst way. But he did not just get the victory against "The Polish Experiment;" he and his opponent engaged in an instant classic that saw the Las Vegan emerge victorious via a second-round TKO. It was a

night to remember, but it wouldn't take long to see another one.

In fact, another thriller occurred just a month later on August 7, in Oakland, California. On that night, Chael Sonnen promised to give UFC middleweight champion Anderson Silva a fight in their UFC 117 main event, and he lived up to his word as he dominated the first four rounds of their bout. But in the fifth, it was Silva pulling off an incredible triangle choke that allowed him to retain his title and get the last word on the challenger.

"I knew that I was losing the first four rounds," said Silva, who made the seventh successful defense of his title. "Chael put on a hell of a fight tonight."

"It was a tough fight; he's a tough guy; I came in second," said Sonnen, whose pre-fight trash talk reached epic proportions and also made this one of the most highly anticipated bouts of the year—and one that lived up to its billing.

KYLE NOKE
DUBBO, AUSTRALIA

DEBUT: THE ULTIMATE FIGHTER: TEAM LIDDELL VS TEAM ORTIZ FINALE, JUNE 19, 2010

A former member of "The Crocodile Hunter" Steve Irwin's security team, as well as a rugby player, Australia's Kyle Noke began training in mixed martial arts simply as a way to keep busy in the off season.

Eight years later, after fighting his way up the ranks on the local scene at home and abroad, he finally earned a spot in the Octagon. A strong effort on *The Ultimate Fighter* season 11 culminated in an impressive TKO victory over Josh Bryant in June 2010. Noke later came full circle as a coach on *The Ultimate Fighter Nations* series in 2014.

FABIO MALDONADO
SOROCABA, SÃO PAULO, BRAZIL

DEBUT: UFC 120, OCTOBER 16, 2010

A popular slugger known as "Hillbilly Steel," Fabio Maldonado is a stellar mixed martial artist but was also a rising star in boxing, compiling an impressive 22-0 record after turning pro in 2002.

But if he has learned anything, it's that when you're in an MMA fight, the action can go anywhere, so you must be prepared. And he has been, showing off all his skills in exciting battles against Kyle Kingsbury, Glover Teixeira, Gian Villante, Hans Stringer and Rampage Jackson, that latter of which saw Maldonado survive "everything but the kitchen sink" in a decision loss.

CHARLES OLIVEIRA
GUARUJÁ, SÃO PAULO, BRAZIL

DEBUT: UFC LIVE: JONES VS MATYUSHENKO, AUGUST 1, 2010

Charles "Do Bronx" Oliveira entered UFC in 2010 as one of the organization's youngest fighters, and he turned into one of its most charismatic when it came to delivering exciting fights. Whether he was slamming opponents, submitting them or knocking them out, Oliveira always brought the heat, compiling an impressive 14-0 record in his first two years as a pro.

That record included one of the most spectacular UFC debuts seen in a long time, as he scored a 41-second submission win over Darren Elkins in August 2010. He then followed up that victory with an equally memorable finish of Efrain Escudero.

BRAD TAVARES
KAILUA, HI

DEBUT: THE ULTIMATE FIGHTER: TEAM LIDDELL VS TEAM ORTIZ FINALE, JUNE 19, 2010

Brad Tavares made a fast but memorable impression on fans on *The Ultimate Fighter* season 11, making it all the way to the semifinals. That run set the stage for the season finale card, where Tavares defeated Seth Baczynski.

It also earned him a spot on the UFC roster, and there was no turning back then for the talented prospect, who has defeated Phil Baroni, Dongi Yang, Tom Watson, Bubba McDaniel, and Lorenz Larkin in the Octagon.

COURT McGEE
OGDEN, UT

DEBUT: THE ULTIMATE FIGHTER: TEAM LIDDELL VS TEAM ORTIZ FINALE, JUNE 19, 2010
THE *ULTIMATE FIGHTER 11* WINNER

An inspiration to fans for his ability to rebound from the ravages of drug addiction, Court "The Crusher" McGee also got a second chance in fighting when he was brought back to *The Ultimate Fighter* season eleven after losing a controversial decision to Nick Ring. In response, McGee won three in a row, finishing all of his opponents.

To top everything off, he defeated Kris McCray via second round-submission in the season finale to earn a UFC contract, proving that fighters are made, not born.

"I didn't do it because I wanted people to think of me as an MMA fighter; I did it because I loved the sport," said McGee.

JAKE SHIELDS
SUMMERTOWN, TN

DEBUT: UFC 121, OCTOBER 23, 2010
STRIKEFORCE MIDDLEWEIGHT CHAMPION

The talent-rich UFC welterweight division got richer in 2010 when Jake Shields, whose grappling prowess placed him among the best in the world, made his Octagon debut with a three-round win over Martin Kampmann.

A standout high school wrestler, Shields began his fighting career in 1999. He went on to compile a stellar record that included wins over a "Who's Who" of modern MMA, including Hayato "Mach" Sakurai, Carlos Condit, Mike Pyle and Jason Miller. Shields has also defeated middleweight standouts Dan Henderson, Robbie Lawler, Dave Menne, and Yushin Okami. In his first UFC title shot, however, Shields could not add Georges St-Pierre's name to his list, losing a five-round decision at UFC 129.

It was one of those rare times when there were no losers, and a star was born in Sonnen. Another young man whose star was rising was Frankie Edgar. The newly minted lightweight champion repeated his win over BJ Penn on August 28 in Boston, this time even more decisively.

That UFC 118 card also featured the first UFC bout between a world-class boxer and an equally proficient mixed martial artist, and it went as most expected. Randy Couture impressively sent three-division world champ James "Lights Out" Toney to defeat via submission in the first round.

After events in Austin, Indianapolis and London, it was Brock Lesnar time again at UFC 121 in Anaheim on October 23. This time, however, the big man would not have any miracle comebacks. Despite giving up more than 20 pounds to the champ, Cain Velasquez held off an initial charge from the 6'3", 265-pounder to take the Minnesotan down and then finish him off in the first round to win the UFC heavyweight championship. In the process, he became the first fighter of Mexican descent to earn a major heavyweight title in combat sports.

UFC's next two numbered events, UFC 122 in Oberhausen, Germany and UFC 123 in Auburn Hills, Michigan, were relatively uneventful. Yushin Okami defeated Nate Marquardt via decision, and Rampage Jackson scored a controversial decision win over Lyoto Machida. In the finale of *The Ultimate Fighter: Team GSP vs Team Koscheck* on December 4, fans saw Jonathan Brookins earn the series title.

The Octagon was back in Montreal on December 11 to close out the year, and its favorite son, Georges St-Pierre, was still in dominant form. He repeated his victory over number-one contender Josh Koscheck, this time by way of a shutout five-round unanimous decision in the main event of UFC 124.

Five champions began the year. Only two of them, Silva and St-Pierre, remained on top heading into 2011.

GSP takes down Josh Koscheck during the welterweight title bout at UFC 124.

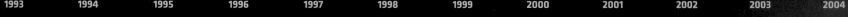

FIGHTS OF THE YEAR   KNOCKOUTS OF THE YEAR   SUBMISSIONS OF THE YEAR

UFC 117

SILVA   WSUB5   SONNEN

UFC 121

VELASQUEZ   TKO1   LESNAR

UFC 117

SILVA   WSUB5   SONNEN

UFC 166

LEBEN   WSUB3   AKIYAMA

UFC 113

RUA   KO1   MACHIDA

UFC 108

MILLER   WSUB1   LAUZON

UFC 116

BONNAR   TKO2   SOSZYNSKI

UFC 123

PENN   KO1   HUGHES

UFC 117

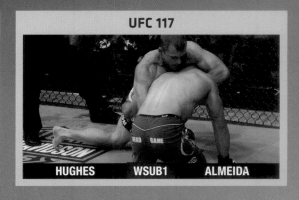

HUGHES   WSUB1   ALMEIDA

UFC 116

LESNAR   WSUB2   CARWIN

UFC 114

RUSSOW   KO3   DUFFEE

UFC 110

LYTLE   WSUB1   FOSTER

UFC 119

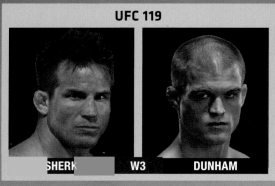

SHERK   W3   DUNHAM

THE ULTIMATE FIGHTER: TEAM GSP VS TEAM KOSCHEK

GARZA   KO1   PAIXAO

UFC 124

BOCEK   WSUB1   HAZELETT

DEBUTS

UFC 108

GILBERT YVEL

JOHN GUNDERSON

UFC 109

RONYS TORRES

PHIL DAVIS

JOEY BELTRAN

ROLLES GRACIE

UFC 110

JAMES TE HUNA

UFC 111

GREG SOTO

UFC 112

RENZO GRACIE

UFC 114

WAYLON LOWE

CYRILLE DIABATE

UFC 115

CLAUDE PATRICK

UFC 116

RICARDO ROMERO

DAVE BRANCH

KARLOS VEMOLA

UFC 117

TODD BROWN

CHRISTIAN MORECRAFT

UFC 118

JAMES TONEY

AMILCAR ALVES

UFC LIVE: VERA VS JONES

DARREN ELKINS

DANIEL ROBERTS

JULIO PAULINO

UFC LIVE: JONES VS MATYUSHENKO

CHARLES OLIVEIRA

UFC 119

PAT AUDINWOOD

MARK HUNT

SEAN MCCORKLE

UFC 120

FABIO MALDONADO

CURT WARBURTON

PAUL SASS

VINICIUS QUEIROZ

ROB BROUGHTON

UFC 121

DONGI YANG

JAKE SHIELDS

UFC 122

ALEXANDRE FERREIRA

PASCAL KRAUSS

MARK SCANLON

CARLOS EDUARDO ROCHA

UFC 123

MAIQUEL FALCAO

MIKE LULLO

EDSON BARBOZA

TJ O'BRIEN

UFC 124

JESSE BONGFELDT

SEAN PIERSON

JOHN MAKDESSI

UFC FIGHT NIGHT: MAYNARD VS DIAZ

MIKE GUYMON

RORY MacDONALD

JOHN SALTER

GERALD HARRIS

UFC FIGHT NIGHT: FLORIAN VS GOMI

TAKANORI GOMI

MARIO MIRANDA

CHARLIE BRENNEMAN

JASON HIGH

UFC FIGHT NIGHT: MARQUARDT VS PALHARES

RAFAEL NATAL

TJ WALDBURGER

DAVID MITCHELL

THE ULTIMATE FIGHTER: TEAM LIDDELL VS TEAM ORTIZ FINALE

COURT McGEE

KRIS MCCRAY

JAMIE YAGER

RICH ATTONITO

MARK HOLST

BRAD TAVARES

SETH BACZYNSKI

KYLE NOKE

JOSH BRYANT

JAMES HAMMORTREE

CHRIS CAMOZZI

TRAVIS BROWNE

THE ULTIMATE FIGHTER: TEAM GSP VS TEAM KOSCHECK FINALE

JONATHAN BROOKINS

MICHAEL JOHNSON

NAM PHAN

CODY MCKENZIE

AARON WILKINSON

TYLER TONER

IAN LOVELAND

SAKO CHIVITCHIAN

KYLE WATSON

WILL CAMPUZANO

NICK PACE

FREDSON PAIXAO

PABLO GARZA

COMPLETE AS OF UFC 188

UFC HEAVYWEIGHT TITLE (206 TO 265 LBS)

1. Mark Coleman – Defeats Dan Severn at UFC 12 (2/7/97) to become the first UFC heavyweight champion.

2. Maurice Smith – Defeats Mark Coleman at UFC 14 (7/27/97). Smith defends the title once, against Tank Abbott.

3. Randy Couture – Defeats Maurice Smith at Ultimate Japan (12/21/97). Couture loses his title after a contract dispute.

4. Bas Rutten – Defeats Kevin Randleman at UFC 20 (5/7/99) to win the vacant title. Rutten vacates the title to move down in weight.

5. Kevin Randleman – Defeats Pete Williams at UFC 23 (11/19/99) to win the vacant UFC heavyweight title. He defends the title once, against Pedro Rizzo.

7. Josh Barnett – Defeats Randy Couture at UFC 36 (3/22/02) to win the title. Barnett loses his belt after testing positive for steroids.

8. Ricco Rodriguez – Defeats Randy Couture at UFC 39 (9/27/02) to claim the UFC heavyweight title.

9. Tim Sylvia – Stops Ricco Rodriguez at UFC 41 (2/28/03) to become champion. Sylvia successfully defends his title against Gan McGee, but later relinquishes his belt after testing positive for steroids.

10. Frank Mir – Defeats Tim Sylvia for the vacant title at UFC 48 (6/19/04). Mir is seriously injured in a motorcycle accident and forced to give up his belt while he recovers from his injuries.

11. Andrei Arlovski – Defeats Tim Sylvia in the first round at UFC 51 (2/5/05) to claim the interim title, which is later upgraded to the full championship. Arlovski defends the title twice, against Justin Eilers and Paul Buentello.

12. Tim Sylvia – Becomes only the second man to regain the heavyweight championship when he knocks out Andrei Arlovski at UFC 59 (4/15/06). Sylvia defends the title against Arlovski and Jeff Monson.

13. Randy Couture – Becomes the first man to win the heavyweight title three times when he decisions Tim Sylvia over five rounds at UFC 68 (3/3/07). Couture defends the title against Gabriel Gonzaga. After a period of inactivity, Minotauro Nogueira and Tim Sylvia are selected to fight for the interim title. Couture subsequently returns to active status in November 2008.

6. Randy Couture – Returns to UFC and regains his title by defeating Kevin Randleman at UFC 28 (11/17/00). He defends the title twice, against Pedro Rizzo.

14. Minotauro Nogueira – Defeats Tim Sylvia in the third round to win the interim heavyweight championship at UFC 81 (2/2/08).

15. Frank Mir – Defeats Minotauro Nogueira via TKO in the second round at UFC 92 (12/27/08) to win the interim heavyweight championship. Loses to Brock Lesnar at UFC 100.

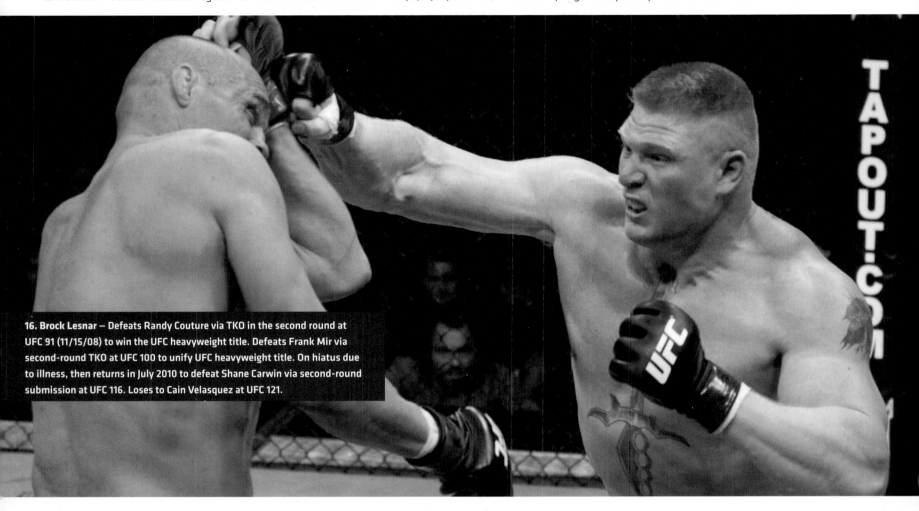

16. Brock Lesnar – Defeats Randy Couture via TKO in the second round at UFC 91 (11/15/08) to win the UFC heavyweight title. Defeats Frank Mir via second-round TKO at UFC 100 to unify UFC heavyweight title. On hiatus due to illness, then returns in July 2010 to defeat Shane Carwin via second-round submission at UFC 116. Loses to Cain Velasquez at UFC 121.

17. Shane Carwin – Defeats Frank Mir via first-round KO at UFC 111 (3/27/10) to win interim UFC heavyweight title. Loses to Brock Lesnar via second-round submission at UFC 116.

18. Cain Velasquez – Defeats Brock Lesnar via TKO in the first round at UFC 121 (10/23/10) to win the UFC heavyweight title. Loses to Junior Dos Santos at UFC on FOX: Velasquez vs Dos Santos.

19. Junior Dos Santos – Defeats Cain Velasquez via knockout in the first round at UFC on FOX: Velasquez vs Dos Santos (11/12/11) to win the UFC heavyweight title. Successfully defends the title against Frank Mir. Loses title to Cain Velasquez at UFC 155.

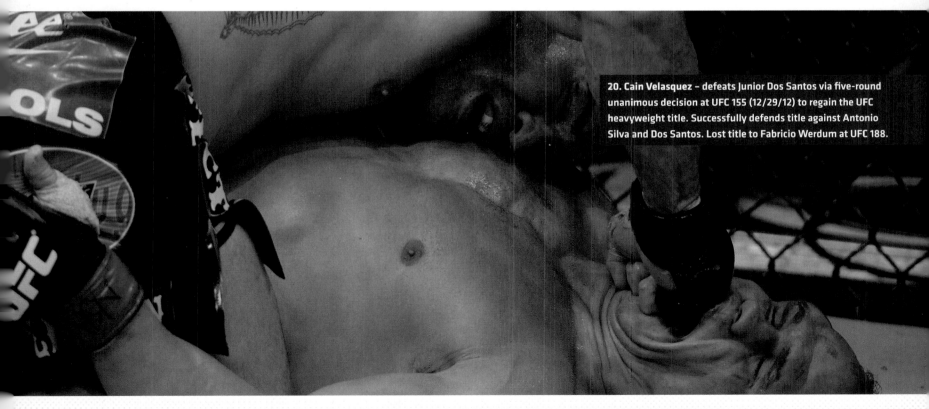

20. Cain Velasquez – defeats Junior Dos Santos via five-round unanimous decision at UFC 155 (12/29/12) to regain the UFC heavyweight title. Successfully defends title against Antonio Silva and Dos Santos. Lost title to Fabricio Werdum at UFC 188.

21. Fabricio Werdum - defeats Mark Hunt via knockout at UFC 180 (11/15/14) to win interim UFC heavyweight title. Submits Cain Velasquez at UFC 188 (6/13/15) to unify title and become undisputed heavyweight champion.

LIGHT HEAVYWEIGHT TITLE (186 TO 205 LBS)

1. Frank Shamrock – Defeats Kevin Jackson at Ultimate Japan (12/21/97) to become the first UFC light heavyweight champion (although the title is called middleweight at the time). Shamrock defends his title against Igor Zinoviev, Jeremy Horn, John Lober and Tito Ortiz. He retires from UFC in November of 1999.

2. Tito Ortiz – Defeats Wanderlei Silva at UFC 25 (4/14/00) to win the vacant title. Ortiz defends his crown against Yuki Kondo, Evan Tanner, Elvis Sinosic, Vladimir Matyushenko and Ken Shamrock. After a period of inactivity, Chuck Liddell and Randy Couture are selected to fight for the interim title.

3. Randy Couture – Defeats Chuck Liddell at UFC 43 (6/6/03) for the interim title. He defeats Tito Ortiz at UFC 44 (9/26/03) to claim the undisputed crown.

4. Vitor Belfort – Defeats Randy Couture at UFC 46 (1/31/04) to win the title.

5. Randy Couture – Regains the championship by defeating Vitor Belfort at UFC 49 (8/21/04).

6. Chuck Liddell – Wins the light heavyweight title by defeating Randy Couture at UFC 52 (4/16/05). Liddell defends the title against Jeremy Horn, Randy Couture, Renato Sobral and Tito Ortiz.

7. Rampage Jackson– Wins the light heavyweight title by defeating Chuck Liddell in the first round at UFC 71 (5/26/07). Jackson defends the title against Dan Henderson.

8. Forrest Griffin – Wins the light heavyweight title by defeating Rampage Jackson at UFC 86 (7/5/08).

9. Rashad Evans – Wins the light heavyweight title with a third-round TKO of Forrest Griffin at UFC 92 (12/27/08).

10. Lyoto Machida – Wins the light heavyweight title with a second-round knockout of Rashad Evans at UFC 98 (5/23/09). Defends the title against Shogun Rua.

11. Shogun Rua – Wins the light heavyweight title with a first-round KO of Lyoto Machida at UFC 113 (5/8/10).

12. Jon Jones – wins the light heavyweight title with a third round TKO of Shogun Rua at UFC 128 (3/19/11). Successfully defends title against Rampage Jackson, Lyoto Machida, Rashad Evans, Vitor Belfort, Chael Sonnen, Alexander Gustafsson, Glover Teixeira and Daniel Cormier. Stripped of title in April of 2015

13. Daniel Cormier – wins vacant UFC light heavyweight title with submission win over Anthony Johnson at UFC 187 (5/23/15).

MIDDLEWEIGHT TITLE (171 TO 185 LBS)

1. Dave Menne – Defeats Gil Castillo at UFC 33 (9/28/01) to win the UFC middleweight championship.

2. Murilo Bustamante – Defeats Dave Menne at UFC 35 (1/11/02) to win the title. Bustamante defends the title against Matt Lindland, and then vacates the title when he leaves the organization.

3. Evan Tanner – Defeats David Terrell at UFC 51 (2/5/05) to win the vacant middleweight title.

4. Rich Franklin – Defeats Evan Tanner at UFC 53 (6/4/05) to win the title. Franklin defends the title against Nate Quarry and David Loiseau.

5. Anderson Silva – Defeats Rich Franklin at UFC 64 (10/14/06) to win the title. Silva defeats Travis Lutter in what should have been his first title defense, but Lutter came in overweight, rendering the bout a non-title affair. Successfully defends the title against Nate Marquardt, Rich Franklin, Dan Henderson, Patrick Cote, Thales Leites, Demian Maia, Chael Sonnen (twice), Vitor Belfort and Yushin Okami. Loses title to Chris Weidman at UFC 162.

6. Chris Weidman – defeats Anderson Silva via second round knockout at UFC 162 (7/6/13). Successfully defended title against Anderson Silva, Lyoto Machida and Vitor Belfort.

1. Pat Miletich – Defeats Mikey Burnett at UFC Brazil (10/16/98) to win the UFC welterweight championship, which is called lightweight at the time. Miletich defends the title against Jorge Patino, Andre Pederneiras, John Alessio and Kenichi Yamamoto.

2. Carlos Newton – Defeats Pat Miletich at UFC 31 (5/4/01) to win the title.

3. Matt Hughes – Defeats Carlos Newton at UFC 34 (11/2/01) to win the title. Hughes successfully defends against Hayato Sakurai, Carlos Newton, Gil Castillo, Sean Sherk and Frank Trigg.

4. BJ Penn – Defeats Matt Hughes at UFC 46 (1/31/04) to win the championship. Penn subsequently leaves the organization, rendering the title vacant.

5. Matt Hughes – Regains the championship by defeating Georges St-Pierre at UFC 50 (10/22/04) to win the vacant title. Hughes defends the title against Frank Trigg and BJ Penn.

6. Georges St-Pierre – Defeats Matt Hughes at UFC 65 (11/18/06) to win the championship.

7. Matt Serra – Finishes Georges St-Pierre in the first round at UFC 69 (4/7/07) to win the welterweight title.

8. Georges St-Pierre – Wins interim title with win over Matt Hughes at UFC 79. Regains the undisputed title by stopping Matt Serra in the second round at UFC 83 (4/19/08). GSP successfully defends title against Jon Fitch, BJ Penn, Thiago Alves, Dan Hardy, Josh Koscheck, Jake Shields, Carlos Condit, Nick Diaz and Johny Hendricks.

9. Carlos Condit – With Georges St-Pierre injured, Condit wins interim UFC welterweight title at UFC 143 (2/4/12) with win over Nick Diaz. Loses title in unification bout against Georges St-Pierre at UFC 154 (11/17/12).

10. Georges St-Pierre – Relinquishes UFC welterweight title on December 13, 2013, to take hiatus from the sport.

11. Johny Hendricks – Defeats Robbie Lawler via decision at UFC 171 (3/15/14) to win vacant UFC welterweight title. Loses title to Lawler in rematch at UFC 181.

12. **Robbie Lawler** – Defeats Johny Hendricks via decision at UFC 181 (12/6/14) to win UFC welterweight title.

1. Jens Pulver – Defeats Caol Uno at UFC 30 (2/23/01) to win the UFC lightweight championship. Pulver defends his title against Dennis Hallman and BJ Penn before leaving the organization and vacating the title. From 2002 to 2003, a four-man tournament featuring BJ Penn, Caol Uno, Matt Serra and Din Thomas is held to determine a new champion, but the title remains vacant after a five-round draw between Penn and Uno in the final match at UFC 41. The division is then used sporadically until the UFC 49 bout between Yves Edwards and Josh Thomson in 2004. The division doesn't return until UFC 58 in 2006.

3. BJ Penn – Defeats Joe Stevenson in the second round at UFC 80 (1/19/08) to win the vacant UFC lightweight title. Penn defends his title against Sean Sherk, Kenny Florian and Diego Sanchez.

2. Sean Sherk – Defeats Kenny Florian at UFC 64 (10/14/06) to win the vacant UFC lightweight title. He defends the title against Hermes Franca but is subsequently stripped of the belt after testing positive for steroids.

4. Frankie Edgar – Defeats BJ Penn via unanimous decision at UFC 112 (4/10/10) to win the UFC crown. Edgar successfully defends the title against BJ Penn and Gray Maynard twice. Loses title to Benson Henderson at UFC 144.

5. Benson Henderson – Defeats Frankie Edgar via decision at UFC 144 (2/26/12) to win the UFC lightweight title. Successfully defends the title against Edgar, Nate Diaz and Gilbert Melendez. Loses title to Anthony Pettis at UFC 164.

6. Anthony Pettis – Defeats Benson Henderson at UFC 164 (8/31/13) to win the UFC lightweight title. Successfully defends title against Gilbert Melendez. Lost title to Rafael dos Anjos at UFC 185.

7. Rafael dos Anjos – Defeats Anthony Pettis via unanimous decision at UFC 185 (3/14/15) to win the UFC lightweight title.

FEATHERWEIGHT TITLE (136 TO 145 LBS)

1. Jose Aldo — Declared first UFC featherweight champion after WEC-UFC merger in 2010. Awarded belt before UFC 123 in November of 2010. Defends title successfully against Mark Hominick, Kenny Florian, Chad Mendes (twice), Frankie Edgar, Chan Sung Jung and Ricardo Lamas.

BANTAMWEIGHT TITLE (126 TO 135 LBS)

1. Dominick Cruz — The former WEC bantamweight champion defeats Scott Jorgensen at WEC 53 on December 16, 2010, to win the first UFC bantamweight championship. Successfully defends title against Urijah Faber and Demetrious Johnson. Forced to relinquish title on January 6, 2014, due to injury.

2. Renan Barão — With Dominick Cruz injured, Barão defeats Urijah Faber at UFC 149 (7/21/12) to win interim UFC bantamweight title. Promoted to undisputed champion on January 6, 2014. Successfully defends title against Michael McDonald, Eddie Wineland and Urijah Faber. Loses title to TJ Dillashaw at UFC 173.

3. TJ Dillashaw — Defeats Renan Barão at UFC 173 (5/24/14) to win UFC bantamweight title. Successfully defends title against Joe Soto.

WOMEN'S BANTAMWEIGHT TITLE
(126 TO 135 LBS)

1. Ronda Rousey — Declared first UFC women's bantamweight champion on December 6, 2012. Successfully defends title against Liz Carmouche, Miesha Tate, Sara McMann, Alexis Davis and Cat Zingano.

FLYWEIGHT TITLE
(116 TO 125 LBS)

1. Demetrious Johnson — Defeats Joseph Benavidez via decision at UFC 152 (9/22/12) to win the UFC flyweight title. Successfully defends title against John Dodson, John Moraga, Joseph Benavidez, Ali Bagautinov and Chris Cariaso.

WOMEN'S STRAWWEIGHT TITLE
(106 TO 115 LBS)

1. Carla Esparza — Defeats Rose Namajunas via third-round submission at The Ultimate Fighter: A Champion Will Be Crowned Finale (12/12/14) to win the UFC women's strawweight title. Loses the title to Joanna Jedrzejczyk at UFC 185.

2. Joanna Jedrzejczyk — Defeats Carla Esparza via second-round TKO at UFC 185 (3/14/15) to win the UFC women's strawweight title.

UFC TOURNAMENT CHAMPIONS

OPEN WEIGHT

UFC 1 – Royce Gracie (defeats Gerard Gordeau in final)

UFC 2 – Royce Gracie (defeats Pat Smith in final)

UFC 3 – Steve Jennum (defeats Harold Howard in final)

UFC 4 – Royce Gracie (defeats Dan Severn in final)

UFC 5 – Dan Severn (defeats Dave Beneteau in final)

UFC 6 – Oleg Taktarov (defeats Tank Abbott in final)

UFC 7 – Marco Ruas (defeats Paul Varelans in final)

Ultimate Ultimate '95 – Dan Severn (defeats Oleg Taktarov in final)

UFC 8 – Don Frye (defeats Gary Goodridge in final)

UFC 10 – Mark Coleman (defeats Don Frye in final)

UFC 11 – Mark Coleman (wins by forfeit over Scott Ferrozzo)

Ultimate Ultimate '96 – Don Frye (defeats Tank Abbott in final)

HEAVYWEIGHT

UFC 12 – Vitor Belfort (defeats Scott Ferrozzo in final)

UFC 13 – Randy Couture (defeats Steven Graham in final)

UFC 14 – Mark Kerr (defeats Dan Bobish in final)

UFC 15 – Mark Kerr (defeats Duane Cason in final)

UFC Japan – Kazushi Sakuraba (defeats Marcus Silveira in final)

NON-HEAVYWEIGHT TOURNAMENTS

UFC 12 – Jerry Bohlander (defeats Nick Sanzo in under 199 lbs. final)

UFC 13 – Guy Mezger (defeats Tito Ortiz in under 199 lbs. final)

UFC 14 – Kevin Jackson (defeats Anthony Fryklund in under 199 lbs. final)

UFC 16 – Pat Miletich (defeats Chris Brennan in under 170 lbs. final)

UFC 17 – Dan Henderson (defeats Carlos Newton in middleweight final, which is 171-199 lbs. at the time)

UFC 23 – Kenichi Yamamoto (defeats Katsuhisa Fuji in middleweight final, which is 171-199 lbs. at the time)

UFC SUPERFIGHT CHAMPIONS

1. Ken Shamrock – Wins title with submission victory over Dan Severn at UFC 6. Defends title with draw against Oleg Taktarov at UFC 7 and submission win over Kimo Leopoldo at UFC 8.

2. Dan Severn – Wins title with split decision over Ken Shamrock at UFC 9. Title becomes UFC heavyweight championship in unification bout with Mark Coleman at UFC 12.

2011

Late in 2010, UFC made an announcement that altered the organization forever when it declared that the World Extreme Cagefighting (WEC) promotion would hold its last event on December 16 of that year.

That was the bad news for the legion of fans who loved the lighter-weight action taking place in the blue cage. The good news was that the top fighters from the 155-pound weight class, including Anthony Pettis and Benson Henderson, were coming to UFC. Even better, UFC was going to introduce the featherweight and bantamweight divisions, as well. That meant fighters like Urijah Faber, Jose Aldo, Renan Barão, Demetrious Johnson, Dominick Cruz and Miguel Angel Torres were going to be gracing the Octagon in 2011 and beyond.

But first, there was some housekeeping to take care of. Cruz's last WEC title defense against Scott Jorgensen at WEC 53 was going to double as a UFC title match, with the winner becoming the first UFC bantamweight champion. Cruz won, picking up a second belt. Also moving over with a new championship belt was Brazil's Jose Aldo, who became the UFC featherweight champion.

Anthony Pettis

At WEC 53, Dominick Cruz battles Scott Jorgensen for the WEC bantamweight title.

Ben Henderson

IURI ALCANTARA
MARAJÓ, MANAUS, BRAZIL

DEBUT: UFC 134, AUGUST 27, 2011

Calling it the "realization of a dream," Iuri "Marajo" Alcantara made his long-awaited United States debut in December 2010 against Ricardo Lamas. He amazed fans at the final WEC event in Arizona by knocking out his highly regarded foe in the first round.

That type of result has been par for the course for Alcantara, who made a move to the bantamweight division in UFC in 2013, defeating Iliarde Santos, Wilson Reis, Vaughan Lee and Russell Doane.

RAPHAEL ASSUNCÃO
RECIFE, PERNAMBUCO, BRAZIL

DEBUT: UFC 128, MARCH 19, 2011

One of the most respected featherweight fighters in the world, Raphael Assuncão has won 23 of 27 pro bouts heading into 2015, with the only losses coming against Jeff Curran, Urijah Faber, Erik Koch and Diego Nunes. A Brazilian jiu-jitsu black belt from Recife, Brazil, Assuncão has been dazzling fight fans since his debut in 2004, defeating the likes of Joe Lauzon and Jorge Masvidal along the way.

In the WEC, Assuncão, the brother of UFC vet Junior Assuncão, made his presence known by defeating Jameel Massouh, Yves Jabouin and LC Davis. While he lost his UFC debut via knockout against Erik Koch at UFC 128, he used the setback as fuel, winning his next seven bouts.

DENNIS BERMUDEZ
SAUGERTIES, NY

DEBUT: THE ULTIMATE FIGHTER: TEAM BISPING VS TEAM MILLER FINALE, DECEMBER 3, 2011

Dennis "The Menace" Bermudez' road to the finale of *The Ultimate Fighter* season 14 against Diego Brandão began back in his wrestling days at Bloomsburg University, where he built up the mental toughness that has become his trademark. Although Dennis "The Menace" lost a thrilling battle to Brandão that night in 2011, he won his next seven bouts against Pablo Garza, Tommy Hayden, Matt Grice, Max Holloway, Steven Siler, Jimy Hettes and Clay Guida, making him one of the featherweight division's leading contenders.

DOMINICK CRUZ

DEBUT: UFC 132, JULY 2, 2011
UFC AND WEC BANTAMWEIGHT CHAMPION

TUCSON, AZ

A high school wrestling standout, San Diego's Dominick "The Dominator" Cruz wanted to keep competing after graduation, so he smoothly transitioned to mixed martial arts in 2005. He won his first nine professional fights, instantly stamping him as a fighter to watch as he showed a mix of ground-fighting ability, aggressiveness, power and heart.

In his tenth fight, though, Cruz hit a wall when he lost his WEC debut in 2007 via submission to featherweight champion Urijah Faber.

Undeterred, Cruz went right back to the gym. With a new attitude and a new weight class, bantamweight, he returned to the WEC and scored back-to-back wins over Charlie Valencia and Ian McCall. He had found his place.

"Once I got here, I knew this is where I should have been," said Cruz of fighting at 135 pounds. "Everything fit just right for me at 135."

After the McCall fight, Cruz continued to impress fight fans and baffle opponents defeating Ivan Lopez and previously unbeaten Joseph Benavidez via decision in back-to-back bouts. It was clear that he was on his way to the title.

He got his shot in March 2010 and made the most of it, stopping Brian Bowles in two rounds. A title defense victory over Benavidez followed five months later. On December 16, 2010, he closed out the year in the last WEC event ever, shutting out tough Scott Jorgensen over five rounds to retain his WEC belt and add a new one to his trophy case as the first-ever UFC bantamweight champion.

It should have been the start of something big for Cruz, and it was at first, as he successfully defended his title against Demetrious Johnson and Urijah Faber. But before his rubber match with Faber, whom he coached against on *The Ultimate Fighter: Live*, he suffered the first of two knee injuries that kept him sidelined for more than two years. A subsequent groin injury kept him out even longer.

When Cruz returned without the belt in September 2014, he was in championship form as he knocked out Takeya Mizugaki in 61 seconds, but another knee injury put him on the shelf again. Nevertheless, Cruz remains positive as he awaits his next move.

"This path has been chosen for me," he said. "Realistically, the way I get through this is I think about the people out there who have real problems. I still have a job, I'm still promoted by the UFC, I still have a job with FOX, and I still can be in the gym and help these guys get better. I can still elevate the sport of mixed martial arts, which is my passion, I can still come back and fight and win. There are people out there that are waking up, God bless them, and they have cancer, and they didn't expect it. There are people going through so much worse, and they need support and they need help. I've got an ACL problem, it's another mountain to climb, and I'm fully capable of handling this mountain."

JOSE ALDO

DEBUT: UFC 129, APRIL 30, 2011
UFC AND WEC FEATHERWEIGHT CHAMPION

MANAUS, AMAZONAS,
BRAZIL

A dynamic fighter with myriad weapons to put opponents away, Jose Aldo had a rapid rise up the mixed martial arts ranks. After winning 10 of his first 11 pro bouts on the local circuit (with his only loss coming via submission to Luciano Azevedo in 2005), he established himself as one of the sport's best, pound-for-pound. He arrived in the United States and took the WEC featherweight title from Mike Brown in November 2009, and he was named the first 145-pound champion in UFC history a year later.

What may have been more impressive, however, is that despite holding a black belt in Brazilian jiu-jitsu, winning numerous grappling titles and learning his craft under world-renowned ground fighter André Pederneiras, Aldo did not make his name with armbars or chokes. Instead, it was his striking ability that led him to seven KO victories in eight WEC bouts, three of which won Knockout of the Night honors.

"The thrill of knocking out an opponent is one of the best things in the world; your work is done," said the Manaus, Brazil, native, who followed up his WEC debut win over Alexandre Nogueira with knockouts of Jonathan Brookins, Rolando Perez, Chris Mickle, Cub Swanson and Mike Brown.

Aldo did not rest on his laurels. After scoring a lopsided five-round win over WEC superstar Urijah Faber—one dominated by Aldo's ferocious leg kicks—and knocking out durable contender Manny Gamburyan in his final two WEC bouts, he made his transition to UFC. He continued his reign of excellence at UFC 129 in April 2011 by winning an exciting five-round battle over Canada's Mark Hominick that earned the two 145-pound warriors Fight of the Night honors.

Next, he went on to face the rest of the featherweight division and has cleaned house, defeating Kenny Florian, Chad Mendes (twice), Frankie Edgar, Chan Sung Jung and Ricardo Lamas. But he's not through yet.

"I'm an employee, and whoever the boss wants me to fight, that's who I've got to fight and take out," said Aldo. "I'm prepared to fight whoever they put in front of me anytime."

DIEGO BRANDÃO
FORTALEZA, CEARÁ, BRAZIL

DEBUT: THE ULTIMATE FIGHTER:
TEAM BISPING VS TEAM MILLER FINALE, DECEMBER 3, 2011
THE ULTIMATE FIGHTER 14 WINNER

Diego "DB" Brandão was going down the wrong path in life as a teenager after his father's death, but eventually, a friend showed him the error of his ways, and he found a positive outlet in the sport of MMA.

Turning pro in 2005, Brandão built his reputation the hard way, eventually submitting Dennis Bermudez to win *The Ultimate Fighter* season fourteen title. Three post-*The Ultimate Fighter* wins followed for "DB," over Joey Gambino, Pablo Garza, and Daniel Pineda, before he experienced back-to-back losses to Dustin Poirier and Conor McGregor.

ALEX CACERES
MIAMI, FL

DEBUT: UFC FIGHT NIGHT: NOGUEIRA VS DAVIS,
MARCH 26, 2011

Best remembered for his entertaining stint on *The Ultimate Fighter* season twelve, Alex "Bruce Leeroy" Caceres submitted Paul Barrow and Jeff Lentz on the show before losing in the quarterfinals to Michael Johnson.

After a rough UFC start, he rebounded with wins over Cole Escovedo, Damacio Page, Motonobu Tezuka, Roland Delorme, and Sergio Pettis. You can bet that every time "Bruce Leeroy" enters the Octagon, he'll pull out all the stops in search of another victory.

BRYAN CARAWAY
YAKIMA, WA

DEBUT: THE ULTIMATE FIGHTER:
TEAM BISPING VS TEAM MILLER FINALE, DECEMBER 3, 2011

A talented collegiate wrestler, Bryan "Kid Lightning" Caraway saw his athletic outlet shut off when his school discontinued its wrestling program in 2004. Caraway soon discovered the world of MMA, though, and he smoothly made the transition to his new sport.

In 2011, he earned a spot on *The Ultimate Fighter* season fourteen. While he lost in the semifinals, UFC wins over Dustin Neace, Mitch Gagnon, Erik Perez and Johnny Bedford forecast a bright future for him.

With two new divisions and more events than ever, cards were filling up quickly. Aldo was slated to defend his new belt against Josh Grispi in the first event 2011 in Las Vegas on January 1. Unfortunately, an injury scrapped Aldo from the bout, and upstart newcomer Dustin Poirier removed Grispi from the number-one contender's slot at UFC 125 with a shutout decision win.

Even with all these changes, the epic lightweight title fight that headlined the card more than made up for everything. By all rights, Frankie Edgar never should have made it out of the first round of that title defense against Gray Maynard. After surviving multiple knockdowns in the opening frame, however, Edgar roared back to retain his belt with a five-round draw, in an exciting bout that kicked off the 2011 fight year in style.

A month later, it was Anderson Silva's time to shine. After a tumultuous 2010 campaign in which he drew UFC president Dana White's wrath for a lackluster effort against Demian Maia and then nearly lost his middleweight title to Chael Sonnen before roaring back to win in the fifth round, Silva was back in top-notch "Spider" form. Silva knocked out his heated rival Vitor Belfort with a first-round front kick that stands immortalized in UFC lore forever.

On that card, rising star Jon Jones defeated fellow up-and-comer Ryan Bader and was then presented with an interesting proposition following the bout. Jones was told that his teammate Rashad Evans was injured and unable to fight light heavyweight champion Shogun Rua on March 19 in Newark, New Jersey, and was then offered the bout on short notice. "Bones" accepted, and six weeks later, the New Yorker was ready for the biggest fight of his career.

There was just one hitch, an attempted robbery in a Paterson, New Jersey, park that Jones and his coaches, Greg Jackson and Mike Winklejohn, helped foil. After that incident, it was remarkable that the challenger was able to keep his focus, but he did. Jones stopped Shogun in the third round to become the youngest champion in UFC history at age 23.

While Jones etched his name in the record books for the first, but not the last, time, one of UFC's longest-reigning titleholders, welterweight champion Georges St-Pierre, made history of a different sort at UFC 129 on April 30. He helped bring in more than 55,000 fans, a UFC record, to Rogers Centre in Toronto to watch him retain his title for the sixth time. Also in action that night was Jose Aldo, who defended his UFC title for the first time by defeating Mark Hominick, and Lyoto Machida, who sent Randy Couture into retirement with a highlight-reel head kick.

Silva and Belfort face off before their bout for the middleweight championship at UFC 126.

UFC 129 at the Rogers Center in Toronto, Ontario.

URIJAH FABER

DEBUT: UFC 128, MARCH 19, 2011
WEC FEATHERWEIGHT CHAMPION

ISLA VISTA, CA

One of the most amazing aspects of mixed martial arts is that no one is invincible. Somewhere, at some time, everyone's number eventually comes up. For a while, though, it looked like no one was going to get close to former WEC featherweight champion "The California Kid" Urijah Faber.

Just look at the facts: 13 straight wins, six in the WEC, with 12 of those wins not making it to the final horn. Faber also had victories over Jens Pulver, Jeff Curran, Dominick Cruz and Charlie Valencia, among others.

However, on November 5, 2008, Mike Brown caught lightning in a bottle and upset Faber via a first-round TKO that earned him the 145-pound title and made "The California Kid" just a challenger again. What was most striking after the defeat, however, was not only Faber's class, but his determination to get the belt back.

"It's one mistake, and he capitalized on it," said Faber, who suffered the second loss of his pro career that night. "Congratulations to Mike Brown. I love life and I'm a happy person, and I'll be back to get that belt."

Two months later, Faber was back in action, and he needed just 94 seconds to submit Pulver with a guillotine choke in their rematch. The stage was set for 2009's Brown vs Faber II, and though he came up short a second time against the veteran champion, his gritty effort in going five rounds with a broken hand and a dislocated thumb earned him even more fans.

Following a comeback win over Raphael Assuncão in January 2010, a second attempt at regaining the 145-pound belt was foiled by new champion Jose Aldo in a five-round decision in the biggest WEC fight of all time on April 24, 2010. Faber was at a crossroads in his career, so he decided to drop 10 pounds to chase after the world title in the bantamweight division.

That decision has been a wise one, with nine victories thus far over a host of top contenders. Faber has fallen short of championship gold against Dominick Cruz and Renan Barão (twice), but he is not finished chasing that goal.

"You've got to ask champions how many times things haven't gone their way and how many times they've got back up, dusted themselves off and kept going on the straight and narrow," he said. "That's what a champion does, and that's what life's about. What are you going to do: sit around and feel sorry for yourself all day, or cut off your nose to spite your face and stop working hard because it didn't work out? I just don't have that in me, and I learned that from my parents, who learned it from their parents, and the people I've been surrounded by. I don't ever want to be a victim. That's the worst thing: people feeling sorry for you. I'm not a victim. I'm a guy that creates my own destiny in this world. It didn't go my way, there's always a second chance. Until I'm off the planet, there's a second chance."

During their light heavyweight bout at UFC 133, Rashad Evans punches Tito Ortiz.

Rashad Evans and Tito Ortiz after their light heavyweight bout at UFC 133.

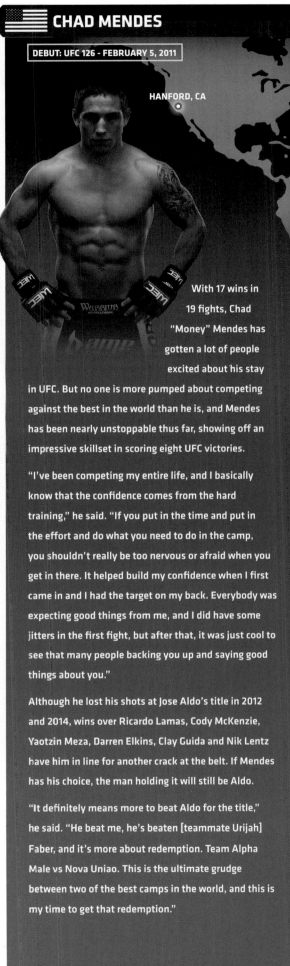

CHAD MENDES

DEBUT: UFC 126 - FEBRUARY 5, 2011

HANFORD, CA

With 17 wins in 19 fights, Chad "Money" Mendes has gotten a lot of people excited about his stay in UFC. But no one is more pumped about competing against the best in the world than he is, and Mendes has been nearly unstoppable thus far, showing off an impressive skillset in scoring eight UFC victories.

"I've been competing my entire life, and I basically know that the confidence comes from the hard training," he said. "If you put in the time and put in the effort and do what you need to do in the camp, you shouldn't really be too nervous or afraid when you get in there. It helped build my confidence when I first came in and I had the target on my back. Everybody was expecting good things from me, and I did have some jitters in the first fight, but after that, it was just cool to see that many people backing you up and saying good things about you."

Although he lost his shots at Jose Aldo's title in 2012 and 2014, wins over Ricardo Lamas, Cody McKenzie, Yaotzin Meza, Darren Elkins, Clay Guida and Nik Lentz have him in line for another crack at the belt. If Mendes has his choice, the man holding it will still be Aldo.

"It definitely means more to beat Aldo for the title," he said. "He beat me, he's beaten [teammate Urijah] Faber, and it's more about redemption. Team Alpha Male vs Nova Uniao. This is the ultimate grudge between two of the best camps in the world, and this is my time to get that redemption."

In June, the finale card of *The Ultimate Fighter* season thirteen saw Tony Ferguson pick up a UFC contract, while veteran Clay Guida spoiled Anthony Pettis' UFC debut in the main event. Later that month, top heavyweight contender Junior Dos Santos stamped his ticket for a shot at champion Cain Velasquez with a punishing three-round win over a returning Shane Carwin at UFC 131 in Vancouver, British Columbia.

Several intriguing storylines were flowing around the promotion's traditional Independence Day weekend event in Las Vegas on July 2, and each one delivered. In the main event, Dominick Cruz's first UFC appearance was a successful one, as he defeated Urijah Faber in their long-awaited bantamweight rematch. Chris Leben scored the biggest win of his career, knocking out Wanderlei Silva in 27 seconds. Finally, former light heavyweight champion Tito Ortiz turned back the clock for one emotional night, as he upset Ryan Bader by submitting him in less than two minutes.

Looking to keep the momentum going from that stirring victory, Ortiz stepped up on short notice to face Rashad Evans in a rematch of their UFC 73 contest. This time, there was no emotional win for Ortiz. "Suga" stopped him in the second round of their UFC 133 main event in Philadelphia on August 6.

CHRIS WEIDMAN

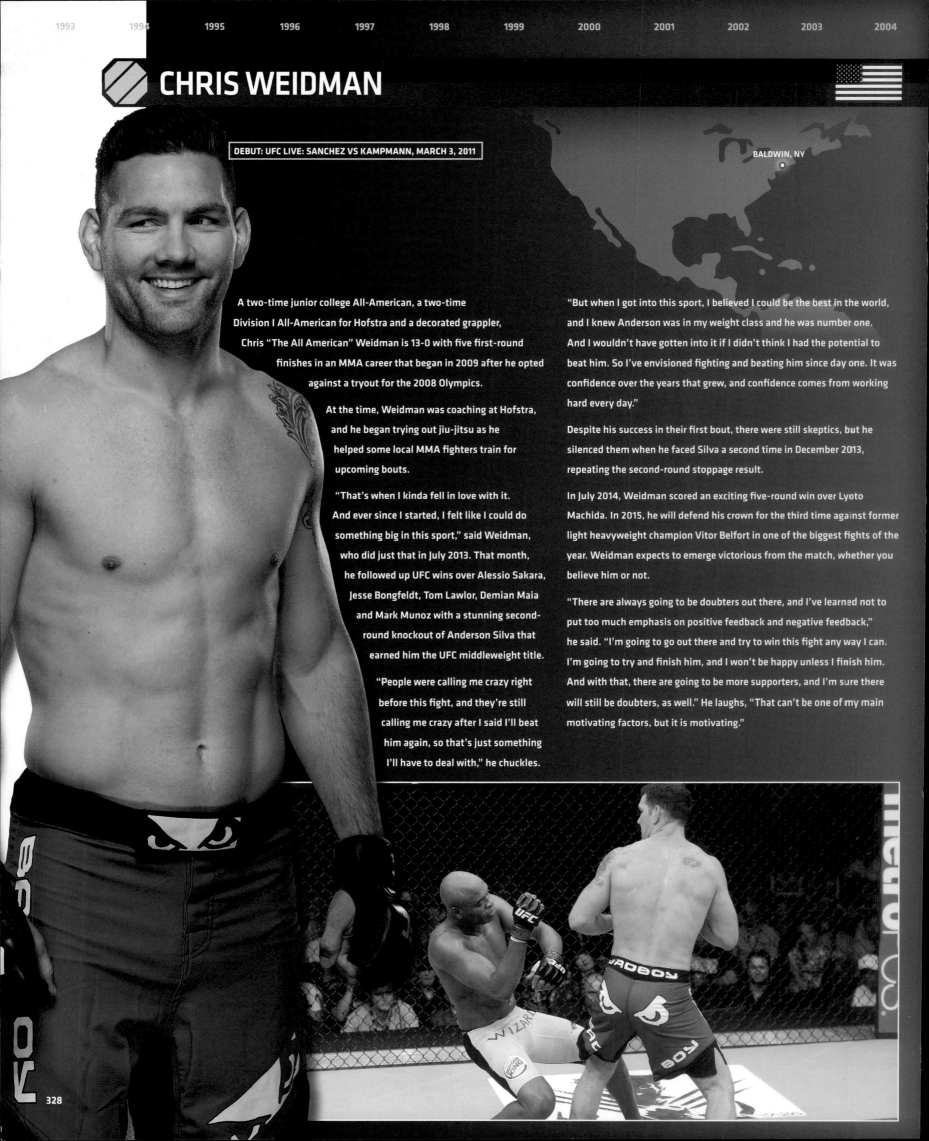

DEBUT: UFC LIVE: SANCHEZ VS KAMPMANN, MARCH 3, 2011

BALDWIN, NY

A two-time junior college All-American, a two-time Division I All-American for Hofstra and a decorated grappler, Chris "The All American" Weidman is 13-0 with five first-round finishes in an MMA career that began in 2009 after he opted against a tryout for the 2008 Olympics.

At the time, Weidman was coaching at Hofstra, and he began trying out jiu-jitsu as he helped some local MMA fighters train for upcoming bouts.

"That's when I kinda fell in love with it. And ever since I started, I felt like I could do something big in this sport," said Weidman, who did just that in July 2013. That month, he followed up UFC wins over Alessio Sakara, Jesse Bongfeldt, Tom Lawlor, Demian Maia and Mark Munoz with a stunning second-round knockout of Anderson Silva that earned him the UFC middleweight title.

"People were calling me crazy right before this fight, and they're still calling me crazy after I said I'll beat him again, so that's just something I'll have to deal with," he chuckles.

"But when I got into this sport, I believed I could be the best in the world, and I knew Anderson was in my weight class and he was number one. And I wouldn't have gotten into it if I didn't think I had the potential to beat him. So I've envisioned fighting and beating him since day one. It was confidence over the years that grew, and confidence comes from working hard every day."

Despite his success in their first bout, there were still skeptics, but he silenced them when he faced Silva a second time in December 2013, repeating the second-round stoppage result.

In July 2014, Weidman scored an exciting five-round win over Lyoto Machida. In 2015, he will defend his crown for the third time against former light heavyweight champion Vitor Belfort in one of the biggest fights of the year. Weidman expects to emerge victorious from the match, whether you believe him or not.

"There are always going to be doubters out there, and I've learned not to put too much emphasis on positive feedback and negative feedback," he said. "I'm going to go out there and try to win this fight any way I can. I'm going to try and finish him, and I won't be happy unless I finish him. And with that, there are going to be more supporters, and I'm sure there will still be doubters, as well." He laughs, "That can't be one of my main motivating factors, but it is motivating."

RENAN BARÃO

DEBUT: UFC 130, MAY 28, 2011
UFC BANTAMWEIGHT CHAMPION

NATAL, RIO GRANDE DO
NORTE, BRAZIL

A training partner of UFC featherweight champion Jose Aldo, Renan "The Baron" Barão joined his teammate at the top of the championship ranks in 2012 when he defeated Urijah Faber for the interim UFC 135-pound title.

The owner of a 35-2 (1 NC) record entering 2015, Barão lost his first pro bout in 2005, and he has only lost once since. He has submitted 15 opponents and knocked out eight of his foes, garnering rave reviews and being marked as a star in the bantamweight division.

In 2009, Barão won five times, and he kicked off 2010 with another victory. But it was his wins in his first two WEC bouts and his UFC victories over Cole Escovedo, Brad Pickett and Scott Jorgensen that really turned heads.

When Dominick Cruz was forced to withdraw from a rubber match against Faber due to a knee injury, the only logical choice to replace him in an interim title fight was Barão, who made the most of his opportunity with a decision win.

Following three successful title defenses and an elevation to undisputed champion, Barão was upset by TJ Dillashaw in 2014, but now, all he wants is a chance to regain his crown.

"There are mixed feelings for me," Barão said. "The first time, I was happy, and I got what I had always dreamed about. When I was champion, I was happy, but now I lost my belt, and every day, I'm thinking about getting this belt back. If I get it back, I'll be really, really happy. But it's complicated."

Jon Jones kicks Rampage Jackson at UFC 135.

Later that month, UFC's international assault brought the Octagon to Brazil for the first time since 1998, and UFC 134 in Rio de Janeiro on August 27 was a good one for the home team. Anderson Silva (over Yushin Okami), Shogun Rua (over Forrest Griffin) and Minotauro Nogueira (over Brendan Schaub) all emerged victorious in emphatic fashion, thrilling the Brazilian fans that packed HSBC Arena.

Jones celebrates his victory over Rampage.

At UFC 135 on September 24, the newly crowned Jones successfully defended his 205-pound title for the first time, submitting Rampage Jackson. That night also saw UFC Hall of Famer Matt Hughes compete in the Octagon for the last time, falling in the first round to Josh Koscheck.

October saw Dominick Cruz defeat Demetrious Johnson to retain his bantamweight title. Additionally, Frankie Edgar and Gray Maynard engaged in another classic before Edgar knocked out "The Bully" to end their trilogy. Jose Aldo turned back Kenny Florian in a featherweight title fight and Nick Diaz pounded out a win over BJ Penn. It was all compelling stuff, seemingly a prelude to a huge November 12 event in Anaheim, California, that changed the landscape of the sport forever.

Earlier in 2011, on August 18, UFC had announced a landmark deal with FOX that would put the promotion on network television, as well as on other FOX channels. This is what you would call a game changer.

"We're excited to be part of the FOX family," said UFC president Dana White. "UFC is finally where it belongs on the number-one network in the country and aligned with the most prestigious sports properties in the world. I've always said that the UFC will be the biggest sport in the world, and with this relationship, it will become a reality."

"My brother Frank, Dana and I always believed that our passion for the sport of mixed martial arts would help us to build the UFC into a successful global brand and ultimately make it one of the premier sports properties in the world," added UFC Chairman and CEO Lorenzo Fertitta. "The partnership with FOX is a major step in making this a reality and also builds on the great relationship that we already have established with FOX in Latin America, Australia and Europe."

The first FOX event was not even scheduled to be part of the deal, but the network brass was eager to introduce UFC to its audience, so Cain Velasquez's title defense against Junior Dos Santos was aired live on network television— the first time that had happened in UFC history. That was great news for the sport and for Junior Dos Santos, who stopped Velasquez in just 64 seconds to become the UFC world heavyweight champion.

With momentum at an all-time high, it was fitting that the promotion's next Pay-Per-View event, UFC 139 in San Jose, California, on November 19, produced perhaps the greatest fight of all time. Former PRIDE legends Shogun Rua and Dan Henderson engaged in a five-round back-and-forth classic that had more twists and turns than a Hollywood thriller. "Hendo" emerged as the winner after 25 minutes of battle, but Shogun was still able to hold his head up high.

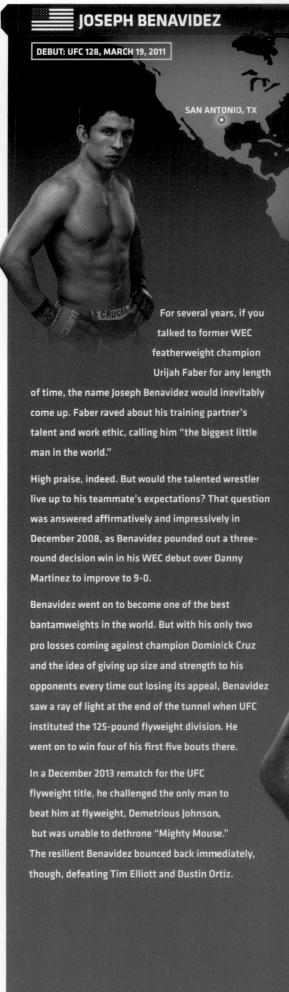

JOSEPH BENAVIDEZ

DEBUT: UFC 128, MARCH 19, 2011

SAN ANTONIO, TX

For several years, if you talked to former WEC featherweight champion Urijah Faber for any length of time, the name Joseph Benavidez would inevitably come up. Faber raved about his training partner's talent and work ethic, calling him "the biggest little man in the world."

High praise, indeed. But would the talented wrestler live up to his teammate's expectations? That question was answered affirmatively and impressively in December 2008, as Benavidez pounded out a three-round decision win in his WEC debut over Danny Martinez to improve to 9-0.

Benavidez went on to become one of the best bantamweights in the world. But with his only two pro losses coming against champion Dominick Cruz and the idea of giving up size and strength to his opponents every time out losing its appeal, Benavidez saw a ray of light at the end of the tunnel when UFC instituted the 125-pound flyweight division. He went on to win four of his first five bouts there.

In a December 2013 rematch for the UFC flyweight title, he challenged the only man to beat him at flyweight, Demetrious Johnson, but was unable to dethrone "Mighty Mouse." The resilient Benavidez bounced back immediately, though, defeating Tim Elliott and Dustin Ortiz.

MIGUEL ANGEL TORRES
EAST CHICAGO, IN

DEBUT: UFC 126, FEBRUARY 5, 2011
WEC BANTAMWEIGHT CHAMPION

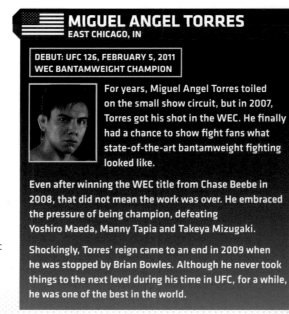

For years, Miguel Angel Torres toiled on the small show circuit, but in 2007, Torres got his shot in the WEC. He finally had a chance to show fight fans what state-of-the-art bantamweight fighting looked like.

Even after winning the WEC title from Chase Beebe in 2008, that did not mean the work was over. He embraced the pressure of being champion, defeating Yoshiro Maeda, Manny Tapia and Takeya Mizugaki.

Shockingly, Torres' reign came to an end in 2009 when he was stopped by Brian Bowles. Although he never took things to the next level during his time in UFC, for a while, he was one of the best in the world.

BENSON HENDERSON

DEBUT: UFC 129, APRIL 30, 2011
UFC AND WEC LIGHTWEIGHT CHAMPION

COLORADO SPRINGS, CO

Two-time NAIA Collegiate All-American wrestler, black belt in taekwondo, brown belt in Brazilian jiu-jitsu, the accolades are impressive and show how well rounded a fighter former WEC and UFC lightweight champion "Smooth" Benson Henderson is. But it is in competition that fans have really seen what "Smooth" can do, as he defeated Anthony Njokuani, Shane Roller, and Donald Cerrone in a spectacular 2009 campaign.

"The mindset of a wrestler is to go out there and attack, attack, attack, and beat your opponent and break his will," he said. "Even in practice, I want to break my opponent. I want my teammates who I love, my brothers who help make me better, I want to break them during practice. Those hard, brutal, tough practices develop and sharpen your killer instinct and that desire to wrestle the best and to beat the best."

Henderson was just getting started. He delivered in his first two fights of 2010, as he unified the 155-pound belt with a win over Jamie Varner and submitted "Cowboy" Cerrone in their rematch.

Although he lost his WEC crown via decision to Anthony Pettis, he kicked off the next chapter of his career in 2011 with a defeat of Mark Bocek in his UFC debut and victories over Jim Miller and Clay Guida. Those wins earned him a shot at Frankie Edgar's UFC lightweight title in February 2012, and he made the most of it. Henderson won the belt in a thrilling five-round battle and subsequently compiled three successful title defenses before losing it to Pettis in their 2013 rematch.

Undeterred, Henderson went on to win three of his next five bouts, including a short-notice win at welterweight against Brandon Thatch. Always ready to fight, Henderson's greatest asset just may be that when the odds are against him, he usually finds a way to win.

"The difference in skill level, especially at 155, between myself and the number 10 guy isn't that big," he said. "Every fight's going to be a tough, hard fight, and if I have a bad night and he has a really good night, guess what, he might win. That's the difference at 155, and to be able to come out on top and get your hand raised every time, I'll do whatever it takes. If I have to run on a treadmill, set the speed at 11, and see who gets off first; if it's holding burning embers in your hand and seeing who can hold on to them the longest; whatever it is to be able to just win, that's something that's hard to categorize or measure. There is no statistic for it: it's just that will, that desire to dig down deep."

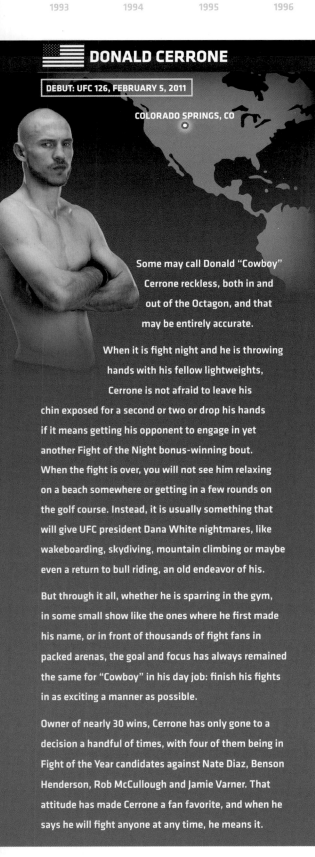

DONALD CERRONE

DEBUT: UFC 126, FEBRUARY 5, 2011

COLORADO SPRINGS, CO

Some may call Donald "Cowboy" Cerrone reckless, both in and out of the Octagon, and that may be entirely accurate.

When it is fight night and he is throwing hands with his fellow lightweights, Cerrone is not afraid to leave his chin exposed for a second or two or drop his hands if it means getting his opponent to engage in yet another Fight of the Night bonus-winning bout. When the fight is over, you will not see him relaxing on a beach somewhere or getting in a few rounds on the golf course. Instead, it is usually something that will give UFC president Dana White nightmares, like wakeboarding, skydiving, mountain climbing or maybe even a return to bull riding, an old endeavor of his.

But through it all, whether he is sparring in the gym, in some small show like the ones where he first made his name, or in front of thousands of fight fans in packed arenas, the goal and focus has always remained the same for "Cowboy" in his day job: finish his fights in as exciting a manner as possible.

Owner of nearly 30 wins, Cerrone has only gone to a decision a handful of times, with four of them being in Fight of the Year candidates against Nate Diaz, Benson Henderson, Rob McCullough and Jamie Varner. That attitude has made Cerrone a fan favorite, and when he says he will fight anyone at any time, he means it.

COSTAS PHILIPPOU
LIMASSOL, CYPRUS

DEBUT: UFC 128, MARCH 19, 2011

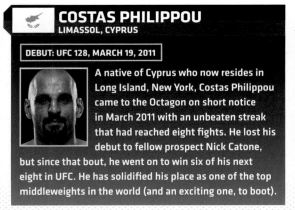

A native of Cyprus who now resides in Long Island, New York, Costas Philippou came to the Octagon on short notice in March 2011 with an unbeaten streak that had reached eight fights. He lost his debut to fellow prospect Nick Catone, but since that bout, he went on to win six of his next eight in UFC. He has solidified his place as one of the top middleweights in the world (and an exciting one, to boot).

The week before Jon Jones made another successful defense of his title against Lyoto Machida at UFC 140 on December 10, John Dodson and Diego Brandão became the next *The Ultimate Fighter* winners after winning their final season fourteen bouts in Las Vegas. Little did anyone know that one of the fighters who lost in the finals, TJ Dillashaw, would go on to become a world champion less than three years later.

Also making the news in 2011 was UFC's purchase of the STRIKEFORCE organization in March. While the San Jose-based promotion continued to run its own shows, one of its top stars, heavyweight Alistair Overeem, made his way to the Octagon to close out the year in a UFC 141 main event against the returning Brock Lesnar. It was a debut to remember for "The Reem," as he knocked Lesnar out in less than three minutes on December 30, capping off another historic year for UFC.

Alistair Overeem during the UFC 141 Open Workouts.

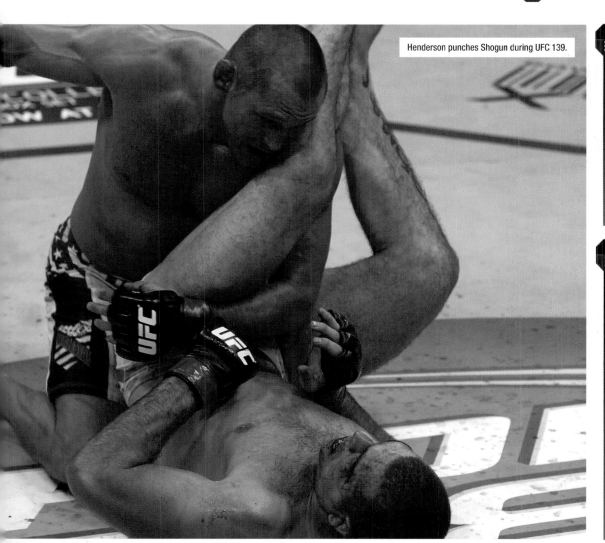

Henderson punches Shogun during UFC 139.

 ### RICARDO LAMAS
CHICAGO, IL

DEBUT: UFC LIVE: KONGO VS BARRY, JUNE 26, 2011

 A Division III All-American wrestler for Elmhurst College, Chicago native Ricardo "The Bully" Lamas never lost that competitive drive after graduation in 2005, so his next step was a career in mixed martial arts. He went on to make an impact in the WEC and UFC, eventually earning a world title shot against Jose Aldo after winning four consecutive bouts in the Octagon from 2011 to 2013.

STIPE MIOCIC
EUCLID, OH

DEBUT: UFC 136, OCTOBER 8, 2011

 When you think of great athletes who made their mark in Cleveland, the names of Jim Brown, Bob Feller, Otto Graham and Tris Speaker immediately come to mind. Well, if things keep progressing the way they are for Stipe Miocic, you may one day add his name to that list.

A standout baseball player and wrestler for Cleveland State University, as well as a Golden Gloves boxing champ, Miocic eventually found mixed martial arts, turning pro in 2010.

A little over a year later, Miocic was in UFC. He has become an elite heavyweight in the Octagon, winning six of eight bouts, including three straight over Roy Nelson, Gabriel Gonzaga and Fabio Maldonado.

 ## TJ DILLASHAW

DEBUT: THE ULTIMATE FIGHTER: TEAM BISPING VS TEAM MILLER FINALE, DECEMBER 3, 2011
UFC BANTAMWEIGHT CHAMPION

SONORA, CA

As a member of the renowned Team Alpha Male fight squad, UFC bantamweight champion TJ Dillashaw is no stranger to the spotlight or to high-level competition.

A three-time Division I national wrestling qualifier for Cal State Fullerton, Dillashaw's post-college association with Urijah Faber and Team Alpha Male immediately put expectations on his shoulders and a target on his back when it came to MMA. So far, the 29-year-old has handled everything well, from his 4-0 run in local shows to his stint on *The Ultimate Fighter* season fourteen, where he earned a spot in the finals with wins over Matt Jaggers, Roland Delorme, and Dustin Pague.

Dillashaw lost in the *The Ultimate Fighter* season fourteen bantamweight final against John Dodson in 2011. But he got back in the win column with victories against Walel Watson, Vaughan Lee, Issei Tamura, Hugo Viana, and Mike Easton. Then, he shocked the world in May 2014 by knocking out Renan Barão for the undisputed UFC bantamweight title.

"Obviously, in my own mind, I knew that I could win," he said. "I had the recipe to do it and [knew] that I was good enough to do it. Otherwise, there's no point in even stepping into that Octagon. I can definitely see why I was an underdog, but anybody who's trained with me or knows who I am knew that I had a shot and that everyone was underestimating me. Those are the people who matter anyways, and I was glad to prove everyone wrong."

It was a stirring victory, to say the least. After defending his belt successfully against Joe Soto at UFC 177 in August 2014, he now awaits the opportunity to attempt to repeat his win over Barão in one of the most eagerly anticipated rematches in bantamweight history.

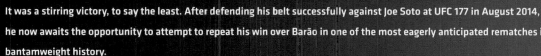

333

DEMETRIOUS JOHNSON

DEBUT: UFC 126, FEBRUARY 5, 2011
UFC FLYWEIGHT CHAMPION

MADISONVILLE, KY

Inspired by the first season of *The Ultimate Fighter*, Demetrious "Mighty Mouse" Johnson took his talents and work ethic to MMA in 2005, and he has not looked back yet. Entering the WEC in 2010, Johnson defeated Nick Pace and Damacio Page and earned an invitation to UFC, where he has taken his game to the next level.

"My coaches are always pushing me to keep on evolving. They say, 'Don't let the sport pass you up; you've got to keep on evolving and getting better.'"

In 2011, Johnson scored a debut win over "Kid" Yamamoto, and three months later, he defeated Miguel Angel Torres. Though he lost a tough five-rounder against Dominick Cruz in an October 2011 title fight, the flyweight division allowed "Mighty Mouse" to compete on a level playing field, and he was excited to help introduce the weight class to the masses.

In March 2012, Johnson and Ian McCall, his opponent in the semifinals of the UFC flyweight tournament, delivered all that and more en route to a three-round draw. Johnson eliminated McCall in their June rematch, though, setting up a UFC 152 showdown with Joseph Benavidez in which "Mighty Mouse" became UFC's first-ever flyweight champion.

"I'm not satisfied," Johnson said. "I always want to be better and improve. We made history on September 22, 2012, and that one's in the books. Now it's time to build a legacy, keep hunting these guys down and keep putting on great performances against the top athletes in the world. And I might never be satisfied, but we'll find out."

Following his title-winning effort, Johnson put his belt on the line five times and won each time, defeating John Dodson, John Moraga, Chris Cariaso, Ali Bagautinov and Benavidez in their rematch. These wins earned him a spot on UFC's Pound-for-Pound list, and it does not look like "Mighty Mouse" will be surrendering anytime soon, even if he remains one of the sport's most humble champions.

"I don't look at myself as a dominant champion," he said. "I think [then light heavyweight champion] Jon Jones is in the lead with that. He's beaten the best of the best in his weight class. Granted, people can say I have too by beating Joseph twice and John Dodson, John Moraga and Ian McCall, so I guess you can put me in the same category as Jon Jones, but I think he's a little bit ahead of me for dismantling [Lyoto] Machida and all the guys he's beaten. But when it's time for me to fight, I just go out there and fight, and if it comes out to be a dominant performance, then that's fantastic. I did my job, and I did my homework in the gym."

ANTHONY PETTIS

MILWAUKEE, WI

With world-renowned kickboxer Duke Roufus in his corner, it goes without saying that Anthony "Showtime" Pettis has been taught the importance of being a well-rounded fighter.

"A big reason why I'm with Duke is because he allows me to be myself," said Pettis. "He doesn't want to make me a Muay Thai guy. He doesn't want to make me a wrestler or a basic jiu-jitsu guy. He allows me to create my own style and make my own Anthony Pettis. So he's supportive, but he's still smart about it. He's not like, 'OK, go out there and do a jump spin kick and see what happens.' Everything's set up, and he just helps me make it more effective."

Of course, when the horn sounds, it's up to the native of Milwaukee, Wisconsin, to perform. So far, he has lived up to his nickname of "Showtime" by winning the WEC and UFC lightweight titles.

"It's how I always was," he said. "Being a little kid on the playground jumping off the monkey bars, I always had to one-up somebody.

If somebody was jumping off the monkey bars, I'm jumping off the next higher monkey bar. I was that guy that always had to one-up everybody, and I think that plays into my fighting style. It's just me. I like to be different, and I'm not gonna change now. This is what I've been doing my whole life."

In December 2010, Pettis became a household name when he defeated Benson Henderson for the WEC lightweight title, aided by a kick off the cage that was heard around the world. The maneuver earned him a spot in MMA's eternal highlight-reel. Though he lost his UFC debut to Clay Guida in 2011, Pettis bounced back with a decision win over Jeremy Stephens and a head-kick knockout of Joe Lauzon that led him into a January 2013 bout with Donald Cerrone. In that fight, Pettis put on a striking clinic for the 2:35 the match lasted, and with yet another Knockout of the Night victory, "Showtime" earned a shot at the UFC lightweight title against WEC rival Henderson. He won that battle by first-round submission.

Pettis successfully defended his belt in December 2014 with a submission of Gilbert Melendez. Though he lost the title in a UFC 185 upset to Rafael dos Anjos, "Showtime" is ready to take the road back to the top. He has already achieved something no other MMA fighter ever has: in 2015 he won a fan-vote to become the first mixed martial artist to land on the coveted Wheaties Box.

Overeem punches Lesnar at the MGM Grand Garden.

🇯🇵 TAKEYA MIZUGAKI
MIURA, KANAGAWA PREFECTURE, JAPAN

DEBUT: UFC LIVE: SANCHEZ VS KAMPMANN, MARCH 3, 2011

 A terror on the Japanese fight scene, Takeya Mizugaki left the comforts of home in 2009 to tackle the best the United States had to offer. Mizugaki knew that he was going to be stepping into a shark tank from the start, but with bouts against Miguel Angel Torres, Urijah Faber, Jeff Curran, Erik Perez, Dominick Cruz and Scott Jorgensen, Mizugaki has certainly proven himself worthy of being called one of the best in the world.

🇬🇧 BRAD PICKETT
LONDON, ENGLAND

DEBUT: UFC 138, NOVEMBER 5, 2011

One of England's top fighters, Brad "One Punch" Pickett took his game to the United States and the WEC in 2009, debuting with a win over Kyle Dietz.

The victory upped his record to 19-4, and after a win over Demetrious Johnson, he earned victory number 21 against Ivan Menjivar in 2010. But then, it was time for him to make his mark in UFC. After five post-fight bonus-winning efforts, he's done just that.

🇺🇸 DUSTIN POIRIER
LAFAYETTE, LA

DEBUT: UFC 125, JANUARY 1, 2011

 A former lightweight standout, Dustin "The Diamond" Poirier was eager to enter the Octagon for his UFC debut at featherweight in 2011. Few expected the clinic Poirier put on during his match with Josh Grispi, en route to victory. Taking risks has never been an issue for "The Diamond." He raced out to a 17-4 record while earning what he calls "a doctorate from the school of hard knocks." In 2015, he returned to the 155-pound weight class with a win over Diego Ferreira.

NORIFUMI YAMAMOTO
KAWASAKI, KANAGAWA PREFECTURE, JAPAN

DEBUT: UFC 126, FEBRUARY 5, 2011

A Japanese superstar who has thrilled fight fans for nearly 15 years, Norifumi "Kid" Yamamoto is a charismatic fighter in and out of the Octagon, possessing world-class wrestling skills as well as knockout power. These traits make him one of the most exciting competitors in the bantamweight division.

After headline-making wins over Royler Gracie, Caol Uno and Genki Sudo, he was long rumored for superfights with Urijah Faber and Miguel Angel Torres before finally making his move stateside in 2011 to compete in UFC.

CUB SWANSON
PALM SPRINGS, CA

DEBUT: UFC ON FOX: VELASQUEZ VS DOS SANTOS, NOVEMBER 12, 2011

With his Brazilian jiu-jitsu black belt around his waist, Cub Swanson is ready to take on the world, one featherweight contender at a time, until he gets to put on a different belt, one representing a UFC championship.

Owner of a stellar record that includes UFC knockouts of Dennis Siver, George Roop, Ross Pearson and Charles Oliveira, Swanson knows that each passing victory sends a strong message to his 145-pound peers that he's ready for the next step in his career.

EDDIE WINELAND
HOUSTON, TX

DEBUT: UFC 128, MARCH 19, 2011
WEC BANTAMWEIGHT CHAMPION

Eddie Wineland earned his stripes in the WEC with a first-round knockout of Antonio Banuelos in May 2006 that garnered him the first-ever WEC bantamweight crown.

Though he lost that title to Chase Beebe, Wineland did not stop on his quest to get to the top. In 2012, Wineland's UFC wins over Scott Jorgensen and Brad Pickett earned him a shot at Renan Barão's interim UFC bantamweight title.

Alistair Overeem claims the victory over Brock Lesnar at UFC 141.

CHRIS CARIASO
SAN JOSE, CA

DEBUT: UFC FIGHT FOR THE TROOPS 2, JANUARY 22, 2011

A pro since 2006, Chris "Kamikaze" Cariaso has drawn rave reviews from fight insiders for his talent, determination and exciting style. In January 2011, Cariaso entered the UFC Octagon for the first time, notching an impressive win over Will Campuzano. By July 2012, Cariaso was competing in his optimum weight class at 125 pounds. Although he lost his first title fight against Demetrious Johnson in 2014, he has already started his march toward a second world title shot.

DANNY CASTILLO
SACRAMENTO, CA

DEBUT: UFC LIVE: SANCHEZ VS KAMPMANN, MARCH 3, 2011

Fight fans first got to know Danny "Last Call" Castillo back in the WEC, where he scored wins that showed off his wrestling ability, punching power and desire to win.

The victories earned him a call to UFC, and he seized the opportunity with both hands as he defeated Joe Stevenson via decision in 2011. He went on to deliver more impressive wins over Anthony Njokuani, John Cholish, Paul Sass, Tim Means and Charlie Brenneman, making "Last Call" one of the last people that lightweights want to see on fight night.

JOHN DODSON
ALBUQUERQUE, NM

DEBUT: THE ULTIMATE FIGHTER:
TEAM BISPING VS TEAM MILLER FINALE, DECEMBER 3, 2011
THE ULTIMATE FIGHTER 14 WINNER

After winning season fourteen of *The Ultimate Fighter*, John "The Magician" Dodson dropped to his original weight class of 125 pounds and began his trek to the top with exciting wins over Tim Elliott and Jussier Formiga. These wins kicked off his post-*The Ultimate Fighter* career and earned him a shot at Demetrious Johnson's championship. Dodson lost a close decision to "Mighty Mouse," but with his subsequent wins over Darrell Montague and John Moraga, he could be in line for a rematch.

BRIAN EBERSOLE
LA PORTE, IN

DEBUT: UFC 127, FEBRUARY 27, 2011

A free spirit who follows his heart to wherever it leads him, Brian "Bad Boy" Ebersole took on the nickname "Bad Boy" for some of his early antics growing up and fighting on the Midwest fight circuit. But these days, while the name remains, you will not find a more serious student of the game than Ebersole. He has won five of his first seven Octagon bouts, beating Chris Lytle, Dennis Hallman and John Howard.

ERIK KOCH
CEDAR RAPIDS, IA

DEBUT: UFC 128, MARCH 19, 2011

Winner of 14 out of 18 pro mixed martial arts contests as he heads into 2015, Erik "New Breed" Koch takes a no-nonsense approach to the sport, an attitude that has made him a popular young contender. Included on his slate is a submission win over Bendy Casimir and highlight-reel knockout victories over Francisco Rivera and Raphael Assuncão. With the help of his coach, Duke Roufus, and teammate Anthony Pettis, he's got his sights set ambitiously on the top of the lightweight division.

HATSU HIOKI
NAGOYA, AICHI PREFECTURE, JAPAN

DEBUT: UFC 137, OCTOBER 29, 2011

Former Shooto and Sengoku champion Hatsu Hioki dominated the Japanese scene in recent years, going 12-1-1 while establishing himself as one of the top featherweights in the sport. But after wins over Rumina Sato, Mark Hominick (twice), Jeff Curran and Marlon Sandro, he began his quest for a UFC title in 2011, with the stakes higher than they have ever been. He has since won three times in the Octagon, defeating George Roop, Bart Palaszewski and Ivan Menjivar.

TONY FERGUSON
OXNARD, CA

DEBUT: THE ULTIMATE FIGHTER:
TEAM LESNAR VS TEAM DOS SANTOS FINALE, JUNE 4, 2011
THE ULTIMATE FIGHTER 13 WINNER

A former national champion and two-time All-American wrestler for Grand Valley State University, Tony "El Cucuy" Ferguson was a natural fit in mixed martial arts. His performance on *The Ultimate Fighter* season thirteen did not disappoint anyone as he achieved the season title with a win over Ramsey Nijem. Victories against veterans Aaron Riley and Yves Edwards followed. After an injury-induced layoff, he went on to defeat Mike Rio, Katsunori Kikuno, Danny Castillo, Abel Trujillo and Gleison Tibau.

CHAN SUNG JUNG
POHANG, SOUTH KOREA

DEBUT: UFC FIGHT NIGHT:
NOGUEIRA VS DAVIS, MARCH 26, 2011

With a nickname like "The Korean Zombie," you just knew that Chan Sung Jung was going to be a hit with fight fans. Before the hard-hitting prospect from Po-Hang, South Korea, made his stateside debut, he promised that he would deliver when the bell rang. But no one expected the war he waged with Leonard Garcia in April 2010, a bout television commentator Joe Rogan dubbed "the fight of the decade." Although Jung lost by a close split decision, he became an instant fan favorite, going on to earn a UFC contract and a 2013 shot at Jose Aldo's featherweight title.

MICHAEL MCDONALD
MODESTO, CA

DEBUT: UFC FIGHT NIGHT:
NOGUEIRA VS DAVIS, MARCH 26, 2011

The youngest fighter in UFC at age 19 when he debuted in the Octagon, Michael "Mayday" McDonald amazed veteran observers in 2010 with three finishes of fellow bantamweight standouts Manny Tapia, Cole Escovedo and Clint Godfrey that made him a hardcore fan favorite. But it was in March 2011 that really got people talking, as he pounded out a three-round win over Edwin Figueroa that earned him Fight of the Night honors. Three more wins got him a world title shot against Renan Barão, but McDonald was submitted in the fourth round in their 2013 bout.

SCOTT JORGENSEN
PAYSON, UT

DEBUT: THE ULTIMATE FIGHTER:
TEAM LESNAR VS TEAM DOS SANTOS FINALE, JUNE 4, 2011

An aggressive battler whose greatest attribute may be his determination to always find a way to win in the cage, Scott "Young Guns" Jorgensen has generated some serious buzz in a career that began in 2006.

A former WEC standout, Jorgensen has continued his run in UFC, with a 2012 win over John Albert earning him both Submission and Fight of the Night honors. After a brief run at flyweight, Jorgensen returned to the bantamweight division where he made his name in 2015.

ALISTAIR OVEREEM
HOUNSLOW, LONDON, ENGLAND

DEBUT: UFC 141, DECEMBER 30, 2011

The former king of the STRIKEFORCE heavyweight division, Alistair "The Reem" Overeem has done what many thought was impossible in the rapidly changing world of MMA: he has established the aura of Mike Tyson, in his prime, as a fearsome force, and a knockout artist who can end anybody's night with a fist, foot or knee. A pro since 1999, Overeem arrived in UFC in 2011. He immediately proved himself with a first-round TKO of Brock Lesnar and followed up with victories against Frank Mir, Stefan Struve and Roy Nelson.

CUNG LE
HO CHI MINH CITY, VIETNAM

DEBUT: UFC 139, NOVEMBER 19, 2011
STRIKEFORCE MIDDLEWEIGHT CHAMPION

A renowned knockout artist, Sanshou master Cung Le always went toe-to-toe with anyone willing to test himself against one of combat sport's top strikers. A native of Saigon who now resides in San Jose, California, Le was unbeaten in kickboxing at 17-0. For years, fans speculated about how Le would fare in the world of mixed martial arts. He did just fine, winning the STRIKEFORCE middleweight title and then becoming a star in UFC, where he knocked out Rich Franklin in 2012. Le, who has starred in several action movies, retired in 2015.

FIGHTS OF THE YEAR

UFC139

HENDERSON	W5	RUA

UFC 125

EDGAR	DRAW 5	MAYNARD II

UFC ON FOX

HENDERSON	W3	GUIDA

UFC 132

CRUZ	W5	FABER II

UFC 136

EDGAR	KO4	MAYNARD III

KNOCKOUTS OF THE YEAR

UFC LIVE: KONGO VS BARRY

KONGO	KO1	BARRY

UFC 131

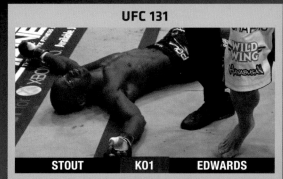

STOUT	KO1	EDWARDS

UFC 129

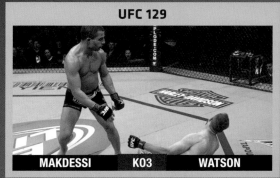

MAKDESSI	KO3	WATSON

UFC 141

HENDRICKS	KO1	FITCH

UFC 126

SILVA	KO1	BELFORT

SUBMISSIONS OF THE YEAR

UFC 140

MIR	WSUB1	NOGUEIRA

UFC FIGHT NIGHT: NOGUEIRA VS DAVIS

JUNG	WSUB1	GARCIA

UFC 129

GARZA	WSUB1	JABOUIN

UFC LIVE 4

LAUZON	WSUB1	WARBURTON

UFC 135

DIAZ	WSUB1	GOMI

DEBUTS

UFC 125
- JOSH GRISPI
- DUSTIN POIRIER
- DIEGO NUNES
- ANTONIO MCKEE

UFC 126
- MIGUEL ANGEL TORRES
- ANTONIO BANUELOS
- DONALD CERRONE
- CHAD MENDES
- NORIFUMI "KID" YAMAMOTO
- DEMETRIOUS JOHNSON
- KENNY ROBERTSON

UFC 127
- BRIAN EBERSOLE
- NICK RING
- RIKI FUKUDA
- TOM BLACKLEDGE
- TIEQUAN ZHANG
- MACIEJ JEWTUSZKO

UFC 128
- RAPHAEL ASSUNCÃO
- ERIK KOCH
- COSTAS PHILIPPOU
- JOSEPH BENAVIDEZ
- ANTHONY NJOKUANI
- KAMAL SHALORUS
- URIJAH FABER
- EDDIE WINELAND

UFC 129
- CHARLIE VALENCIA
- BENSON HENDERSON
- JOSE ALDO

UFC 130
- RENAN BARÃO
- COLE ESCOVEDO

UFC 131
- DAVE HERMAN
- JOHN-OLAV EINEMO
- VAGNER ROCHA
- JAMES HEAD
- JASON YOUNG
- AARON ROSA

UFC 131
- DAVE HERMAN
- JOHN-OLAV EINEMO
- VAGNER ROCHA

UFC 132
- DONNY WALKER
- JEFF HOUGLAND
- DOMINICK CRUZ

UFC 133
- PAUL BRADLEY

UFC 134
- STANISLAV NEDKOV
- JOHNNY EDUARDO
- ERICK SILVA
- LUIS RAMOS
- IURI ALCANTARA
- FELIPE ARANTES

UFC 135
- EDDIE YAGIN

UFC 136
- STIPE MIOCIC

UFC 137
- DUSTIN JACOBY
- HATSU HIOKI
- BART PALASZEWSKI
- FRANCIS CARMONT
- CLIFFORD STARKS

UFC 138
- JOHN MAGUIRE
- BRAD PICKETT
- PAPY ABEDI
- PHIL DE FRIES
- CHE MILLS
- VAUGHAN LEE

UFC 139
- CUNG LE
- ALEX SOTO

UFC 140
- JAKE HECHT
- JOHN CHOLISH
- MITCH CLARKE

UFC 141
- ALISTAIR OVEREEM

UFC LIVE: SANCHEZ VS KAMPMANN
- CHRIS WEIDMAN
- BRIAN BOWLES
- DAMACIO PAGE
- DANNY CASTILLO
- SHANE ROLLER
- REUBEN DURAN
- TAKEYA MIZUGAKI

UFC LIVE: KONGO VS BARRY
- JAVIER VAZQUEZ
- RICARDO LAMAS
- MATT GRICE
- EDWARD FAALOLOTO

UFC LIVE: HARDY VS LYTLE
- RONNY MARKES
- JIMY HETTES

UFC LIVE: CRUZ VS JOHNSON
- WALEL WATSON
- JOSEPH SANDOVAL
- MIKE EASTON
- BYRON BLOODWORTH

UFC ON FOX: VELASQUEZ VS DOS SANTOS
- MATT LUCAS
- CUB SWANSON
- DARREN UYENOYAMA

THE ULTIMATE FIGHTER: TEAM BISPING VS TEAM MILLER FINALE
- DIEGO BRANDÃO
- DENNIS BERMUDEZ
- JOHN DODSON
- TJ DILLASHAW
- JOHNNY BEDFORD
- LOUIS GAUDINOT
- MARCUS BRIMAGE
- STEPHEN BASS
- JOHN ALBERT
- DUSTIN PAGUE
- ROLAND DELORME
- JOSH FERGUSON
- STEVEN SILER
- JOSH CLOPTON
- BRYAN CARAWAY
- DUSTIN NEACE

UFC FIGHT FOR THE TROOPS 2
- RANI YAHYA
- WILLAMY FREIRE
- CHRIS CARIASO

UFC FIGHT NIGHT: NOGUEIRA VS DAVIS
- MICHAEL MCDONALD
- EDWIN FIGUEROA
- ALEX CACERES
- MACKENS SEMERZIER
- CHAN SUNG JUNG

UFC FIGHT NIGHT: SHIELDS VS ELLENBERGER
- ROBBIE PERALTA
- JORGE LOPEZ
- LANCE BENOIST
- MIKE STUMPF

THE ULTIMATE FIGHTER: TEAM LESNAR VS TEAM DOS SANTOS FINALE
- TONY FERGUSON
- RAMSEY NIJEM
- CHRIS COPE
- CHUCK O'NEIL
- DAN DOWNES
- RYAN McGILIVRAY
- CLAY HARVISON
- JUSTIN EDWARDS
- SCOTT JORGENSEN
- KEN STONE
- FRANCISCO RIVERA
- ANTHONY PETTIS

OCTAGON GIRLS

ALL-TIME OCTAGON GIRL ROSTER

- Jhenny Andrade
- Luciana Andrade
- Carly Baker
- Chrissy Blair
- Kahili Blundell
- Jessica Cambensy
- Arianny Celeste
- Aline Caroline Franzoi

- Red Dela Cruz
- Vanessa Hanson
- Edith Labelle
- Rachelle Leah
- Su Jung Lee
- Holly Madison
- Kristie McKeon
- Amber Nichole Miller

- Azusa Nishigaki
- Camila Oliveira
- Brittney Palmer
- Chandella Powell
- Ali Sonoma
- Logan Stanton
- Natasha Wicks
- Kang Ye-Bin

JHENNY ANDRADE

Sao Paulo's Jhenny Andrade had a successful career as a presenter and model in her native Brazil, but things really took off when she began writing a popular column for the men's magazine *VIP*. Now, her fans can see her Octagon side for UFC Brazil events. "In the beginning, it was all new and different," she said. "Today, I am part of the delicious adrenaline, and I am in love with fighting."

CARLY BAKER

London's Carly Baker is a multimedia threat in the entertainment business as a model, actress and even a pop star, having been part of the pop duo Mynxters. She's also a former beauty queen, representing Wimbledon in the Miss Great Britain competition. These days, UFC fans can see her on fight nights, supporting the leading brand in mixed martial arts.

THE ULTIMATE FIGHTER
A CHAMPION WILL BE CROWNED

CHRISSY BLAIR

Actress and Octagon Girl Chrissy Blair first came to the attention of fight fans when she worked for the STRIKEFORCE organization. Now in UFC, Chrissy continues to chase her dreams daily. "I have high expectations of myself, so my goals are more like dreams...some of them have already come true, but I still keep them a secret until they happen. Let's just say my goals are to keep pushing for more, and I love every minute of it."

NOS ENERGY DRINK

ARIANNY CELESTE

Arianny Celeste became a UFC Octagon Girl in typical fashion—through a modeling casting call. Ever since she made her debut in 2006, life has been anything but typical for the Las Vegas native, who saw her first live mixed martial arts fight that night. Since then, this striking Latina has become a fixture at UFC events. This fan favorite has also appeared on the covers of *Playboy* and *Maxim*.

RACHELLE LEAH

Rachelle Leah first made her name in UFC as an Octagon Girl, but since then, the Bay Area-born beauty has become a multimedia powerhouse. She has hosted UFC programming, appeared in modeling and acting gigs and was featured on the cover of *Playboy*. But Rachelle has never abandoned her first love, resuming her Octagon duties for select shows over the years.

VANESSA HANSON

Los Angeles model Vanessa Hanson was a popular part of the STRIKEFORCE promotion before making the move to UFC, where she continues to thrill fight fans with her statuesque beauty and grace. As far as what she considers the perks of the job, they are simple: "I love the traveling, the fans, and of course, all the action."

CAMILA OLIVEIRA

A model since age 16 who has appeared in television commercials and in high-fashion runway shows, Brazilian beauty Camila Oliveira has been a UFC Octagon Girl since 2013. Although she cried when Anderson Silva lost his title at UFC 162, it is usually all smiles for Camila, who enjoys giving back to her community every chance she gets. "Helping people is something wonderful," she said.

BRITTNEY PALMER

Las Vegas' Brittney Palmer first came to mixed martial arts after a stint as a boxing ring card girl. Once she got her first dose of WEC action, she was hooked. "There's really no comparison," said Brittney. "When you're watching MMA, it's just so much better." Now gracing the UFC Octagon, nothing makes this bombshell happier than working a big room, like she does every night when UFC takes its show on the road.

2012

2011 featured sweeping changes in UFC, with a FOX television deal, the first full year of bantamweights and featherweights in the Octagon and the purchase of the STRIKEFORCE promotion. In contrast, 2012 was going to focus on maintaining this pace and keeping fans happy with the fights and fighters they wanted to see. That wasn't limited to United States fans, but those around the world, as well.

So it was no surprise that 2012 began in the promotion's new hotbed, Brazil. With UFC returning to Rio de Janeiro after its ultra-successful UFC 134 event, UFC 142 on January 14 saw Jose Aldo successfully defend his featherweight title with a first-round knockout of Chad Mendes. After the bout ended, Aldo ran into the crowd to celebrate with his fans, a memorable moment to say the least for the hometown hero.

The first "official" event of UFC's landmark deal with FOX took place at the United Center in Chicago on January 28. The network-televised card featured Rashad Evans' win over Phil Davis, a victory by Chael Sonnen over Michael Bisping and an opener that saw Chris Weidman defeat Demian Maia. It was not the most aesthetically pleasing set of results, but FOX viewers would get plenty of compelling action in the following months and years.

Mendes takes down Aldo during their featherweight bout at UFC 142.

Jose Aldo and Chad Mendes prior to their bout.

BIGFOOT SILVA
CAMPINA GRANDE, PARAÍBA, BRAZIL

DEBUT: UFC 146, MAY 26, 2012

An imposing heavyweight with not only size and strength, but also the world-class skill to be a tough opponent for anyone he faces, Antonio "Bigfoot" Silva skyrocketed to prominence with his one-sided stoppage of longtime superstar Fedor Emelianenko in February 2011.

This was no overnight success, however. Silva, a native of Brazil who now resides in Florida, has been working for years to reach the top. And now that he's in UFC, he is not about to stop.

A Brazilian jiu-jitsu black belt who has also achieved that honor in judo and karate, Silva owns wins over Octagon vets Wesley Correira, Ricco Rodriguez, Justin Eilers, Andrei Arlovski and Mike Kyle. After a stellar run in STRIKEFORCE, he entered UFC in 2012.

In the Octagon, Silva stumbled at times, including twice against Cain Velasquez. With knockouts of a previously unbeaten Travis Browne and number-one contender Alistair Overeem, as well as a classic draw with Mark Hunt, however, he has still earned himself a high level of respect.

Carlos Condit kicks Nick Diaz.

Joseph Benavidez and Yasuhiro Urushitani compete for the flyweight title.

Alexander Gustafsson defeats Thiago Silva via decision at UFC on Fuel TV.

With Georges St-Pierre sidelined by injury, top contenders Nick Diaz and Carlos Condit squared off for the interim welterweight title at UFC 143 on February 4. Condit scraped out a hard-fought five-round decision win to take the belt.

On February 26, UFC's international team traveled to Japan for the first event in the Land of the Rising Sun since 2000. UFC 144 was another rousing success, as former WEC lightweight champion Benson Henderson dethroned Frankie Edgar, Ryan Bader defeated Rampage Jackson, Mark Hunt knocked out Cheick Kongo and Anthony Pettis stopped Joe Lauzon on an action-packed, star-studded card.

In March, a new weight class officially arrived in UFC, and the Fight Night event in Sydney, Australia saw the first two bouts of the 125-pound flyweight division. Four of the top competitors in the world—Demetrious Johnson, Ian McCall, Joseph Benavidez and Yasuhiro Urushitani—battled it out for the first UFC flyweight crown. While Benavidez easily punched his ticket to the tournament final with a knockout of Urushitani, his opponent took a little longer to determine, as Johnson and McCall fought to a draw.

Swedish star Alexander Gustafsson was the obvious choice to headline UFC's first visit to Stockholm on April 14, and he did not disappoint as he defeated Thiago Silva via decision, kicking off his move into the contenders' race at 205 pounds. Of course, the champion of that division, Jon Jones was not slowing down. He proved his determination when he defeated Rashad Evans in the main event of UFC 145 on April 21, defusing the feud between the former friends and teammates.

MICHAEL CHIESA
AURORA, CO

DEBUT: THE ULTIMATE FIGHTER: LIVE FINALE, JUNE 1, 2012
THE ULTIMATE FIGHTER: LIVE **WINNER**

Michael "Maverick" Chiesa has represented the fighting hotbed of the Pacific Northwest well thus far, losing just twice in a pro MMA career that began in 2008.

He's come a long way, and supporting him throughout was his father, Mark, who tragically passed away after a battle with leukemia. His death happened while Chiesa was on The Ultimate Fighter: Live Finale in 2012, but in honor of his dad, "Maverick" courageously fought on and won the season title, beginning his UFC journey in the process.

MAX HOLLOWAY
WAIANAE, HI

DEBUT: UFC 143, FEBRUARY 4, 2012

Considering that he's been training in MMA since he was a sophomore in high school, it's really no surprise that featherweight contender Max Holloway is among the best in UFC, where he remains one of the youngest fighters currently on the roster.

"This was a dream since I first started fighting," said Holloway, who holds UFC wins over Cole Miller, Akira Corassani, Andre Fili and Leonard Garcia. "I'm living my dream doing what I love to do. It's hard to explain how I feel."

RONY JASON
QUIXADÁ, CEARÁ, BRAZIL

DEBUT: UFC 147, JUNE 23, 2012
THE ULTIMATE FIGHTER: BRAZIL 1 **WINNER**

As a black belt in jiu-jitsu and kickboxing and an orange belt in judo, Ceara's Rony Jason has a list of accolades that stretches a mile long, including several mixed martial arts victories and the season title for *The Ultimate Fighter: Brazil* season one. Not surprisingly, his biggest early influence was Brazil's first family of fighting.

"I started in jiu-jitsu because I was a fan of the Gracies and always liked to test myself," said Jason, who has defeated the likes of Godofredo Pepey, Sam Sicilia and Steven Siler.

Junior Dos Santos punches Frank Mir at UFC 146.

At UFC 146 in May, another young champion with a bright future, Junior Dos Santos, made it look easy in his first title defense, knocking out former two-time titleholder Frank Mir in the second round. Waiting in the wings for "Cigano," however, was Cain Velasquez, the man he had beaten for the title. Velasquez made a triumphant return in the co-feature, stopping the debuting former STRIKEFORCE star, Bigfoot Silva in the first round.

On June 1, a successful but stressful experiment came to a close, as the first live season of The Ultimate Fighter finished up with Michael Chiesa defeating Al Iaquinta. The finale show capped off a 13-week season—the longest in The Ultimate Fighter h story.

A week later, Johnson and McCall met again, with Johnson taking a decisive decision win to earn a spot alongside Benavidez in UFC's first flyweight title fight later in the year. Although that business settled smoothly, that was not the case for UFC 147 in Belo Horizonte, Brazil, as several changes to the card left fans wondering what was going to happen on fight night. Eventually, things settled with Rich Franklin defeating Wanderlei Silva a second time and Brazil's first two Ultimate Fighters, Cezar Ferreira and Rony Jason, being crowned.

MYLES JURY
HAZEL PARK, MI

DEBUT: THE ULTIMATE FIGHTER: LIVE FINALE, JUNE 1, 2012

Myles Jury is a jiu-jitsu black belt and member of the respected Alliance MMA team. After stints on *The Ultimate Fighter*'s 13th and 15th seasons, he transitioned smoothly into UFC, submitting Chris Saunders in June 2012. He then defeated Michael Johnson, Diego Sanchez and Mike Ricci via decision, and he knocked out Ramsey Nijem and Takanori Gomi. In the process, he became one of the lightweight division's top candidates for world title honors.

JOHN LINEKER
PARANAGUÁ, PARANÁ, BRAZIL

DEBUT: UFC ON FOX: DIAZ VS MILLER, MAY 5, 2012

Several years ago, John Lineker decided to take his love of boxing to a different level and began training in MMA. Soon, the teenager turned to the pro game in 2008 at age 18.

The rest was history. He bounced back from a rocky 6-5 start to his career to win his next 13 bouts, earning him a call to become Brazil's first representative in UFC's flyweight division. In the Octagon, he continued to crush the competition, thrilling fans with knockout wins over Azamat Gashimov, Jose Maria, Phil Harris and Alptekin Ozkilic.

HECTOR LOMBARD
MATANZAS, CUBA

DEBUT: UFC 149, JULY 21, 2012

Long considered one of the top middleweights on the planet, and without question one of UFC's key acquisitions, Hector "Showeather" Lombard made his Octagon debut at UFC 149 in 2012.

A member of Cuba's Olympic judo team in 2000, Lombard craves competition, and his record in mixed martial arts proves it. Owner of wins over James Te Huna, Eiji Ishikawa, Brian Ebersole, Kalib Starnes, Jay Silva, Joe Doerksen, Falaniko Vitale, Jesse Taylor and Trevor Prangley, the black belt in judo and Brazilian jiu-jitsu was glad to finally test himself in the Octagon.

"It means everything," said Lombard of fighting in UFC.

There would be no upheaval in the UFC 148 card in Las Vegas on July 7, though, as the most highly anticipated rematch in history took place. Anderson Silva and Chael Sonnen had engaged in a classic the first time around in 2010, but in the return bout, "The Spider" put it on Sonnen and stopped him early in the second round. In the co-main event, Forrest Griffin defeated newly minted UFC Hall of Famer Tito Ortiz via decision in the final bout of their trilogy.

Sidelined by a knee injury that forced him out of his UFC 148 rubber match with Urijah Faber, Dominick Cruz revealed that he was going to be out for a while. This prompted the promotion to establish an interim title fight between Faber and Renan Barão that took place at UFC 149 on July 21. The unheralded Barão was dazzling that night in Calgary, winning both a clear-cut five-round unanimous decision and the belt.

Rich Franklin defeats Wanderlei Silva at UFC 147.

After an action-packed FOX show on August 4 that saw Shogun Rua outlast a talented Brandon Vera en route to a fourth-round knockout win, lightweight stalwarts Benson Henderson and Frankie Edgar met again at UFC 150 on August 11. The rematch had the same result: a razor-thin decision win for "Smooth" Benson.

At this point, the year was going as seamlessly as possible, despite some key injuries causing fight card shifts. But on August 23, everything hit a stop when Dan Henderson was forced from his UFC 151 main event on September 1 against Jon Jones due to injury. Jones opted against a short-notice fight against Chael Sonnen, prompting UFC to cancel the event.

It was the first time in history that UFC made such a move. The company needed to come back strong with its next event on September 22, so it did just that. In the headliner of UFC 152 in Toronto, Jones returned to face Vitor Belfort, and after some early rough moments, he submitted "The Phenom" in the fourth round. Also that night, Demetrious Johnson became UFC's first flyweight champion, as he defeated Joseph Benavidez via decision in a five-round instant classic that showed precisely why the promotion brought the flyweights in.

Several changes rocked the organization's UFC 153 event in Rio de Janeiro on October 13, so who came to the rescue? Middleweight superstar Anderson Silva, who agreed to move up to light heavyweight for the third time as a UFC fighter to face Stephan Bonnar on short notice. That decision certainly left the fans happy, as "The Spider" was in vintage form in scoring a first-round TKO of "The American Psycho."

China became the newest international destination on UFC's itinerary on November 10, with a trip to Macao, highlighted by a Cung Le knockout of former middleweight champion Rich Franklin. But a week later, all eyes were on Montreal's Bell Centre, as Georges St-Pierre fought, for the first time since his knee surgery, against Carlos Condit. Would GSP still be the same fighter after the long layoff? The answer was yes, as the welterweight champion rose from an early knockdown to win a dominant five-round unanimous decision victory over Condit.

FOX viewers got another championship fight on network television on December 8, but this time, it lasted longer than 64 seconds. Benson Henderson's clinic against Nate Diaz went the distance but still kept the title belt firmly around the defending champion's waist.

Anderson Silva stops Sonnen in the second round of their middleweight championship bout.

IAN MCCALL
COSTA MESA, CA

DEBUT: UFC ON FX: ALVES VS KAMPMANN, MARCH 3, 2012

With many regarding him as one of the best flyweights in the world, Ian "Uncle Creepy" McCall finally found a home in UFC. A pro since 2002, McCall made his UFC debut against Demetrious Johnson in the organization's first-ever flyweight tournament in March 2012. After a three-round war, a majority draw verdict was rendered. Johnson won their rematch via close decision, but McCall bounced back with wins over Iliarde Santos and Brad Pickett that put him back at the top of the division.

GUNNAR NELSON
AKUREYRI, ICELAND

DEBUT: UFC ON FUEL TV: STRUVE VS MIOCIC, SEPTEMBER 29, 2012

A jiu-jitsu black belt under Renzo Gracie, Gunnar "Gunni" Nelson is a decorated grappler with several titles and medals on his résumé, but in 2007, he began to seek out new challenges in MMA. After a draw in his first bout, he won 13 bouts in a row, with four of them occurring in UFC against DaMarques Johnson, Jorge Santiago, Omari Akhmedov and Zak Cummings before he lost to Rick Story via split decision in October 2014. Not surprisingly, nine of his first 13 victories came via submission.

KHABIB NURMAGOMEDOV
MAKHACHKALA, RUSSIA

DEBUT: UFC ON FX: GUILLARD VS MILLER, JANUARY 20, 2012

Khabib "The Eagle" Nurmagomedov is one of the top talents to emerge from Russia in years. Fight game insiders regard him as having a bright future in the sport, and his remarkable record is proof of that. A three-time Russian combat sambo champion, Nurmagomedov turned pro in September 2008. He has been blasting through all challengers ever since, defeating such top foes as Rafael dos Anjos, Gleison Tibau and Abel Trujillo along the way.

In Queensland, Australia, a week after Henderson vs. Diaz, *The Ultimate Fighter*'s *Smashes* competition came to an end, with Robert Whittaker picking up a season title for Australia and Norman Parke doing the same for the UK. In the American version of *The Ultimate Fighter*, Colton Smith won the season sixteen crown.

Now all that was left was for the heavyweights to make their final statement of the year. At UFC 155 in Las Vegas on December 29, Cain Velasquez regained his title with a shutout five-round decision win over Junior Dos Santos, setting the stage for a 2013 rubber match.

Cain Velasquez regains the heavyweight title from Junior Dos Santos.

Demetrious Johnson becomes UFC's first flyweight champion.

Velasquez punches Dos Santos at UFC 155.

NORMAN PARKE
BUSHMILLS, UNITED KINGDOM

DEBUT: UFC ON FX: SOTINOPOULOS VS PEARSON, DECEMBER 15, 2012

Already considered by his Team UK coach Ross Pearson to be a UFC-level fighter in terms of skill, Northern Ireland's "Stormin" Norman Parke took advantage of his opportunity to fulfill his Octagon dreams in December 2012 when he defeated Colin Fletcher to win the first season of *The Ultimate Fighter: The Smashes*. The judo expert was just getting started, though. He went unbeaten in his next four UFC fights before a decision loss to Gleison Tibau in 2015.

GLOVER TEIXEIRA
SOBRÁLIA, MINAS GERAIS, BRAZIL

DEBUT: UFC 146, MAY 26, 2012

For years, he was one of the mixed martial arts world's most coveted free agents, but in May 2012, Brazil's Glover Teixeira finally stepped into the Octagon for the first time to begin his UFC career against Kyle Kingsbury. This veteran has over a decade of experience in mixed martial arts and is always looking to deliver a fight to remember when the bell rings. Teixeira fell short in his UFC light heavyweight title bout against Jon Jones in 2014, but he is determined to get back to the top as soon as possible.

ROBERT WHITTAKER
MIDDLEMORE, NEW ZEALAND

DEBUT: UFC ON FX: SOTINOPOULOS VS PEARSON, DECEMBER 15, 2012

The lone member of Team Australia in the finals of UFC on FX: Sotinopoulos vs Pearson, Robert Whittaker had the hopes of his country's MMA community on his shoulders, and he delivered with flying colors in December 2012. He defeated Bradley Scott to win the season title. Whittaker split his next four fights in UFC at welterweight, but a move to middleweight late in 2014 appeared to be the right one, as he knocked out Clint Hester in the second round.

FIGHTS OF THE YEAR

UFC 155

MILLER   W3   LAUZON

UFC ON FUEL TV: KOREAN ZOMBIE VS POIRER

JUNG   WSUB4   POIRIER

UFC 145

YAGIN   W3   HOMINICK

UFC 144

HENDERSON   W5   EDGAR

UFC 154

ST-PIERRE   W5   CONDIT

KNOCKOUTS OF THE YEAR

UFC 142

BARBOZA   KO3   ETIM

UFC ON FUEL TV: FRANKLIN VS LE

LE   KO1   FRANKLIN

UFC 144

PETTIS   KO1   LAUZON

UFC ON FUEL TV: GUSTAFSSON VS SILVA

BAHADURZADA   KO1   THIAGO

THE ULTIMATE FIGHTER: TEAM CARWIN VS TEAM NELSON FINALE

BARRY   KO2   DEL ROSARIO

SUBMISSIONS OF THE YEAR

UFC ON FUEL TV: KOREAN ZOMBIE VS POIRER

JUNG   WSUB4   POIRIER

UFC ON FUEL TV: STRUVE VS MIOCIC

WIMAN   WSUB1   SASS

UFC ON FOX: EVANS VS DAVIS

OLIVEIRA   WSUB1   WISELY

UFC ON FOX: DIAZ VS MILLER

DIAZ   WSUB2   MILLER

THE ULTIMATE FIGHTER: TEAM CARWIN VS TEAM NELSON FINALE

WALDBURGER   WSUB2   CATONE

DEBUTS

UFC 142
- EDNALDO OLIVEIRA
- ANTONIO CARVALHO
- CARLO PRATER

UFC 143
- STEPHEN THOMPSON
- DAN STITTGEN
- HENRY MARTINEZ
- MICHAEL KUIPER
- MAX HOLLOWAY

UFC 144
- EIJI MITSUOKA
- ISSEI TAMURA

UFC 145
- CHAD GRIGGS
- CHRIS CLEMENTS
- MAXIMO BLANCO

UFC 146
- BIGFOOT SILVA
- SHANE DEL ROSARIO
- GLOVER TEIXEIRA

UFC 147
- CEZAR FERREIRA
- SERGIO MORAES
- RONY JASON
- GODOFREDO PEPEY
- ANISTAVIO MEDEIROS
- FRANCISCO TRINALDO
- DELSON HELENO
- HUGO VIANA

- JOHN TEIXEIRA
- THIAGO PERPETUO
- LEONARDO MAFRA
- MARCOS VINICIUS
- WAGNER CAMPOS
- HACRAN DIAS
- RODRIGO DAMM
- MILTON VIEIRA

UFC 149
- HECTOR LOMBARD
- RYAN JIMMO
- MITCH GAGNON

UFC 150
- CHICO CAMUS

UFC 152
- ROGER HOLLETT

UFC 153
- RENEE FORTE

UFC 154
- AZAMAT GASHIMOV

UFC 155
- DEREK BRUNSON

UFC ON FX: GUILLARD VS MILLER
- TOMMY HAYDEN
- JARED PAPAZIAN
- DANIEL PINEDA
- NICK DENIS
- KHABIB NURMAGOMEDOV
- PAT SCHILLING

UFC ON FX: ALVES VS KAMPMANN
- ANDREW CRAIG
- OLI THOMPSON
- SHAWN JORDAN
- YASUHIRO URUSHITANI
- IAN MCCALL
- NICK PENNER

UFC ON FX: JOHNSON VS MCCALL
- CAIO MAGALHAES
- BUDDY ROBERTS

UFC ON FX: MAYNARD VS GUIDA
- JOEY GAMBINO
- BROCK JARDINE
- CJ KEITH

UFC ON FX: BROWNE VS BIGFOOT
- PHIL HARRIS
- JUSSIER FORMIGA

UFC ON FOX: EVANS VS DAVIS
- LAVAR JOHNSON
- ERIC WISELY

UFC ON FOX: DIAZ VS MILLER
- TIMOTHY ELLIOTT
- JOHN LINEKER

UFC ON FOX: SHOGUN VS VERA
- WAGNER PRADO
- JOHN MORAGA
- ULYSSES GOMEZ

UFC ON FOX: HENDERSON VS DIAZ
- ABEL TRUJILLO

THE ULTIMATE FIGHTER 15 FINALE
- MICHAEL CHIESA
- AL IAQUINTA
- JUSTIN LAWRENCE
- JOHN COFER
- DARON CRUICKSHANK
- CHRIS TICKLE
- MYLES JURY
- CHRIS SAUNDERS
- SAM SICILIA
- CRISTIANO MARCELLO
- JOE PROCTOR
- JEREMY LARSEN
- ERIK PEREZ

THE ULTIMATE FIGHTER: THE SMASHES FINALE
- ROBERT WHITTAKER
- BRADLEY SCOTT
- NORMAN PARKE
- COLIN FLETCHER
- YAOTZIN MEZA
- BENNY ALLOWAY
- MANUEL RODRIGUEZ
- MIKE WILKINSON
- BRENDAN LOUGHNANE
- CODY DONOVAN

THE ULTIMATE FIGHTER: TEAM CARWIN VS TEAM NELSON FINALE
- COLTON SMITH
- MIKE RICCI
- MIKE RIO
- JOHN COFER
- RUSTAM KHABILOV
- VINC PICHEL

UFC ON FUEL TV: SANCHEZ VS ELLENBERGER
- BERNARDO MAGALHAES
- JUSTIN SALAS
- ANTON KUIVANEN
- TIM MEANS

UFC ON FUEL TV: GUSTAFSSON VS SILVA
- REZA MADADI
- SIMEON THORESEN
- BESAM YOUSEF
- SIYAR BAHADURZADA
- TOM DEBLASS
- MAGNUS CEDENBLAD
- YOISLANDY IZQUIERDO

UFC ON FUEL TV: KOREAN ZOMBIE VS POIRIER
- MARCUS LEVESSEUR

UFC ON FUEL TV: STRUVE VS MIOCIC
- GUNNAR NELSON
- TOM WATSON
- ANDY OGLE
- AKIRA CORASSANI
- JIMI MANUWA

UFC ON FUEL TV: FRANKLIN VS LE
- MOTONOBU TEZUKA
- JON TUCK

WEC

These names are synonymous with mixed martial arts excellence: Jose Aldo, Urijah Faber, Benson Henderson, Anthony Pettis, Renan Barão, Dominick Cruz, Carlos Condit, Nate Diaz and Donald Cerrone. What do they all have in common? At one time or another, they all graced the World Extreme Cagefighting organization, a breeding ground for not only consistently exciting fights, but for the best lighter weight fighters in the world.

Founded in 2001 by Scott Adams and Reed Harris, the WEC was revered by hardcore fans for producing many instant classics. But for years, the organization was also MMA's best kept secret, like that great band you used to see at a local club that you knew would hit it big. In late 2006, the WEC became the Rolling Stones.

Under the ownership of Zuffa, the WEC secured a national television deal, made Las Vegas its home base and focused its energies on not only MMA's established weight classes, but the featherweight and bantamweight divisions that rarely received exposure in the United States.

The impact was immediate, aided in great part by the organization's featherweight champion Urijah Faber. Faber was a talented and charismatic fighter whose appeal cut across all demographics and brought in fans by the truckload, especially in Sacramento, California, the hometown of "The California Kid." Luckily, Faber was on board to do whatever was necessary to show the world just how exciting the lighter weight fighters were.

"People are gonna fall in love with our weight classes," said Faber during a media stop in New York before his 2007 bout against Chance Farrar. "You're going to find that it's faster, it's more explosive and it's extremely entertaining."

> "YOU'RE GOING TO FIND THAT IT'S FASTER, IT'S MORE EXPLOSIVE AND IT'S EXTREMELY ENTERTAINING."
> —URIJAH FABER

Faber had plenty of help in his quest, as some of the early stars of the Zuffa-owned WEC were current household names like Donald Cerrone and Carlos Condit—exciting battlers willing to put it all on the line once the horn sounded.

The WEC was just getting started. As a new breed of dynamic fighters started to filter into the organization, the fights featuring these standouts were routinely finding their way onto the end of year "best of" lists.

Classics like Leonard Garcia vs Chan Sung Jung, Miguel Angel Torres vs Takeya Mizugaki, Urijah Faber vs Jens Pulver I, Benson Henderson vs Donald Cerrone I and Anthony Pettis vs Benson Henderson captivated fans and made any WEC event a must-see for the true fight fan.

In October 2010, Zuffa announced that UFC would be adding the featherweight and bantamweight divisions and merging the remainder of the WEC fighters into the world's premier MMA organization. Although the organization no longer exists, the excitement the WEC brought to fight fans will never be forgotten.

"As UFC continues to evolve and grow globally, we want to be able to give fans title fights in every weight division," said UFC president Dana White in 2010. "This is a big day for the sport and the athletes who will have the opportunity to fight on the biggest stage in the world."

WEC CHAMPIONSHIP ROSTER

SUPER HEAVYWEIGHT
- RON WATERMAN

HEAVYWEIGHT
- JAMES IRVIN
- BRIAN OLSEN

LIGHT HEAVYWEIGHT
- STEVE CANTWELL
- LODUNE SINCAID
- JASON LAMBERT
- SCOTT SMITH
- DOUG MARSHALL
- BRIAN STANN
- FRANK SHAMROCK

MIDDLEWEIGHT
- PAULO FILHO
- JOE RIGGS
- CHRIS LEBEN

WELTERWEIGHT
- SHONIE CARTER
- KARO PARISYAN
- CARLOS CONDIT
- MIKE PYLE
- NICK DIAZ

LIGHTWEIGHT
- HERMES FRANCA
- ANTHONY PETTIS
- BENSON HENDERSON
- GABE RUEDIGER
- ROB MCCULLOUGH
- JAMIE VARNER
- GILBERT MELENDEZ

FEATHERWEIGHT
- JOSE ALDO
- COLE ESCOVEDO
- MIKE BROWN
- URIJAH FABER

BANTAMWEIGHT
- CHASE BEEBE
- DOMINICK CRUZ
- BRIAN BOWLES
- MIGUEL ANGEL TORRES
- EDDIE WINELAND

NOTABLE WEC ALUMNI

- JOSE ALDO
- JOHN ALESSIO
- OLAF ALFONSO
- RAPHAEL ASSUNCAO
- ANTONIO BANUELOS
- RENAN BARÃO
- CHASE BEEBE
- JOSEPH BENAVIDEZ
- BRIAN BOWLES
- JONATHAN BROOKINS
- MIKE BROWN
- STEVE CANTWELL
- CHRIS CARIASO
- SHONIE CARTER
- SHANE CARWIN
- GIL CASTILLO
- DANNY CASTILLO
- DONALD CERRONE
- DAN CHRISTISON
- CARLOS CONDIT
- KIT COPE
- WESLEY CORREIRA
- RICH CRUNKILTON
- DOMINICK CRUZ
- JEFF CURRAN
- MAC DANZIG
- LC DAVIS
- NATE DIAZ
- NICK DIAZ
- JOE DOERKSEN
- DAN DOWNES
- YVES EDWARDS
- COLE ESCOVEDO
- URIJAH FABER
- WAGNNEY FABIANO
- PAULO FILHO
- HERMES FRANCA
- MANNY GAMBURYAN
- LEONARD GARCIA

- PABLO GARZA
- TIKI GHOSN
- JOSH GRISPI
- CLAY GUIDA
- BENSON HENDERSON
- JOHNY HENDRICKS
- JAY HIERON
- MARK HOMINICK
- JEREMY HORN
- CHRIS HORODECKI
- MATT HORWICH
- BRAD IMES
- JAMES IRVIN
- YVES JABOUIN
- DEMETRIOUS JOHNSON
- SCOTT JORGENSEN
- ALEX KARALEXIS
- TIM KENNEDY
- ROB KIMMONS
- ERIK KOCH
- MIKE KYLE
- JASON LAMBERT
- BROCK LARSON
- CHRIS LEBEN
- CHRIS LYTLE
- DOUG MARSHALL
- TERRY MARTIN
- ROB McCULLOUGH
- GILBERT MELENDEZ
- CHAD MENDES
- IVAN MENJIVAR
- MICAH MILLER
- JASON MILLER
- TAKEYA MIZUGAKI
- MARK MUNOZ
- ANTHONY NJOKUANI
- DIEGO NUNES
- JAKE O'BRIEN
- NICK PACE

- DAMACIO PAGE
- BART PALASZEWSKI
- KARO PARISYAN
- KURT PELLEGRINO
- ANTHONY PETTIS
- NAM PHAN
- BRAD PICKETT
- CARLO PRATER
- JENS PULVER
- MIKE PYLE
- JOE RIGGS
- ANDRE ROBERTS
- RICCO RODRIGUEZ
- SHANE ROLLER
- GEORGE ROOP
- GABE RUEDIGER
- MACKENS SEMERZIER
- DAN SEVERN
- KAMAL SHALORUS
- FRANK SHAMROCK
- AARON SIMPSON
- WES SIMS
- SCOTT SMITH
- RAMEAU SOKOUDJOU
- CHAEL SONNEN
- BRIAN STANN
- CHAN SUNG JUNG
- CUB SWANSON
- MIKE SWICK
- MIGUEL ANGEL TORRES
- CHARLIE VALENCIA
- JAMIE VARNER
- JAVIER VAZQUEZ
- RON WATERMAN
- MARK WEIR
- VERNON WHITE
- EDDIE WINELAND
- RANI YAHYA
- TIEQUAN ZHANG

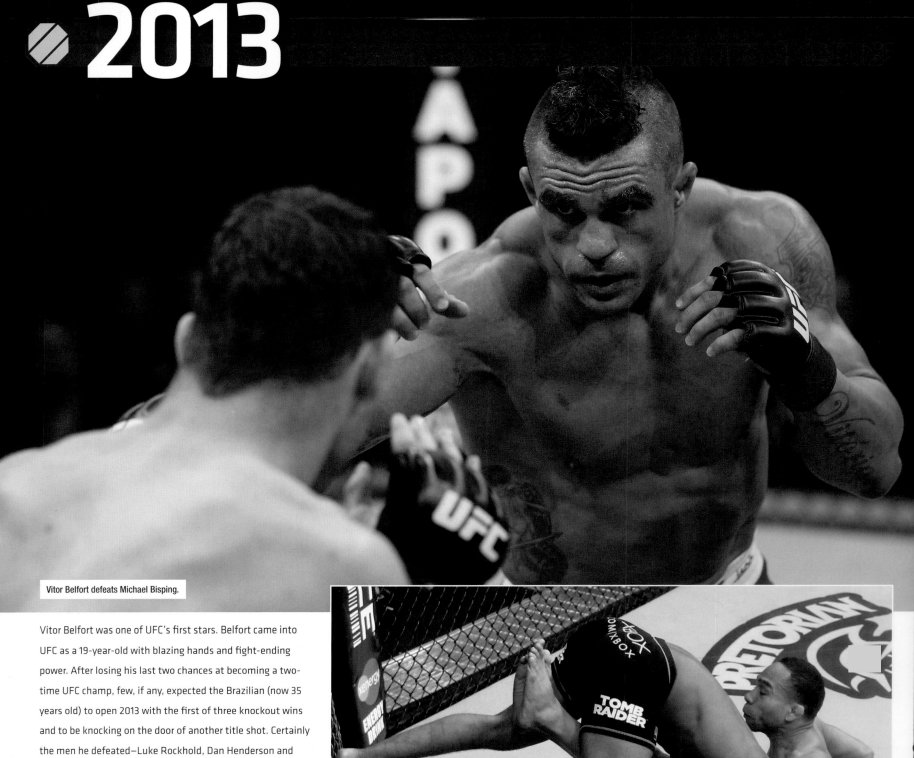

Vitor Belfort defeats Michael Bisping.

Vitor Belfort was one of UFC's first stars. Belfort came into UFC as a 19-year-old with blazing hands and fight-ending power. After losing his last two chances at becoming a two-time UFC champ, few, if any, expected the Brazilian (now 35 years old) to open 2013 with the first of three knockout wins and to be knocking on the door of another title shot. Certainly the men he defeated—Luke Rockhold, Dan Henderson and Michael Bisping, the fighter he kicked off UFC's year with on January 19 in Brazil—did not.

That UFC on FX card started 2013 off explosively. When you consider that a week earlier, the STRIKEFORCE promotion held its final show, opening the door for several more top stars to make their way to the Octagon, it was going to be quite a year for UFC.

2013's first FOX event took place on January 26 at the United Center in Chicago. Demetrious Johnson and John Dodson continued putting the flyweight division in a positive light as they battled for five fast-paced rounds. "Mighty Mouse" came from behind to take a close, but unanimous, decision and retain his 125-pound crown.

Johnson vs Dodson at UFC on FOX.

YOEL ROMERO
PINAR DEL RÍO, CUBA

DEBUT: UFC ON FOX: HENDERSON VS MELENDEZ, APRIL 20, 2013

An Olympic silver medalist in freestyle wrestling, Cuba's Yoel "Soldier of God" Romero transitioned to mixed martial arts after his wrestling career ended. In 2009, he made his pro debut with a 48-second knockout of Sascha Weinpolter. Three wins later, Romero received a call from STRIKEFORCE, and though he lost to Rafael Cavalcante, he made good on his second chance to make a first impression when he knocked out Clifford Starks in his first UFC bout.

Four more wins over Ronny Markes, Derek Brunson, Brad Tavares and Tim Kennedy followed in rapid succession, putting the "Soldier of God" at the top of the middleweight division.

Alistair Overeem and Bigfoot Silva at the UFC 156 weigh-in.

GEGARD MOUSASI
TEHRAN, IRAN

DEBUT: UFC ON FUEL TV: MOUSASI VS LATIFI, APRIL 6, 2013
STRIKEFORCE LIGHT HEAVYWEIGHT CHAMPION

Current UFC middleweight standout Gegard Mousasi was once one of STRIKEFORCE's top stars, an international success that earned the promotion's light heavyweight title in 2009 with a knockout win over Renato "Babalu" Sobral. He has won numerous big fights since then: he submitted Mark Munoz, Jake O'Brien, Mike Kyle and Tatsuya Mizuno, won TKO victories over Hiroshi Izumi and Dan Henderson and defeated Ovince Saint-Preux and Ilir Latifi via decision. With his reputation as one of the best secure, he can now go about the business of contending for a UFC title at 185 pounds.

Pay-Per-View viewers received a superfight to kick off the year on February 2, as Jose Aldo successfully defended his featherweight title with a close decision win over former lightweight champion Frankie Edgar. Bigfoot Silva also made a statement in his bout that night in Las Vegas, knocking out Alistair Overeem in the third round.

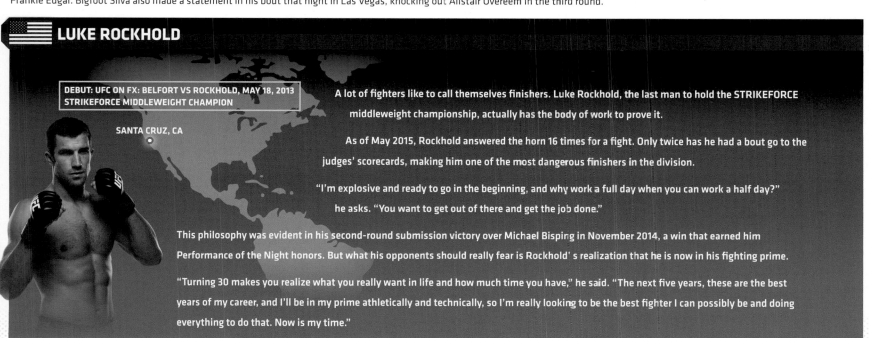

LUKE ROCKHOLD

DEBUT: UFC ON FX: BELFORT VS ROCKHOLD, MAY 18, 2013
STRIKEFORCE MIDDLEWEIGHT CHAMPION

SANTA CRUZ, CA

A lot of fighters like to call themselves finishers. Luke Rockhold, the last man to hold the STRIKEFORCE middleweight championship, actually has the body of work to prove it.

As of May 2015, Rockhold answered the horn 16 times for a fight. Only twice has he had a bout go to the judges' scorecards, making him one of the most dangerous finishers in the division.

"I'm explosive and ready to go in the beginning, and why work a full day when you can work a half day?" he asks. "You want to get out of there and get the job done."

This philosophy was evident in his second-round submission victory over Michael Bisping in November 2014, a win that earned him Performance of the Night honors. But what his opponents should really fear is Rockhold's realization that he is now in his fighting prime.

"Turning 30 makes you realize what you really want in life and how much time you have," he said. "The next five years, these are the best years of my career, and I'll be in my prime athletically and technically, so I'm really looking to be the best fighter I can possibly be and doing everything to do that. Now is my time."

RONDA ROUSEY

DEBUT: UFC 157, FEBRUARY 23, 2013
UFC WOMEN'S BANTAMWEIGHT CHAMPION
STRIKEFORCE WOMEN'S BANTAMWEIGHT CHAMPION

RIVERSIDE COUNTY, CA

Pound-for-pound and punch-for-punch—or, more accurately, armbar-for-armbar—"Rowdy" Ronda Rousey is the undisputed queen of female mixed martial arts. Each time she fights, she brings the sport to more and more people. But how does she manage life in the public eye, where she is not only a world champion, a star in blockbuster Hollywood films and featured in magazines such as *ESPN The Magazine*'s Body Issue and *Sports Illustrated*?

"I'm dealing with it fine," said Rousey. "Before, I was working three jobs and training fulltime, and now because everything has been going so well, it's the same amount of work, but it's just different work. I don't have to do graveyard shifts anymore or show up for a 9-to-5 job; I just have more media obligations. But I've trained more than I ever have for anything before, even for the Olympics. This is the peak of my athletic career, and having to deal with some extra media and all those other things, the only challenges are multi-tasking, organization, getting help with my schedule and getting enough rest. But thankfully, I have a very professional team behind me now that's really helping me coordinate everything, so that's pretty much how I'm dealing with it—I get a lot of outside help with organization. But I always put my training first, and all the other things come second."

In 2012, Ronda took the STRIKEFORCE bantamweight title from Miesha Tate, and after defending it against Sarah Kaufman, she became the first women's champion in UFC history. She has since defended the title successfully against Liz Carmouche, Miesha Tate, Sara McMann, Alexis Davis and Cat Zingano, becoming a pioneer and a role model in the process.

"A lot of progress has been made, but there's still a lot of progress left to make," Rousey said. "I know that we don't live in a utopian society where everyone is treated equally. People are a lot more tolerant than they used to be, but they're not as tolerant as they should be. And so I'm not surprised that we still have progress to make, but it gives me goals to get after."

The Californian's athletic journey began on the judo mats several years ago. The daughter of AnnMaria De Mars, a World Champion judo competitor, Rousey took home gold medals in the 2004 and 2005 Pan Ams and in the 2004 and 2006 Junior World Championships. She then earned a silver medal in the 2007 World Championships and made two United States Olympic teams, winning a bronze medal in the 2008 Beijing Games. That 2008 Olympic medal was the first ever won by an American woman in judo.

The next step was MMA. She has won three amateur and 11 pro bouts, the most recent being a 16-second knockout over Davis at UFC 175 and a 14-second submission of Zingano at UFC 184. It's a devastating track record, one that has people saying she is the new Mike Tyson of combat sports. She prefers to be the first Ronda Rousey.

"I try to think about having my own thing," she said. "There are people that I respect and admire and try to mold myself after as an athlete, but no one's going to be able to have his [Tyson's] style better than he had it, because it was his. He's definitely one of the inspirations and people that I pull from. But I can have my style better than anybody else."

And what a style it is: Hollywood glamorous outside of the Octagon, and ferociously competitive inside of it. Yet make no mistake, Ronda Rousey is all fighter.

"These fights are real; it's not a sport to me," she said. "I don't like going out there and dancing and timing and checking out what everybody else has got. I'm trying to finish them, and I'm trying to show myself that I'm indestructible. It's very real to me. I don't know how else to describe it. It's self-defense: me using these disciplines that I've learned to not be hurt by someone and to hurt them in return instead."

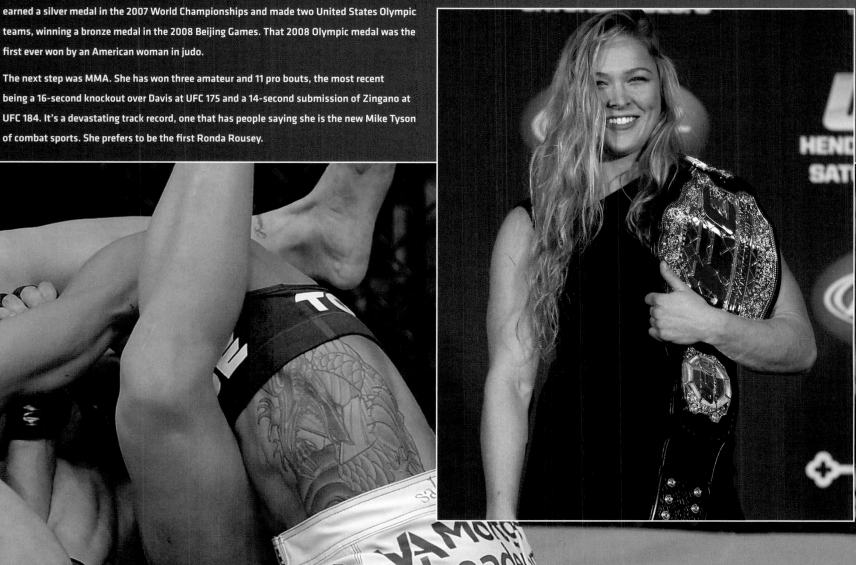

Two weeks later, Renan Barão submitted Michael McDonald in the fourth round to retain his interim bantamweight title. History was then made on February 23, as UFC welcomed women into the Octagon for the very first time.

Unsurprisingly, the woman chosen to lead the revolution was former STRIKEFORCE champion Ronda Rousey. This Olympic bronze medal winner had the talent, charisma and attitude to take all the pressure on her shoulders and not just survive, but thrive. "Rowdy" Ronda Rousey experienced a stern test early on in her UFC 157 main event against Liz Carmouche. Moments after surviving a rear-naked choke attempt, Rousey finished Carmouche with her trademark armbar in the closing seconds of the very first round. The first UFC women's bantamweight titleholder said that she finally felt like a true champion.

Rousey and her peers produced much more Octagon magic, but the men didn't want to be excluded. What better fight could headline UFC 158 in Montreal on March 16 than the welterweight grudge match between Georges St-Pierre and Nick Diaz? Seemingly years in the making, the two finally met at the Bell Centre, and once again, GSP made it look easy. He dominated from start to finish, earning a five-round unanimous decision victory. That's not to say there was no one to challenge the Canadian star, as Johny Hendricks, who defeated Carlos Condit in the co-main event that night, was closing in quickly.

In April, Kelvin Gastelum completed an upset-filled run through the field on *The Ultimate Fighter* season seventeen by defeating the highly touted Uriah Hall to win the season title. Benson Henderson won a superfight over former STRIKEFORCE champion Gilbert Melendez to retain his UFC lightweight title.

Silva punches Overeem during their heavyweight bout at UFC 156.

Ronda Rousey and Liz Carmouche face off prior to the UFC 157 women's bantamweight title bout.

DEBUT: THE ULTIMATE FIGHTER: TEAM JONES VS TEAM SONNEN FINALE, APRIL 13, 2013

An accomplished high school and college wrestler, "Alpha" Cat Zingano parlayed her skill on the mats into a new passion in 2007 when she discovered Brazilian jiu-jitsu. A quick study in the gentle art, Zingano eventually decided to give MMA a try in 2008. Since then, she has been virtually unstoppable, winning all but one of her bouts, including devastating knockout wins over Carina Damm, Takayo Hashi and Miesha Tate.

In her first bout following a stirring TKO of Amanda Nunes in September 2014, the number-one bantamweight contender challenged for Ronda Rousey's world title in February 2015, but was submitted after only fourteen seconds in the first round. Disappointed but not deterred, Zingano looks forward to a comeback, and she will not be happy with anything but a finish.

"I don't want a decision—ever—in a fight," Zingano said. "Decisions, to me, are a loss because organically, you would not know how that fight would have ever went had it gone another 20 minutes, had it gone another hour. In nature, you would not know what happened, and I don't like that. I want to get to the bottom of things, and for a fight to go to a decision, it bothers me."

Then, Jon Jones and Chael Sonnen, coaches of *The Ultimate Fighter* season seventeen, finally met in Newark, with "Bones" Jones stopping the "Gangster from West Linn" late in the first round.

The UFC 160 event on May 25 featured heavyweight rivals Cain Velasquez and Junior Dos Santos in separate bouts, and the two secured their rubber match. Velasquez stopped Bigfoot Silva for the second time to retain his title, and Dos Santos knocked out Mark Hunt in the final round of a bout that earned Fight of the Night honors.

Georges St-Pierre flips Nick Diaz at their UFC 158 bout.

Dos Santos knocks down Hunt during their bout at UFC 160.

MIESHA TATE
TACOMA, WA

**DEBUT: THE ULTIMATE FIGHTER: TEAM JONES VS TEAM SONNEN FINALE, APRIL 13, 2013
STRIKEFORCE WOMEN'S BANTAMWEIGHT CHAMPION**

Miesha "Cupcake" Tate has been a competitive athlete for most of her life, with a 2005 state high school wrestling championship serving as a precursor of things to come for the Tacoma, Washington, native. But while most successful high school athletes move on to more sedate pursuits after graduation, Tate had other ideas. By 2007, she had turned pro in mixed martial arts with a decision win over Jan Finney. Two fights later, she was in the prestigious STRIKEFORCE organization, where she defeated Elaina Maxwell.

Over the next three years, Tate was on a mission, going 10-1 and winning the STRIKEFORCE bantamweight title with a stirring fourth-round submission of Marloes Coenen. Her title reign ended in March 2012 at the hands of Ronda Rousey, but Tate's courageous effort garnered her even more fan support and steeled her resolve for another shot at someone who would become her most heated rival.

In 2013, Tate coached against Rousey on *The Ultimate Fighter* season 18, intensifying their rivalry even further. Although she lost in their rematch for the UFC women's bantamweight championship in December 2013, wins over Liz Carmouche, Rin Nakai and Sara McMann have put her back in the title picture.

In June, *The Ultimate Fighter: Brazil*'s second season produced a veteran winner, as Leonardo Santos replaced the injured Santiago Ponzinibbio and submitted William Macario in the second round. Rashad Evans also picked up a win over Dan Henderson in the UFC 161 main event in Winnipeg, Manitoba, Canada.

At UFC 162 on July 6, many expected it to be business as usual when Anderson Silva defended his middleweight title against unbeaten Chris Weidman. Yet, it was anything but that. A showboating Silva got caught with a flush punch by Weidman in the second round and dropped to the canvas. A follow-up barrage brought in referee Herb Dean to stop the fight. Weidman was the new 185-pound champ, and an era in UFC history had ended.

Chris Weidman catches Anderson Silva with a flush blow.

Despite the shock of "The Spider's" first-ever UFC loss, the show must go on. Demetrious Johnson remained on top as he put another title defense in the bank on July 27, this one via fifth-round submission over John Moraga. Also remaining untouchable was featherweight king Jose Aldo, who defeated "The Korean Zombie," Chan Sung Jung, via fourth-round TKO in the UFC 163 main event on August 3.

Another UFC first took place in Boston on August 17, as the launch of the new FOX Sports 1 channel featured a Fight Night card packed with stars. In the main event, Chael Sonnen stunned Shogun Rua, submitting him in the first round. Also victorious were Travis Browne, Urijah Faber, Matt Brown and "The Notorious" Conor McGregor, a young man from Dublin, Ireland who had been making a lot of noise in UFC ever since his debut win in Sweden in April.

By late August, it was time for another eagerly anticipated title fight, this one a rematch of a WEC bout between Benson Henderson and Anthony Pettis. Since their first meeting in 2010, which Pettis won, Henderson had won the UFC lightweight title and successfully defended it three times. But that would be all, as Pettis submitted Henderson in the first round to be crowned the new lightweight champ.

It was now "Showtime" at 155 pounds, but 50 pounds north in the light heavyweight division, Jon Jones was also having a dominant and seemingly unstoppable reign at the top. In the main event of UFC 165 in Toronto on September 21, however, "Bones" faced the toughest test of his career in the form of Swedish contender Alexander Gustafsson. Just when it seemed that "The Mauler" was about to upset the champion and take the title, Jones rallied down the stretch to take a hard-earned unanimous decision victory.

In other UFC 165 action, Renan Barão retained his interim bantamweight title with a second-round TKO of Eddie Wineland.

The rubber match between Cain Velasquez and Junior Dos Santos took place in Houston on October 19. In the featured UFC 166 bout, it was all Velasquez, as he ran through "Cigano" en route to a fifth-round TKO win. The performance was perhaps the most impressive of Velasquez's career, but perhaps even more exciting was the three-round brawl between Gilbert Melendez and Diego Sanchez that "El Nino" won the hard way.

Alexander Gustafsson lands a blow against Jon Jones during their UFC light heavyweight championship bout.

GILBERT MELENDEZ
SANTA ANA, CA

DEBUT: UFC ON FOX: HENDERSON VS MELENDEZ, APRIL 20, 2013
STRIKEFORCE LIGHTWEIGHT CHAMPION

The last man to hold the STRIKEFORCE lightweight championship, Gilbert "El Nino" Melendez is not flashy; he doesn't make a lot of noise. But he trains, he fights and he wins. And he does it better than most. The Santa Ana, California native has put together a résumé any fighter would envy, with more than 20 wins and a list of victims that includes Diego Sanchez, Shinya Aoki, Jorge Masvidal, Josh Thomson (twice), Clay Guida and Rumina Sato. In the last few years, however, more casual fans have started to realize that Melendez is one of the best lightweights in the game today—an odd phenomenon for the veteran of over a decade in the sport.

"I feel like I've always got respect from my peers, and I think a lot of the real fans and the journalists have known," Melendez said. "I've had a lot of entertaining fights, and I would like a lot of people to check those out."

In UFC, "El Nino" has his biggest audience to date, and he will thrill them every step of the way when he fights.

Dana White looks on as GSP and Hendricks face off at the UFC 167 weigh-in.

GSP kicks Hendricks during their bout for the UFC welterweight championship.

KYOJI HORIGUCHI
GUNMA PREFECTURE, JAPAN

DEBUT: UFC 166, OCTOBER 19, 2013

A protégé of Japanese great Norifumi "Kid" Yamamoto, Kyoji Horiguchi made his highly anticipated UFC debut in 2013 against Dustin Pague. He didn't disappoint, halting his foe in the second round.

Owner of a devastating striking attack that led him to knockouts in nine of his first 15 wins, Horiguchi brought a nine-fight winning streak that included four UFC victories into his first UFC championship bout against Demetrious Johnson at UFC 186 on April 25, 2015 in Montreal.

Although Horiguchi received his first UFC loss that night, he will be part of history for the rest of time because Johnson submitted Horiguchi with an armbar with only one second left in the fifth and final round, making it the latest UFC finish ever, a record that can only be matched, but never broken.

As for his key to success both at home and internationally, he knows what it takes: "Fight the best, as usual, and finish the fight to get a lot of attention from the fans; I want them to look at me as a finisher," said Horiguchi.

CONOR McGREGOR
DUBLIN, IRELAND

DEBUT: UFC ON FUEL TV: MOUSASI VS LATIFI, APRIL 6, 2013

The brightest talent to ever emerge from Ireland, "The Notorious" Conor McGregor immediately showed himself to be a top candidate for world title honors after his debut UFC knockout of Marcus Brimage.

"One of my favorite things to do in life is say I'm gonna do something and then go out and do it," he said. "There's no better feeling for me than doing that. It's a beautiful thing."

But "The Notorious" was just getting started. McGregor's impressive wins over Max Holloway, Diego Brandão, Dustin Poirier and Dennis Siver piled up and built anticipation for a bout between the fighting pride of Dublin and featherweight champion Jose Aldo that will take place in July 2015.

As for fight night, McGregor remains as cool as ever. "It's just another day for me," he said. "I've been the star since Day 1. It's just another day in the life of a king, and it feels normal. Everything is the same. In my head, it was always like this, no different. And I'm going to perform like that, as well. People think there's pressure; I don't feel pressure, I never did. I've been in a UFC main event every fight of my career."

In November, UFC celebrated its 20th anniversary with UFC 167 in Las Vegas. It was a main event worthy of such an occasion. Johny Hendricks pushed Georges St-Pierre to the brink in their welterweight title bout. When it was over, many felt that Hendricks had done enough to win, but the split decision went to GSP. A month later, St-Pierre announced that he was taking a break from the sport, leaving the 170-pound title vacant.

The Ultimate Fighter season 18, coached by rivals Ronda Rousey and Miesha Tate, was the first season to feature men and women competing for individual titles. At the season finale show on November 30, Julianna Pena won the women's side and Chris Holdsworth took the honors for the men.

A bout that initially flew under the radar in Brisbane, Australia, Mark Hunt and Bigfoot Silva woke up the universe with their five-round war on December 7. Showing heart, determination and fight-altering power, the two heavyweights left it all in the Octagon in a fight neither of them deserved to lose. And neither did because the fight was, appropriately, deemed a draw.

Hunt-Silva was a tough act to follow for flyweight champ Demetrious Johnson in his rematch against Joseph Benavidez on FOX on December 14. While he and his challenger didn't match the heavyweights in terms of action, "Mighty Mouse" did leave jaws hanging open with his first-round knockout win.

The biggest card of the year was still yet to come, and fittingly, it was the last event of 2013. UFC 168 featured two world title rematches on December 28. In the main event, Chris Weidman and Anderson Silva would meet again, while the co-main event would see Rousey defend her belt against Tate.

Hendricks lands a blow on GSP during UFC 167.

ALEXIS DAVIS
PORT COLBORNE, CANADA

DEBUT: UFC 161, JUNE 15, 2013

Alexis Davis was one half of an epic 2012 fight with Sarah Kaufman that many believe was the greatest female fight ever. Ontario's Davis is proud of that bout, but she is determined to ensure that her legacy contains more than just one classic fight.

With Davis winning over top contenders Jessica Eye, Liz Carmouche, Amanda Nunes and Shayna Baszler, her presence in the 135-pound UFC women's mix has clearly made a talent-rich division even more intriguing and competitive.

SARAH KAUFMAN
VICTORIA, CANADA

DEBUT: UFC 166, OCTOBER 19, 2013
STRIKEFORCE WOMEN'S BANTAMWEIGHT CHAMPION

Sarah Kaufman grew from an unknown prizefighter from Victoria, British Columbia, to one of the top 135-pound fighters in the world, earning a STRIKEFORCE bantamweight title in the process.

She's consistently tough against the best contenders in the world, with a list of victims that includes Miesha Tate, Alexis Davis (twice), Liz Carmouche, Shayna Baszler and Roxanne Modafferi. Don't expect Kaufman to ever suffer from any nerves when it's time to put the gloves on and fight.

JULIANNA PEÑA
SPOKANE, WA

DEBUT: THE ULTIMATE FIGHTER:
TEAM ROUSEY VS TEAM TATE FINALE, NOVEMBER 30, 2013
THE ULTIMATE FIGHTER 18 WINNER

The first pick of coach and longtime training partner Miesha Tate on The Ultimate Fighter season 18, Julianna "Venezuelan Vixen" Peña may have been an underdog when the competition started, but by the time she submitted Team Rousey's first pick Shayna Baszler, everyone knew who "The Venezuelan Vixen" was. Following a win over Jessica Rakoczy that earned her the crown on The Ultimate Fighter and an injury-induced layoff, Peña made a triumphant return to the Octagon in April 2015, defeating Milana Dudieva.

LIZ CARMOUCHE
LAFAYETTE, LA

DEBUT: UFC 157, FEBRUARY 23, 2013

Hailing from San Diego, California, Liz "Girlrilla" Carmouche is a veteran of the United States Marine Corps who brings a powerful ground-and-pound attack and championship experience into all of her fights in the Octagon.

One of the many young women who grew up idolizing soccer players, Carmouche's journey eventually took her to mixed martial arts after her time in the Marine Corps. She is one of the top contenders in the ultra-competitive 135-pound weight class.

JESSICA EYE
ROOTSTOWN TOWNSHIP, OH

DEBUT: UFC 166, OCTOBER 19, 2013

One of the top flyweights in mixed martial arts for several years, Cleveland's Jessica "Evil" Eye moved 10 pounds north in 2013. She delivered a stellar effort in her UFC debut at bantamweight against former STRIKEFORCE champion Sarah Kaufman.

A veteran with an impressive record that includes several wins over high-level competition, Eye even compiled some pre-UFC victories that were some of her biggest, defeating Zoila Frausto Gurgel and Carina Damm in back-to-back bouts.

SARA McMANN
TAKOMA PARK, MD

DEBUT: UFC 159, APRIL 27, 2013

One of the most decorated athletes to ever set foot in the Octagon, 2004 Olympic silver medal winner Sara McMann has proven herself on the international stage as a freestyle wrestler. Now, she is looking forward to doing the same thing in UFC, a journey that began with her wins over Sheila Gaff and Lauren Murphy. Losses to Ronda Rousey and Miesha Tate slowed her progress, but this former Olympian is not easily deterred from her goals.

TIM KENNEDY
SAN LUIS OBISPO, CA

DEBUT: UFC 162, JULY 6, 2013

A true American hero who represented his country as a Special Forces sergeant in the United States Army, Tim Kennedy has received plenty of acclaim for the sacrifices he has made over the years. But while he was performing his military duties, some forgot the strides he has made as a middleweight mixed martial artist.

UFC noticed, though, signing the former STRIKEFORCE standout. He made his Octagon debut in 2013 and promptly won three straight bouts over Roger Gracie, Rafael Natal and Michael Bisping.

JORGE MASVIDAL
MIAMI, FL

DEBUT: UFC ON FOX:
HENDERSON VS MELENDEZ, APRIL 20, 2013

Jorge "Gamebred" Masvidal has been fighting for much of his life, but it has only been in recent years that his passion is starting to pay off. He has become one of the top lightweights in the world, moving closer to a UFC title shot with each passing victory.

Born and raised in Miami, Masvidal preferred prizefighting to club hopping. From the time he turned pro in 2003, he has taken on all opponents, with a list including the names Gilbert Melendez, Al Iaquinta, Michael Chiesa, KJ Noons, Yves Edwards and Joe Lauzon.

KELVIN GASTELUM
SAN JOSE, CA

DEBUT: THE ULTIMATE FIGHTER:
TEAM JONES VS TEAM SONNEN FINALE, APRIL 13, 2013
THE ULTIMATE FIGHTER 17 WINNER

A jiu-jitsu purple belt who loves to stand and trade, or work his ground-and-pound attack, Kelvin Gastelum showed it all during his stint on *The Ultimate Fighter* season 17. En route to the season title, Gastelum defeated Uriah Hall and Kito Andrews via decision, submitted Bubba McDaniel and Josh Samman, and knocked out Collin Hart. While his toughest tests may be yet to come, UFC wins over Rick Story and Jake Ellenberger have Gastelum—a coach on season two of *The Ultimate Fighter: Latin America*—ready for anything.

TYRON WOODLEY
FERGUSON, MO

DEBUT: UFC 156, FEBRUARY 2, 2013

A two-time Division I All-American wrestler for the University of Missouri, Tyron "The Chosen One" Woodley scored more than 100 victories on the mat during his college career. These wins proved that when it comes to competition, Woodley is not used to coming in second. In 2009, he turned pro in MMA, and he has gone on to big things both in STRIKEFORCE and UFC. Five of his wins in the Octagon were over challenging opponents Jay Hieron, Josh Koscheck, Carlos Condit, Dong Hyun Kim and Kelvin Gastelum.

OVINCE SAINT PREUX
MIAMI, FL

DEBUT: UFC 159, APRIL 27, 2013

A former defensive standout for the University of Tennessee's football team, Ovince Saint Preux parlayed his athletic ability and work ethic into what has been a successful mixed martial arts career thus far. The Haitian-American, who has won five UFC bouts heading into 2015, including a November 2014 knockout of Shogun Rua, cannot stop now. He must defeat anyone and everyone put in front of him if he wants to continue on his road to a world light heavyweight title.

JACARE SOUZA
VILA VELHA, ESPÍRITO SANTO, BRAZIL

DEBUT: UFC ON FX: BELFORT VS ROCKHOLD, MAY 18, 2013
STRIKEFORCE MIDDLEWEIGHT CHAMPION

The gold standard for ground fighters, Brazilian jiu-jitsu and judo black belt Jacare Souza was a quick study on the canvas, winning five world championships in jiu-jitsu. In 2003, he made his MMA debut, and by 2010, he had earned the STRIKEFORCE middleweight title. In 2013, he entered the Octagon for the first time. After wins over Chris Camozzi, Francis Carmont, Yushin Okami, Ed Herman and Gegard Mousasi, Souza earned the number-one contender's spot in UFC's 185-pound division.

The co-feature went as expected, with Rousey getting a tough go from Tate before submitting her in the third round. In the main event, however, Weidman's repeat second-round stoppage of Silva was anything but ordinary. A checked kick thrown by the Brazilian broke Silva's leg in a horrendous fashion, prompting the fight to be halted. Yet even more devastating was the possibility that "The Spider" would never fight again. That possibility was eliminated as soon as he reached the hospital and asked the doctor not if, but when he could return to the Octagon. That's a true champion, belt or no belt.

Silva kicks Weidman during their championship bout.

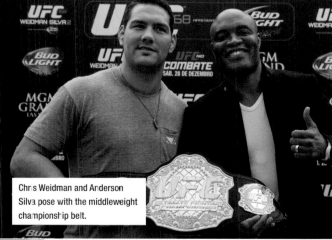

Chris Weidman and Anderson Silva pose with the middleweight championship belt.

DANIEL CORMIER

DEBUT: UFC ON FOX:
HENDERSON VS MELENDEZ, APRIL 20, 2013
UFC LIGHT HEAVYWEIGHT CHAMPION
STRIKEFORCE HEAVYWEIGHT GRAND PRIX WINNER

LAFAYETTE, LA

In the MMA universe, there are world-class wrestlers, and then there's Daniel Cormier, one of the most decorated rulers of the mat to hit the sport in the modern era.

But after his wrestling days were over, there was a new mountain to climb as a professional fighter. It wasn't easy, but a competitor like Cormier wasn't going to be scared away by a little hard work.

"It's rough, but it's humbling," said Cormier, who began training in MMA in August 2009. "I honestly was top five in the world almost every year I competed at the world level and was on two Olympic teams. So to go back and be the guy in the gym that actually can't do anything, it was real humbling. You go from walking into any wrestling room in the country and being the guy that everybody looked to for technique to the guy that's kinda dumped off in the corner trying not to get noticed because I'm throwing punches wrong or throwing punches off the wrong foot, and I'm trying to mimic stuff that I saw on TV for years, but it's not as easy as it looks."

Yet once the two-time U.S. Olympian from Oklahoma State University got his legs under him, he quickly made an impression as a fighter to watch, first as a heavyweight with wins over Antonio Silva, Josh Barnett, Frank Mir and Roy Nelson.

But it was at 205 pounds that "DC" was determined to win his first world title, and he immediately set his sights on champion Jon Jones. Devastating wins over Patrick Cummins and Dan Henderson followed, setting up the biggest light heavyweight title fight in years against Jones at UFC 182 in January 2015. And while Cormier wasn't able to take the belt from "Bones" that night, he was determined to scale the 205-pound ladder once more and take the belt home. Getting there required keeping everything in perspective.

"You don't want to be lying to yourself going into the cage," he said. "Anybody can beat anybody on any given night and I'm fully aware of that. It allows me to be completely open and honest with myself that if I do something wrong, I'll get beat, and I don't want to get beat. And if I believe that this guy can beat me at any moment or over the course of 15 minutes, it allows me to make him bigger and badder than he can ever possibly be, and then I train better for him."

In April 2015, an out of the Octagon incident forced the UFC to suspend Jones and strip him of the light heavyweight title, and a phone call was made to Cormier to see if he was willing to step up and face Anthony Johnson for the vacant crown at UFC 187 on May 23. The answer was a no brainer for "DC."

"If you get an opportunity to fight for a championship, you gotta take it," he said. "My ultimate goal is to be the champion of the UFC. Regardless of how that comes about, that's always been the goal, and that's what drives me. That's why I do this sport and that's why I compete. I want to be the best and now I get an opportunity to actually hold the belt that, after January, it was hard to imagine at what point I would actually get back there."

Cormier did get back there though, and when the horn sounded against Johnson, he took advantage of his second chance, dominating "Rumble" en route to a third-round submission victory.

Daniel Cormier was now a world champion. Just as he pictured it all those years ago.

FIGHTS OF THE YEAR

UFC 165

JONES   W5   GUSTAFSSON

UFC ON FUEL TV: SILVA VS STANN

SILVA   KO2   STANN

UFC FIGHT NIGHT: HUNT VS BIGFOOT

HUNT   DRAW5   SILVA

UFC 166

MELENDEZ   W3   SANCHEZ

UFC 158
HENDRICKS   W3   CONDIT

KNOCKOUTS OF THE YEAR

UFC 162

WEIDMAN   KO2   SILVA

UFC FIGHT NIGHT: BELFORT VS HENDERSON

BELFORT   KO1   HENDERSON

UFC FIGHT NIGHT: HUNT VS BIGFOOT

RUA   KO1   TE HUNA

UFC 165

BARÃO   TKO2   WINELAND

UFC 160

DOS SANTOS   KO3   HUNT

SUBMISSIONS OF THE YEAR

UFC 164

PETTIS   WSUB1   HENDERSON

UFC 157
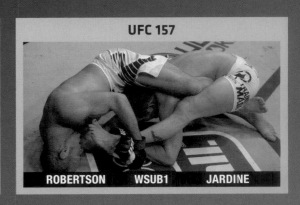
ROBERTSON   WSUB1   JARDINE

UFC ON FX: BELFORT VS ROCKHOLD

SOUZA   WSUB1   CAMOZZI

UFC 157

ROUSEY   WSUB1   CARMOUCHE

UFC ON FUEL 10

NETO   WSUB1   SMITH

DEBUTS

UFC ON FX: BELFORT VS BISPING

DANIEL SARAFIAN
LUCAS MARTINS
PEDRO NOBRE
ILDEMAR ALCANTARA

UFC ON FX: BELFORT VS ROCKHOLD

LUKE ROCKHOLD
RONALDO SOUZA
JOAO ZEFERINO
ILIARDE SANTOS
MICHEL PRAZERES

UFC ON FOX: JOHNSON VS DODSON

SEAN SPENCER

UFC ON FOX: HENDERSON VS MELENDEZ

GILBERT MELENDEZ
DANIEL CORMIER
JORGE MASVIDAL
ROGER BOWLING
YOEL ROMERO
LORENZ LARKIN

UFC ON FOX: JOHNSON VS MORAGA

BOBBY VOELKER
JESSICA ANDRADE
TREVOR SMITH
GERMAINE DE RANDAMIE
JULIE KEDZIE

UFC ON FOX: JOHNSON VS BENAVIDEZ 2

ZACH MAKOVSKY
ALPTEKIN OZKILIC

UFC: FIGHT FOR THE TROOPS 3

BRIAN HOUSTON

DEBUTS

UFC 156

TYRON WOODLEY

BOBBY GREEN

ISAAC VALLIE-FLAGG

DUSTIN KIMURA

UFC 157

RONDA ROUSEY

LIZ CARMOUCHE

CAROS FODOR

NEIL MAGNY

JON MANLEY

NAH-SHON BURRELL

YURI VILLEFORT

UFC 158

JORDAN MEIN

QUINN MULHERN

UFC 159

KURT HOLOBAUGH

SARA MCMANN

SHEILA GAFF

OVINCE SAINT PREUX

GIAN VILLANTE

YANCY MEDEIROS

UFC 160

ESTEVAN PAYAN

UFC 161

ALEXIS DAVIS

ROSI SEXTON

JAMES KRAUSE

UFC 162

ROGER GRACIE

BRIAN MELANCON

UFC 163

JOSE MARIA

THIAGO SANTOS

AMANDA NUNES

SHEILA GAFF

FRANCIMAR BARROSO

VISCARDI ANDRADE

UFC 164

NIKITA KRYLOV

UFC 165

NANDOR GUELMINO

JESSE RONSON

DANIEL OMIELANCZUK

UFC 166

JESSICA EYE

SARAH KAUFMAN

ANDRE FILI

KYOJI HORIGUCHI

DARRELL MONTAGUE

UFC 167

ANTHONY LAPSLEY

SERGIO PETTIS

UFC FIGHT NIGHT: SHOGUN VS SONNEN

JAMES VICK

UFC FIGHT NIGHT: CONDIT VS KAMPMANN 2

BRANDON THATCH

ZAK CUMMINGS

UFC FIGHT NIGHT: TEIXEIRA VS BADER

JUNIOR HERNANDEZ

ALI BAGAUTINOV

KEVIN SOUZA

IVAN JORGE

PIOTR HALLMANN

UFC FIGHT NIGHT: MAIA VS SHIELDS

IGOR ARAUJO

ALAN PATRICK

GARETT WHITELEY

YAN CABRAL

UFC FIGHT NIGHT: MACHIDA VS MUNOZ

NICO MUSOKE

ROB WHITEFORD

UFC FIGHT NIGHT: BELFORT VS HENDERSON

OMARI AKHMEDOV

ADRIANO MARTINS

DUSTIN ORTIZ

SANTIAGO PONZINIBBIO

UFC FIGHT NIGHT: HUNT VS BIGFOOT

BETHE CORREIA

ALEX GARCIA

BEN WALL

JUSTIN SCOGGINS

RICHIE VACULIK

KRZYSZTOF JOTKO

BRUNO SANTOS

DEBUTS

UFC ON FUEL TV: SILVA VS STANN

MIZUTO HIROTA

KAZUKI TOKUDOME

KYUNG HO KANG

HYUN GYU LIM

UFC ON FUEL TV: MOUSASI VS LATIFI

RYAN COUTURE

TOR TROENG

ADAM CELLA

ADLAN AMAGOV

CHRIS SPANG

CONOR MCGREGOR

RYAN LAFLARE

ILIR LATIFI

GEGARD MOUSASI

UFC ON FUEL TV: NOGUEIRA VS WERDUM

LEONARDO SANTOS

WILLIAM MACARIO

RAFAEL CAVALCANTE

EDDIE MENDEZ

LEANDRO SILVA

ANTONIO BRAGA NETO

ANTHONY SMITH

THE ULTIMATE FIGHTER: TEAM JONES VS TEAM SONNEN FINALE

KELVIN GASTELUM

URIAH HALL

CAT ZINGANO

MIESHA TATE

BUBBA MCDANIEL

GILBERT SMITH

JOSH SAMMAN

KEVIN CASEY

LUKE BARNATT

COLLIN HART

DYLAN ANDREWS

JIMMY QUINLAN

CLINT HESTER

BRISTOL MARUNDE

THE ULTIMATE FIGHTER: TEAM ROUSEY VS TEAM TATE FINALE

JULIANNA PENA

JESSICA RAKOCZY

CHRIS HOLDSWORTH

DAVEY GRANT

JESSAMYN DUKE

PEGGY MORGAN

RAQUEL PENNINGTON

ROXANNE MODAFFERI

TOM NIINIMAKI

WALT HARRIS

JARED ROSHOLT

DREW DOBER

JOSH SAMPO

RYAN BENOIT

371

STRIKEFORCE

Much like PRIDE and the WEC, the STRIKEFORCE mixed martial arts promotion may not have been UFC, but it had more than its share of loyal followers during its run from 2006 to 2013. Those fans were thrilled to watch action-packed fights and several stars who left it all in the cage during every match they fought.

Created by Scott Coker in 1985 as a kickboxing organization, it soon evolved into an MMA promotion that had its first show at the HP Pavilion in San Jose, California, on March 10, 2006. The bout pitted former UFC champion Frank Shamrock against renowned jiu-jitsu practitioner Cesar Gracie.

That first main event lasted just 21 seconds, with Shamrock winning by knockout. Despite that abbreviated outcome, STRIKEFORCE was off and running. The affectionately nicknamed "Shark Tank" in San Jose became the promotion's unofficial home arena and host to 15 of its 63 events.

Alistair Overeem in St. Louis, MO.

Gilbert Melendez strikes Tatsuya Kawajiri to retain the STRIKEFORCE Lightweight Championship.

With names like Shamrock, Cung Le, Alistair Overeem, Tank Abbott, Phil Baroni and Vitor Belfort stocking early shows, STRIKEFORCE certainly brought in crowds who wanted to see these international and former UFC stars in action. But as the years went by, STRIKEFORCE's pool of young talent began to carry the promotion and attract a loyal following.

Among the fighters building the promotion were Gilbert Melendez and Josh Thomson, who engaged in a memorable series of bouts. Other fighters like Cain Velasquez, Clay Guida and Nate Diaz, who graduated to big things in UFC, also made appearances in the early STRIKEFORCE days.

By 2008, the premium cable network Showtime began airing STRIKEFORCE events, giving the fighters even more exposure. The promotion also became the biggest stage at the time for women's MMA, with Gina Carano leading the way.

The biggest time for the company came in 2009-2010. During those years, the promotion aired two shows on CBS network television. When fighters from PRIDE like Fedor Emelianenko made their move to STRIKEFORCE, everyone stood up and took notice.

Despite STRIKEFORCE's success and growing roster of world-class fighters, on March 14, 2011, it was announced that Coker and his partners sold the promotion to Forza, LLC, a subsidiary of UFC owners, Zuffa.

"We have worked hard to make mixed martial arts the fastest-growing sport in the world," UFC president Dana White said at the time. "We've spent countless hours getting this sport regulated and taking the Octagon all over the world. Acquiring the STRIKEFORCE assets allows us to continue to develop this sport into a global force."

Forza kept STRIKEFORCE running until its final show in January of 2013. All the way through, the promotion kept putting on compelling cards while stars like Ronda Rousey, Miesha Tate, Luke Rockhold, Ronaldo "Jacare" Souza and Ovince Saint Preux made their names known on the world stage.

It was quite the legacy to leave, and if there's one thing for certain, it is that STRIKEFORCE will always remain a part of mixed martial arts lore.

Gina Carano

2014

The UFC world may have still been reeling from the injury that ended Anderson Silva's UFC 168 bout against Chris Weidman, but a week later, the Octagon was back up and ready to go. UFC was going to Singapore for the first time, with a Fight Night event that saw the launch of the promotion's digital streaming service: UFC FIGHT PASS.

Headlined by Tarec Saffiedine's win over Hyun Gyu Lim, the 10-bout card was aired exclusively on the new service, which allowed fans to see both live fights in real time and extensive fight libraries on their computer, gaming console, tablet or smartphone.

This new technology showed just how far UFC had come since 1993. But as always, the best part of watching the sport had nothing to do with technological advances; it was the fights that mattered.

In February, the first title fights of the year took place on the UFC 169 card in Newark, New Jersey. Originally scheduled to feature the long-awaited bout for the undisputed bantamweight title between Dominick Cruz and Renan Barão, Cruz was unfortunately injured again. His absence elevated Barão from interim to undisputed champion, and opened the door for Urijah Faber to step in for a title fight. Barão left no doubt in their rematch, though, stopping "The California Kid" in the first round. Barão's teammate Jose Aldo, was also on the card and kept his featherweight crown intact with a five-round decision win over Ricardo Lamas.

The championship fireworks kept coming at UFC 170 on February 22. Ronda Rousey stopped Sara McMann in 66 seconds to retain her women's bantamweight title in a clash of former Olympians. March got off to a solid start, as well, with the crowning of the first *The Ultimate Fighter: China* champion, Zhang Lipeng.

Tarec Saffiedine defeats Hyun Gyu Lim during their welterweight bout.

Renan Barão punches Urijah Faber at UFC 169.

Rousey defeats McMann to retain her title.

Ronda Rousey and Sara McMann face off during the UFC 170 weigh-in.

EDDIE ALVAREZ
PHILADELPHIA, PA

DEBUT: UFC 178, SEPTEMBER 27, 2014

Eddie Alvarez has competed around the world, fighting everywhere from Russia and Costa Rica to Canada and Japan. As one of the top lightweights in mixed martial arts, he picked up wins against Shinya Aoki, Michael Chandler, Roger Huerta, Josh Neer, Tatsuya Kawajiri, Aaron Riley and Joachim Hansen. In September 2014, the best 155-pounder who wasn't in UFC joined the roster and entered the Octagon for the first time.

"It's just another step toward my goal of being recognized by not just some fans, but all fans, as being the best lightweight in the world," he said.

TAREC SAFFIEDINE
BRUSSELS, BELGIUM

DEBUT: UFC FIGHT NIGHT:
SAFFIEDINE VS LIM, JANUARY 4, 2014
STRIKEFORCE WELTERWEIGHT CHAMPION

Inspired by the Japanese manga *TOUGH*, Belgium's Tarec "Sponge" Saffiedine found his way into a gym at the age of 16, and as far as mixed martial arts fans are concerned, the rest is history for the talented welterweight contender. He won the STRIKEFORCE title by beating Nate Marquardt in 2013, and he then went on to defeat Hyun Gyu Lim in his UFC debut in January 2014.

On March 15, the vacancy at the top of the 170-pound division created by Georges St-Pierre's sabbatical from the sport was filled by the 2014 Fight of the Year. Johny Hendricks outpointed Robbie Lawler in an epic five-round bout that saw both men go for broke in their quest for championship gold.

The first season of *The Ultimate Fighter Nations* concluded in Quebec City on April 16 with Elias Theodorou and Chad Laprise picking up UFC contracts. Three days later in Orlando, Florida, Fabricio Werdum earned a shot at Cain Velasquez' heavyweight title with a five-round win over Travis Browne. This hectic schedule kept UFC staffers running from coast to coast and across the globe, but the fans loved every minute of it, now that UFC events could be seen on an almost-weekly basis. The next stop was Baltimore on April 26, with Jon Jones turning back yet another challenger for his light heavyweight title. This time, Glover Teixeira fell at the hands of "Bones," who bounced back from his grueling late 2013 battle with Alexander Gustafsson in style.

Jon Jones retains his title with a win over Glover Teixeira.

TJ Dillashaw punches Renan Barão during their championship bout at UFC 173.

CARLA ESPARZA
TORRANCE, CA

DEBUT: *THE ULTIMATE FIGHTER:*
A CHAMPION WILL BE CROWNED, DECEMBER 12, 2014
UFC WOMEN'S STRAWWEIGHT CHAMPION

It was almost shocking to see that former Invicta FC strawweight champion Carla "Cookie Monster" Esparza was the underdog heading into her first world title fight against Rose Namajunas in December 2014.

Widely considered to be the top 115-pound fighter in the world, Esparza didn't disappoint on *The Ultimate Fighter: A Champion Will Be Crowned*, defeating Angela Hill, Tecia Torres and Jessica Penne to earn a spot in the finals against Rose Namajunas. But Esparza wasn't going to let her chance to make history in the Octagon pass her by. At 1:26 of the third round, she submitted her opponent to become the first UFC women's strawweight champion.

"When I got the belt, it didn't even feel real," Esparza said. "I kept waiting to wake up from a dream. It was such an unreal feeling, and it didn't hit me how significant this was. Even the day after, I was blowing my own mind, thinking, 'Oh my God, I cannot believe this.' It's crazy."

At UFC 185 in March 2015, Esparza lost her belt to unbeaten Polish standout Joanna Jedrzejczyk, but she vows to be back on top in no time.

PAIGE VANZANT
DAYTON, OR

DEBUT: UFC FIGHT NIGHT: EDGAR VS SWANSON,
NOVEMBER 22, 2014

When 20-year-old "12 Gauge" Paige VanZant entered the Octagon for the first time in November 2014, she did so as the second youngest female fighter in UFC. But with wins in three of her first four pro fights, she was ready for the step up to the big leagues against unbeaten Kailin Curran. What followed next was a blistering TKO win that earned her Fight of the Night honors and made her an overnight sensation that had fans eagerly awaiting her next move in the strawweight division.

At UFC 173 in Las Vegas on May 24, it was expected to be another successful title defense for Renan Barão as he took on the talented but unheralded TJ Dillashaw. Those expectations went south in a hurry for Barão, as Dillashaw dropped him early and kept the heat on throughout. He eventually knocked out the Brazilian in the fifth round to become the UFC bantamweight champion in one of the sport's great upsets.

Chris Weidman retains his middleweight title against Lyoto Machida.

Dillashaw's win should have been ringing in the heads of *The Ultimate Fighter: Brazil* season three winners Antonio Carlos Junior and Warlley Alves, as it was the Californian's stint on *The Ultimate Fighter* season 14 that propelled him into UFC and paved the way for him to eventually win a world title.

One fighter who didn't have *The Ultimate Fighter* on his résumé but was inspired by the first season to start training in MMA was Demetrious Johnson. "Mighty Mouse" didn't let any upsets cross his path at UFC 174 in June, as he easily turned back the challenge of Ali Bagautinov.

Another champion who kept his title secure in the summer 2014 was Chris Weidman. Fresh off two wins over Anderson Silva, the New Yorker got a chance to see a different face for the first time in a while when he battled former light heavyweight champion Lyoto Machida at UFC 175 on July 5. The end result was yet another win, as Weidman held off a spirited effort from "The Dragon" to retain his middleweight title. Also defending a title successfully was Ronda Rousey, who needed only 16 seconds to knock out Canadian challenger Alexis Davis.

JOANNA JEDRZEJCZYK
OLSZTYN, POLAND

DEBUT: UFC FIGHT NIGHT: LAWLER VS BROWN, JULY 26, 2014
UFC WOMEN'S STRAWWEIGHT CHAMPION

In the lead-up to Joanna Jedrzejczyk's UFC debut in July 2014, the question wasn't whether the unbeaten strawweight was ready for prime time in the Octagon, but whether anyone here in the United States was going to be able to pronounce her name.

She wasn't offended. In fact, if worst comes to worst the native of Olsztyn, Poland has a way around it for those who are phonetically challenged.

"My family name is typical Polish and contains so many difficult letters," she said. "But soon, everyone will know how to pronounce my name. Or I can just be JJ."

If her first UFC performance was any indication, fight fans need to start figuring out how to say "Jedrzejczyk." While the pre-bout talk was about her name, the post-fight banter was all about her unanimous decision win over Brazil's Juliana Lima. It was a dominant effort that showed off her Muay Thai attack both at range and in close. If beating Lima weren't enough, Jedrzejczyk added another win to her record in December 2014, defeating Claudia Gadelha to earn a shot at Carla Esparza's UFC women's strawweight title.

At UFC 185, Jedrzejczyk made the most of her opportunity, stopping Esparza in two rounds to earn a title belt and a new name: Joanna Champion.

TJ Dillashaw reacts after his victory over Joe Soto.

Joe Rogan interviews Joe Soto at the UFC 177 weigh-in.

The day after UFC 175, there was yet another fight card in Las Vegas. While *The Ultimate Fighter* season 19 winners Corey Anderson and Eddie Gordon got their share of the spotlight, it was BJ Penn who received the lion's share of it, and rightfully so, as he announced his retirement following his loss to Frankie Edgar in the card's main event. It had been a great career for "The Prodigy," but he knew it was time to move on.

The new breed of UFC was more than willing to take up the mantle for fighters like Penn, though. No fighter was more vocal about it than Ireland's Conor McGregor, who tested his appeal on July 19 when the Octagon returned to Dublin for the first time since 2009. Suffice to say that it was a success, with the sold-out crowd of more than 9,500 fans sounding like 90,000 as they cheered McGregor on to a first-round TKO over Diego Brandão. It was a seminal day for Irish MMA, and "The Notorious" one was leading the way, saying after the bout, "We're not here to take part; we're here to take over."

McGregor had his sights on featherweight champion Jose Aldo, but Aldo first had pressing matters to deal with from former opponent Chad Mendes. Mendes had soared back to the number-one contender's spot after a series of knockout wins, and the two were scheduled to meet again at UFC 176 in Los Angeles on August 2. But an injury to Aldo scrapped the bout, and later the entire card, with Aldo-Mendes II moving to UFC 179 later in the year.

The brief title fight drought ended on August 30, as TJ Dillashaw prepared to defend his title against the man he had beaten for the belt, Renan Barão. But after a bad weight cut forced Barão out of the bout on weigh-in day, debuting undercard fighter Joe Soto stepped up to face the champion on a day's notice. It was a gutsy decision, and Soto gave a supreme effort in the UFC 177 main event. But there was no Hollywood ending in Sacramento, as Dillashaw retained his title with a fifth-round knockout.

By now, bad blood was brewing between Jon Jones and unbeaten Daniel Cormier, but first, the light heavyweight champ had business to attend to with former foe Alexander Gustafsson. The two were slated to meet at UFC 178 on September 27, but a Gustafsson injury forced him out of the bout. Cormier stepped in, and a subsequent press conference brawl with Jones ignited even more interest in the fight. But soon, a Jones leg injury prompted the postponement of the bout to UFC 182 in January 2015.

Working quickly, UFC moved the UFC 177 bout between Demetrious Johnson and Chris Cariaso into the UFC 178 main event slot. Johnson was mighty once more, submitting his foe in the second round. That card also saw comeback wins by Dominick Cruz and Cat Zingano, another knockout win by Conor McGregor and a victory by Donald Cerrone over highly regarded newcomer Eddie Alvarez.

On October 25 in Rio de Janeiro, Jose Aldo and Chad Mendes finally met again. Their first bout had been a quick knockout win for champion Aldo, but in the UFC 179 rematch, Aldo had to fight tooth and nail to keep his featherweight belt in one of the best UFC title fights ever.

With the euphoria from Aldo–Mendes II keeping fight fans asking for more, they got it on November 15, as UFC visited Mexico for the first time. Unfortunately, injuries also plagued this UFC 180 card, with fights like Diego Sanchez vs Joe Lauzon and the main event of Cain Velasquez vs Fabricio Werdum falling by the wayside. The main event delivered plenty of excitement, though, as Werdum won the interim heavyweight title with a second-round knockout of late replacement Mark Hunt.

Mark Hunt punches Fabricio Werdum at UFC 180.

Hunt and Werdum trade strikes during their interim championship bout.

Werdum celebrates his victory over Hunt.

Robbie Lawler

Robbie Lawler kicks Johny Hendricks during their UFC welterweight championship bout.

It had definitely been a rollercoaster year, but UFC made sure that it was going to finish strong in December. Indeed, on December 1, it was announced that UFC had signed a deal with Reebok for the global fitness leader to become UFC's exclusive outfitter and apparel provider.

"This will be the biggest non-broadcast partnership that our company has ever signed," UFC Chairman and CEO Lorenzo Fertitta said. "So it is significant."

In the Octagon, the action ended the year on a high note. At UFC 181 on December 6, the welterweight title changed hands when Robbie Lawler defeated Johny Hendricks via decision in another closely contested showdown. Also, Anthony Pettis successfully defended his lightweight belt for the first time against Gilbert Melendez, his rival coach on *The Ultimate Fighter: A Champion Will Be Crowned*.

Speaking of *The Ultimate Fighter: A Champion Will Be Crowned*, that season was the first to feature all women and UFC's newest weight class, the 115-pound women's strawweight division. Even more notable was the fact that the winner would be crowned UFC's first women's strawweight champion. That first champ on was Carla Esparza, who beat Rose Namajunas in the finals on December 12 in Las Vegas.

It was a thrilling ride for sure, and UFC fans love that kind of excitement.

Carla Esparza celebrates after submitting Rose Namajunas for the UFC women's strawweight title.

Lawler punches Hendricks at UFC 181.

FIGHTS OF THE YEAR

UFC 171

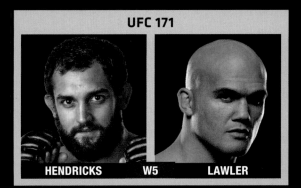

HENDRICKS   W5   LAWLER

UFC 179

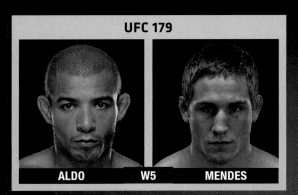

ALDO   W5   MENDES

UFC FIGHT NIGHT: DOS SANTOS VS MIOCIC

DOS SANTOS   W5   MIOCIC

UFC FIGHT NIGHT: BROWN VS SILVA

BROWN   TKO3   SILVA

UFC 169

TRUJILLO   KO2   VARNER

KNOCKOUTS OF THE YEAR

UFC FIGHT NIGHT: BISPING VS LE

KIM   KO3   HATHAWAY

UFC 172

BEAL   KO1   WILLIAMS

UFC 181

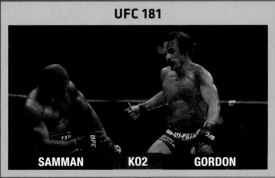

SAMMAN   KO2   GORDON

UFC FIGHT NIGHT: HUNT VS NELSON

HUNT   KO2   NELSON

UFC FIGHT NIGHT: NOGUEIRA VS NELSON

NELSON   KO1   NOGUEIRA

SUBMISSIONS OF THE YEAR

UFC FIGHT NIGHT: TE HUNA VS MARQUARDT

OLIVEIRA   WSUB2   HIOKI

UFC 181

PETTIS   WSUB2   MELENDEZ

UFC FIGHT NIGHT: HENDERSON VS DOS ANJOS

SAUNDERS   WSUB1   HEATHERLY

UFC 172

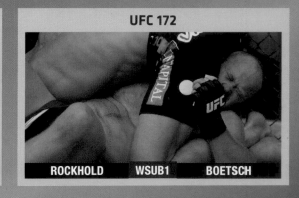

ROCKHOLD   WSUB1   BOETSCH

UFC 173

CLARKE   WSUB2   IAQUINTA

Timeline years: 2005 | 2006 | 2007 | 2008 | 2009 | 2010 | 2011 | 2012 | 2013 | 2014 | 2015

DEBUTS

UFC FIGHT NIGHT: SAFFIEDINE VS LIM

- TAREC SAFFIEDINE
- TATSUYA KAWAJIRI
- SEAN SORIANO
- LUIZ DUTRA
- SHUNICHI SHIMIZU
- WILL CHOPE
- ROYSTON WEE
- DAVE GALERA
- TAE HYUN BANG
- JON DELOS REYES
- KIICHI KUNIMOTO
- KATSUNORI KIKUNO
- MAIRBEK TAISUMOV
- RUSSELL DOANE
- LEANDRO ISSA

UFC FIGHT NIGHT: ROCKHOLD VS PHILIPPOU

- LOUIS SMOLKA
- BENEIL DARIUSH

UFC FIGHT NIGHT: MACHIDA VS MOUSASI

- TAKENORI SATO
- ALBERT TUMENOV
- ZUBAIRA TUKHUGOV
- DOUGLAS SILVA DE ANDRADE

UFC FIGHT NIGHT: GUSTAFSSON VS MANUWA

- MATS NILSSON
- DANNY MITCHELL
- CLAUDIO SILVA

UFC FIGHT NIGHT: SHOGUN VS HENDERSON 2

- HANS STRINGER
- NOAD LAHAT

UFC FIGHT NIGHT: NOGUEIRA VS NELSON

- JIM ALERS
- ALAN OMER

UFC FIGHT NIGHT: BROWN VS SILVA

- RUAN POTTS

UFC FIGHT NIGHT: MUNOZ VS MOUSASI

- NIKLAS BACKSTROM
- NICK HEIN
- PAWEL PAWLAK
- RUSLAN MAGOMEDOV
- VIKTOR PESTA

UFC FIGHT NIGHT: HENDERSON VS KHABILOV

- JAKE LINDSEY
- ROGER NARVAEZ

UFC FIGHT NIGHT: TE HUNA VS MARQUARDT

- JAKE MATTHEWS
- DASHON JOHNSON
- ROLDAN SANGCHA-AN
- DAN HOOKER
- IAN ENTWISTLE

UFC FIGHT NIGHT: SWANSON VS STEPHENS

- JAMES MOONTASRI
- DIEGO FERREIRA
- ALEXEY OLIYNYK
- ANTHONY HAMILTON
- SHANE HOWELL

UFC FIGHT NIGHT: CERRONE VS MILLER

- LEONARDO MAFRA
- JERROD SANDERS
- CLAUDIA GADELHA
- TINA LAHDEMAKI

UFC FIGHT NIGHT: McGREGOR VS BRANDÃO

- CHRIS DEMPSEY
- MIKE KING
- CATHAL PENDRED
- PADDY HOLOHAN

UFC FIGHT NIGHT: BADER VS SAINT PREUX

- LAUREN MURPHY
- SAM ALVEY
- FRANKIE SAENZ
- NOLAN TICMAN
- ALAN JOUBAN

UFC FIGHT NIGHT: BISPING VS LE

- BRENDAN O'REILLY
- NING GUANGYOU
- JIANPING YANG
- ALBERTO MINA
- SHINSHO ANZAI
- ULKA SASAKI
- YAO ZHIKUI
- MILANA DUDIEVA

UFC FIGHT NIGHT: HENDERSON VS DOS ANJOS

- VALMIR LAZARO
- CHRIS HEATHERLY
- JOBY SANCHEZ
- COLBY COVINGTON

UFC FIGHT NIGHT: JACARÉ VS MOUSASI

- TATEKI MATSUDA

UFC FIGHT NIGHT: BIGFOOT VS ARLOVSKI

- WENDELL OLIVEIRA
- LARISSA PACHECO

UFC FIGHT NIGHT: HUNT VS NELSON

- RIN NAKAI
- MASANORI KANEHARA
- JOHNNY CASE

UFC FIGHT NIGHT: NELSON VS STORY

- JAN BLACHOWICZ
- SCOTT ASKHAM
- CHARLES ROSA
- MARCIN BANDEL

UFC FIGHT NIGHT: MacDONALD VS SAFFIEDINE

- ROMAN SALAZAR
- CHRIS KELADES
- MATT DWYER

UFC FIGHT NIGHT: SHOGUN VS SAINT PREUX

- LEON EDWARDS
- JORGE DE OLIVEIRA
- NINA ANSAROFF
- DIEGO RIVAS
- RODOLFO RUBIO
- THOMAS ALMEIDA

UFC FIGHT NIGHT: EDGAR VS SWANSON

- JOSH COPELAND
- PAIGE VANZANT
- KAILIN CURRAN
- DOO HO CHOI

UFC FIGHT NIGHT: MACHIDA VS DOLLAWAY

- ANTONIO DOS SANTOS
- RENATO MOICANO
- JAKE COLLIER

DEBUTS

UFC FIGHT NIGHT: DOS SANTOS VS MIOCIC

WILLIE GATES
BRYAN BARBERENA
ANTHONY BIRCHAK
HENRY CEJUDO

UFC FIGHT NIGHT: KIM VS HATHAWAY

ZHANG LIPENG
WANG SAI
YUI CHUL NAM
WANG ANYING
ALBERT CHENG
MARK EDDIVA
JUMABIEKE TUERXUN

UFC FIGHT NIGHT: BISPING VS KENNEDY

ELIAS THEODOROU
SHELDON WESTCOTT
CHAD LAPRISE
OLIVIER AUBIN-MERCIER
LESLIE SMITH
MIKE DE LA TORRE
NORDINE TALEB
VIK GRUJIC
RICHARD WALSH
CHRIS INDICH
TIM GORMAN

UFC FIGHT NIGHT: MIOCIC VS MALDONADO

ANTONIO CARLOS JUNIOR
VITOR MIRANDA
WARLLEY ALVES
MARCIO ALEXANDRE
ALEXANDER YAKOVLEV
RICARDO ABREU
WAGNER SILVA
MARCOS ROGERIO DE LIMA
RICHARDSON MOREIRA
MATT HOBAR

UFC 169

ANDY ENZ
KEVIN LEE
RASHID MAGOMEDOV
TONY MARTIN
GASAN UMALATOV
DANNY MARTINEZ

UFC 170

PATRICK CUMMINS
PEDRO MUNHOZ
ALJAMAIN STERLING
CODY GIBSON
ERNEST CHAVEZ
YOSDENIS CEDENO

UFC 171

SEAN STRICKLAND

UFC 172

CHRIS BEAL
PATRICK WILLIAMS

UFC 173

LI JINGLIANG
DAVID MICHAUD
AARON PHILLIPS

UFC 174

VALERIE LETOURNEAU
ELIZABETH PHILLIPS
KAJAN JOHNSON
JASON SAGGO
JOSH SHOCKLEY
MICHINORI TANAKA

UFC 175

ROB FONT
GUILHERME VASCONCELOS
BUBBA BUSH

UFC 177

JOE SOTO
SHAYNA BASZLER
DAMON JACKSON
CHRIS WADE
CAIN CARRIZOSA

UFC 178

EDDIE ALVAREZ

UFC 179

CHRISTOS GIAGOS

UFC 180

AUGUSTO MONTANO
HECTOR URBINA
YAIR RODRIGUEZ
LEONARDO MORALES
ALEJANDRO PEREZ
JOSE QUINONEZ
GABRIEL BENITEZ
HUMBERTO BROWN
HENRY BRIONES
GUIDO CANNETTI
MARCO BELTRAN
MARLON VERA

UFC 181

JUSTIN JONES
ASHLEE EVANS-SMITH

DEBUTS

UFC ON FOX: HENDERSON VS THOMSON

- GEORGE SULLIVAN
- MIKE RHODES

UFC ON FOX: WERDUM VS BROWNE

- LUKE ZACHRICH
- HERNANI PERPETUO
- RAY BORG
- MIRSAD BEKTIC
- CHAS SKELLY
- DERRICK LEWIS
- JACK MAY
- ALEX WHITE

UFC ON FOX: LAWLER VS BROWN

- BRIAN ORTEGA
- AKBARH ARREOLA
- GILBERT BURNS
- JOANNA JEDRZEJCZYK
- JULIANA LIMA
- TIAGO TRATOR
- ANDREAS STAHL

EDGAR VS PENN: THE FINALE

- COREY ANDERSON
- MATT VAN BUREN
- EDDIE GORDON
- DHIEGO LIMA
- JUAN PUIG
- PATRICK WALSH
- DANIEL SPOHN
- SARAH MORAS
- ALEXIS DUFRESNE
- ROBERT DRYSDALE
- KEITH BERISH

THE ULTIMATE FIGHTER FINALE: A CHAMPION WILL BE CROWNED

- CARLA ESPARZA
- ROSE NAMAJUNAS
- JESSICA PENNE
- RANDA MARKOS
- FELICE HERRING
- LISA ELLIS
- HEATHER JO CLARK
- BEC RAWLINGS
- JOANNE CALDERWOOD
- SEOHEE HAM
- TECIA TORRES
- ANGELA MAGANA
- AISLING DALY
- ALEX CHAMBERS
- ANGELA HILL
- EMILY KAGAN

BIZARRE MOMENTS

DIAZ LOSES FIGHT BEFORE THE OPENING HORN

Oh that Nick Diaz, always marching to the beat of his own drummer. It's an attitude that has endeared him to his fans, but it hasn't always been the best thing for his career. Case in point: The 2011 Las Vegas press conference for his challenge of UFC welterweight champion Georges St-Pierre, a presser Diaz didn't show up to. When he didn't make it, UFC president Dana White had an emphatic response; he pulled Diaz from the fight. Diaz would eventually get his shot at GSP, but it took until March 2013 in Montreal for him to finally step in the Octagon with the champ.

GERARD GORDEAU GIVES TEILA TULI FREE DENTAL WORK

It was the world's first exposure to the UFC in November of 1993, and what an impression it was. Gerard Gordeau sent Teila Tuli's tooth flying from his mouth with a kick—while Tuli was down, no less—that let everyone know that this wasn't some gimmick—this event was for real.

THE "JUST BLEED" GUY

Shirtless, drink in hand, painted with "UFC" on his forehead and "Just Bleed" on his chest, this audience member probably hit all the bases when it came to the stereotypical early UFC fan. Luckily, we all got to see him immortalized when he was put on camera during the introduction of the Mark Kerr vs. Greg Stott bout at UFC 15 in Bay St. Louis, Mississippi. Mention him to any long-time fan, and they'll remember him. Current UFC middleweight Tom Lawlor even paid homage to him during the weigh-in for his UFC 100 bout against CB Dollaway.

BJ PENN HAS LEFT THE BUILDING

How do you top an 11-second knockout over a world-class contender like Caol Uno? If you're BJ Penn, you finish the job and immediately run out of the Octagon and back to your locker room without interviews, congratulatory handshakes or poses for the camera. This was Penn getting caught up in the emotion of the moment, and it firmly established him as one of UFC's legendary free spirits.

KEVIN RANDLEMAN TAKES ON PIPES—AND LOSES

Former Ohio State wrestling star Kevin Randleman was the UFC heavyweight champion, and big things were expected from "The Monster." But first, he had to get past Pedro "The Rock" Rizzo in his first title defense at UFC 24. Unfortunately, Randleman had another issue to deal with before he even made it to the Octagon. He slipped on some pipes backstage and hit his head on the concrete floor, knocking him unconscious and making him the first fighter in UFC history to get knocked out *before* his fight.

KEITH HACKNEY SLAYS THE GIANT

When 5'11", 200-pound Keith Hackney was matched up against 6' 8", 600-pound Emmanuel Yarborough at UFC 3 in 1994, fans had three thoughts: someone didn't like Keith Hackney; the matchmaker certainly had a sense of humor; and how will Hackney avoid getting destroyed by this mountain of a man? But then the horn sounded, and Hackney dropped Yarborough with the first right hand he landed. A seemingly endless array of punches followed, with Hackney eventually winning at the 1:59 mark. David 1, Goliath 0.

PETE SELL SNATCHES DEFEAT FROM THE JAWS OF VICTORY

There was never such a swing in emotions than when Pete Sell fought Scott Smith in 2006. It was the second round of what had been an action-packed standup battle. The two buddies continued to throw caution to the wind, much to the delight of the crowd. While it looked like Smith was pulling into the lead, Sell fired back with a shot to the body that hurt Smith and sent him reeling backwards. The end was probably a punch or two away, and Sell knew it. But in his haste to finish, Sell got careless, and Smith—who admitted he had only one punch left in him—swung for the fences and scored the improbable KO win.

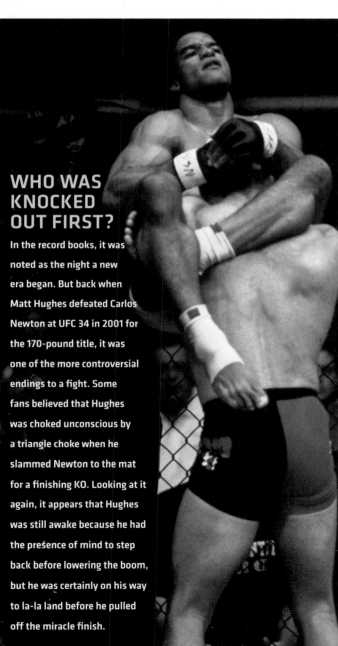

WHO WAS KNOCKED OUT FIRST?

In the record books, it was noted as the night a new era began. But back when Matt Hughes defeated Carlos Newton at UFC 34 in 2001 for the 170-pound title, it was one of the more controversial endings to a fight. Some fans believed that Hughes was choked unconscious by a triangle choke when he slammed Newton to the mat for a finishing KO. Looking at it again, it appears that Hughes was still awake because he had the presence of mind to step back before lowering the boom, but he was certainly on his way to la-la land before he pulled off the miracle finish.

THE BUFFER 360

UFC 100 was the biggest event in UFC history. In the weeks leading up to the bout, many wondered whether Octagon announcer Bruce Buffer would up the ante on his 180 technique of introducing the fighters to do what was dubbed "The Buffer 360." Well, during his introduction of heavyweight champion Brock Lesnar, it happened, and The Buffer 360 became the talk of MMA message boards around the Internet.

BUSTAMANTE GETS TWO TAPS FOR THE PRICE OF ONE

Renowned ground fighter Murilo Bustamante has the jiu-jitsu skills to force anyone to submit. But when he defended his UFC middleweight title against Matt Lindland at UFC 37 in May 2002, he had to do it twice in one fight. Early in the bout, he caught Lindland in an armbar, and after an apparent tap, he released the hold. Lindland protested, and referee John McCarthy decided to restart the action. Regardless, Bustamante was able to pull off another submission, this time via guillotine choke in the third round.

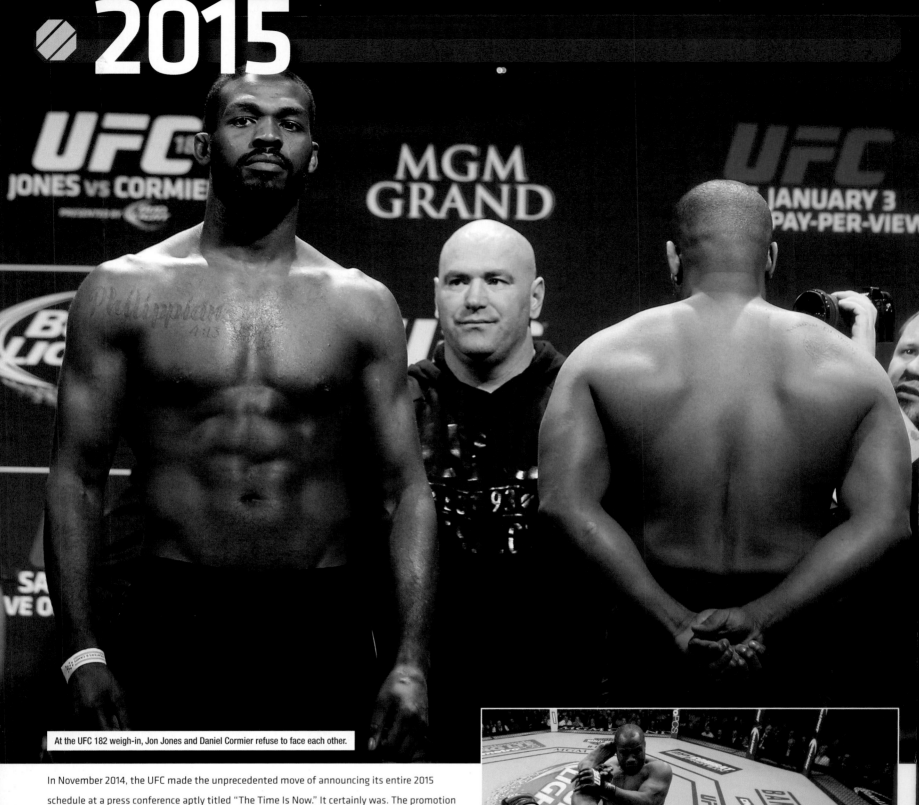

At the UFC 182 weigh-in, Jon Jones and Daniel Cormier refuse to face each other.

In November 2014, the UFC made the unprecedented move of announcing its entire 2015 schedule at a press conference aptly titled "The Time Is Now." It certainly was. The promotion unveiled 41 events that would take the Octagon from Japan to Canada, Brazil to Mexico, the Philippines to Poland, and all points in between.

It was an ambitious undertaking, but when has UFC ever played it safe? Never. The 2015 season got off to a spectacular start. On January 3, the MGM Grand Garden Arena played host to the highly-anticipated showdown between UFC light heavyweight champion Jon Jones and unbeaten challenger Daniel Cormier. The rivalry between the two had produced a press conference brawl, heated staredowns, and plenty of ill will. When it came down to the UFC 182 main event, however, none of that mattered.

All that counted was what happened in the Octagon, and when the dust settled, Jones had his eighth successful title defense, as he won a hard-fought, but unanimous, decision over Cormier.

Jon Jones kicks Daniel Cormier during their UFC light heavyweight championship bout.

Cormier kicks Jones at UFC 182.

Nick Diaz taunts Anderson Silva during their middleweight bout at UFC 183.

2015 was just heating up. Before January was even over, Irish sensation Conor McGregor secured a shot at the featherweight title with a thrashing of Dennis Siver in Boston, and Anthony "Rumble" Johnson shocked Alexander Gustafsson in Stockholm. This allowed the resurgent American to leap "The Mauler" and get a crack at the light heavyweight championship belt.

The second biggest fight of January was the UFC 183 main event on January 31, featuring the return of Anderson Silva against Nick Diaz. The five round bout was often bizarre thanks to Diaz's taunting In the end, however, Silva had his hand raised once more, thrilling his fans around the world.

Silva defeats Diaz to win the bout.

Joanna Jedrzejczyk punches Carla Esparza at UFC 185.

HOLLY HOLM
SANDIA HEIGHTS, NM

DEBUT: UFC 184, FEBRUARY 28, 2015

A multiple-time world champion considered to be one of the best female boxers to ever lace up the gloves, Holly Holm held a 33-2-3 record in the sweet science before moving to MMA in 2011. After going unbeaten in her first seven pro bouts, she earned a call to UFC, where she will make history, if she has her way.

"When I first started doing MMA, people asked me what my goal was in this, and my goal is to be the first female that has titles in both MMA and boxing because nobody's done that," Holm said.

At UFC 184, the young lady who had become the UFC's biggest star, Ronda Rousey, continued to dominate the women's bantamweight division, this time defending her title with a 14-second submission of unbeaten number one contender Cat Zingano. With that victory, Rousey had finished her last three opponents in a combined 96 seconds.

While there seemed no championship belt more secure than the one around Rousey's waist, two titles changed hands two weeks later at UFC 184. Poland's Joanna Jedrzejczyk dethroned women's strawweight champion Carla Esparza, and Rafael dos Anjos took the lightweight title from Anthony Pettis' grasp. Those UFC 185 upsets proved that on any given night in the UFC, any of these world-class athletes can win.

In April 2015, in Montreal, UFC 186 was absolutely historic. First, this event marked the triumphant return of the legendary Quinton "Rampage" Jackson who defeated Fabio Maldonado. On the same night, Demetrious Johnson set an unbreakable record.

"Mighty Mouse" Johnson defeated Kyoji Horiguchi via submission when the contender was forced to tap out to an arm bar with one second remaining in the fifth, and final round, making this title defense the latest UFC finish ever, a record that may someday be matched, but can never be broken.

The shakeup among the Octagon elite continued throughout the spring, with Daniel Cormier submitting Anthony "Rumble" Johnson to take the UFC light heavyweight title vacated by the suspension of Jon Jones at UFC 187 in May, and Fabricio Werdum dethroning Cain Velasquez at UFC 188 in May to unify the world heavyweight title.

The excitement of these upsets, thrilling knockouts and slick submissions show precisely why this is the fastest growing sport in the world and one that will continue to thrill fans around the globe, more than two decades after its birth in Colorado.

Ronda Rousey triumphs over Cat Zingano during their UFC women's bantamweight championship bout.

DEBUTS*

UFC 182

- CODY GARBRANDT
- JARED CANNONIER
- MARION RENEAU

UFC 184

- HOLLY HOLM
- MASIO FULLEN
- ALEX TORRES

UFC 185

- JOSEPH DUFFY

UFC 186

- SHANE CAMPBELL

UFC 187

- ISLAM MAKHACHEV
- LEO KUNTZ

UFC FIGHT NIGHT: MCGREGOR VS SIVER

- RON STALLINGS
- FRANKIE PEREZ

UFC FIGHT NIGHT: HENDERSON VS THATCH

- CODY PFISTER

UFC FIGHT NIGHT: MENDES VS LAMAS

- TIMOTHY JOHNSON
- SHAMIL ABDURAKHIMOV

UFC FIGHT NIGHT: MAIA VS LAFLARE

- ALEX OLIVEIRA
- FREDY SERRANO
- BENTLEY SYLER

UFC FIGHT NIGHT: GONZAGA VS CRO COP 2

- MARYNA MOROZ
- BARTOSZ FABINSKI
- GARRETH MCLELLAN
- MICKAEL LEBOUT
- DAMIAN STASIAK
- ALEXANDRA ALBU
- IZABELA BADUREK
- STEVIE RAY
- TAYLOR LAPILUS
- ROCKY LEE

UFC FIGHT NIGHT: MIOCIC VS. HUNT

- JONAVIN WEBB
- BEN NGUYEN

UFC FIGHT NIGHT: EDGAR VS. FABER

- LEVAN MAKASHVILI

UFC ON FOX: GUSTAFSSON VS JOHNSON

- ANTHONY CHRISTODOULOU
- PAUL REDMOND
- KONSTANTIN EROKHIN
- SULTAN ALIEV
- MAKWAN AMIRKHANI

INDEX

394

A VISUAL HISTORY

Written by Thomas Gerbasi

DK/Prima Games, a division of Penguin Random House LLC
6081 East 82nd Street, Suite #400
Indianapolis, IN 46250

ISBN: 978-1-4654-3695-5

Printing Code: The rightmost double-digit number is the year of the book's printing; the rightmost single-digit number is the number of the book's printing. For example, 15-1 shows that the first printing of the book occurred in 2015.

18 17 16 15   4 3 2 1

Printed in China.

CREDITS

Senior Development Editor
Jennifer Sims

Book Designer
Tim Amrhein

Production Designers
Julie Clark
Wil Cruz

Copy Editor
Angie Lawler

Indexer
Ken Johnson

PRIMA GAMES STAFF

VP & Publisher
Mike Degler

Editorial Manager
Tim Fitzpatrick

Design and Layout Manager
Tracy Wehmeyer

Licensing
Aaron Lockhart
Christian Sumner

Marketing
Katie Hemlock
Paul Giacomotto

Digital Publishing
Julie Asbury
Tim Cox
Shaida Boroumand

Operations Manager
Stacey Beheler

ACKNOWLEDGMENTS

Prima Games would like to thank Stacey Allen, Brandon Magnus, Rachel Greene, Rob Tonelete, Feather Lake and the rest of the amazing team at UFC for all their help and support in creating this book.

ABOUT THE AUTHOR

Currently the Editorial Director for Ultimate Fighting Championship, Thomas Gerbasi has covered combat sports for various publications for over 15 years. An award-winning member of the Boxing Writers Association of America, his work has also appeared in *The Independent*, YahooSports.com, The DailyBeast.com, *The Ring* and ESPN.com. In addition, Mr. Gerbasi is the author of three boxing books, and his amateur boxing record was 0-1.